Transition Assessment

Planning Transition and IEP Development for Youth with Mild to Moderate Disabilities

Robert J. Miller
Minnesota State University, Mankato

Richard C. Lombard
University of Wisconsin, Whitewater

Stephanie A. Corbey
Burnsville-Eagan-Savage School District

Boston New York San Francisco
Mexico City Montreal Toronto London Madrid Munich Paris
Hong Kong Singapore Tokyo Cape Town Sydney

Executive Editor: Virginia Lanigan
Editorial Assistant: Matthew Buchholz
Marketing Manager: Kris Ellis-Levy
Composition and Prepress Buyer: Linda Cox
Manufacturing Manager: Megan Cochran
Cover Coordinator: Elena Sidorova
Editorial-Production Coordinator: Mary Beth Finch
Editorial-Production Service: Stratford Publishing Services
Electronic Composition: Stratford Publishing Services

For related titles and support materials, visit our online catalog at www.ablongman.com

Between the time Website information is gathered and then published, it is not unusual for some sites to have closed. Also, the transcription of URLs can result in unintended typographical errors. The publisher would appreciate notification where these errors occur so that they may be corrected in subsequent editions.

Library of Congress Cataloging-in-Publication Data

Miller, Robert J. (Robert Joseph)
Transition assessment: planning transition and IEP development for youth with mild to moderate disabilities/Robert J. Miller, Richard C. Lombard, Stephanie A. Corbey.
p. cm.
Includes bibliographical references and index.
ISBN 0-205-32727-3
1. Youth with disabilities— Services for—Planning. 2. Students with disabilities—Services for —Planning. 3. Vocational evaluation. 4. School-to-work transition. 5. Individualized education programs. I. Lombard, Richard C. II. Corbey, Stephanie A. III. Title.
HV1569.3.Y68M55 2006
371.9'0473—dc22
2005056688

Printed in the United States of America.

18 2022

This book is dedicated to my wife, Diane, and my sons, Dylan and Alec. Their love and support sustain me at a personal level. Their kindness, caring, and generosity are the basis for my professional accomplishments.

Robert J. Miller

In appreciation for their endless support of my professional and personal achievements, I dedicate this book to my children, Cassie, Sacha, Jordan, and Hannah.

Richard C. Lombard

I have dedicated this book to my husband Mark, for his undying love and confidence in me. He provides the sustenance I need to contribute to the field in this manner.

Stephanie A. Corbey

Contents

To the Reader

The purpose of *Transition Assessment: Planning Transition and IEP Development for Youth with Mild to Moderate Disabilities* is to provide a practical text that is comprehensive in the area of transition assessment. It is intended for both practitioners who are already in the field of transition service delivery and for university students at the graduate and undergraduate levels.

In this text, we provide a Transition Assessment Model for evaluating the transition service needs of youth with mild disabilities. We have framed the text to address each component of the model. As a result, each chapter not only illustrates how the particular assessment component can be used to evaluate the transition needs of students with mild disabilities, but also provides examples and tools for immediate application, as well as a thorough discussion of the theory regarding how each assessment component fits into the complete model.

Each of us has a broad array of experiences across special education, vocational education, and general education, in various settings. These experiences, along with a solid knowledge base in transition planning and service delivery, have helped us create a text that is applicable to an interdisciplinary audience. The focus of this text is on students with mild disabilities, however, many of the concepts used can be applied to a wide range of student populations.

The term *mild disabilities* is meant to cover a wide range of students, including students with emotional/behavioral disabilities, learning disabilities, mild to moderate cognitive disabilities, physical and sensory disabilities, etc. In general, this text focuses on students who can benefit from transition planning that targets competitive employment and/or postsecondary training and education outcomes. The examples and tools were designed and selected specifically to address the need to meet the focus of transition planning and IEP development for these individuals.

You need not come to the text with a wealth of knowledge about transition planning and services, although a basic understanding of disability-related services and etiology is beneficial. We anticipate that you will be in a position now or in the future to use the tools we offer to identify and assess transition needs of individuals in the areas outlined in the text including: future planning, self-determination and self-advocacy, academic and behavioral skills, functional life skills, and vocational and career planning.

The ultimate purpose of this text is to assist you with learning methods of gathering transition assessment information regarding student interests, preferences, and transition needs, and then to move you forward to using the assessment data to design meaningful transition goals for inclusion in your own students' IEPs. Ultimately, evaluation of transition needs is only as useful as the resulting transition plan designed by the IEP team.

The text culminates with the design of a comprehensive transition plan that spans an entire high school career (see Chapter 9). This plan incorporates all aspects of transition assessment and transition planning, including future planning, and is documented in the Individual Education Program (IEP). All team members involved in transition planning will be able to relate to their role in the interagency aspect of transition service delivery that stems from identified student needs and personal interests and preferences. Parents and students with disabilities are key players in effective transition planning, and through use of the tools encompassed in this text will become active participants in the process.

Acknowledgements

We would like to thank the following reviewers for their contributions: Jeffrey Bakken, Illinois State University; Patrick Brennan II, Armstrong Atlantic State University; Inge Jacobs, Capital Region BOCES, Albany, New York; Debbie Case, Southwestern Oklahoma State University, Sondra Dastoli, Edinboro University of Pennsylvania; Kimberly Fatata-Hall, North Central Unversity; Joseph George, Columbus State University; Susan Severson, Minnesota State University–Moorhead; and James Yanok, Ohio University.

I The Foundation of Transition Assessment

CHAPTER 1

Transition Planning and Transition Assessment

What Is It? Why Do We Do It?

Historical Overview

A seminal event that led to the inclusion of students with disabilities in the public schools in the United States can be traced to the passage of The Education of All Handicapped Children Act of 1975 (EAHCA), P. L. 94–142. The EAHCA required participating states to provide free appropriate public education (FAPE) for all qualified students with disabilities between the ages of three and eighteen by September 1, 1978, and for all students with disabilities up to age twenty-one by September 1, 1980 (Yell, 1998). Sitlington, Clark, and Kolstoe (2000) suggest that there is little historical evidence that people with disabilities were considered capable of participating in traditional schooling or competitive employment, or were valued as citizens of the community prior to the 1970s.

The transition planning movement is in many ways an outgrowth of the marriage of the EAHCA and the career education movement of the 1970s and early 1980s. Ken Hoyt (1975) defined career education as "the totality of experiences through which one learns about and prepares to engage in work as part of her or his way of living" (p. 4). Hoyt (1977) further elaborated in his definition of career education as "an effort at refocusing education and the actions of the broader community in ways that will help individuals acquire and utilize the knowledge, skills, and attitudes necessary for each to make work a meaningful, productive and satisfying part of his or her way of living" (p. 5). The career education movement was an education movement for all students. It represented an attempt at making the public school experience more meaningful and to tie academic education to real world experience. Career education included paid and nonpaid work as well as the many roles of the individual including family member, citizen, student, etc. It included the social skills, interpersonal skills, work habits, and attitudes toward work that students need to make appropriate adjustments to work and community life (Levinson, 1993). The career education movement was never fully implemented on a national basis (Sitlington, et al. 2000).

Since the 1970s, there have been many competing and complementary educational initiatives identified by scholars and community members which compete for the focus of educational and political leaders and vie for federal funding and support. A reemerging theme of interest in educational policy is the importance of preparation of all students for meaningful vocational education opportunities. The School-to-Work Opportunities Act of 1994 was another attempt at systemic change in public education with the expressed framework of preparing all students for work and further education, and to increase the opportunities for all students to enter first jobs in high-skill, high-wage careers (U.S. Department of Education, 1994). The School-to-Work Opportunities Act of 1994 was never fully implemented on a national basis and was overshadowed by competing and more academically-focused educational initiatives.

However, the goal of infusing meaningful career education and vocational preparation into the public schools and merging academic instruction with career preparation continues. This reemergence is influenced by numerous factors including: (a) high national dropout rates for all students, (b) continuing criticism by employers that students are leaving high school without the skills necessary to find and maintain meaningful work, and (c) systemic changes in the nature of work in America (Lombard, Miller, & Hazelkorn, 1998).

Field, et al. (1998) noted that studies have confirmed that many students with disabilities are making the transition to adult life without the skills required to be successful members of society. While students with disabilities are graduating or completing high school with less preparedness to participate in the labor market, the labor market is requiring more skill and maturity for employment. Gone are the days of low skill, high-wage employment (Lombard, Hazelkorn, & Miller, 1995). High quality employment in the twenty-first century will require high skills for high wages. Too few persons with disabilities live independently, are employed at a living wage, or are competitively employed in a full-time capacity (see, for example, Hasazi, Gordon, & Roe, 1985; Siegel, et al., 1992; Sitlington, Frank, & Carson, 1992). Too few persons with disabilities are continuing in postsecondary education to learn the employment skills needed for the twenty-first century (Fairweather & Shaver, 1991). While few students with disabilities are entering high-tech career fields in science, engineering, and technology, the attrition rate is high for those students who do attempt to enter these postsecondary career fields (National Science Foundation, 2000). According to results of the Harris Poll reported by the National Organization on Disability, 71% of adults with disabilities are unemployed, compared to 20% of the general population (Louis Harris and Associates, 2000).

IDEA and Transition Planning

In 1990, P.L. 101–476, the Individuals with Disabilities Education Act (IDEA) was passed by Congress. With the passage of this legislation, educators were required to address the transition needs of all students with disabilities as a portion of their Individual Education Program (IEP) no later than age sixteen and as early as age fourteen if needed. In this legislation, **transition services** were defined as:

> A coordinated set of activities for a student, designed within an outcome oriented process, which promotes movement from school to postschool activities, including post-secondary education, vocational training, integrated employment (including supported employment), continuing and adult education, adult services, independent living, or community participation (20 U.S. C. 1401(19)).

IDEA (1990) also addressed the importance of assessment of transition needs. Specifically, this legislation required that, "The coordinated set of activities shall be based upon the individual student's needs, taking into account the student's preferences and interests and shall include instruction, community experiences, the development of employment and other postschool adult living objectives, and when appropriate, acquisition of daily living skills and functional vocational evaluation" (20 U.S.C. 1401(19)).

The importance of preparation for life and transition planning was reconfirmed with the passage of the IDEA Amendments of 1997. With the passage of the IDEA Amendments of 1997, transition was once again identified as a key component of school preparation. The purpose of the legislation is defined as:

> . . . to ensure that all children with disabilities have available to them a free appropriate public education that emphasizes special education and related services designed to meet their

> unique needs and prepare them for employment and independent living (Section 601 (d) Purposes (1) (A)).

In this purpose statement, the IDEA Amendments of 1997 once again confirmed that the purpose of education is to prepare students with disabilities for participation in adult life. To do less would be to abdicate the responsibility of educators to provide each student with a free appropriate public education. Transition assessment in the development of the student's IEP is again addressed in this legislation and is required by the law (Section 602. Definitions (30) (A-C)).

In December 2004 P.L. 108–446, the Individuals with Disabilities Education Improvement Act of 2004 (IDEA 2004), was reauthorized by Congress and signed into law by President Bush. IDEA 2004 went into effect in July 2005 except for the highly qualified teacher requirements that went into effect in December 2004. While the mandate for doing transition assessment and developing transition plans to assist the student to plan for life after high school are reaffirmed in the law, there are several notable changes in IDEA 2004 with regard to transition planning.

- Transition planning must begin no later than the first IEP to be in effect when the child is sixteen, and updated annually thereafter (Section 614(d)(1)(A)(i)(VIII)).
- Appropriate measurable postsecondary goals based upon age appropriate **transition assessments** related to training, education, employment, and where appropriate, independent living skills must be developed (Section 614(d)(1)(A)(i)(VIII)(aa)).
- Transition services (including courses of study) needed to assist the child in reaching postsecondary goals must be developed (Section 614(d)(1)(A)(VIII)(bb)).
- Beginning not later than one year before the child reaches the age of majority under state law, a statement that the child has been informed of the child's rights under this title, if any, that will transfer to the child on reaching the age of majority under section 615(m) (Section 614(d)(1)(A)(i)(VIII)(cc)).
- The term **transition services** is defined in IDEA 2004 as a coordinated set of activities for a child with a disability that
  (A) is designed to be within a results-oriented process, that is focused on improving the academic and functional achievement of the child with a disability to facilitate the child's movement from school to postschool activities, including postsecondary education, vocational education, integrated employment (including supported employment), continuing and adult education, adult services, independent living, or community participation;
  (B) is based on the individual child's needs, taking into account the child's strengths, preferences, and interests; and
  (C) includes instruction, related services, community experiences, the development of employment and other postschool adult living objectives, and, when appropriate, acquisition of daily living skills and functional vocational evaluation (Section 602. Definitions (34)(A-C)).

Transition, as defined by the IDEA, represents an attempt to make education relevant and meaningful to students with disabilities and their families, as well as an attempt to integrate the student into the planning process and harness the natural motivation of the student. This book is based on the premise that middle- and high school education becomes relevant to the student if the student believes the educational progam is based on his or her goals and aspirations. Transition planning is the process of empowering the student and family to make decisions regarding the student's future. It is a process of gathering and using information to identify goals and develop strategies to increase the likelihood that the young adult with disabilities will succeed in life after high school. Now, more than ever, effective transition planning is needed for all students as they leave high school and take on the responsibilities of adult life.

The purpose of this book is to assist educators in assessing the transition needs of their students so they may assist each student and their family to develop an effective transition plan and as such, prepare the student to plan for near and distant futures.

Transition Assessment

Transition assessment can be defined as the process of determining a student's abilities, attitudes, aptitudes, interests, work behaviors, levels of self-determination and self-advocacy skills, interpersonal skills, academic skill level, and independent living skills over an extended period of time for the purpose of planning an appropriate individual education program (IEP).

Transition assessment provides the student, parents, teachers, and school personnel with information needed for future planning for life after high school. Transition assessment provides information regarding the strengths, limitations, and motivations of a specific student so the student and significant others can make wise choices both in terms of school curriculum and life planning. It is the continuous gathering of information rather than a one-time event. The components of the process are: (1) assessment, (2) intervention, and (3) evaluation. Evaluation of the success or failure of a given intervention is used as assessment information to modify and implement new interventions, which will in turn be evaluated again. Transition assessment can be viewed as ongoing and circular in nature. Transition assessment represents assessment and evaluation of the entire young person across the life span and includes assessment at home, in school, and in the community.

Since transition planning represents a holistic approach to preparing the student for adult life, transition assessment information must also be comprehensive. The Division on Career Development and Transition of the Council for Exceptional Children has endorsed the following definition of transition assessment:

> Transition assessment is the ongoing process of collecting data on the individual's needs, preferences, and interests as they relate to the demands of current and future working, educational, living, and personal and social environments. Assessment data serve as the common thread in the transition process and form the basis for defining goals and services to be included in the Individual Education Plan (Sitlington, Neubert, & Leconte, 1997).

Assessment may be formal or informal depending on the information needed for decision making. Figure 1.1 displays the types of assessment information that must be gathered for effective transition planning. Assessments included in an effective transition evaluation are:

1. assessment of future planning needs and goals,
2. assessment of self-determination and self-advocacy skills,
3. assessment of academic strengths and deficits, including the student's learning style as well as behavioral assessment as warranted,
4. assessment of life skills instruction needs,
5. assessment of vocational interests, aptitudes, and abilities both in the classroom (e.g., technical preparation and in-school vocational coursework) and in the community (e.g., work-based learning).

Each of these five assessment components is intertwined and is woven into a complex interrelationship. Academic strengths and deficits affect future plans. The levels of self-determination and self-advocacy skills affect the ability of the student to function

Transition Assessment Model

Using Assessment Data to Create an Effective Transition Plan

EFFECTIVE TRANSITION PLANNING

Vocational Assessment

1. Interests
2. Abilities
3. Aptitudes

Formal and Informal

1. Tech-prep/School-to-work assessment
2. Community-based assessment
3. Situational/Workplace assessment

General and Specific Occupational Skills

Academic and Behavioral Assessment in All Relevant Areas

1. Criterion-referenced testing
2. Norm-referenced testing
3. Learning style assessment

Life Skills Assessment

1. Daily living skills
2. Social skills

Formal and Informal Environments

1. Home
2. School
3. Community

Assessment of Future Planning Needs and Goals

1. Home living
2. Community participation
3. Jobs and job training
4. Recreation and leisure
5. Postsecondary education and training

Assessment of Student Self-Determination and Self-Advocacy Skills

1. Academic
2. Jobs and job training
3. Postsecondary education and training

< < < PREPARATION FOR ANTICIPATED ENVIRONMENTS > > >

< < < PLANNING FOR NEAR AND DISTANT FUTURES > > >

TRANSITION ASSESSMENT

Figure 1.1

independently in the academic setting. Social skills affect the ability of the student to find and maintain employment or to request needed accommodations. The young adult's goal to be employed in a particular field after graduation impacts the student's need to consider a particular type of curriculum (e.g., tech prep or college prep). The five assessment components together provide a holistic view of the student and provide the context for educational decision-making.

The remaining chapters will discuss the five components of the Transition Assessment Model as well as topics which provide context to the transition assessment process. In each remaining chapter you will find strategies for collecting and using transition assessment information. In several chapters you are provided with an informal assessment tool for your use in gathering and assessing student transition needs. In the appendices you will also find information regarding additional assessment instruments which may be acquired to assist you in assessing the transition needs of your students. In short, this book includes methods, materials, and strategies to do effective and comprehensive transition assessment with a student and the family of that student.

We have based this work on the belief that transition assessment and transition planning must center on ten fundamental tenets.

1. Education in the twenty-first century must be relevant to the student. As such, the IEP must be a student-driven document and effective transition assessment is critical to identifying and addressing the student's needs and goals.

2. The student must identify their goals, interests, and aspirations to plan for near and distant futures.

3. The student must be able to state their goals, summarize their strengths and limitations, and articulate needed accommodations.

4. The student must learn to be self-determined. Therefore, planning skills, choice making, and decision making are critical components of the curriculum as well as critical components of career development.

5. The student must possess the skills of self-advocacy including learning to advocate for needs, wants, and aspirations.

6. The student must develop ownership in future planning to enhance strengths and remediate limitations, and to develop strategies to accommodate these limitations.

7. The student must develop a real sense of academic strengths and limitations as well as a real sense of strengths and limitations in vocational skills and life skills. The IEP should build upon the student's strengths and identify strategies to address student limitations.

8. The student, family, and educators must be contributors in the transition assessment process.

9. While IDEA 2004 does not require transition planning to begin until age sixteen, it is our opinion that transition planning should begin no later than age fourteen to provide the time for identifying goals and acquiring experiences and skills to prepare the student for adult life. As a result, initial transition assessment must take place when the student is age thirteen or younger.

10. The transition plan is the engine of the IEP process for secondary-aged students. The transition plan drives all curricular decisions as well as helps the IEP team to define instructional goals.

Relationship of the Transition Plan to Other IEP Goals and Objectives

The importance of the transition plan to the IEP process can be visualized through a review of Figure 1.2. Through the transition assessment process the transition plan is initially developed. This transition plan is a collaborative effort between the student, family, community, and involved educators. The transition plan identifies the short-term goals (academic year) for the student as well as develops the longer-term plan for the student (high school and beyond). As such, the transition plan provides a structure to plan for near and distant futures. While Figure 1.1 identified the five components needed

Infusing Transition into the Individual Education Plan (IEP)

TRANSITION ASSESSMENT				
Future Planning Goals and Objectives	**Self-Determination and Self-Advocacy Goals and Objectives**	**Academic and Behavioral Goals and Objectives**	**Life Skills Goals and Objectives**	**Vocational Goals and Objectives**
• Assessment of future planning needs • Structured information-gathering process • Future planning inventories 1. Student 2. Family 3. Special education teacher	• Self-determination and self-advocacy assessment • Self-determination and self-advocacy skills 1. Student 2. Family 3. Special education teacher	• Academic skill assessment • Criterion-referenced testing, norm-referenced testing and learning style assessment • Behavioral skills assessment	• Life skill assessment • Formal and informal environments 1. Home 2. School 3. Community 4. Workplace	• Vocational assessment • Formal and informal community-based, situational assessment and evaluation 1. Interests 2. Aptitudes 3. Abilities
AREAS				
1. Home living 2. Community participation 3. Jobs and job training 4. Recreation and leisure 5. Postsecondary education and training	1. Academic 2. Jobs and job training 3. Postsecondary education and training	In all relevant academic and behavioral areas	1. Daily living 2. Social skills 3. General employment	1. General occupational skills 2. Specific occupational skills
PREPARATION FOR ANTICIPATED ENVIRONMENTS				

Figure 1.2

to complete an effective and holistic transition assessment, Figure 1.2 identifies the relationship of the transition plan to the instructional goals and objectives found in the student's IEP.

Self-determination and self-advocacy goals, academic goals, life skills goals, and vocational goals are developed based on the interests, aptitudes, abilities, strengths, and limitations identified through the transition assessment process and as identified as significant and relevant to the student and family in the transition plan.

For example, John and his family identify his future employment goal to be a history teacher and coach after high school. This long-term transition goal will immediately effect the kinds of academic courses that John will need to take throughout high school. As a result of his career decision, John will need to commit to a college preparation curriculum during high school and this will effect curriculum decisions for John as early as ninth grade. John will need to focus on developing the academic skills needed to be successful in college and beyond. In addition, John will need to identify and practice any needed academic accommodations to maximize his success in the transition from high school to a four-year college. This decision has important ramifications for the self-advocacy skills that John will need to be successful in the future. After graduation, protection under IDEA will no longer be provided to John; he will have only the protections available under Section 504 of the Rehabilitation Act of 1973 as well as the Americans with Disabilities Act (ADA).

To be afforded academic accommodation at a four-year college, John will need to self-identify as a person with a disability and provide documentation of that disability to be entitled to the protections under the law. In addition, John must be able to articulate the specific accommodations that he will need to be successful in postsecondary education. These are self-advocacy skills that must be addressed to maximize the likelihood of John's future success.

To be successful at a four-year college, John may need specific life skills instruction. Too often educators believe that students with mild disabilities do not need any life skills training or that life skills instruction will be learned by the student through experiences at home. Occasionally, educators even believe that life skills instruction is only for students with more substantial levels of disabilities. This could not be further from the truth.

In a recent conversation with the mother of a high school graduate with a learning disability, the mother recalled how her daughter had gone to college in a nearby city with fine academic skills (with accommodation) but with no training in independent living skills. Her parents provided the daughter a diesel truck for transportation to the four-year college. The daughter immediately filled the diesel truck with gasoline thereby causing great damage to the vehicle. When renting her apartment for college the young adult ordered an unlisted phone number so she could focus on her studies. She did not realize that her parents and friends could not get her phone number and could not call her. This young adult signed up for cable television for her new apartment and signed up for every possible channel. She was unaware that there was a direct relationship between the cost of the service and the number of channels and premium channels ordered. Part of the young adult's disability was a problem with following directions. The young adult could not find her classes and she was too embarrassed to ask others for help with finding classrooms. She did not identify herself as a person with a disability at the college and her lack of attendance was perceived to be a lack of interest or commitment by her professors. As a result of the number and level of problems in the area of life skills and self-advocacy, this young adult with strong academic skills was unsuccessful in her attempt to attend a four-year college. As her mother later stated, the daughter "received a 4–0 grade point. She received four zeros for the classes taken."

The IEP must provide the opportunity and necessary supports for the student to explore career interests and to gather needed information to make career choices. In our example with John, he wanted to be a history teacher and coach. While the IEP team should applaud John's identification of a long term goal, John may or may not have a realistic understanding of the responsibilities of a history teacher and coach. Situational assessment and continued assessment of interests and abilities are in order. The transition plan may provide John the opportunity to visit a four-year college or to work as an aide to a history teacher or coach and thereby gather needed self-assessment information. As we have already stated, students often lack life experiences on which to base career decisions. At any rate, in this model of transition planning, the transition plan is the capstone for planning for high school and life after high school. The transition plan drives all curricular decisions as well as helps the IEP team to define student-focused goals and objectives. Figure 1.3 includes a review of the critical components of IDEA 2004 regarding transition planning.

IDEA 2004—Critical Components for Transition Planning

Section 602. Definitions.

(34) *TRANSITION SERVICES* The term "transition services" means a coordinated set of activities for a child with a disability that

(A) is designed to be within a results-oriented process, that is focused on improving the academic and functional achievement of the child with a disability to facilitate the child's movement from school to postschool activities, including postsecondary education, vocational education, integrated employment (including supported employment), continuing and adult education, adult services, independent living, or community participation;

(B) is based on the individual child's needs, taking into account the child's strengths, preferences, and interests; and

(C) includes instruction, related services, community experiences, the development of employment and other postschool adult living objectives, and, when appropriate, acquisition of daily living skills and functional vocational evaluation.

Section 614 (d)(1) Individual Education Programs

(i) In General the term "individualized education program" or "IEP" means a written statement for each child with a disability that is developed, reviewed, and revised in accordance with this section and that includes

(VIII) beginning not later than the first IEP to be in effect when the child is 16, and updated annually thereafter

(aa) appropriate measurable postsecondary goals based upon age appropriate transition assessments related to training, education, employment, and when appropriate, independent living skills;

(bb) the transition services (including courses of study) needed to assist the child in reaching those goals; and

(cc) beginning no later than one year before the child reaches the age of majority under State law, a statement that the child has been informed of the child's rights under this title, if any, that will transfer to the child on reaching the age of majority under Section 615(m).

Figure 1.3

CHAPTER SUMMARY

Chapter 1 explored the reasons for transition planning and transition assessment and provided a review of both past and current legal requirements to do transition planning for students with disabilities. We found that:

- Transition planning is an outgrowth of the career education movement of the 1970s and 1980s.
- Transition planning and transition assessment have been mandated in the IEP process since IDEA 1990 (P.L. 101:476).
- Transition planning continues to be a required component of the IEP today (IDEA 2004).
- Transition assessment is required for transition planning (IDEA 2004).
- Transition assessment is a holistic assessment process which includes (1) assessment of future planning needs and goals, (2) assessment of self-determination and self-advocacy skills, (3) assessment of academic strengths and deficits including the student's learning style as well as behavioral assessment as warranted, (4) assessment of life skills instruction needs, (5) assessment of vocational interests, aptitudes, and abilities both in the classroom (e.g., technical preparation, in-school vocational coursework) and in the community (e.g., work-based learning).
- The transition plan is the engine of the IEP process for secondary-aged student. The transition plan drives all curricular decisions as well as helps the IEP team to define instructional goals.

CHAPTER ACTIVITIES

Turn to Appendix B, part 1 (B-1). There you will find the **Critical Part 300 Regulations Regarding Transition Planning for IDEA 1997**. Compare and contrast transition planning components of IDEA 2004 found in Figure 1.3 with the components Part 300 Regulations Regarding Transition Planning for IDEA 1997. How are the components in each law similar? What differences do you see? What are the possible effects of the changes in the law between IDEA 1997 and IDEA 2004?

CHAPTER REFERENCES

Fairweather, J. S., & Shaver, D. M. (1991). Making the transition to postsecondary education and training. *Exceptional Children, 5*, 264–270. (ERIC Document Reproduction Service No. EJ 517 928)

Field, S., Martin, J., Miller, R., Ward, M., & Wehmeyer, M. (1998). *A practical guide for teaching self-determination.* Reston, VA: Council for Exceptional Children.

Hasazi, S., Gordon, L., & Roe, C. (1985). Factors associated with the employment status of handicapped youth exiting high school from 1979–1983. *Exceptional Children, 51*, 455–469. (ERIC Document Reproduction Service No. EJ 316 948)

Hoyt, K. B. (1975). *An introduction to career education.* Policy Paper of the United States Office of Education, DHEW Publications No. (OE) 75-00504. Washington, DC: U.S. Government Printing Office.

Hoyt, K. B. (1977). *A primer for career education.* Washington, DC: U.S. Government Printing Office.

Individuals with Disabilities Education Act of 2004, P.L. 108–466 [Online], Retrieved March 28, 2005, from http://thomas.loc.gov/cgi-bin/query/z?c108h.1350.enr:

Individuals with Disabilities Education Act of 1997, P.L. 105–17[Online], 111, 37. Available: Lexis-Nexis Database: PL 105-17 [1999, May 21].

Individuals with Disabilities Education Act of 1990, Public Law 101–476 (October 30, 1990). Title 20, U.S.C. 1400–1485: U.S. Statutes at large, 104, 1103–1151.

Levinson, E. M. (1993). *Transdisciplinary vocational assessment. Issues in school-based programs.* Brandon, VT: Clinical Psychology Publishing.

Lombard, R.C., Hazelkorn, M.N., & Miller, R.J. (1995). Special populations and tech-prep: A national study of state policies and practices. *Career Development for Exceptional Individuals, 18*(2), 145–156.

Lombard, R.C., Miller, R.J., & Hazelkorn, M.N. (1998). School-to-work and technical preparation: Teacher attitudes and practices regarding the inclusion of students with disabilities. *Career Development for Exceptional Individuals, 21*(2), 161–172.

Louis Harris and Associates. (2000). *Closing the gaps.* Washington, DC: National Organization on Disability.

National Science Foundation. (2000). *Women, minorities, and persons with disabilities in science and engineering.* Arlington, VA: Author. Retrieved May 2, 2003, from http://www.nsf.gov/pubs/20002/nsf0225/nsf0225.html

Siegel, S., Robert, M., Waxman, M., & Gaylord-Ross, R. (1992). A follow-along study of participants in a longitudinal transition program for youths with mild disabilities. *Exceptional Children, 58,* 346–356. (ERIC Document Reproduction Service No. EJ 442 994)

Sitlington P. L., Clark, G. M., & Kolstoe, O.P. (2000). *Transition education and services for adolescents with disabilities.* (3rd ed.). Needham Heights, MA: Allyn & Bacon.

Sitlington, P. L., Frank, A., & Carson, R. (1992). Are adolescents with learning disabilities successfully crossing the bridge into adult life? *Learning Disabilities Quarterly, 13,* 97–111. (ERIC Document Reproduction Service No. EJ 411 771)

Sitlington, P., Neubert, D., & Leconte, P. (1997). Transition assessment: The position of the Division on Career Development and Transition. *Career Development for Exceptional Individuals, 20*(1), 69–80.

U. S. Department of Education. (1994). School-to-Work Opportunities Act of 1994, Pub.L. No. 103–239. [Online]. Available at http://www.stw.ed.gov/factsht/act.htm.

Yell, M. L. (1998). *The law and special education.* Upper Saddle River, NJ: Prentice Hall.

CHAPTER

Career Development and Transition Assessment

A comprehensive understanding of the career development of adolescents with disabilities is critically important to the development of a systemic, sequential, and purposeful approach to design and implementation of career counseling interventions and transition programming (Rojewski, 1994). An understanding of career development is critical when choosing the methods, instruments, and strategies to be used in transition assessment. Career development is the process through which an individual comes to understand themselves as they relate to the world of work and their role in it (National Occupational Information Coordinating Committee, 1992).

The study of career decision making and the attempt to understand and describe why an individual makes career decisions is a young field of study. From 1900 through 1950 career theorists considered career decision making a one-time event based on matching the requirements of the job with the strengths and limitations of the individual (Trait-Factor theory of career development). For all practical purposes, this field of study began with the work of Frank Parsons (1909). It was not until the 1950s that career development theorists Ginzberg, Ginsburg, Axelrad, and Herma (1951) asserted that occupational choice was developmental in nature, that occupational choice was not a simple decision, but rather a series of decisions made over a period of years. Ginzberg, et al. (1951) identified a series of life stages through which all youth moved toward career choice. These stages were labeled as (a) *fantasy* (through age ten to twelve), (b) *tentative* (age twelve to eighteen) and (c) *realistic* (age eighteen to twenty-four).

Based on the work of Buehler (1933), Donald Super (1957) suggested five stages to the individual's career life. These life stages include *growth* (from birth thorough childhood), *exploration* (adolescence through young adulthood), *establishment* (adulthood through middle age), *maintenance* (middle age through retirement), and *decline* (retirement and beyond). Super theorized that the exploration stage of career development could be divided into the *tentative*, *transition*, and *trial* substages of development. In the *transition* substage of the exploration stage of career development, Super suggested that career decisions become increasingly realistic based on vocational thought and actions. In short, experience, interests, values, capacities, needs, and opportunities all assist the individual in making the transition from the exploration of careers into career choice, realistic career decision making, and finally into the establishment of a career.

Osipow (1975) suggested that the idea of self-concept implementation is a more or less unifying construct describing the process in which personal characteristics are included in thinking about careers. Super (1957, 1983) suggested that individuals with high self-esteem have clearer, more certain perceptions of themselves and their vocational goals when compared to individuals with low self-esteem. As a result, individuals with high self-esteem would be better prepared to identify needs, interests, values, and abilities, and to make more appropriate career choices. Super (1957, 1983) suggested that motivation is a function of drive, expectancy of success, and the incentive or attractiveness of the goal. As such, both achievement motivation and motivation to avoid failure impact human behavior. Since students with disabilities are often at high risk with regards to self-esteem, one might surmise that there is less risk of failure if one chooses not to risk attempting achievement. Therefore, low self-esteem and avoidance to risk are potential areas of concern for students with disabilities (Miller, 1988; Patton & Polloway, 1982; Bingham, 1980). Szymanski and Parker (1996) suggested that the process of career development is essentially the development and implementation of occupational self-concept.

According to Osipow (1973), the work of Tiedeman and O'Hara forms a link between the theories of Ginzberg and Super. All three groups share the view that career development is an aspect of general development. O'Hara and Tiedeman (1959) found aptitude, interest, social class, values, and understanding of one's own ability to be significant factors in vocational self-concept. Career decisions are made as a result of the totality of the individual's experiences. These experiences include the environmental realities and an ever-changing ability to estimate one's own abilities, interests, and psychological needs.

Tiedeman and O'Hara (1963) found occupational choice to be both developmental and systemic in that it is a process of decision making and subsequent adjustment. Crucial decisions occur at unequal intervals. Examples would include graduation from high school, college, marriage, first full-time job, etc. Career decision making is not a straight line but rather a process of three steps forward and two steps back. According to Tiedeman and O'Hara (1963), the individual arrives at an occupational choice with a perception of what that occupation will be like. Since the reality of the job and the expectations of the individual are never totally congruent, the individual and the job both tend to adjust to make an appropriate fit. However, if the job is too far beyond the individual's ability to flex, then the person will move to a new job. The decision making process includes anticipation, implementation, and adjustment. Career choices and the necessary conformity to others already in the field shape the individual's personality. Individuals with an inaccurate self-evaluation are more prone to make inappropriate or inadequate career decisions. (Tiedeman & O'Hara, 1963).

Ginzberg (1972) restated this theory of occupational choice based on twenty additional years of research. The restated theory suggested occupational choice was a life-long process of decision making in which the individual seeks to find the optimal fit between career preparation, goals, and realities of the world of work. According to Ginzberg (1972), career development is a life-span phenomenon which should be viewed as a series of decisions that have a shaping or cumulative effect on career development. These decisions shape career behavior hand-in-hand with continuing changes in the work place and life in general.

Career Maturity

Super (1957, 1983, 1990, 1994) suggested that self-concept and career maturity were key constructs in the career development of youth. Super and his colleagues were the first researchers to emphasize the importance of maturity in the ability to make wise occupational choices (Super & Overstreet, 1960), and are credited with developing the operational definition of career maturity (Jordaan & Heyde, 1979). The hypothetical construct that represents the constellation of physical, psychological (both cognitive and affective), and social characteristics that reflect the readiness or ability of the individual to participate in the career decision making process is called *career maturity*. (Szymanski & Parker, 1996). Gray (2000) stated "postsecondary success depends on both academic skills and commitment, which comes from career maturity and direction" (p. 124).

In 1983, Super identified attitudinal and cognitive factors that represented the readiness of young adults to make career choices and focus on career goals. Attitudinal factors in career maturity included:

- the ability to plan for near and distant futures;
- the ability to accept responsibility for one's own life (locus of control);

- a healthy perception of one's self-worth;
- an understanding of goal attainment and the time that goal attainment may require;
- the ability and willingness to explore careers;
- the willingness to ask questions and seek solutions;
- the willingness to seek out resources and utilize resources; and
- the willingness to participate in community-based and school-based activities.

Super (1983) identified cognitive factors of career maturity as (a) information for decision making, (b) rational decision making skills, and (c) a reality orientation based on the information gathered and decision making skills. In order to make appropriate career decisions the individual must have a realistic picture of strengths and limitations. This includes a realistic picture of one's self as worker and citizen. This realistic picture of self is enhanced by work experience in the community, stabilization of values, interests and goals, as well as consistency of personal preferences. Crystallization of interests, values, and personal preferences are key to choosing a career path. A career has been conceptualized as a series of related jobs over time, organized around a particular knowledge base and set of skills (Gray, 2000).

Career Development and Disability

It is clear that the nature of disability impacts the career development of adolescents with disabilities. The effects of disability on career development are varied and potentially substantial. Career maturity of the individual may be impaired or delayed, (LoCascio, 1974) and does not correspond directly to the age of the individual (Super, 1990). Career development for adolescents with disabilities is impacted by (a) limitations in early career exploration experiences, (b) limited opportunities to develop decision-making abilities, and (c) a negative self-concept resulting from societal attitudes toward persons with disabilities. (Conte, 1983; Curnow, 1989). Super (1994) suggested disability in children and adolescents is incorporated into the person's development of self-concept. Early dependency experiences may make a person fear competition or chance of failure during job search. Further, a lack of career experience and environmental factors may make obtaining employment more difficult. In a study exploring the role played by self-efficacy and career decision making involving postsecondary students with physical disabilities as they engaged in the career planning process, ELHessen (2002) found a high correlation between perception/acceptance of disability and self-efficacy which in turn showed strong correlation to career exploration behavior. Disability status has been found to have a strong, consistent, and negative influence on occupational aspirations of high school seniors with learning disabilities (Rojewski, 1996). Gottfredson (1986) identified career development risk factors for students with learning disabilities compared to a general population. These risk factors included poor academic skill, functional limitations, poor social skills, and low self-esteem. Kortering and Braziel (2000) found many adolescents with learning disabilities have unrealistic career ambitions or no career ambitions. In a review of research studies regarding the career development of persons with disabilities, Biller (1985) found students with learning disabilities were less prepared than their non-disabled peers to participate fully in adult life. Specifically, research has found students with learning disabilities to:

- exhibit an external locus of control,
- exhibit low self-esteem,
- exhibit poor planning skills,
- participate least in extra-curricular activities,
- have difficulty in obtaining information or to possess low amounts of information regarding real job duties of occupations,

- be weak in specific career decidedness, and
- as a result of the previous characteristics, have a weak reality orientation regarding their strengths and limitations.

The cumulative effect of these characteristics of career development of persons with disabilities is that adolescents with disabilities are often less career mature than non-disabled peers and as a result are less ready to make career decisions and may be less prepared for adult responsibilities (Field, et al., 1998; Sitlington, et al., 1996; Rojewski, 1993). However, there is neither the need nor the possibility for a separate theory of career development for persons with disabilities (Beveridge, et al., 2002; Conte, 1983). Persons with disabilities represent a highly diverse population of individuals. While disability impacts career development, disability is a single factor that influences and impacts the career development of that individual. While we may generalize regarding possible impacts of disability on career development, the real impact of disability must be measured on an individual student level and each adolescent's career development and career maturity will vary. Gauging the impact of disability on career development is one of the purposes of transition assessment.

Career Development and Transition Assessment

While career development and career assessment have been rich areas for research regarding non-disabled populations, Rojewski (2002) noted that attention to career and transition-related assessment issues for individuals with mild disabilities has been relatively limited in comparison. One of the first steps in any transition assessment process is to obtain a fundamental understanding of the individual students' strengths and limitations in the career development process (Sitlington, et al., 1996). Sitlington, et al. (1996) suggest assessment within a career development context will assist the student in beginning to understand the interdependent relationship among adult roles. Based on the career development model of Donald Super, Figure 2.1 includes a list of sample questions that the student, family, and special education case manager should consider during this initial phase of transition assessment to gauge the career maturity of the student. The assessment results garnered by these questions concerning career development of the student will assist in identifying areas in which transition goals and objectives may be considered.

"Readiness" to Make Career Decisions

Since career decision making is a developmental process, the "readiness" of a student to make career choices is not an issue that should limit an individual's participation in career development activities. While IDEA 2004 does not require that transition planning begin before age sixteen, we strongly advocate that transition assessment begin at age thirteen and transition planning at age fourteen. Some teachers have registered concerns that age fourteen is "too early" for transition assessment and transition planning with students with disabilities. At this age, students with disabilities often do not have a clear idea of career interests, may lack a vision of future goals, are often immature, and may have unrealistic career goals such as becoming a professional football player, baseball player, or fashion model. Educators may be unsure of the value of collecting transition assessment information regarding what are considered to be unrealistic or fantasy goals of students. As a result, these educators may view

Transition Assessment: Questions to Ask to Gauge the Career Maturity of a Student

1. Can you (student) name two jobs that you are interested in finding out more information about for a career after high school? (career decidedness and reality orientation)
2. Can you (student) list three reasons (rational) why you are interested in each of the two jobs listed above? (information regarding career interests, maturity of choice)
3. Can you (student) list two reasons why you believe you would be good at the job you are interested in? Do you have any limitations that you would need to address or accommodate to get and keep a job in this area? (strengths and limitations, reality orientation)
4. You (student) got a "C-" on an English assignment that you thought you had done really well on. What are two questions you might ask your English teacher to improve your grade on the next assignment? (willingness and ability to ask questions and seek solutions)
5. A friend asks you (student) to go to the lake for the weekend with his or her family. The friend says you will have a great time fishing and boating. What are five questions you need to ask your friend in order to get the information for your parents so you and your parents can decide if you will go? (willingness and ability to ask questions, planning for near and distant futures)
6. Pick out one of the careers you were interested in getting more information about in question one (e.g., plumber or cosmetologist). If you had the opportunity to talk to a person in this field, what are five questions that you would ask that professional to find out if that job were right for you? (gathering information, understanding goal attainment, willingness to ask questions and seek solutions)
7. Would you like to spend one afternoon in the business community watching this professional work and asking him or her questions about the career? If yes, why? If no, why not? (ability and willingness to explore careers, willingness to ask questions, willingness to seek out and use resources, willingness to participate in community-based activity)

Figure 2.1

assessment of transition needs, preferences, and interests of students as premature or even untimely.

It is, however, precisely for these reasons that transition assessment and transition planning must begin at this early age. Transition assessment and transition planning are designed to begin early to address these very concerns. Career development literature strongly supports the importance of *information* and *experience* as key variables in providing the individual with the experiential base to make decisions and develop a realistic vision of one's strengths and limitations. This realistic vision of one's strengths and limitations are the building blocks of a *reality orientation*. Understanding one's strengths and limitations assists the individual to establish a *realistic plan for near and distant futures* and enhances career maturity. Englert, Tarrant, and Mariage (1992) identify the following as effective cognitive interventions for use with adolescents with learning disabilities:

- goal setting;
- clear demonstrations of self-talk and task-specific strategies;
- opportunities for students to practice both behavior and thinking skills in authentic situations;
- feedback and giving and listening to explanations; and
- teaching students to generalize and apply knowledge across various settings and conditions.

Gottfredson (1986) suggested that everyone, not just special populations, experience some type of career related problems based on the degree to which certain risk factors are present. A lack of career development is a concern for many middle school students including adolescents with disabilities. The U.S. Department of Education (1990) conducted a National Education Study which included 23,000 eighth grade students. Results revealed:

- approximately 1/3 of eighth grade students had little knowledge about different occupations, or the relevance of school to future work and career selection.
- 64% of eighth grade students had never discussed their future high school program with their guidance counselor.
- 50–66% of eighth grade students plan to complete college but only 25% planned to take any college preparation courses.

Jencks, et al. (1979) found teachers' ratings of tenth graders' executive ability (e.g., planning skills) to be a better predictor of a student's future adult earnings than teacher ratings of students as "industrious." To delay the implementation of transition assessment and transition planning may only delay the development of realistic career goals and the corresponding vision of the value of education in attaining these goals.

Crystallization of career choice may or may not be dramatically effected by disability. For example, a student with a serious visual impairment is not going to become an airline pilot. The student with significant visual impairments does not meet the fundamental physical vision requirement for this career. There is no accommodation that is required or appropriate for any individual who does not meet this physical requirement under the law. However, a student who is deaf may aspire to become a composer. While the student's hearing impairment would seem to make a career in music composition unlikely, it does not make it impossible.

In a study examining the relationship between disability status, career indecision, and the beliefs that individuals have regarding the world of work, Enright (1994) found significant correlation between self-doubt of the individual and career indecision. In addition, this researcher found a small interactive relationship between self-doubt and disability status. In a study of the interactive relationship between career indecision, age, and disability status, Tseng (1992) found older students with disabilities had significantly higher levels of career indecision when compared to their non-disabled peers. Clearly, students with disabilities need information and experience for decision making. Students with disabilities need to learn to plan for near and distant futures as a key component of establishing realistic career goals. Early assessment in career development is necessary to determine the career maturity and career development of the student.

CHAPTER SUMMARY

Chapter 2 has explored career development and the possible impact of disability on the career development of adolescents with disabilities. We found out that

- self-concept and career maturity are key constructs in gauging the career development of all students including students with disabilities.
- career development is a life-long and developmental process.
- disability impacts career development. However, career development and disability are specific to the individual. As such, assessment of the student's career development is necessary to determine the career maturity and career development of the student.
- many middle school students including adolescents with disabilities are in need of career development activities as a portion of their school experience.
- the ability to participate in career decision making is impacted by the student's career maturity. Donald Super (1983) has identified cognitive and attitudinal factors influencing career maturity.

CHAPTER ACTIVITIES

Included in Appendix A, part 1 (A-1) you will find a form titled "Questions to Ask to Gauge Career Maturity of Student." These are the same questions found in Figure 2.1. Please use this informal assessment instrument and ask these questions of a student with a mild disability age fourteen to twenty-one. What information did you learn regarding the career maturity of the student using this informal assessment process?

DISCUSSION QUESTIONS

Discuss strategies and techniques for explaining to families how career development fits into transition planning for students with mild disabilities. Next, explain how career development fits into the general education curriculum.

CHAPTER REFERENCES

Beveridge, S., Craddock, S. H., Lieserver, J., Stapleton, M., & Hershenson, D. (2002). Income: A framework for conceptualizing the career development of persons with disabilities. *Rehabilitation Counseling Bulletin, 45*(4). Retrieved June 2004 from http://www.worksupport.com/main/proed16.asp

Biller, E.F. (1987). *Career decision making for adolescents and young adults with learning disabilities: Theory, research, and practice*. Springfield, IL: Charles C. Thomas.

Biller, E. F. (1985). *Understanding and guiding the career development of adolescents and young adults with learning disabilities*. Springfield, IL: Charles C. Thomas.

Bingham, G. (1980). Career maturity of learning disabled adolescents. *Psychology in the school, 17*, 135–139.

Buehler, C. (1933). *Der menschilche lebenslau als psychologiches problem*. Lepzig: Hirzel.

Conte, L. E. (1983). Vocational development theories and the disabled person: Oversight or deliberate omission? *Rehabilitation Counseling Bulletin, 27*, 316–328.

Curnow, T. C. (1989). Vocational development of persons with disability. *Career Development Quarterly, 37*, 269–278.

ELHessen, S. (2002). A new paradigm to career counseling: Self-efficacy and career choice among students with disabilities in postsecondary education. Retrieved September 9, 2003 from http://icdl.uncg.edu/ft/060603-5.html

Englert, C. S., Tarrant, K. L., & Mariage, T. V. (1992). Defining and redefining instructional practice in special education: Perspectives on good teaching. *Teacher Education and Special Education, 15*(2), 62–86.

Enright, M. S. (1994). *The relationship between disability status, career beliefs, and career indecision*. Unpublished doctoral dissertation. University of Wisconsin—Madison.

Field, S., Martin, J., Miller, R., Ward, M., & Wehmeyer, M. (1998). *A practical guide for teaching self-determination*. Reston, VA: Council for Exceptional Children.

Ginzberg, E. (1972). Toward a theory of occupational choice: A restatement. *Vocational Guidance Quarterly, 20*, 169–176.

Ginzberg, E., Ginzburg, S.W., Axelrad, S., & Herma, J. L. (1951). *Occupational choice: An approach to a general theory*. New York: Columbia University.

Gottfredson, L. S. (1986). Special groups and the beneficial use of vocational interest inventories. In W. B. Walsh & S. H. Osipow (Eds.), *Advances in vocational psychology, Volume 1: The assessment of interests* (pp. 127–198). Hillsdale, NJ: Erlbaum.

Gray, K. C. (2000). *Getting real: Helping teens find their future*. Thousand Oaks, CA: Corwin.

Jencks, C., Barrtlett, S., Corcoran, M., Crouse, J., Eaglesfield, D., Jackson, G., McClelland, K., Mueser, P., Olneck, M., Schwartz, J., Ward, S., & Williams, J. (1979). *Who gets ahead? The determinants of economic success in America*. New York: Basic Books.

Jordaan, J. P., & Heyde, M. B. (1979). *Vocational maturity during the high school years*.

New York: Teachers College Press, Teachers College, Columbia University.

Kortering, L., & Braziel, P. (2000). A look at the expressed career ambitions of youth with disabilities. *Journal for Vocational Special Needs Education, 23*(1), 24–33.

LoCascio, R. (1974). The vocational maturity of diverse groups: Theory and measurement. In D. E. Super (Ed.), *Measuring vocational maturity for counseling and evaluation* (pp. 122–133). Washington, DC: Division of American Personnel and Guidance Association.

Miller, R. J. (1988). *The effects of selected characteristics on the learning disabled subject's decision to participate in post-secondary education opportunities*. Unpublished doctoral dissertation, University of Iowa, Iowa City, Iowa.

National Occupational Information Coordinating Committee. (1992). *The national career development guidelines.* Washington, DC: Author.

O'Hara, R. P., & Tiedeman, D. V. (1959). Vocational self concept in adolescence. *Journal of Counseling Pschology, 60*, 292–301.

Osipow, S. H. (1975). The relevance of theories of career development to special groups: Problems, needed data, and implications. In J. S. Picou & R. E. Campbell (Eds.). *Career behavior of special groups*. Columbus, OH: Merrill.

Osipow, S. H. (1973). Theories of career development. (2nd ed.). New York: Meredith Corporation.

Parsons, F. (1909). *Choosing a vocation.* Boston: Houghton Mifflin.

Patton, J. R., & Polloway, E. A. (1982). The learning disabled: The adult years. *Topics in Learning and Learning Disabilities, 2*(3), 79–88.

Rojewski, J. W. (2002). Career assessment for adolescents with mild disabilities: Critical concerns for transition planning. *Career Development for Exceptional Individuals, 25*(1), 73–95.

Rojewski, J. W. (1996). Educational and occupational aspirations of high school seniors with learning disabilities. *Exceptional Children, 62*, 463–476. (ERIC Document Reproduction Service No. EJ 519 867)

Rojewski, J. W. (1994). Applying theories of career behavior to special populations: Implications for vocational transition programming. In P. M. Retish (Ed.), *Issues in Special Education and Rehabilitation, 9*(1), 7–26. Israel: University of Haifa.

Rokewski, J. W. (1993). Theoretical structure of career maturity for rural adolescents with learning disabilities. *Career Development for Exceptional Individuals, 16*, 39–52.

Sitlington, P. L., Neubert, D. A., Begun, W., Lombard, R. C., & Leconte, P. J. (1996). *Assess for success: Handbook on transition assessment.* Reston, VA: Council for Exceptional Children.

Super, D. E. (1994). A life-span, life-space perspective on convergence. In M. L. Sanvickas & R. W. Lent (Eds.)., *Convergence in career development theories: Implications for science and practice* (pp. 63–74). Palo Alto, CA: Consulting Psychologists Press.

Super, D. E. (1990). A life-span, life-space approach to career development. In D. Brown & L. Brooks, & Associates, *Career choice and development: Applying contemporary theories to practice.* (2nd ed., pp. 197–261). San Francisco: Jossey-Bass.

Super, D. E. (1983). Assessment in career guidance: Toward truly developmental counseling. *The Personnel and Guidance Journal, 61*(9), 555–561.

Super, D. E. (1957). *The psychology of careers.* New York: Harper & Row.

Super, D. E., & Overstreet, P. L. (1960). *The vocational maturity of ninth grade boys.* New York: Bureau of Publications, Teachers College, Columbia University.

Szymanski, E. M., & Parker, R. M. (Eds.). (1996). *Work and disability: Issues and strategies in career development and job placement.* Austin, TX: PRO-ED.

Teideman, D. V., & O'Hara, R. P. (1963). *Career development: Choice and adjustment.* New York: College Entrance Examination Board.

Tseng, C. C. (1992). A study of the relationship of disability status and life experience among college students. (Doctoral dissertation, University of Wisconsin—Madison). *Dissertation Abstracts International, 53*, 1883A.

U. S. Department of Education (1990). The conditions of education. Washington, DC: National Center for Education Statistics.

CHAPTER 3

Assessment of Future Planning Needs

The Relationship of Career Planning, Future Planning, and Transition Assessment

In the transition assessment process, the first step is future planning assessment (see Figure 3.1). This makes future planning assessment a critically important component of the transition assessment process. Future planning is a person-centered planning process and is the starting point in the assessment of goals, interests, preferences, and aspirations for life after high school. Future planning assessment can help the student, family, and educator develop a longitudinal plan to reach career goals as well as goals regarding lifestyle after high school. Career planning is the core assessment component of the larger and more encompassing future planning process (see Figure 3.2). Career planning is an essential component of career development and future planning. It is critical for effective transition planning and is the cornerstone of making appropriate career, educational, and occupational choices. Career planning requires specific, systematic, and formal planning (Cunanan & Maddy-Bernstein, 1995). Cunanan and Maddy-Bernstein (1995) suggest that the process of career planning include:

1. information—presenting students with current and predictive data regarding market trends in employment to facilitate career decisions;
2. assessment of interests, abilities, aptitude, and preferences;
3. parental involvement;
4. intra- and interagency collaboration;
5. development of a career plan that reflects the career planning process; and
6. evaluation of the career plan on an annual basis.

Career planning assessment identifies the interests, preferences, and future career goals of the student and is a critical component of the broader future planning process. Depending on the age and career maturity of the student, the student may have no clear career focus, the student may have a foggy concept of his or her future career, or the student may have a mature, crystallized vision of his or her future career goals. Any of these visions is appropriate and it is the goal of transition planning and assessment to move the student forward toward the development of specific career goals around which we can develop the transition plan and identify the education and training necessary for high school and beyond.

Wehmeyer, Agran, and Hughes (1998) suggest that educators can use observation, interview, and assessment instruments to identify the interests, preferences, choices, and expectations of students and that this information will facilitate the student's transition to adulthood. It is in the future planning process that the student is asked as a component of formal transition assessment and planning: What career do you want after high school? Where do you want to live after high school? What supports will you need to succeed during high school and after high school? What recreational and leisure activities will you participate in after high school?, etc. The cumulative effect of asking these questions develops a vision

Transition Assessment Model

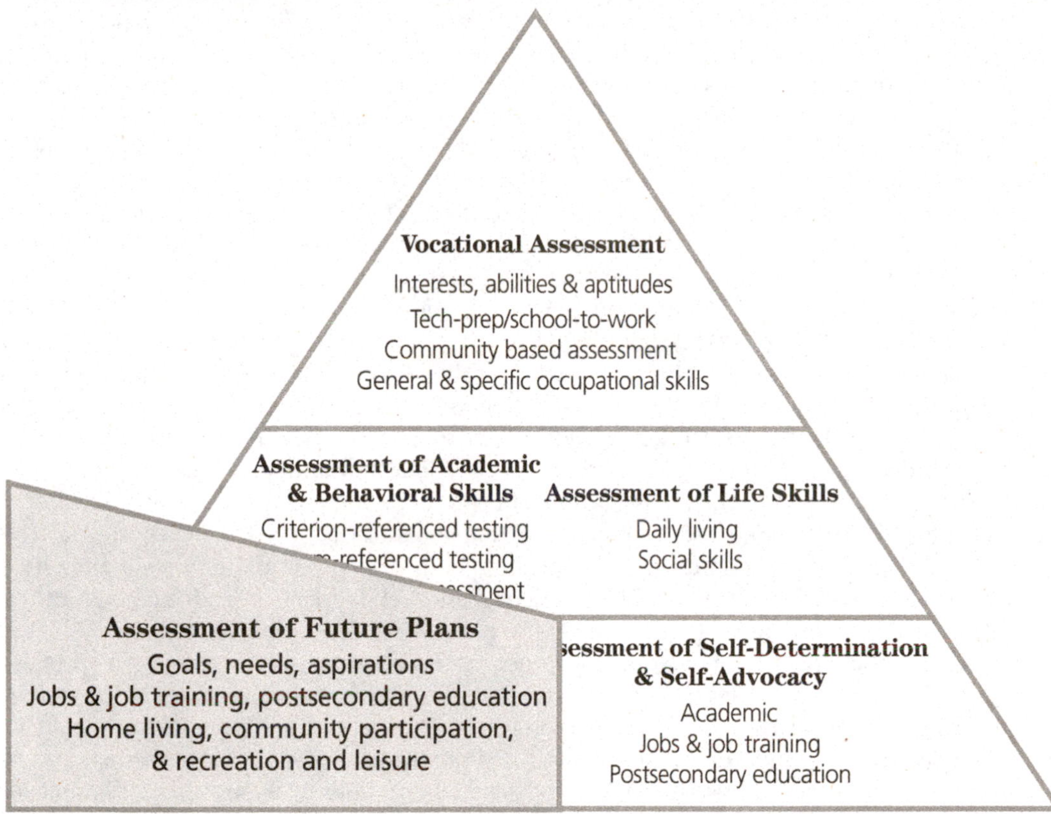

Figure 3.1

Assessment of Future Planning Needs

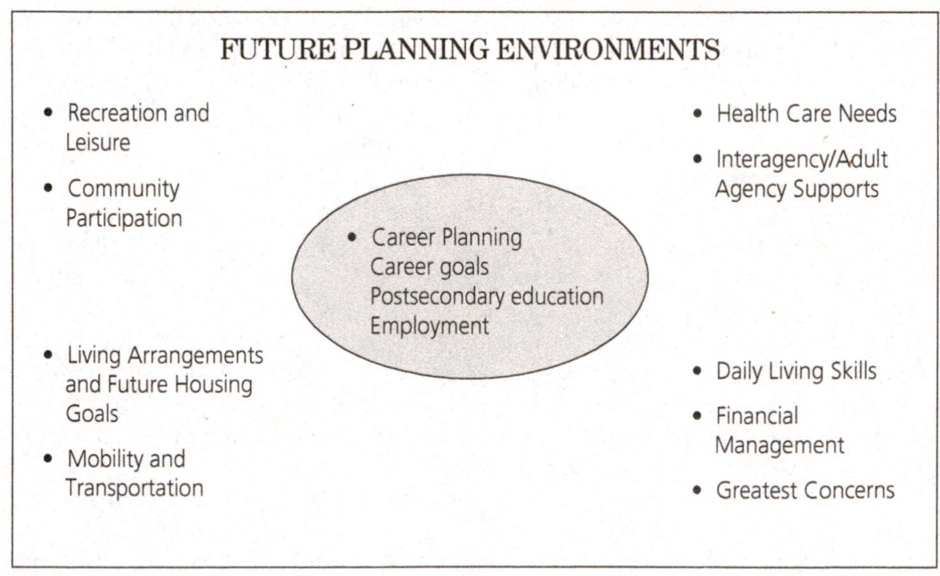

Figure 3.2

of who the student will be after high school so a plan can be developed to address these future goals. The importance of this future planning process can not be overstated. Future planning is the component of the transition assessment process in which the student articulates his or her vision of their future life and begins the process of developing plans to accomplish these goals. It is through this process that educators can begin to harness the natural motivation of the student to take charge of their own life and future. Envisioning the future leads to decisions regarding future plans—to choice making—which motivates the student to accomplish his or her plan. According to Van Reusen and Bos (1994), students who choose their own activities are more motivated to participate in those activities and complete those activities.

Nearly one third (32.5%) of students with disabilities drop out of high school on a national basis (Valdes, Williamson, & Wagner, 1990). According to these researchers, almost half (49.5%) of all young adults with emotional disturbance/behavior disorders drop out of high school. Researchers hypothesize that one reason students with disabilities drop out of high school is the lack of success they feel in the public schools, as well as a student-perceived lack of relevance of the public school experience. Future planning acts as a catalyst to provide the student ownership of their educational program and the IEP process. If done properly, the process helps the student and family to identify and report interests, preferences, goals, and aspirations. Future planning ensures that the educational program considers the interests, preferences, and goals of the student as required by the IDEA. If, as we believe, the purpose of education is to prepare students for life after high school, then assessment of future planning goals and needs must be an initial step in the development of a consumer-driven and person-centered IEP process.

While the strength of having a consumer-driven and person-centered IEP process seems self-evident for students with mild disabilities, one must also be aware of the potential limitations of any process that focuses on the student with disabilities to provide direction for future planning. The student with a disability may fear their unknown future (Menchetti & Sweeney, 1994–1995). Students may be unable to effectively communicate their interests and preferences, be unwilling to reveal their aspirations and plans, or have no idea of their long-term goals (O'Brien & Lovett, 1992). Clark (1998) suggested that person-centered planning requires trained, knowledgeable, and committed persons to facilitate the planning process. Further, Clark (1998) suggested that the person-centered process may be a product of a mostly white, middle-class advocacy community and may fail to fully consider cultural and ethnic group differences with the concept of establishing a vision of the future. Finally, one must remember that future planning is a process and not a one-time event. The process assists students to develop knowledge of self as well as goals for near and distant futures and must be used on a longitudinal basis to be effective. Future planning assessment can not stand alone as a comprehensive transition assessment.

Assessment based on future goals is effected by both planned and unplanned student life experiences, which provides a context for potential changes in student transition choices. As a result, needs derived from the assessment of future goals should be revisited on at least a yearly basis to ensure that the direction charted by this assessment still reflects the goals, aspirations, and interests of the student and family, as well as the additional life experience that each adolescent receives in the daily living and educational process.

Future planning is directly linked and interwoven to the assessment of the self-determination and the self-advocacy skills of the student. Together, future planning and self-determination assessments provide the foundation for all transition assessment activities (see Figure 3.3). Further, future planning assessment is dependent on the data gathered in the other assessment processes including assessment of self-determination and self-advocacy skills, as well as academic and learning style assessment, life skill assessment, and vocational assessment. In a study of the perceptions of students, parents, and educators, regarding the transition IEP process, Friedland (1999) found that some students with mild intellectual disabilities had difficulty communicating future plans with their parents and had

Foundations of Transition Assessment	
Assessment of Future Planning Needs and Goals	Assessment of Student Self-Determination and Self-Advocacy Skills
• Home living • Community participation • Recreation and leisure • Jobs and job training • Postsecondary education and training	• Academic environment • Jobs and job training • Postsecondary education and training

Figure 3.3

difficulty communicating their future plans in general. In addition, Friedland found no systematic training of students was taking place in self-determination skills. Self-determination and self-advocacy assessment will be discussed in the next chapter.

Resources for Assessing Future Planning Needs of Students with Mild to Moderate Disabilities

Over the past several years, assessment processes and materials have been published to assist the IEP team in gathering relevant information regarding future planning goals of the student and family. The following is a brief overview of several future planning processes and materials. You may wish to review each of these for possible use in the transition assessment process. The initial assessment of future planning goals should be in place before the student turns fourteen years of age.

Future Planning Inventory System

The Future Planning System (FPS) was first published as a component of transition assessment by the Minnesota Department of Education in 1993 (Corbey, et al., 1993) and was updated in 1998. This future planning system was designed for use with students with mild disabilities and their families. (A set of the FPS inventories is included in Appendix A, part 2 (A-2). The FPS is comprised of three interrelated inventories to be completed by the student, the parent(s)/guardian, and the special educator. We suggest that you copy each of the three inventories on a different color paper to easily discriminate among assessment information provided by the student, parent(s)/guardian, and educator.

These inventories gather future planning information in the following areas:

- vocational/postsecondary education options
- home living options
- recreation/leisure options
- transportation options

- financial support
- health-related needs
- greatest future concerns

These future planning areas are consistent with the transition planning requirements as identified in the IDEA 2004.

Each of the three inventories requires the completer to respond to similar items regarding future planning goals and needs from their unique perspective. It is imperative that the student, parent(s)/guardian, and educator each complete their inventories independently in order to ensure that only their vision of the future is reflected in the responses on the inventory. The student, parent(s)/guardian, and educator could have considerably different visions of the student's employment, postsecondary education, or independent living in the years after high school.

The inventories are designed to be used as an integral part of an ongoing assessment of transition needs and aspirations. The data gathered from these inventories are discussed at IEP meetings or are reported in a comprehensive evaluation report and can elicit student needs which in turn can be used to formulate transition goals and objectives in the IEP process. The interview and discussion with the student, parent(s)/guardian, and educator regarding the information in the FPS provides for clarification of information found in the future planning documents as well as an opportunity to *negotiate* what future goals will be the focus for transition planning. We suggest that inventories are completed and updated by the student, parent(s)/guardian, and educator on an annual or biannual basis and that each participant's inventory be completed and brought to the IEP meeting to provide direction for planning the student's academic year and beyond. Successful transition planning is based on the IEP team possessing a common vision for the young adult's future given their strengths, limitations, hopes, and dreams for their life after high school. The Future Planning System inventories will be useful tools to achieve this end.

Student Inventory

The primary purpose of the student inventory is to identify the goals and aspirations of young adults both during high school and in planning for life after high school. A second purpose of the student inventory is to begin the process of educating the student in the terminology of transition (e.g., supported employment, ASVAB test, Pell grant) as well as information for the student in the names of important adult service providers (e.g., Division of Rehabilitation Services [vocational rehabilitation], supplemental security income [social security], technical college) that offer services in each transition planning area. Before students can make choices regarding their future, they must have information regarding options and supports for the future as well as an understanding of the criteria to receive services from adult providers that may be useful or needed in life after high school. Starting before age fourteen, and with the use of the student inventory, special education personnel can begin to inservice the student as to options and choices. Certainly, the curriculum of the student with a mild disability must also include exposure to these community resources as well as training in the appropriate use of these resources. The student inventory provides an opportunity for the student to articulate their future and to begin the process of identifying needed support services.

No attempt was made in the design of this student inventory to reduce the reading level at the expense of needed transition vocabulary. Reading level can easily be accommodated and we believe that appropriate accommodation is imperative if needed. However, students (and their families) must learn the terminology of adult service providers as well as the names of agencies that provide needed services. As such, these inventories provide needed inservice for the student (and family) as well as gathering important planning information.

If the student needs assistance in completing the student inventory, referral to a high school guidance counselor or school social worker will be helpful. If the special education teacher has any concerns regarding the ability or readiness of the young adult to complete the inventory independently, the teacher could assist the student in setting up an appointment with a high school guidance counselor or social worker to complete the inventory. This could alleviate several potential concerns. First, students would gain access to a professional guidance counselor or school social worker when identifying preferences and aspirations. Second, this process would involve the high school guidance counselor or social worker as a resource in the planning process. Third, involving the counselor or social worker in establishing future planning goals will insure that the student's interests and goals are presented at the IEP meeting. Young adults with disabilities should complete an inventory and bring the completed form to their IEP/transition meeting.

Parent/Guardian Inventory

Before the student reaches the age of fourteen, this inventory should be sent to parents or guardians annually or bi-annually and at least two full weeks prior to a scheduled IEP meeting. Parents should be instructed to complete the inventory and to bring it to the IEP meeting. While the primary purpose is to gather information for future planning, a secondary purpose of the inventory is to begin the process of inservice of the family in the names and services provided by adult providers.

The inventories in this future planning system may be used in many fashions. For example, you may wish to include a copy of the previous year's parent inventory as well as a new (clean) copy of the inventory. Some parents may choose to review and update the previous year's inventory by simply initialing sections of the inventory that remain the same and crossing out and making additional comments on inventory areas that have changed over the past year. Remember that the purpose is to gather data on an annual or biannual basis for assessment and planning. Any method of gathering this assessment information that works for the student, family, and educator is appropriate.

It is possible that the family (or student) may be unaware of some or all of the adult providers and the services offered by those providers early in the future planning assessment process. As such, the initial inventory from the parents or student (age fourteen) may have very limited information. It is important that the IEP/ transition team members understand that this is a longitudinal process and that planning improves with the age and career maturity of the student as does the opportunity for the family and IEP team to participate in the planning process.

Educator Inventory

Special educators should complete the educator inventory before reviewing the contents of the parent or student forms. The educator's perceptions of the student will be helpful in negotiating the most appropriate transition plan. As with all participants, the special educator should complete the inventory annually or biannually and prior to each student's IEP/transition meeting.

Students with disabilities many times lack experience in processing information for future planning or thinking beyond the present moment. Therefore, the development of future goals is something that may not occur naturally and must be orchestrated. The same thing can be said for parents/guardians since having the student complete high school may be foremost in their minds. The FPS inventories provide an opportunity to think beyond the present and supplies specific information for future planning to begin.

Oftentimes the various perceptions—the student's, the parent's, and the educator's—don't gel into a common vision of the future. Students may view their disability as limiting them more than it actually will, or the student may have on over-inflated idea of what the future may hold for them. This phenomenon may be equally true of many young adults without disabilities who are thirteen to twenty-two years of age with limited life experience. However, students with disabilities may have less time than their peers without disabilities to choose and prepare for adult roles (see Chapter 2 for a review of career maturity issues). Parents may or may not have difficulty viewing their child as an adult with all the related responsibilities and privileges. As a result, a yearly opportunity to discuss, realign, and refine the common vision is imperative at the time of the IEP meeting. In the absence of a common vision of the future, the student, parent(s)/guardian, and educator have a responsibility to work together to negotiate common ground so that a meaningful plan can be developed.

The following sets of scenarios are designed to illustrate the flexibility and opportunity afforded the IEP/transition team through the use of the FPS or similar informal future planning assessment.

Using Future Planning Assessment Information to Develop IEP Goals

Scenario 1: Considering Future Plans and High School Curriculum

Akram, a sixteen-year-old student (beginning of 10th grade) with a learning disability completed the Student Future Planning Inventory with the assistance of the school social worker. Last year, Akram wanted to be a plumber. During his freshman year he did several reports for English class on plumbing as a career. Through this process he gathered information regarding future job opportunities in plumbing as well as information regarding the typical day of a plumber. He also job-shadowed a plumber for three hours on two different school days during the school year. Based on this experience, Akram is no longer interested in becoming a plumber. He was surprised at how dirty plumbers seemed to get while doing their job. He was also surprised at the amount of time that the plumbers seem to work by themselves. Akram is now sure he wants to work with people.

Akram is now really excited about attending a community college or four-year college and studying law enforcement to become a police officer (see Figure 3.4, Section I, parts A–F of Akram's 10th grade Future Planning Inventory). Akram's parents are aware that he is interested in law enforcement and are very supportive. They are aware that he is no longer interested in plumbing as a career. All parties (student, teacher and parents) are in agreement that Akram is a motivated student with strong academic motivation and potential. A review of Akram's student inventory (Section I, parts A–F), found in Figure 3.4, suggests that Akram does not fully understand the relationship between college preparation curriculum and college attendance. This change in career goal was addressed at the IEP team meeting and an appropriate transition plan was written to reflect Akram's new career goal. This change in career paths required a change in some of Akram's coursework for the 10th grade. Akram's educational program was changed from a vocationally focused and "hands-on" high school curriculum to a more academic and college preparation curriculum. Akram's academic strength is in mathematics. His disability manifests itself in written and oral communication. Akram is in need of social skills training and enhanced communication skills. IEP goals and transition activities were written as follows to address this career plan.

Postsecondary Education

Future Goal After graduation, I (Akram) plan to attend a community college or university and major in law enforcement so I can train to become a police officer.

Akram's Future Planning Inventory

Education Options

What kind of courses do you want to take during high school? (Be sure you choose the kind of coursework that will meet your future planning goals!)

_X_ College preparation
_X_ Vocational/Technical preparation
___ General education (Minimum graduation requirements)
_X_ I don't know

I. Vocational/Postsecondary Education Options

A. Upon graduation, I want to go on for future education and training.

_X_ Yes ___ No

If yes, please check each kind of postsecondary education or training that interests you.

_X_ Four-year college/university
_X_ Community college
_X_ Technical college
___ Private occupational training program
___ Military service
___ Adult education program

What do you want to study or train to be? _Police Officer_

My level of motivation to succeed in the academic setting:
_X_ high ___ medium ___ low

The level of control I have over decision making and my individual success:
___ high _X_ medium ___ low

My ability to identify what I need and how to get it:
___ high _X_ medium ___ low

B. Upon graduation I am going to get a job right away.

_X_ Yes ___ No

If yes, please check the kind of job you expect to have.
_X_ Competitive employment: ___ Full-time _X_ Part-time
___ Self-employed
___ Supported employment: ___ Full-time ___ Part-time
___ Sheltered employment: ___ Full-time ___ Part-time

C. In what type of job/occupation will you be working one year after graduation?
Food Worker

D. In what type of job/occupation will you be working in five years after graduation?
Police Officer

E. What courses do you need to take in high school this year that will help you attain your employment or postsecondary education goals?
Woodworking _Not sure_
English

F. Do you want information on testing required to get into postsecondary education (e.g., ASVAB, SAT, ACT, PSAT)? _Yes, what do I need?_

Figure 3.4

(continued)

Scenario 1: Considering Future Plans and High School Curriculum (continued)

Transition Needs Akram and the transition team agree that Akram needs (1) information regarding law enforcement careers; (2) information regarding the relationship between college preparation curriculum and college attendance; (3) improved social and communication skills.

Transition Services/Activities

1. With the support of his parents, Akram and (educator) will visit with the police department and set up a job-shadowing experience for Akram.
2. Akram will join the Police Explorers student organization.
3. Akram will visit the community college or university and find out what courses and grades are required to get into college. He will also visit with at least one student who is majoring in law enforcement.
4. Akram will research careers in law enforcement and will explore the supply and demand for police officers and other careers in law enforcement over the next decade.
5. During English or Social Studies, when given an opportunity to write a report, Akram will do a report on the Miranda Act or other legal issues of importance to law enforcement.

IEP Goal The ability to communicate freely and to gather and provide information is very important in law enforcement. Akram will increase his communication skills from a level of having difficulty starting and maintaining conversations with individuals he does not know well to a level of communicating freely and gathering information from persons he does not know well.

Instructional Objectives

1. With use of the accommodations listed on the IEP, Akram will receive a grade of at least a "B" in his sophomore communications class.
2. On three consecutive trials, Akram will have a five-minute conversation with three individuals he does not know well. During each conversation Akram will provide three items of information and collect three items of information. The adults with whom Akram has these conversations will rate Akram's conversation skills on a five-point Likert scale with a rating of (1) as "not adequate," (3) as "adequate," and (5) as "outstanding communication skills".
3. Given instruction in social skills communication strategies, Akram will list the ten steps and behaviors with 90% accuracy on two consecutive trials.

Scenario 2: Capturing and Considering Different Visions

Karen, an eighteen-year-old 11th grade student with an emotional behavior disorder, completed the Student Future Planning Inventory without assistance (during the spring term of 11th grade). Based on the results of the future planning assessment, Karen is planning to move from her small hometown to a large urban metropolitan area approximately 100 miles from her home once she graduates (see Figure 3.5, Home Living Options in Karen's Future Planning Inventory). Based on conversation during the IEP meeting regarding her plans for home living, Karen now hopes to live in an apartment with a female friend. Based on other sections of the FPS, Karen has no plans to continue in postsecondary education after high school and she is planning to "get a job" once she moves to the large metropolitan area. The kind of employment seems less important to Karen than moving to the large urban community.

This is a big surprise to Karen's parents. Last year, based on the 10th grade IEP/transition meeting, Karen was planning to live at home after she graduated and work in her hometown. Her parents were not aware she had changed her independent living goals. Based on the current future planning inventory (11th grade) completed by her parents, Karen would remain at home and live in her hometown after high school. In the 10th grade, the parties were in agreement that Karen would remain in the small community after graduation. In this case, Karen's parents are very concerned that the student does not have the daily living skills or the emotional and social skills to live independently in a large city without family support.

In situations such as this, it is important to remember that the IEP team must attempt to negotiate a transition and educational plan that all parties can find acceptable. It is also important to remember that the student's plans must lead the way in the development of a meaningful transition plan. First, remember that this is the student's transition plan. The student must be heard and his or her goals and aspirations must be strongly considered. Families and educators may want to consider developing a "layered transition plan." A layered transition plan develops a "safety net" of transition objectives and skills to ensure that the student's goals as well as adult concerns are addressed. A layered transition plan addresses the student's goals and aspirations and then questions: What will happen if this goal does not work? In the following scenario regarding Karen's transition plan, the reader will note that the IEP focuses on preparing Karen for a potential move to the urban center. This is Karen's plan. In this scenario, the team will plan for Karen's potential move with the caveat that Karen will need to demonstrate that she has developed independent living skills (as demonstrated by reaching her annual goals and short-term objectives) in order to gain the support of family and educators for the move. If Karen does not develop the skills listed on the IEP she may decide she is not ready to live independently. Karen may also change her mind to move to the urban center over the next academic year.

This does not mean to suggest that Karen could not move with or without the support of family and educators. It is important to remember several realities regarding Karen's plan to move after high school. Under the *Transfer of Rights* provision of IDEA,

Karen's Future Planning Inventory

Home Living Options

II. Home Living Options

A. Where do you plan to live after graduation?
(Please check one from this list.)

_X_ Large urban (100,000 population plus) What city? Minneapolis
___ Urban/Suburban (30,000 to 100,000) What city? ___
___ Rural/Small city (under 30,000) What town? ___
___ Farm

B. Please check one from this list:

_X_ Live independently in apartment or home
___ With a family member (who?) ___
___ With support
___ Supervised apartment (which one?) ___
___ Group home (which one?) ___
___ College dorm (where?) ___
_X_ Other, please describe My friend Sara and me

Figure 3.5

In a State that transfers rights at the age of majority, beginning at least one year before a student reaches the age of majority under State law, the student's IEP must include a statement that the student has been informed of his or her rights under Part B of the Act, if any, that will transfer to the student on reaching the age of majority, consistent with Section 300.517. (Section 300.347 (c)).

In Section 300.517, it states that there is a *Transfer of parental rights at age of majority*.

> 2. *General*. A State may provide that, when a student with a disability reaches the age of majority under State law that applies to all students (except for a student with a disability who has been determined to be incompetent under State law):
>
> (1)(i) The public agency shall provide any notice required by this part to both the individual and the parents; and (ii) All other rights accorded to parents under Part B of the Act transfer to the student; and
>
> (2) All rights accorded to parents under Part B of the Act transfer to students who are incarcerated in an adult or juvenile, State or local correction institution.
>
> (3) Whenever a State transfers rights under this part pursuant to paragraph (a)(1) or (a)(2) of this section, the agency shall notify the individual and the parents of the transfer of rights.
>
> 3. *Special rule*. If, under State law, a State has a mechanism to determine that a student with a disability, who has reached the age of majority under State law that applies to all children and has not been determined incompetent under State law, does not have the ability to provide informed consent with respect to his or her educational program, the State shall establish procedures for appointing the parent, or if the parent is not available another appropriate individual, to represent the educational interests of the student through-out the student's eligibility under Part B of the Act. (Authority: 20 U.S.C. 1415(m)).

Therefore, unless the student has been found to be incompetent to function independently under State law (e.g., parents file for, and are granted guardianship) or some issue(s) were present that would necessitate the implementation of Section 300. 517(b), to assist the student with informed consent with regards to the Individual Education Program, then at the age of majority each student with a disability is in charge of their own educational program decision making.

In our scenario it is important to remember that many young adults, with and without disabilities, plan to live independently, make purchases, or make career choices that are risky or concerning to their parents, teachers, or adults that care about them. Regardless of whether the parents or educator believe Karen is ready to live independently, it is Karen's right to *plan* to live independently. Karen is viewed as an adult and is in charge of her own educational program now that she is eighteen years of age in all states where age eighteen is the age of majority.

At this point, the rights and responsibilities for the educational program are Karen's, with her parents and educators in support. Karen signs her own IEP and is in charge of her educational program. Regarding Karen's plan to move to the urban center, the focus of the educational program should be on assisting Karen to identify and develop the daily living skills, interpersonal skills, and decision making skills to live independently, if, in fact, she does move after high school. Finally, even if the parents and educators were strongly opposed to Karen's plan to live independently, it would be prudent to gather information and work toward developing the skills that the student will need for independent decision making and independent living. The educational team can use Karen's plan to assist Karen to accept ownership and responsibility for her future plan. Finally, it is worth noting that the independent living goals of many young adults change rapidly. The opportunity for the student to plan for a future that she perceives as viable is an important opportunity. The IEP team should take advantage of this to plan for a future that the student views as relevant and realistic. The following are sample goals, objectives, and activities that might have been developed with Karen and her family to address her independent living goals as well as address the concerns of the family regarding Karen's independent living skills.

Scenario 2: Capturing and Considering Different Visions (continued)

Independent Living

Future Adult Goal I (Karen) want to move to Minneapolis to live after I graduate. I plan to get a job and an apartment, and to live with a girlfriend.

Transition Needs Living independently requires many independent living skills. Karen needs to learn independent living skills including (1) proper use of credit and credit cards; (2) responsibilities and opportunities of apartment living including leasing, contracts, etc.; (3) costs involved with renting an apartment; and (4) social and communication skills needed to get along with a roommate and other adults.

Transition Services/Activities (Senior Year)

1. Karen will explore jobs in the Minneapolis newspaper and identify three jobs that she would be interested in and qualified to do when she moves to Minneapolis (jobs and job training transition activity).
2. With the use of the newspaper, Karen will identify two possible apartments that she and her roommate could afford to rent and that they would find acceptable.
3. Karen and her parents will visit two apartments in the Minneapolis area that were identified by Karen as apartments of interest. Karen will gather information regarding the costs of renting the apartment (e.g., monthly rent, utilities, deposit, lease features).

Annual Goal in Independent Living Given Karen's plan to live independently in Minneapolis in the year after high school, Karen will demonstrate the daily living skills needed to live independently in the community.

Instructional Objectives

1. Given lease contracts to read regarding two different apartments, Karen will independently read the contracts and correctly answer six of six questions regarding the leases. Questions will include: What is the monthly rent for the apartment? Are utilities included as part of the rent payment? Can you have pets in the apartment? What is the deposit cost to rent the apartment? How and when do you get your deposit back after you leave the apartment? How or why can you break this lease? Other specific features of the lease will also be reviewed.
2. When asked to list costs of renting an apartment, Karen will list at least five realistic costs of renting an apartment.
3. When given a hypothetical job of her choice (as found in the newspaper), Karen will create a realistic budget for independent living including identifying approximate monthly net income as well as approximate monthly expenses including rent, utilities, food costs, entertainment, and auto or transportation expenses.
4. On a test regarding independent living, Karen will list three positive and three negative consequences or concerns associated with having a roommate.
5. Given a hypothetical credit card bill, Karen will identify (a) the total amount due, (b) the minimum payment, (c) date the payment is due, (d) finance charges for balance carried forward, and (e) credit limit. Karen will do this on three of three occasions with 100 percent accuracy.
6. On an exam, Karen will list three positive reasons to use a credit card as well as three consequences of misusing a credit card.

Scenario 3: Greatest Future Concern

John, a 14-year-old student (end of 8th grade) with a mild mental disability completed the Student Future Planning Inventory with the assistance of the school counselor. It was not surprising that John did not know much about the adult services listed in different sections of the Future Planning Inventory. It was also not surprising that John did not have a strong vision of employment after high school. At least, John did not have a strong vision that he could articulate at this time. It was not until John answered the final question on his inventory that the IEP team got a significant surprise regarding John's future plans. John suggested his "Greatest Concern" for the future was that he might not be able to play professional football after he graduated from high school (see section VIII of the Student Future Planning Inventory in Appendix A, part 1 (A-1, Form 1). This was quite a surprise to John's family and educators as John had never participated in organized football and he had never before articulated a desire to play the sport. Further, John was not a particularly large student. At the end of eighth grade John was 5'4" and weighed approximately 120 pounds.

As a result of conversations during the IEP meeting, the transition team found that John was playing football with a group of 5th and 6th grade boys after school and enjoying the activity quite a lot. However, John's football experience was not necessarily age appropriate and additional information for the student regarding participation in football was needed. Based on the IEP meeting, and with the help of a high school teacher, John was scheduled to visit a high school football practice (transition activity) to decide if he wanted to play football in high school on the freshman team. While John's parents were concerned regarding John's size, there were other young men of a smaller stature who were trying out for the football team and the IEP team agreed that John should be allowed to try the sport based on his interest. Becoming part of the high school football team could be listed in the IEP as a transition activity if found to be appropriate for John. The high school football team had a "no cut" policy and every student who would try out for the team would get to be a member of one of the high school football squads (varsity, junior varsity, or freshman team).

As a result of the IEP meeting and with the use of the information solicited with the use of the Future Planning System, John identified football as a recreation and leisure activity in which he was interested. In addition, John identified an interest in exploring a career in athletics with a particular interest in football. Based on this information the IEP/transition team implemented a transition plan in the area of recreation and leisure and vocational interests based on the assessment information. IEP transition planning activities, goals, and objectives were included in John's 9th grade IEP.

The "Greatest Concern" section of the FPS as completed by the student is an interesting one and may provide meaningful information for team discussion at the IEP meeting. Based on years of using these instruments, we have included the following real-student responses to this "Greatest Concern" question from student's perspective. Sample student responses include:

- Will I be able to get a good job after high school?
- Will I be able to get into college and graduate?
- Where will I live after high school?
- How will I make a living after high school?

All of these student responses, including John's concern regarding whether he would be able to be a professional football player, all provide insight into the students' concerns as they look toward transition from school to adult life. The responses provided by John in his future planning provide a discussion opportunity for educators and parents when planning for his first year of high school.

Recreation and Leisure

Future Adult Goal I (John) will explore recreation and leisure activities in high school football and other sports through the YMCA program.

Transition Needs John is now interested in playing on the high school football team. John needs skills to interact with his high school teammates. Specifically, John needs social skills and communication skills including (1) identifying the topic of discussion, (2) staying on topic, (3) reciprocal communication skills, and (4) strategies to close conversations.

Transition Activities (Freshman Year)

1. John and his parents will contact the YMCA regarding the potential to act as a team manager for the 5th or 6th grade YMCA boys football team for fall.
2. John will sign up for freshman football for fall of his freshman year.
3. John will identify two YMCA activities or sports that he is interested in joining in winter or spring of his freshman year.
4. John will participate in high school football as a member of the freshman high school team.
5. John will visit with the freshman football coach to find out about the time of practices, the number of practices per week, and the coach's expectations of freshman players at the beginning of practice in the fall. John will collect this information and share a written report regarding what he found with the special education teacher.
6. John will sign up and participate in one YMCA winter or spring activity.

Annual Goal in Recreation and Leisure John will increase his communication skills from the inability to independently start, maintain, and close a conversation with a same-age peer, to the ability to independently initiate, maintain a conversation on the initial topic for at least five minutes, and effectively close that conversation on five of five trials.

Instructional Objectives

1. Given a topic of his choice, John will independently initiate a conversation with a high-school-aged peer on five of five trials.
2. Given a topic of his choice, John will independently initiate a conversation and will maintain that conversation for three minutes on five of five trials.
3. Given a football topic of his choice, John will independently initiate a conversation and will independently maintain that conversation on the initial topic for three minutes on five of five trials.
4. Given a football topic of his choice, John will independently begin, maintain, and close a conversation of five or more minutes on the initial topic of the conversation on five of five trials.

Resources for Assessing Future Planning Needs of Students with Mild Disabilities

My Future My Plan: A Transition Planning Resource for Life After High School

My Future My Plan (Sheets & Gold, 2003) is a comprehensive future planning resource for students with mild and moderate disabilities. This future planning system includes (1) a student notebook, (2) videotape of students in the transition process, and (3) a *Parent/Family Member and Teacher Guide*. In this comprehensive planning material, the student's future planning notebook includes information to assist students in successful future planning. The student notebook includes informal future planning assessment instruments, as well as information regarding resources for planning for life after high school. The student notebook system includes a place for inclusion of the student's future planning records. The *Parent/Family Member and Teacher Guide* (Stenhjem & Scholeller, 2003), is designed to assist parents and teachers to support students with disabilities to plan for life after high school. Each chapter outlines major topics followed by a series of action steps for teachers and family members. My Future My Plan videotape and notebook are also available in a Spanish language version.

I PLAN: The Self-Advocacy Strategy

An important future planning system for students with mild disabilities is I PLAN (Van Ruesen & Bos, 1990), the self-advocacy strategy. I PLAN is a person-centered planning strategy which combines the process of planning for near and distant futures with the development of self-advocacy skills. This mnemonic strategy focuses on preparing the student to participate in and to lead their own IEP meeting and to present his or her own goals and preferences for learning (Van Ruesen & Bos, 1990). "I PLAN" stands for:

I—Inventory your strengths, weaknesses, and preferences for learning
P—Provide your inventory
L—Listen and respond
A—Activate your thinking
N—Name your goals

In 1994, I PLAN became the Self-Advocacy Strategy (Van Reusen, et al., 1994). The Self-Advocacy Strategy provides the student with structured opportunities to simulate leading the IEP team meeting as well as giving the student appropriate tools to develop and practice the social and self-advocacy skills needed to participate in and lead a group meeting. The goal of this strategy is for the student to lead his or her own IEP meeting and present his or her own academic and learning strengths, limitations, goals, and aspirations. This is a strong and useful learning strategy in the area of future planning and self-advocacy training. The focus of the strategy is to motivate the student to take charge of the IEP process (Van Reusen & Bos, 1994). We feel the Self-Advocacy Strategy is a well-designed tool and process that would be beneficial to students with mild disabilities at the middle school or high school level.

Dare to Dream: A Guide to Planning Your Future

Dare to Dream (Webb, et al., 1999) is a workbook designed to assist students with disabilities to plan their post high school futures. Among the topics included in the comprehensive planning workbook are: planning my personal transitions; identifying my dreams and considering how to attain those dreams; participating in my IEP; considering where to live and how to get around and involved in the community; and a comprehensive look at my strengths, limitations, aptitudes, and skills. This future planning workbook is a comprehensive planning document well-designed for use with students with mild disabilities. This material is available online through the Transition Center at the University of Florida at www.thetransitioncenter.org/page

FUTURE Planning Strategy

Sitlington, et al., (1996) found the FUTURE Planning Strategy developed by Wynne Begun (1995) to be effective. The Future Planning Strategy is based on the mnemonic FUTURE. The six steps of FUTURE that lead to student-directed planning include:

F—Find facts about yourself
U—Understand and value your dreams, differences, rights, and abilities
T—Think what is required and tell what is needed to achieve your goals

U—Use the information to make a plan
R—Reach your goals through your plan
E—Evaluate the outcome of the plan

Sitlington, et al. (1996) suggested that the FUTURE Planning Strategy could be used independently by students with mild disabilities.

Resources for Assessing Future Planning Needs of Students with Moderate to Severe Disabilities

The McGill Action Planning System (MAPS)

MAPS (Vandercook & York, Forest, 1989) was originally developed as a planning tool which targeted full inclusion and participation in the general education classroom for students with severe disabilities (Westing & Fox, 1995). With limited modification, such as a focus on planning on future environment, the MAPS process can also be used to provide a means of assessing the student's current and future dreams, strengths, interests, and needs. The MAPS process involves stakeholders in the student's life (e.g., parents, siblings, service providers, peers, and educators) by addressing a series of planning questions which include:

- What is the individual's history?
- What is your dream for the individual?
- What are your nightmares for the individual?
- Who is the individual?
- What are the individual's strengths, gifts, and abilities?
- What are the individual's needs?
- What would the individual's ideal day at school look like and what must be done to make it happen?

This process looks toward friends, family, and other stakeholders who know the student to generate and brainstorm information for educational and career planning. It is through the combined efforts of many participants that a clearer picture of the student's interests, preferences, and skill level is generated. Much literature exists regarding implementation of MAPS for persons with severe disabilities (Forest & Lusthaus, 1989; Forest & Pearpoint, 1992; Vandercook, York, & Forest, 1989). While some writers have suggested MAPS as an appropriate strategy for use with students with mild disabilities, we feel the MAPS process is effective and an appropriate planning process for persons with severe disabilities, but that it may be too intrusive for use with students with mild disabilities.

Personal Futures Planning

Personal futures planning (Mount & Zwernik, 1988) is a three-step planning process developed for students with severe disabilities. The steps involved include developing a personal profile of the student with a disability, developing a future plan for the individual based on the student's personal profile, and forming a network or circle of support from family, friends, educators, and community support persons to ensure the plan is successful. Personal futures planning focuses on the hopes and dreams of the individual as identified by the planning team and seeks to identify methods and supports to implement the student's plans. The planning process seeks to minimize the student's "fit" into community resources. Rather, the planning process establishes an "ideal plan" for the student and seeks innovative ways to meet the goals of the plan.

Comparing Future Planning for Students with Mild, Moderate, and Severe Disabilities

Methods and materials for person-centered planning developed for persons with severe disabilities tend to include a larger group of concerned parties in the future planning process when compared to those processes and assessment instruments developed for students with mild disabilities. The meeting to develop a future plan for a student with a severe disability may include family, friends, educators, service providers, and classmates in the planning process to identify an individual's potential to function in future environments or ways to foster inclusion in the school setting or the community. This wide net of inclusion in the planning process is appropriate for students with severe disabilities but may be too intrusive for students with mild disabilities. When choosing a method or material for future planning or person-centered planning, it is important to consider the ability of the young adult to participate and provide leadership and ownership of the planning process. Therefore, care should be given to match the planning process and assessment with the strengths and limitations of the student in question.

CHAPTER SUMMARY

This chapter explored future planning as a component of effective transition assessment. We found that

- future planning assessment is a critical component of transition assessment as it is critical to developing a consumer-driven and person-centered IEP.
- future planning is an ongoing transition process and is interwoven with all other components of an effective transition assessment.
- many future planning assessment materials and processes exist to assist with gathering future planning assessment information from team participants.
- educators should carefully review future planning assessments to match the assessment method and material with the skill set of the student with a disability.

CHAPTER ACTIVITIES

Susan McMillin is a 9th grade student at Suburban High School. Susan, her parents, and her special education teacher are preparing for Susan's upcoming IEP meeting. In preparation for this team meeting, Susan, her parents, and her special education teacher have all completed the future planning documents. The completed future planning assessment forms for all three parties can be found in Appendix B, part 2 (B-2, Forms 1–3). Please review the future planning inventories completed by the student, the parents, and the educator.

1. Based on your review of these documents, what are three potential transition planning goals to be addressed in Susan's IEP?
2. What are two areas of future planning where Susan, her parents, and the educator are in some level of disagreement regarding future planning goals and options for Susan?
3. At the IEP meeting, Susan, her parents, and the educator reach agreement regarding a transition goal, objectives, and transition activities in the area of Vocational/Postsecondary Education Options. Please write the one IEP goal with three IEP objectives in this transition planning area.
4. What are three transition planning activities that Susan, her parents, or the educator could do to assist the student with gathering information to address this goal area?

DISCUSSION QUESTIONS

Does the disability category (emotional/behavior disorder, learning disabilities, cognitive disability) have any bearing on future planning discussions during the IEP meeting? If so, how?

CHAPTER REFERENCES

Begun, W. H. (1995). The FUTURE strategy. In W. H. Begun, L. Minor, B. Silvers, & P. Witcher (Eds.). *The TRANS-PLAN curriculum*. (pp. 52–53). Desoto, KS: Desoto School District.

Clark, G. (1998). *Assessment for transition planning*. Austin, TX: PRO-ED.

Corbey, S., Miller, R., Severson, S., & Enderle, J. (1993). *Identifying individual transition needs: A resource guide for special educators working with students in their transition from school to adult life*. St. Paul, MN: Minnesota Department of Education.

Cunanan, E. S., & Maddy-Bernstein, C. (1995, May). Individualized career plans: Opening the door for all students. *Office of Student Services: Brief, 7*(1), 1–7.

Friedland, B. (1999). *How are students with mild intellectual disabilities involved in planning their own transitions?* Rural Special Education for the New Millennium: Conference proceedings of the American council on rural special education (ACRES) (19th, Albuquerque, New Mexico, March 25–27, 1999).

Forest, M., & Lusthaus, E. (1989). Promoting educational equality for all students: Circles and maps. In Stainback, S., Stainback, W., & Forest, M. (Eds.). *Educating All Students in the Mainstream of Education*. Baltimore, MD: Paul H. Brookes, pp. 43–57.

Forest, M., & Pearpoint, J. (1992). Putting all kids on the MAP. Educational Leadership, *50*(2), 26–31.

Individuals with Disabilities Education Act of 2004, PL 108–466. Retrieved March 28, 2005 from http://thomas.loc.gov/cgi-bin/query/z?c108h.1350.enr:

Individuals with Disabilities Education Act of 1997, PL 105–17 (1997). [online], 111, 37. Available: Lexis–Nexis Database: PL 105–17 [1999 May 21].

Menchetti, B. M., & Sweeney, M. A. (1994–1995). *Person-centered planning. Technical Assistance Packet #5*. Project CDT, Florida Network: Information and services for Adolescents and Adults with Special Needs. University of Florida Department of Special Education, Gainesville, FL.

Mount, B., & Zwernik, K. (1988). *It's never too early, it's never too late: An overview of personal futures planning*. St. Paul, MN: Governor's Planning Council on Developmental Disabilities.

O'Brien, J., & Lovett, H. (1992). *Finding a way toward everyday lives: The contribution of person-centered planning*. Harrisburg: Pennsylvania Office of Mental Retardation, Pennsylvania Department of Public Welfare.

Sitlington, P. L., Neubert, D. A., Begun, W., Lombard, R. C., & Leconte, P. J. (1996) *Assess for success: Handbook on transition assessment*. Reston, VA: Council for Exceptional Children.

Sheets, D., & Gold, E. (2003). *My future my plan: A transition planning resource for life after high school—For students with disabilities and their families*. Washington, DC: State of the Art, Inc.

Stenhjem, P., & Schoeller, K. (2003). *My future my plan: Parent, family member and teacher guide*. Washington, DC: State of the Art, Inc.

Valdes, K. A., Williamson, C. L., & Wagner, M. M. (1990). *The national transition study of special education students*. Menlo Park, CA: SRI International.

Van Reusen, A. K., & Bos, C. S. (1990). I Plan: Helping students communicate in planning conferences. *Teaching Exceptional Children, 22*(4), 30–32.

Van Reusen, A. K. & Bos, C. S. (1994). Facilitating student participation in individual education programs through motivation strategy instruction. *Exceptional Children, 60* (5), 466–475.

Van Reusen, A. K., Bos, C. S., Schumaker, J. B., & Deshler, D. D. (1994). *Self-advocacy strategy for education and transition planning*. Lawrence, KS: Edge Enterprises.

Vandercook, T., York, J., & Forest, M. (1989). The McGill Action Planning System (MAPS): A strategy for building the vision. *Journal of the Association for Persons with Severe Handicaps, 14* (3), 205–215

Webb, K., Repetto, J., Beutel, A., Perkins, D., Bailey, M., & Schwartz, S. (1999). *Dare to dream: A guide to planning your future. Revised*. Tallahassee, FL: Florida State Department of Education. Retrieved August 12, 2005 from http//www.thetransitioncenter.org/page

Wehmeyer, M. L., Agran, M., & Hughes, C. (1998). *Teaching self-determined students with disabilities: Basic skills for successful transition*. Baltimore, MD: Paul H. Brookes.

Westing, D. L, & Fox, L. (1995). *Teaching students with severe disabilities*. Englewood, NJ: Prentice Hall.

CHAPTER

4 Assessment of Self-Determination and Self-Advocacy Skills

In Chapters 2 and 3, we discussed the importance of goal setting and career planning as critical components of the education of all adolescents, including adolescents with disabilities. Realistic goal setting is an important predictor of success in adulthood (Raskind, et al., 1999; Reiff, Gerber, & Ginsberg, 1997). Goal setting and future planning skills have been conceptualized as critical components of the self-determination process (e.g., Abery, et al., 1997; Bremer, Kachgal, & Schoeller, 2003; Field, et al., 1998b; Wehmeyer, 2002). In Chapter 4 we will discuss assessment of self-determination and self-advocacy skills (see Figure 4.1). There is a critical interrelationship between future planning, the self-determination process, and self-advocacy skills. While assessment is integral to the self-determination process for all students with disabilities (Sitlington, et al., 1996), self-determination is also an essential component of student involvement in all assessment activities across life skills and academic skills (Field, et al., 1998a). In a very real sense, future planning and self-determination assessment represent the foundation of an effective transition plan. The central purpose for these foundation assessments is to harness the natural motivation of the student and to convey ownership of the educational process to the student and family. The fundamental premise for assessment in both these areas is that education must be student-centered and consumer-driven to be effective and relevant. If the goal of education is to develop self-directed learners who can address their own needs, wants, and concerns and can advocate for their goals and aspirations (Miller, 1994), then assessment and instruction in self-determination is critical for all students.

As a concept, self-determination has recently taken on increased importance in the disability community and is particularly evident in the transition from school to adulthood movement (Field, 1996). In 1994, Field and Hoffman developed a model of self-determination based on five major components. These components are: (1) know yourself, (2) value yourself, (3) plan, (4) act, and (5) experience outcomes and learn (see Figure 4.2 on page 40). The experiences learned by the student add to one's knowledge of self and impact one's values and then the process begins again. This model is, therefore, developmental in nature based on the continuing self-evaluation component. In Figure 4.2 both internal affective factors as well as skill components of self-determination are included.

In a position paper published in Career Development for Exceptional Individuals (CDEI), Division on Career Development and Transition (DCDT) has endorsed the following definition of self-determination:

> Self-determination is a combination of skills, knowledge and beliefs that enable a person to engage in goal directed, self-regulated, autonomous behavior. Self-determination is an understanding of one's strengths and limitations together with a belief in oneself as capable and effective. When acting on the basis of these skills and attitudes, individuals have greater ability to take control of their lives and assume the roles of adults in our society (Field, et al., 1998b).

There is a positive relationship between self-determination and improved postschool outcomes. (Wehmeyer & Schwartz, 1998). Unfortunately, many teachers of students with disabilities are not including these important skills in student IEPs (Wood, et al., 2004).

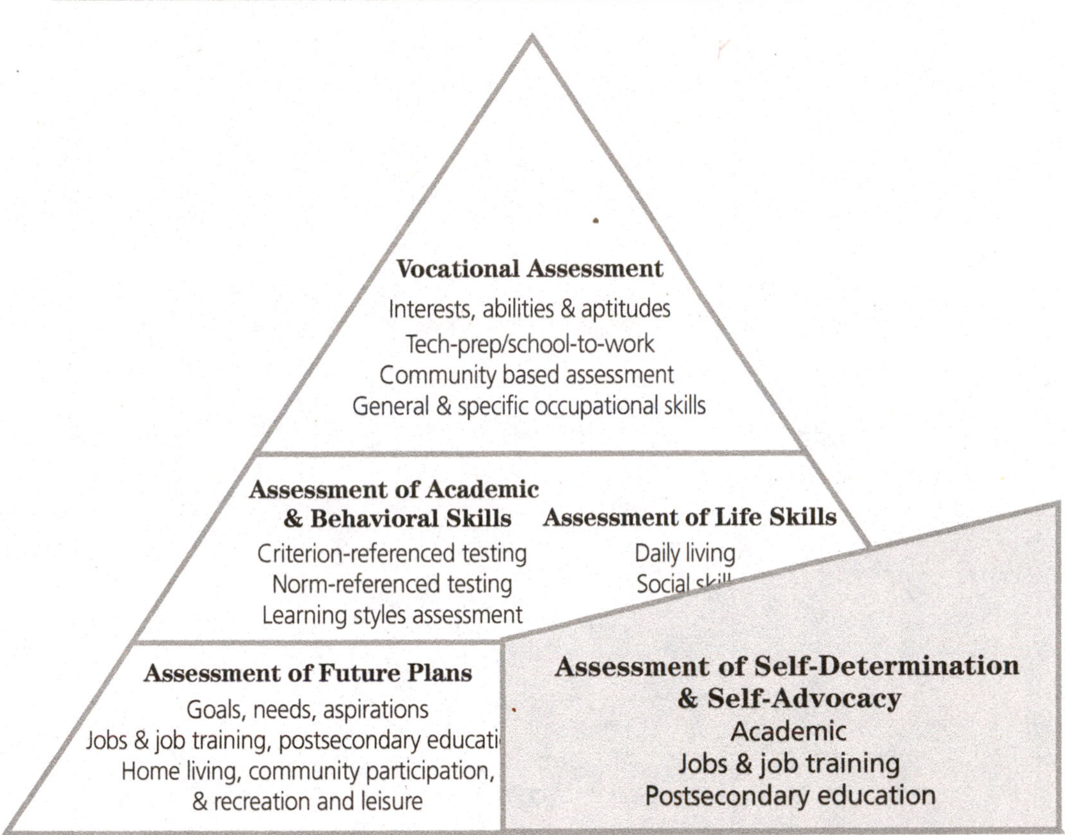

Figure 4.1

Effective self-determination assessment results will promote self-awareness, will assist in identifying instructional goals and needed curricular interventions, and will provide the opportunity for evaluation of the effectiveness of the overall educational program of the student. Wehmeyer (2002) suggests strategies to promote self-determination including assessing interests and preferences of students, probing choice-making skills, encouraging educational planning and educational goal setting, involving the student in problem solving and decision making, and utilizing student-directed learning strategies.

A focus on issues related to self-determination is a central theme in the Individuals with Disabilities Education Act of 1990 (IDEA), the IDEA Amendments of 1997, and IDEA 2004. The self-determination focus is also echoed in the 1992 Amendments to the Rehabilitation Act of 1973. Field (1996) references this relationship in her writings on self-determination and points to the following philosophical statement about disability in our society. According to the 1992 Rehabilitation Amendments:

> Disability is a natural part of the human experience and in no way diminishes the right of the individual to: (a) live independently, (b) enjoy self-determination, (c) make choices, (d) contribute to society, (e) pursue meaningful careers, and (f) enjoy full inclusion and integration into the economic, political, social, cultural and educational mainstream of American society . . . (Section 2, Findings, Purpose, Policy).

With the 1992 Amendments to the Rehabilitation Act of 1973, issues related to self-determination are continued beyond the mandate of IDEA into life after high school. The

Self-Determination

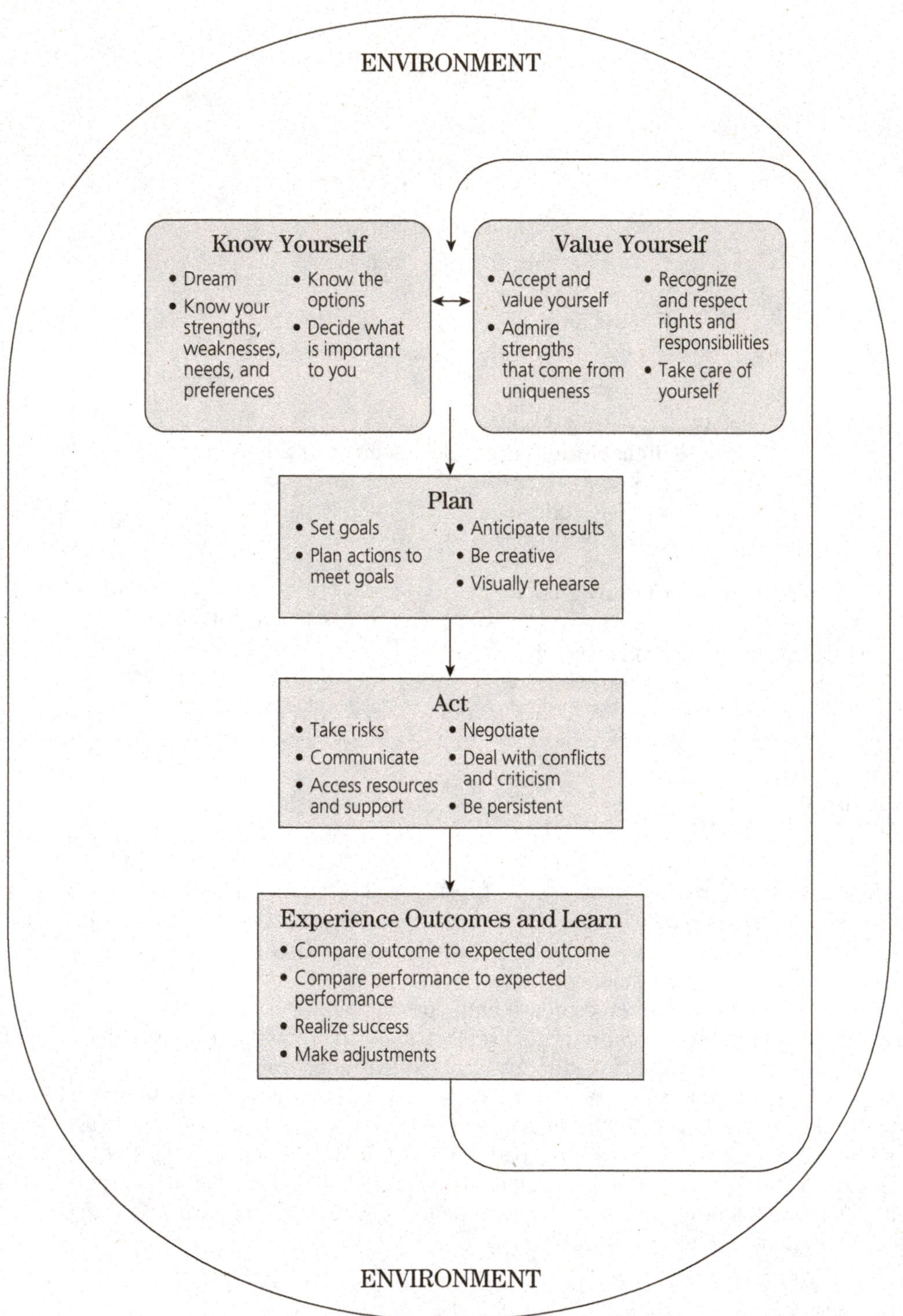

Figure 4.2

Source: Field, S. & Hoffman, A. (1994). Development of a model for self-determination. *Career Development for Exceptional Individuals, 17*, 159–169. Copyright by PRO-ED, Inc. Reprinted with permission.

importance of the self-determined individual is a unifying construct between public education and provision of adult services. To be self-determined, graduates from public education must be able to:

1. identify (choose) adult services they wish to approach for assistance;
2. request adult services;
3. identify themselves as a person with a disability;
4. articulate their needs, wants, and desires;
5. provide needed documentation to meet the requirements for the requested service;
6. identify needed accommodations in employment or postsecondary education to be provided with the services that they deserve; and ultimately,
7. advocate for their rights to identified accommodations as required by law.

While future planning identifies the goals and aspirations of the student, the self-determination process and self-advocacy skills define the student's readiness to participate and perhaps lead the transition planning process. While future planning assessment helps the student to begin to identify and crystallize their vision of near and distant futures, goal setting, and career planning, self-determination assessment provides the student and relevant adults the opportunity to measure the individual's readiness to advocate for those near and distant futures, to make choices, to solve problems, and to self-advocate. Effective transition assessment cannot occur without meaningful assessment in all the components of self-determination. Abery, et al. (1997) have suggested skills, knowledge, and beliefs that make up the self-determination process. (see Figure 4.3).

The Knowledge, Skills, and Beliefs of Self-Determination

Knowledge

- Laws and rights
- Systems and resources
- Self-awareness
- Responsibilities

Skills

- Goal setting
- Decision making
- Problem solving
- Self-regulation
- Independent living skills
- Social skills
- Communication skills

Attitudes and Beliefs

- Self-confidence
- Internal locus of control
- Determination
- Self-esteem

Figure 4.3

The Relationship between Self-Determination and Self-Advocacy

Self-advocacy is often used almost interchangeably with self-determination (Field, 1996). In reality, self-advocacy is a subset of knowledge and skills under a larger umbrella of the self-determination process. Self-advocacy has been defined as:

> An individual's ability to effectively communicate, convey, negotiate or assert his or her own interests, desires, needs, and rights. It involves making informal decisions and taking responsibility for those decisions (Van Reusen, et al., 1994).

Self-advocacy could be summarized as the ability to say what you need and to get what you want. Self-advocacy skills are fundamental to the self-determination process and to future planning and establishing career goals.

Valenti (1989) designed a practical guide and workbook for preparing high school students with the skills of self-advocacy for postsecondary success. Topics of this guide and workbook included understanding specific disability, understanding diagnostic testing, knowing your rights and responsibilities under the law, understanding the transition process to postsecondary education, and developing skills for independent learning. Field, et al. (1998a) suggest that self-advocacy instruction will focus on *how to advocate* and *what to advocate*. In order to instruct in self-advocacy, one must first measure the knowledge and skill level of the student.

Each component of self-advocacy (knowledge [what to advocate] and skills [how to advocate]) is intregal to self-determination. However, without a strong belief in one's own power to control or influence the situation, one cannot be self-determined. One may, however, possess the skills of self-advocacy without the capacity or willingness to use those skills and be self-determined. See Figure 4.4 for an example of the relationship of knowledge, skills, and beliefs in self-determination.

According to Field, et al. (1998a), in the self-determination assessment process students must be active participants "in deciding what needs to be assessed, how those factors will be measured, and how assessment results will be used" (p. 30). Field, et al. (1998b) suggest that in self-determination assessment, students: (a) will help decide the questions the assessment will answer, (b) will participate in the gathering of data, (c) will assemble portfolio information for review, and (d) will utilize the results of the assessment to make informed decisions regarding educational goals. (See Appendix C, part 3, for an example of an Individual Student Transition Portfolio designed to assist students to organize transition assessment and transition planning information.)

Wood, et al. (2004) suggest that methods of assessing knowledge and skill in self-determination go beyond the use of commercially available self-determination tests (both norm-referenced and criterion-reference). Field, et al. (1998a) suggest that methods might also include creation of portfolios to include reviewing records and student background information; interviewing the student and others; observing the student; and using curriculum-based assessment techniques. Wood, et al. (2004) suggest that in the absence of a published self-determination instrument, teachers may develop their own self-determination checklists or questionnaires.

Becoming self-determined is a process of starts and stops, and successes and failures within a context of information-gathering and skill development. As suggested in Chapter 2, career development literature strongly supports the importance of *information* and *experience* as key variables in providing individuals with the experiential base to make decisions and develop a realistic vision of one's strengths and limitations. This realistic vision of one's strengths and limitations are building blocks to a *reality orientation*. However, Wehmeyer and Kelchner (1996) correctly point out that failure experiences are learning experiences only if they are mitigated. Students learn from failure only if they have the opportunity to try the experience

Relationship of Knowledge, Skills, and Beliefs in Self-Determination

Knowledge

Based on your disability, you acquire knowledge that you have protection under the law to request accommodations in academic settings.

Skills

You practice and develop competence in stating your rights and requesting accommodations in the academic setting. In short, you learn the skill of self-advocacy.

Beliefs

You choose to apply the knowledge and skills you possess in all relevant academic situations.

Figure 4.4

again with a different level of intensity and success or with a different strategy. There is a fine line between experiencing the real world and losing one's sense of personal empowerment (Bremer, Kachgal, & Schoeller, 2003). Therefore, a significant component of self-determination for students with disabilities is perception of self and the perception of their skill set. Does the student believe they have the skills or can develop the skills to reach their career goals? Does the student understand the requirements to enter the career? Does the student have a realistic vision of their current academic skill set? In a study regarding the accuracy of academic self-evaluation in adolescents with learning disabilities, Stone and May (2002) found that despite reporting lower academic self-concept, students with learning disabilities overestimated their academic skills relative to the ratings of others and to their actual test performance. Such overestimation was less pronounced among students without learning disabilities. Stone and May (2002) hypothesize that it is possible that overestimation of academic skills serves to protect self-esteem but simultaneously is detrimental to academic achievement and the development of self-advocacy skills.

Resources for Assessing Self-Determination

Self-determination assessment instruments, interviews with students and parents, documentation of existing skills, and observation may be used to help determine the focus of instruction for students with disabilities (Renzaglia, et al., 2003). Over the last few years, several assessment instruments have been published to assist the IEP team in gathering relevant information regarding the student's knowledge, skills, and beliefs in self-determination. The following is a brief overview of some of these instruments. You may wish to review each of these instruments for possible use in the transition assessment process. We suggest that educators may want to consider using different assessment instruments to measure self-determination and self-advocacy at various points in the high school career of the student. The use of multiple instruments may provide the student and IEP team with deeper insight into the knowledge, skills, and beliefs of self-determination. Initial assessment of self-determination, as a component of transition assessment, should be completed before the student turns fourteen years old.

Commercially-Available Self-Determination Assessments

The Arc's Self-Determination Scale

The Arc's Self-Determination Scale (Wehmeyer & Kelchner, 1995) was developed by the Arc of the United States and is currently available online through the Beach Center on Disability at the University of Kansas. The scale requires students to complete a survey which is designed for use by adolescents with mild cognitive disabilities or learning disabilities. This self-report instrument provides an overall measure of self-determination as well as scores in the domain areas of autonomy, self-regulation, psychological empowerment, and self-realization. This instrument can be found on the Beach Center of Disabilities website at www.beachcenter.org.

ChoiceMaker Self-Determination Assessment

The *ChoiceMaker Self-Determination Assessment* (Martin & Marshall, 1994) is a curriculum-based assessment tool which is directly matched to the *ChoiceMaker Instructional Series* (Martin, et al., 1997) curriculum and is designed for use in conjunction with this published curriculum. Published by Sopris West Publisher in Longmont, Colorado, this instrument measures student skill in choosing goals, expressing goals, and taking action. This self-determination instrument is intended for use with middle school to high school students with mild to moderate learning problems or emotional/behavior disorders. Sopris West Publishing can be reached by phone at (800) 547-6747 or (303) 651-2829, or on the web at http://www.sopriswest.com.

The Self-Determination Knowledge Scale

The *Self-Determination Knowledge Scale* (Hoffman, Field, & Sawilowsky, 1995) is a curriculum-based assessment tool published by both the Council for Exceptional Children (CEC) of Reston, Virginia, and PRO-ED Publishing of Austin, Texas. The assessment instrument is a paper and pencil test which uses a multiple choice and true/false format. It also includes a self-determination observation checklist for use by classroom teachers. This pretest–posttest instrument is designed to assess students' knowledge of self-determination skills as taught in the *Steps to Self-Determination: A Curriculum to Help Adolescents Learn to Achieve Their Goals, Second Edition* (Field & Hoffman, 2005). This instrument measures affective, cognitive, and behavioral factors of self-determination. This curriculum, including the assessment tool, can be found at the online PRO-ED publishing catalog at http://proedinc.com or by phone at (800)897-3202. The material can be found on the CEC catalog website at http//www.cec.sped.org/bk/catalog2/self.html. You may also contact the CEC at (888)232-7733.

The Self-Determination and Self-Advocacy Skills Questionnaires

A complete set of the Self-Determination and Self-Advocacy Skills Questionnaires are included in Appendix A (A-3, Forms 1–5). The instruments were initially developed and field tested with secondary-aged students with disabilities who were attending a statewide Self-Advocacy Institute in Minnesota that was held in August 1995. This institute was the second in a series of Transition Institutes designed to empower students in planning for life after high school as well as to empower students to plan for participation in postsecondary education (Miller & Corbey, 1994, Miller, Corbey, & Asher, 1994). Since the initial 1995 field test, these instruments have gone through numerous revisions based on feedback from students and professionals. The Student and Teacher Interview: Performance Battery was added to the assessment tools in 2004. You may photocopy and use this set of SD/SA Skills Questionnaires to begin the self-determination assessment process. These tools are designed to be used with secondary aged students with mild disabilities and their families. The purpose of the SD/SA Skills Questionnaires is to measure the student's self-determination and self-advocacy skills in two areas: (a) knowledge and skills related to self-determination and self-advocacy in secondary/postsecondary academic settings, and (b) knowledge and skills related to self-determination and self-advocacy in employment settings.

There are four separate SD/SA Skills Questionnaires designed to be used with students age sixteen and older. One questionnaire is to be completed by the student, one by the parents, and one by the educator. If substantial differences are found between the perceptions of knowledge and skills between student, parents, and teachers, then a fourth instrument is included to be used in a interview format between student and teacher. The purpose of this fourth instrument is to more specifically identify the student's knowledge and skills in self-determination and self-advocacy. The fourth instrument acts as a performance battery. In this manner, the student may document their knowledge and skills, or the team may document the student's overestimation or underestimation of knowledge and skills in self-determination and self-advocacy skills. It is important that students, parents, and educators complete the questionnaires independently, and prior to the IEP/transition meeting. As with the Future Planning System, it is important that the student, parents, and educators all share their perceptions of areas of strength as well areas in which additional instruction may be needed. We believe that students, parents, and educators all have an important perception of strengths and limitations that need to be heard at the IEP/transition meeting and that any discussion of different perceptions of strengths and instructional needs can only enhance the resulting goals and objectives developed for the Individual Education Program. If assistance in completing the instrument appears to be needed, we suggest the school guidance counselor or school social worker may be an appropriate adult to facilitate the student's completion of the initial self-determination assessment instrument.

The instruments are criterion-referenced and are meant to accomplish three goals. First, the SD/SA Skills Questionnaires are designed to promote student and family self-awareness of strengths and limitations in knowledge and skills of self-determination in the academic and employment arenas. Second, the SD/SA Skills Questionnaires are designed to assist the student and IEP team to identify instructional goals and needed curricular interventions in the arena of self-determination and self-advocacy. Third, they are designed to provide the student and IEP team an opportunity to evaluate the effectiveness of the overall Individual Educational Program in terms of self-determination knowledge and skills. The knowledge and skills identified with the use of the instrument are fundamental to success in the next setting, whether that setting is employment or postsecondary education. Assessment of strengths and limitations in this important area of transition assessment are crucial.

On occasion, students, parents, or teachers may question the importance of inclusion of questions regarding self-determination and self-advocacy in employment settings in these instruments. First, the capacity to use self-determination and self-advocacy skills in an educational setting does not necessarily transfer to the job setting. Second, the student may have significant strength in self-advocating in an educational setting but have little or no experience or skill in advocating for themselves in an employment setting. Finally, if the purpose of transition planning is to prepare students for life after high school, then preparing each student to advocate for themselves in employment situations is a critical skill.

An example of this importance is the case of Ben. Ben had a significant learning disability. His goal in high school was to attend a large state university and major in business.

Ben's learning disability manifested itself in significant impairments in writing and reading skills. At the time of graduation, Ben did not have the grades or ACT scores (with accommodations) to be accepted into the state university. Ben chose to attend a comprehensive community college and major in business. Ben's strengths were a strong work ethic (industrious), high motivation, and a clear and specific career plan. Ben spent three years completing a two-year business program at the comprehensive community college. He worked very hard to develop his academic skills and develop the use of compensatory strategies to assist him in completing his program. He also became an expert in using self-determination and self-advocacy skills in the postsecondary setting. Ben transferred to the four-year state university upon completion of his business program. Ben used his self-advocacy skills to complete his Bachelor's degree in business administration over the next three years. Ben graduated on a full scholarship at the university for "overcoming" his disability. Ben was the poster example of addressing one's disability in the postsecondary setting, compensating for his disability, utilizing accommodations in the postsecondary setting, and advocating for himself (demonstrating self-determination). Ben accomplished what seemed to be nearly impossible for him at the time of graduation from high school . . . a Bachelor's degree in business from a major institution of higher education over a six-year period.

After graduation, Ben applied for jobs in the business community. He accepted a job in real estate management. Ben did not identify himself as a person with a disability upon his employment. He did not believe his disability would interfere with his job and he did not want to be identified as disabled in his place of employment. Ben did not receive any accommodations to assist him to be successful on the job. Ben lost his job within six months. Upon being told during the exit interview of Ben's disability, Ben's employer stated that he wished he had known of Ben's disability so that he could have made accommodations.

While we may or may not be successful in teaching self-determination and self-advocacy skill in academic situations, these skills do not automatically transfer to employment situations. Learning disabilities and other mild disabilites are not resolved when students leave the educational setting. Disability affects all aspects of life after high school.

Using Self-Determination Assessment Information to Develop IEP Goals

James is a seventeen-year-old junior student with a learning disability. James' career goal is to attend the state university, major in respiratory therapy, and become a respiratory therapist. As part of the assessment process in preparation for the junior year IEP meeting, James, his parents, and his special education teacher have all independently completed the Self-Determination and Self-Advocacy Skills Questionnaire. The results indicated significant discrepancies between the skill set identified by James and the skill sets identified by his parents and his special education teacher. While James believed he had excellent skills in the area of self-determination and self-advocacy, James' parents and teacher believed James' skill set in this important curricular area to be very poor. To gather additional information regarding James's ability to perform these skills, James and his special education teacher completed the Self-Determination and Self-Advocacy Skills Questionnaire—Student and Teacher Interview: Performance Battery. The results documented that James was substantially overestimating his ability to self-advocate in an academic setting (see Figure 4.5). Based on this assessment tool, the parties found that James (1) was unable to identify any academic accommodations that he was currently using, (2) was not able to role-play an adequate request for academic accommodations, and (3) was not able to identify any specific rights afforded him under IDEA, Section 504, or the Americans with Disabilities Act (ADA). As a result of these assessment results, IEP goals and transition activities were written as follows to address James' need in the area of self-advocacy.

Assessment Results for James' Self-Determination and Self-Advocacy Skills Questionnaire Student and Teacher Interview: Performance Battery

1. Please list and discuss the academic accommodations you use in high school classes.
   a. Student did not identify any academic accommodations he or she is using. X
   b. Student identified some but not all academic accommodations he or she is using.____
   c. Student provided a comprehensive list of academic accommodations as identified on the student's IEP. ____
   d. Academic accommodations discussed by the student included:
      1. ______
      2. ______
      3. ______

4a. You are starting a new academic class. Let's pretend I am the teacher of that class and I don't know you. Give me an example of how you would request accommodations in that class.
   a. Student was *not able* to role-play an adequate request for accommodations. X
   b. Student was *able* to role play an adequate request for accommodations. ___

6. Please tell me what your rights are for reasonable accommodation under federal law.
   a. Student did not identify any specific right under IDEA, Section 504 or ADA. X
   b. Student identified a few rights under IDEA, Section 504 or ADA.___
   c. Student provided a substantial list of rights under IDEA, Section 504 or ADA.___
   d. Rights identified by the student included:
      1. ______
      2. ______
      3. ______

Figure 4.5

Using Self Determination Assessment Information to Develop IEP Goals (continued)

Postsecondary Education

Future Goal After graduation, I (James) plan to attend a state university and major in respiratory therapy.

Transition Needs James and the IEP/transition team agree that James needs to improve his self-advocacy skills in high school coursework. Specifically, James needs to (1) identify the academic accommodations he is currently using in high school, (2) decide if the academic accommodations on his IEP are adequate or whether other academic accommodations might be of more use to him, (3) be able to state his rights to academic accommodation under IDEA, Section 504 and the ADA.

Transition Services/Activities

1. With his parents' support, James will visit the Disability Services Office at the state university. James will identify the accommodations most used by students with disabilities at the university.
2. James will visit with at least one student with a disability majoring in respiratory therapy at the university. James will find out (a) the types of services the student uses from the Disability Service Office, (b) the types of accommodations used in academic settings by the college student, (c) the process the college student followed to get accommodations in each academic course.
3. When given an opportunity to write a report in Social Studies, Science, or English class, James will do a report on one of the following topics: (a) respiratory health issues for children and

(*continued*)

adults, or (b) career opportunities in the respiratory health fields, including job outlook over the next ten years and wages for this career area.

IEP Goal The ability to advocate for oneself in academic situations is very important in high school and beyond (college). James will increase his capacity to self-advocate for his academic needs and accommodations from a level of having little knowledge regarding specific academic accommodations or his rights under the law, to a level of being able to independently identify his rights under federal law, list and discuss academic accommodations that work for him in academic situations, and independently request accommodations in academic classes.

Instructional Objectives

1. On a written examination, James will identify five legal rights he has under the IDEA.
2. On a written examination, James will identify five legal rights he has under Section 504 or the ADA.
3. After reviewing his IEP, James will identify all academic accommodations he is currently using in high school academic classes.
4. James will review his current academic accommodations and will rank all accommodations used as either (a) very useful, (b) somewhat useful, or (c) not useful at all.
5. James will request his own academic accommodations in each academic course during his junior year of high school. During this process, James will identify himself as a person with a disability and for each instructor he will list the accommodations he will need. Each of his five instructors will rate James' ability to adequately request academic accommodation in their class, using a Likert scale (e.g., 5 = excellent skills and communication, 4 = very good skills and communication, 3 = adequate skills and communication, 2 = marginal skills and communication, and 1 = poor skills and communication). The mean score of all instructors will be a rating of 3.75.

Additional Resources for Self-Determination, Self-Advocacy, and Future Planning

Based on the synthesis of self-determination curricula and other published materials, Wood, et al. (2000) found that dozens of curricula have been developed to address the self-determination needs of students with disabilities. In 2003, Bremer, Kachgal, and Schoeller published a list of curricular resources for teaching self-determination skills based on the work of Wood, et al. (2000). Based on our review, each of the following curricula are commercially available, and each represents a useful, *field-tested* tool for teaching self-determination and assisting students with disabilities to plan for their transition from school to adult life.

ChoiceMaker Instructional Series by J. Martin, L. Marshall, L. Maxson, P. Jerman, W. Hughes, T. Miller, and T. McGill. Published by Sopris West Publishing, 4093 Specialty Place, Longmont, CO 80504. Phone: (303)651-2829 or (800)547-6747. Online at www.sopriswest.com.

My Future, My Plan: A Transition Planning Resource for Life After High School—For Students with Disabilities and Their Families by D. Sheets and E. Gold. Institute on Community Integration, University of Minnesota, 102 Pattee Hall, 150 Pillsbury Drive, S.E., Minneapolis, MN 55455. Phone: (612)624-4512. Online at http://ici.umn.edu

NEXT S.T.E.P.: Student Transition Educational Planning, Second Edition by A. Halpern, C. Herr, B. Doren, and N. Wolf. Published by PRO-ED, 8700 Shoal Creek Boulevard, Austin, TX 78757. Phone: (800)897-3202. Online at www.proedinc.com

Self-Determination for Youth with Disabilities: A Family Education Curriculum by B. Abery, K. Arndt, P. Greger, L. Tetu, A. Eggebeen, J. Barosko, A. Hinga, M. McBride, K. Peterson, and L. Rudrud. Published by the Institute on Community

Integration, University of Minnesota, 102 Pattee Hall, 150 Pillsbury Drive, S.E., Minneapolis, MN 55455. Phone: (612)624-4512. Online at http:// ici.umn.edu.

Steps to Self-Determination: A Curriculum to Help Adolescents Learn to Achieve Their Goals, Second Edition by S. Field and A. Hoffman. Published by PRO-ED, 8700 Shoal Creek Boulevard, Austin, TX 78757. Phone: (800)897-3202. Online at www.proedinc.com.

Student-Led IEPs: A Guide for Student Involvement by M. McGahee, C. Mason, T. Wallace, and B. Jones. Published by the Council for Exceptional Children, 1110 North Glebe Road, Suite 300, Arlington, VA 22201-5704. Phone: (888)232-7733. Online at www.cec.sped.org

Whose Future Is It, Anyway? A Student Directed Transition Process, Second Edition by M. Wehmeyer, M. Lawrence, K. Kelchner, S. Palmer, N. Garner, and J. Soukpu. Published by the Beach Center on Disability, The University of Kansas, 1200 Sunnyside Avenue, Lawrence, KS 66045-7534. Phone: (785)864-7600. Online at www.beachcenter.org.

CHAPTER SUMMARY

Chapter 4 explored the self-determination process and self-advocacy as components of effective transition assessment. We found that

- Together, future planning assessment and self-determination assessment represent the foundation of effective transition planning and transition assessment.
- Self-advocacy is a subset of knowledge and skills under the larger umbrella of the self-determination process.
- Effective self-determination assessment will promote self-awareness, assist in identifying instructional goals and needed curricular interventions, and provide the opportunity to evaluate the effectiveness of the overall educational program.
- In order to be self-determined, the individual must have knowledge and skills of self-determination and self-advocacy strategies. However, a student can not be self-determined without the belief and personal power to request and use self-determination skills.
- The student must be actively involved in the self-determination assessment process.

CHAPTER ACTIVITIES

Sara is a second semester sophomore student. Sara wants to be a journalist. She would like to write for a major urban newspaper. Sara, her parents, and her special education teacher have completed independent copies of the Self-Determination and Self-Advocacy Skills Questionnaire. See Appendix B, part 3 (B-3, Forms 1–3) for the completed forms to assist you with this activity. (Note that Teacher Form B: Employment Skills (B-3, Form 3) was not completed for Sara since she has no community work experience at this time. Also note that the Self-Determination and Self-Advocacy Skills Questionnaire: Student and Teacher Interview—Performance Battery was not completed for Sara given the reasonably strong correspondence between the answers of the student, parent(s), and teacher.)

Strengths

1. Sara is very enthusiastic about her career choice—newspaper journalist.
2. Sara has a very positive self-concept.
3. Sara has a clear and specific career goal.
4. Sara has strength in self-advocacy skills. She identifies herself as a student with a learning disability in academic settings. She will use accommodations in her academic classes as identified on the IEP. However, she does not request her own accommodations.
5. Sara uses a spell-check well and is effective at word processing. She types at 35 words per minute with five errors. She can correct most errors (95%) with spell-check.
6. Sara is motivated and industrious.

7. Sara has gotten A and B grades in her freshman and sophomore English classes. She is considered an average writer in her classes.

Concerns

1. Sara overestimates her academic skills.
2. Sara writes in a laborious fashion. It takes her a long time to complete a writing assignment. In general, the IEP team believes she spends twice as much time completing assignments as her non-disabled peers.
3. In her freshman and sophomore English classes, her assignments have been shortened and often modified.
4. Sara tends to write in simple as opposed to complex sentences. She has no particular problem with present and past tense in her writing assignments.
5. Sara does not request her own accommodations in academic classes.
6. As a sophomore, Sara has not had a paid job or participated in any nonpaid job exploration or service learning.

Assignment

Use the information provided for this activity to do the following three things.

1. Identify three areas of transition need for Sara.
2. Identify three appropriate transition services/activities for Sara.
3. Write two transition goals and corresponding measurable objectives.

DISCUSSION QUESTIONS

How important is self-determination as a curriculum topic for middle school and high school? Discuss strategies for students with disabilities to demonstrate self-advocacy knowledge, skills, and beliefs in the general education classroom.

CHAPTER REFERENCES

Abery B., Arndt, P., Greger, L. Tetu, A., Eggebeen, J., Barosko, A., Hinga, M., McBride, K., Peterson, K., & Rudrud, L. (1994). *Self-advocacy/self-determination.* Minneapolis, MN: University of Minnesota Research and Training Center on Community Living, Institute on Community Integration.

Abery, B. H., Elkin, S. V., Smith, J. G., Springborg, H. L., & Stancliffe, R. J. (2000). *Minnesota self-determination scales.* Minneapolis, MN: University of Minnesota Research and Training Center on Community Living, Institute on Community Integration.

Abery, B., Schoeller, K., Simunds, E., Gaylord, V., & Fahnestock, M. (February 1997). *Yes, I can: A social inclusion curriculum for students with and without disabilities. Instructor's guide.* Minneapolis, MN: University of Minnesota Institute on Community Integration.

Bremer, C. D., Kachgal, M., & Schoeller, M. (April, 2003). *Self-determination: Supporting successful transition: Research to practice brief. 8,* (1). Minneapolis, MN: University of Minnesota Institute on Community Integration.

Field, S. (1996). Self-determination instructional strategies for youth with learning disabilities (pp. 61–84). In J. R. Patton & G. Blalock (Eds.). *Transition and students with learning disabilities*. Austin, TX: PRO-ED.

Field, S., & Hoffman, A. (2005). *Steps to self-determination: A curriculum to help adolescents learn to achieve their goals.* (2nd ed.) Austin, TX: PRO-ED.

Field, S., & Hoffman, A. (1994). Development of a model for self-determination, *Career Development for Exceptional Children, 17*(2). 159–169.

Field, S., Martin, J., Miller, R., Ward, M., & Wehmeyer, M. (1998a). *A practical guide to teaching self-determination*. Reston, VA: Council for Exceptional Children.

Field, S., Martin, J., Miller, R., Ward, M., & Wehmeyer, M. (1998b). Self-determination for persons with disabilities: A position statement of the Division on Career Development and Transition, the Council for Exceptional Children. *Career Development for Exceptional Individuals, 21*(2), 113–128.

Halpern, A. S., Herr, C. M., Doren, B., & Wolf, N. K. (2000). *Next S.T.E.P.: Student transition and educational planning.* (2nd ed.). Austin, TX: PRO-ED.

Hoffman, A., Field, S., & Sawilowsky, S. (1995). *Self-determination knowledge scale.* Austin, TX: PRO-ED

Martin, J. E., Marshall, L. H., Maxon, L., Jerman, P., Hughes, W., Miller, T., & McGill, T. (1997). *ChoiceMaker instructional series.* Longmont, CO: Sopris West.

Martin, J. E., & Marshall, L. H. (1994). *ChoiceMaker self-determination assessment.* Longmont, CO: Sopris West.

McGahee, M., Mason, C., Wallace, T., & Jones, B. (2001). *Student-led IEPs: A guide for student involvement.* Arlington, VA: Council for Exceptional Children.

Miller, R. J., (1994). Preparing for adult life: Teaching students their rights and responsibilities. *CEC Today, 1*(7), 12.

Miller, R. J., & Corbey, S. A. (1994). *Rocketing into the future: A conference launching kit.* [monograph]. St. Paul, MN: Minnesota Department of Education.

Miller, R. J., Corbey, S., & Asher, G. (1994). Promoting postsecondary education for high school-aged youth with disabilities: A model of empowerment. *Rural Special Education Quarterly. 13*(1), 57–63.

Raskind, M. H., Goldberg, R. J., Higgins, E. L., & Herman, K. L. (1999). Predictors of success in individuals with learning disabilities: Results from a twenty-year longitudinal study. *Learning Disabilities Research and Practice, 14*(1), 35–49.

Renzaglia, A., Karvonen, M., Drasgow, E., & Stoxen, C. C. (2003). Promoting a lifetime of inclusion. *Focus on Autism and Other Developmental Disabilities, 18*(3), 1–13.

Reiff, H.B., Gerber, P.J., & Ginsberg, R. (1997). *Exceeding expectations: Highly successful adults with learning disabilities.* Austin, TX: PRO-ED.

Sheets, D., & Gold, E. (2003). *My future my plan: A transition planning resource for life after high school—For students with disabilities and their families.* Washington, DC: State of the Art, Inc.

Sitlington, P. L., Neubert, D. A, Begun, W., Lombard, R. C., & Leconte, P. J. (1996). *Assess for success: Handbook on transition assessment.* Reston, VA: The Council for Exceptional Children.

Stone, A. C., & May, A. L. (2002). The accuracy of academic self-evaluation in adolescents with learning disabilities. *Journal of Learning Disabilities, 35*(4), 370–383.

Valenti, R. A. (1989). *Developing self-advocacy: A practical guide and workbook for preparing high school learning disabled students and their parents.* Columbia, MO: Hawthorne Educational Services.

Van Reusen, A. K., Bos, C. S., Schumaker, J. B., & Deshler D. D. (1994). *The self-advocacy strategy: for education & transition planning: Preparing students to advocate at education and transition conferences.* Lawrence, KS: Edge Enterprises, Inc.

Wehmeyer, M. (2002). *Promoting the self-determination of students with severe disabilities.* Arlington, VA: Eric Clearinghouse on Disabilities and Gifted Education.

Wehmeyer, M., Lawrence, M., Kelchner, K., Palmer, S., Garner, N., & Soukup, J. (2004). *Whose Future is it Anyway? A Student-Directed Transition Planning Process* (2nd ed.). Lawrence, KS: Beach Center on Disability.

Wehmeyer, M., & Kelchner, K. (1996). Perceptions of classroom environments, locus of control and academic attributions of adolescents with and without cognitive disabilities. *Career Development for Exceptional Individuals, 19*(1), 15–29.

Wehmeyer, M., & Kelchner, K. (1995). *The Arc self-determination scale.* Retrieved August 15, 2005 from http://www.beachcenter.org

Wehmeyer, M. L., & Schwartz, M. (1998). The relationship between self-determination and quality of life for adults with mental retardation. *Education and Training in Mental Retardation and Developmental Disabilities, 33*, 3–12.

Wood, W. M., Karvonen, M., Test, D. W., Browder, D., & Algozzine, B. (2004). Promoting student self-determination skills in IEP planning. *Teaching Exceptional Children, 36*(3), 8–16.

Wood, W. M., Test, D., W. Browder, D. M., Algozzine, B, & Karvonen, M. (2000). A summary of self-determination curricula and components. Retrieved March 27, 2005 from http://uncc.edu/sdsp/sd_curricula.asp

II Building Blocks for Effective Transition Assessment and Planning

CHAPTER 5

Using Academic and Behavioral Assessment Information for Transition Planning

For all students, including students with disabilities, academic skills impact capacity and choices regarding life after high school. While impaired academic skills do not necessarily limit student choice of careers after high school, these same academic limitations must be addressed in planning for high school and beyond. In the twenty-first century, employment requires high skill for high-wage employment. Reading, mathematics, and writing skills are more critical today than at any time in the history of our country. Thurlow and Johnson (2000) noted that increasingly, high-stakes testing is significantly affecting student promotion from one grade to the next as well as graduation from high school with a standard diploma. The critical importance of academic skills has been addressed through the passage of the federal No Child Left Behind Act (NCLB). With the passage of NCLB, *all* students are expected to be proficient in these academic areas prior to graduation from high school. Addressing academic limitations for secondary-aged students with disabilities may mean remediation of academic skills. It may mean developing compensatory skills to address academic limitations. It may mean the need for instruction in learning strategies to impact academic concerns. Based on transition assessment information, any or all of these interventions may be appropriate to address a student's academic limitations.

Behavior concerns impact all students' capacity to participate successfully in the general education curriculum. This is particularly true for students labeled with emotional/behavior disorders and learning disabilities. Students labeled with emotional/behavior disorders and learning disabilities have been found to be at great risk for dropping out of high school. According to Blackorby and Wagner (1996), of students who do not complete high school, about 36% are students with learning disabilities and a staggering 59% are students with emotional/behavior disorders. Dropping out of high school is the outcome of a long process of alienation and disengagement preceded by symptomatic types of withdrawal such as course failures and truancy (Finn, 1993). Clearly, not graduating from high school will dramatically impact these young adults' capacity to find meaningful and high-wage employment. Social and behavioral assessment information must be gathered regarding any student for whom behavior and social concerns are impacting their capacity to be successful in high school and beyond. For all students, including students with disabilities, social and behavioral skills impact capacity to succeed in life during and after high school.

The focus of this segment of the chapter will be on interpreting the meaning of educational achievement testing, social and behavioral testing, and integrating this information into the transition assessment process (see Figure 5.1). A comprehensive transition assessment is an evaluation of the entire adolescent. To be complete, an effective transition assessment must include information regarding (a) educational achievement of the student (formal and informal) as well as (b) assessment information regarding the social and behavioral needs of

Transition Assessment Model

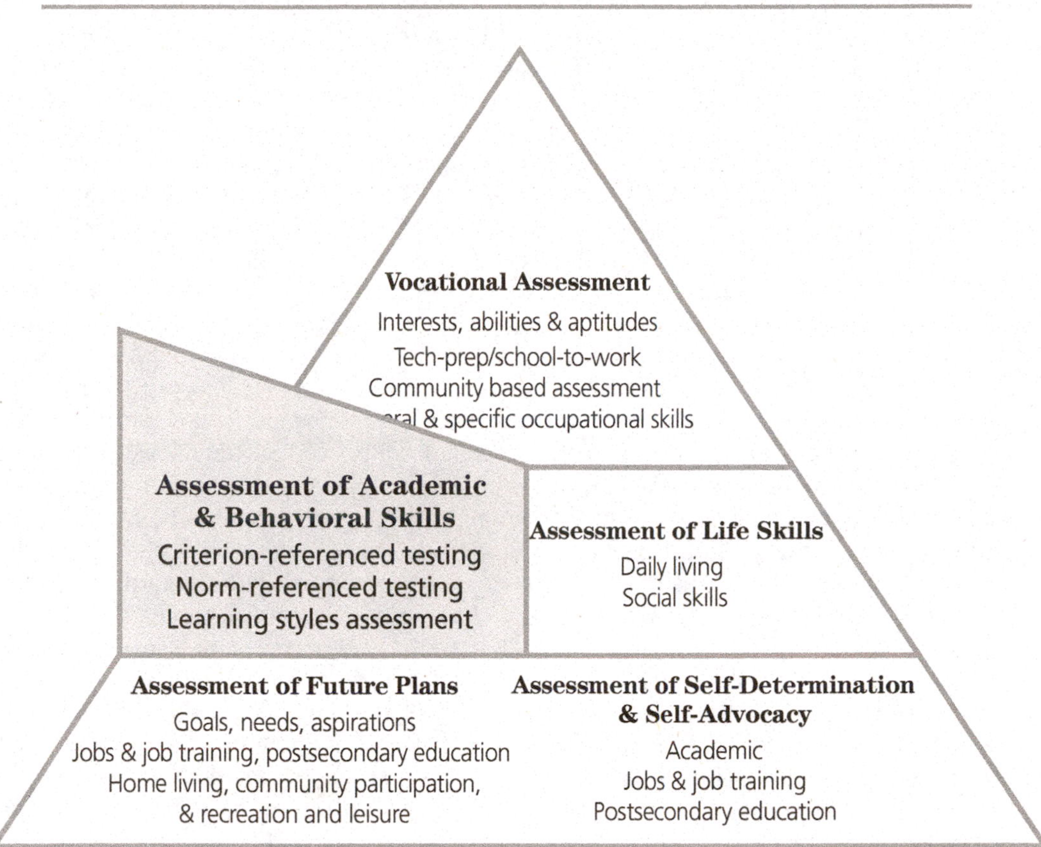

Figure 5.1

students as is warranted. For secondary-aged students with disabilities, transition assessment is a holistic evaluation process that includes academic and behavioral assessment information. Ultimately, any decisions regarding goals and benchmarks in the IEP is an IEP team decision. The school is responsible to ensure that the educational program provides the student a free appropriate public education (FAPE). As such, the IEP must address student interest, preferences, and identified needs.

The time of educational evaluation or reevaluation of the student is an optimal time to consider academic and other diagnostic testing in the transition assessment process. P.L. 108–446 (IDEA 2004) maintains much of the general structure and requirements for evaluation and eligibility found in earlier versions of IDEA. With the passage of IDEA 2004, Local Education Agencies (LEAs) are still required to conduct a full and individual initial evaluation before special education and related services can be provided to the student. However, IDEA 2004 has modified the requirements for student reevaluation. Reevaluations are required if the child's teacher or parent makes a request or if the LEA determines that the student's educational and service needs warrant a reevaluation (academic achievement or functional performance) Section 614(a)(2). Prior versions of the IDEA required that reevaluation take place at least every three years (Three-Year Reevaluation). IDEA 2004 permits the LEA and the parents to override this requirement if they agree that a reevaluation is not necessary. IDEA 2004 also prohibits reevaluation more often than once per year without the agreement of both the parents and the LEA (Apling & Jones, 2005).

While the intent of allowing the parents and LEA to override the requirement of reevaluation (when both the parents and the LEA agree that reevaluation is not necessary) seems reasonable, districts should carefully weigh the costs and benefits of not using a model of continuous assessment to monitor student progress. Special education assessment can be a useful tool in helping to resolve conflicts between parents and LEAs before a dispute ends up in litigation. Current assessment data can help an IEP team to stay focused on student need, interest, and preferences (Janisch & Schreifels, 2001). The purpose of assessment is to enhance student learning and teacher effectiveness (McMillan, 2000).

IDEA 2004 mandates that transition planning begin *no later than* the first IEP to be in effect when the adolescent is sixteen years of age and that it is updated annually thereafter. As a result, assessment of transition needs must begin when the student is fifteen years of age or younger. Based on career development concerns for student with disabilities (see Chapter 2), best practice would dictate that transition evaluation and transition planning begin with the movement of the young person from junior high school to high school, and continue on an ongoing basis throughout high school. As we have discussed in earlier chapters, transition planning is a developmental process and student goals, interests, and preferences may change due to information gathered, life experiences, and the career maturity of the student. Transition assessment is the process of gathering information to assist the student, family, and IEP team with decision making and planning for life both during high school and for adult life after high school. Remember that educational assessment information addresses a broad variety of needs for information including: identifying student strengths and limitations, assisting the student and family in making informed educational and career decisions, monitoring student progress, motivating the student, diagnosising and prescribing for educational need, carrying out curriculum evaluation and refinement, determining student grades, and determination of school accountability (Dietel, Herman, & Knuth, 1991).

When reviewing the results of educational evaluation of students, it is important to consider whether the test given to the student was a standardized test or a criterion-referenced test. Dietel, et al. (1991) defined a **standardized test** as a form of measurement that compares the student's performance to a norm sample. Standardization is obtained by giving the test to the norm sample and then calculating the means, standard deviations, standard scores, and percentile ranks. The individual's score can then be compared to the population that makes up the norm sample. Figure 5.2 demonstrates the relationship among different types of scores in a normal distribution of scores. Most standardized tests provide the evaluator with standard scores. Standard scores that are based on normal distribution have characteristics that allow a student's performance to be related to the mean score and standard deviation of the norm group. These standard scores can then be converted into percentile ranks (McLoughlin & Lewis, 2001). Some examples of standardized testing instruments used in individualized special education testing include the Wechsler Intelligence Scale for Children, Third Edition (WISC–III), Woodcock Johnson Tests of Achievement, Third Edition (WJ–III ACH), and Behavior Assessment System for Children (BASC). A **criterion-referenced test** is a measurement of achievement of a specific skill or criteria with a focus on the performance of the individual against mastery of the skill or criteria as opposed to the criteria of comparing the performance on the test against others who are taking the test. There is no norm sample in criterion-referenced testing (Dietel,et al., 1991). Criterion-referenced testing compares an individual's performance to a preestablished level of performance (e.g., 85%) rather than to compare the performance of the individual to the performance of others (Sitlington & Clark, 2006). The Diagnostic Comprehensive Inventory of Basic Skills—Revised (CIBS-R) by Brigance is an example of an assessment that combines criterion-referenced assessment with a standardized test option for key academic skills (pre-K through grade nine).

Normal Distribution

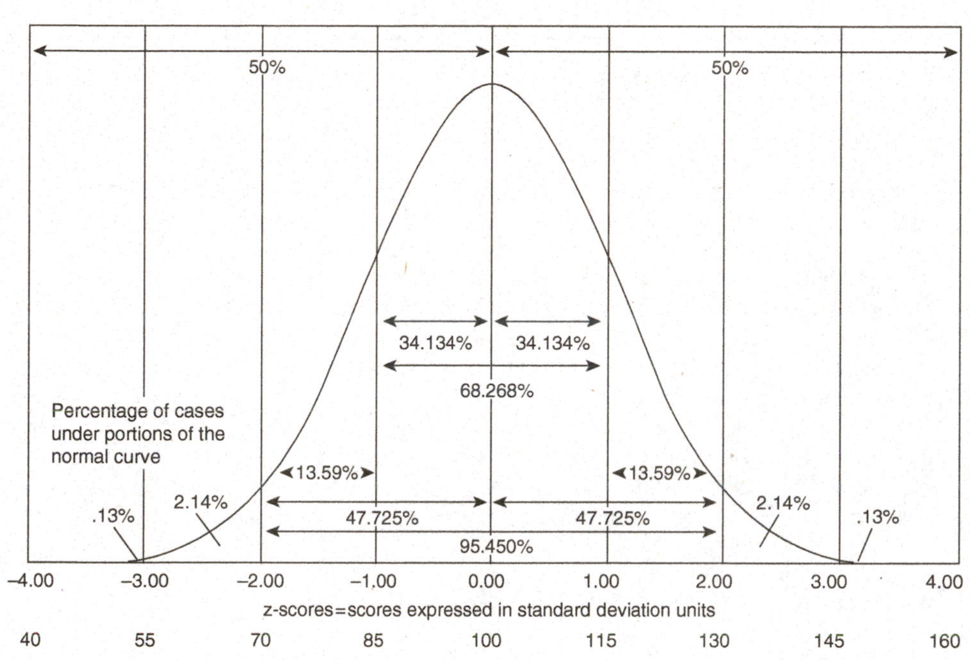

Figure 5.2

Diagnostic Comprehensive Inventory of Basic Skills (CIBS-R) 1999

CIBS-R includes 154 assessments in readiness, speech, listening, reading, spelling, writing, research and study skills, and math. Since it is criterion-referenced its results can be applied directly to planning and individualized instruction. Fourteen of the assessments have two forms—A and B. One form could be used as a pretest and the alternate form as a posttest. The CIBS-R identifies which skills the student has mastered and which skills the student has not mastered, and provides suggested instructional objectives.

The money and time assessments are particularly applicable to functional life skills assessment. Time is assessed pertaining to basic skills and supplemental and related lists/skills sequences. Basic skills include: tells time, knows equivalent units of time, converts units of time, knows equivalent calendar units, converts calendar units, uses a calendar, and writes dates. Supplemental and related lists/skills sequences include: time vocabulary related to the clock, time concepts related to the clock, time vocabulary related to the calendar, and time concepts related to the calendar. Money is assessed for basic skills including recognizes money, knows equivalent values of coins and the dollar bill, totals, values of groups of coins, converts coins, and makes change.

All the assessments can be administered by individual or group written response except "recognizes money". If a student has been observed performing a skill, such as making change when purchasing an item, on a daily basis they are given credit for the skill by recording it in the *Student Record Book* without conducting the assessment. The Student Record Book serves as a means for tracking the progress of the individual student, communicating information in the parent conference, and communicating student data to other school personnel.

Case Study: Joe Site

For the purposes of this text, perhaps the most efficient manner to examine integration of academic and other diagnostic testing into the transition planning process is through a case study of fifteen-year-old Joe Site (see Appendix D). The educational reevaluation of Joe Site occurred in his 9th grade year. Joe Site was originally referred to special education in third grade based on parent and teacher concerns regarding low grades, disrespectful behavior toward school staff, unsent and impulsive behavior. Joe has high levels of off-task behavior and talking-out behavior. During third grade Joe was medically diagnosed with Oppositional Defiant Disorder (ODD) and Attention Deficit with Hyperactivity Disorder (ADHD). Based on the student's educational history and current reevaluation results, the multidisciplinary team had a choice of two disability categories under which Joe could receive special education services. The team chose between a category of Emotional/Behavior Disorders and Other Health Disability. The multidisciplinary team identified Joe for special education services under what is now the disability category of Other Health Disability (OHD). Remember, once one is evaluated and found eligible under the IDEA as a student with a disability (under one of the thirteen disability categories), *the door is opened to all needed special educational and support services*. Therefore, a student's disability category never limits the types of services from which the IEP team may choose when designing an IEP to meet the needs of the student.

Reevaluation Test Results: 9th Grade

Wechsler Intelligence Scale for Children, Standard Scores, Third Edition (WISC–III)

	Standard Scores
Verbal IQ	90
Performance IQ	103
Full Scale IQ	96

Woodcock Johnson Tests of Achievement, Third Edition (WJ–III ACH)

Standard Battery Age Norms

	Standard Score	Percentile
Broad Reading	96	40
Broad Math	98	44
Broad Written Language	90	26
Math Calculation Skills	100	50
Written Expression	90	26

Academic Performance Joe had a GPA of 1.45 out of possible 4.0 in 8th grade. In 8th grade, Joe participated in general education classes and failed classes in reading, science, and social studies. Joe did best in math, art, and physical education courses. Joe had significant problems in social studies and science. During the first three quarters of 9th grade, Joe had a GPA of 1.55 out of a possible 4.0.

Communication Skills According to teacher report, Joe appears to have age-appropriate expressive and receptive communication skills.

Information Processing Based on testing, no concerns regarding storage, organization and acquisition of information, retrieval, expression, or manipulation of information.

Test Interpretations

Intellectual and Academic Achievement Results Joe is currently functioning in the average range of intellectual ability (see Appendix D, pages 296–297). The difference in scores between Joe's verbal IQ and his performance IQ would suggest that Joe has more capacity to use nonverbal strategies rather than verbal strategies for problem solving. This may impact career choice and should be considered in exploring career choices. However, with an IQ very much in the average range, there are no obvious limitations that would affect Joe's options for career decision making for transition planning. In Joe's case, the issues that may limit his success in high school and beyond are clearly behavioral.

Educational achievement testing is consistent with the results of his IQ testing. Broad reading, mathematics, and writing skills are all within the average range of performance and are consistent with the cognitive capacity demonstrated in his IQ testing. Joe's strengths are in math calculation, broad math, and broad reading skills. His lowest academic scores are in broad written language and written expression. Based on this testing, there is no obvious need for IEP goals in the area of academic skill development. If an IEP goal were to be developed for Joe in his 10th grade year, it would probably be developed to address improving his written language skills. This will be an IEP team decision. The IEP team would be wise to carefully consider Joe's input and commitment prior to development of an academic goal to remediate written language skills. There are a limited number of goals that can be addressed in any annual IEP. If Joe wants to improve his writing skills, the IEP team may choose to develop a goal in this area. On the other hand, if Joe is resistive to writing and does not perceive the value of improving his written language skills, then the team may choose to focus on other issues. Again, this is a team decision. Second, the IEP team, including Joe, must consider Joe's career goals or areas of interest. Are improved written language skills important or necessary in a career field in which Joe is interested? If Joe wants to work as a writer in a newspaper then written language skills are critical. If Joe wishes to be a plumber, then other skills are more paramount. It is important that the IEP team lay out options and consequences of choosing or not choosing to develop any particular academic skill.

Joe's academic performance in 8th and 9th grade are not consistent with his cognitive ability or his educational achievement. Academically, Joe is clearly capable of achieving grades that are superior to what he accomplished in 8th and 9th grade. A closer look at assessment results in emotional, social, and behavioral areas of assessment are warranted. It is clear that Joe is underachieving in his academic performance.

Case Study: Joe Site (continued)

Emotional, Social, and Behavioral Assessment Results (see Appendix D, pages 298–300) Joe was admitted to hospital in January of 8th grade year presenting problems of defiance, aggression, irritable mood, and multiple school suspensions. Discharge summary confirms his diagnosis of ODD and ADHD. Joe is currently taking medications to address these issues. Parents report Joe's current school problems center around "defiance and disrespectful behavior." Teachers report Joe is "disrespectful, lashes out, becomes angry, and shuts down" when presented with activities he does not like. Teachers note severe problems with verbal aggression, violent behavior, mood swings, and threatening behavior. Joe has had fourteen days of in-school suspension over the last three years. Absenteeism is trending upward (7th grade—12 days (all reasons); 8th grade—18 days (all reasons); 9th grade—26 days (through April 30)).

Joe reports being "bored" with school. Parents report Joe likes physical activities and prefers to do "hands-on activities." Teachers report behavior incidents occurred most often in academic classes but less often in classes with hands-on activities and during times when movement is allowed (e.g., art, physical education).

(continued)

Behavior Assessment System for Children (BASC)

Bold = Clinically Significant

Asterisk = At Risk

Clinical Scale	Parent	Teacher 1	Teacher 2
Hyperactivity	66*	56	51
Aggression	**71**	63*	50
Conduct Problems	**84**	51	56
EXTERNAL COMPOSITE	**78**	57	53
Anxiety	54	48	52
Depression	**77**	50	49
Somatization	64*	55	43
INTERNALIZING COMPOSITE	68*	51	48
Attention Problems	62*	59	64*
Learning Problems		53	55
SCHOOL PROBLEM COMPOSITE		56	60*
Atypicality	44	43	47
Withdrawal	52	51	47
BEHAVIOR SYMPTOMS INDEX	67*	54	53
Adaptive Skills Scale			
Social Skills	35*	32*	39*
Leadership	40*	42	33*
Study Skills		39*	40*
ADAPTIVE SKILLS COMPOSITE	36*	37*	35*

Teacher ratings of student behavior produced no scores in Clinically Significant range. Parent rating resulted in multiple areas of Clinically Significant (Aggression, Conduct Problems, External Composite score) and At-Risk ratings.

Adaptive Skills Scale All raters (both teachers and parents) rated student At Risk in Social Skills. Both teachers rated Study Skills and Adaptive Skills Composite as At Risk. Scores in Social Skills, Study Skills, and Adaptive Skills Composite suggest deficits in the skills to interact successfully with adults and peers. This scale is a measure of the skills associated with accomplishing academic, social, and community goals including the capacity to work well with others.

BASC Self-Report of Personality This self-report was also completed by the student to examine his own skills and behaviors as perceived by the student. Validity indexes are within acceptable limits.

Bold = Clinically Significant

Asterisk = At Risk

CLINICAL SCALES (student self-report)	T – Scores
Attitude toward School	**75**
Attitude toward Teachers	**73**
Sensation Seeking	66*
SCHOOL MALADJUSTMENT COMPOSITE	**77**
Atypicality	44
Locus of Control	63*
Somatization	49
Social Stress	48
Anxiety	40
CLINCIAL MALADJUSTMENT COMPOSITE	47
Depression	62*
Sense of Inadequacy	51
EMOTIONAL SYMPTOMS INDEX	48

ADAPTIVE SCALES	
Relations with Parents	55
Interpersonal Relations	41
Self-Esteem	50
Self-Reliance	42
PERSONAL ADJUSTMENT COMPOSITE	49

Student's ratings of Attitude toward Teachers, Attitude toward School, and School Maladjustment Composite were in the Clinically Significant range. This is consistent with academic classroom behavior which is often disruptive and aggressive. Student often uses verbal threats as "jokes." Example: "I'm going to sit on you and shave your head." Teachers sometimes hear this or a similar response when the student is given independent seatwork and asked to work independently during class time. Teachers believe this behavior is meant as "attention getting" and represents the student's need for personal power in the academic setting.

Student believes his biggest problem in school is "talking back to teachers and getting in trouble."

Classroom Observations

Math Class In math class a special education paraprofessional did an observation during class time. Out of fifty systematic observations done at thirty-second intervals, student was found to be "on task" 55% of the time compared to 85% by peers. Student blurted out responses in class and was defiant when asked to work. Is out of seat 25% of time.

Art Class Out of fifty systematic observations done at thirty-second intervals, student was "on task" 100% of time as compared to 85% by peers. Student worked independently with no out of seat behavior or inappropriate blurting responses.

Reading Class Out of fifty systematic observations done at thirty-second intervals, student was "on task" 75% of time compared to 85% by peers. Student blurted out questions or comments when he struggled with words in reading assignment or did not understand reading. Is out of seat 20% of time.

Functional Behavioral Assessment (FBA)

An FBA was completed with input from parent, student, and teacher interview, and classroom observation. **Target Behavior**: student refuses to work in class.

Based on assessment data, team hypothesizes that student engages in work refusal behavior as a way to escape/avoid tasks he does not like to do. At the same time, he gains attention from adults and staff for emotional needs.

Behavior Reduction Strategies

1. Provide student with opportunity to move in classroom. Provide two desks for student. One in preferential seating in front of room to minimize distractions and one in back of room to provide a destination for movement in class.
2. Allow student to choose between acceptable alternative tasks.
3. Provide assignments that are "hands-on." If possible include motor activity and use of tools.
4. Involve student in development of a plan to meet his educational goals in the class. Specifically identify what he needs to do to be successful.
5. Clearly identify the consequences of behavioral choices.

Possible Reinforcements

- Building models
- Riding bike
- Working on bike
- Playing basketball/Shooting baskets
- Praise
- Positive comments/Good grades

Learning Style Assessment

In the model of transition assessment found in Chapter 1, transition assessment includes five major assessment components. In this model, one type of assessment information that must be gathered in order to complete a comprehensive transition evaluation is academic and behavioral skills assessment in all relevant academic and behavioral areas. Included in this area of assessment is learning styles assessment. Learning styles refer to the highly individualized way in which all people take in, process, organize, and express information. An individual's learning style is the natural channel used to learn most effectively and most efficiently. Every individual has a mix of learning styles with some individuals having a more dominant style of learning while other individuals having less dominant learning styles or completely different learning styles. There is no "right" mix. (Advanogy, 2003). Learning styles assessment is of particular importance to students with learning disabilities since information processing (acquisition of information, processing of information, organizing and expression of information) is a key component of their disability. Assisting students with identifying the ways in which they learn best and providing the opportunity to practice using those preferred methods of learning can assist learners to be successful in the academic setting.

Dunn and Dunn (1978) identified four types of learners including: visual learners, auditory learners, tactile and kinesthetic learners, and multisensory learners. In an academic environment, visual learners are those who learn best from visual methods of communication such as reading and seeing. Additional visual examples would include overheads, graphs, handouts, and films; the use of color to highlight important information in text books; or the use of preferential student seating to ensure that the student has a clear view of the teacher to see body language and facial expressions. Auditory learners were identified as those persons who learn best from listening and speaking. These individuals often have good verbal skills and often benefit from auditory methods of communication such as lectures, audiotapes, and oral examinations. Other strategies for use with auditory learners might include creation and use of musical jingles or mnemonics to aid memorization; or the use of speeches and presentations as opposed to written papers. Tactile and kinesthetic learners are those learners who learn best by doing an activity. This hands-on type of learning includes movement and manipulation of objects. These learners need to touch and manipulate materials and objects to maximize learning. Some tactile and kinesthetic learners may learn better if allowed to listen to music while studying or perhaps be allowed to work in a standing position. Multisensory learners are those individuals who learn best by combining two or more learning styles.

The importance of learning style assessment should not be underestimated. This importance can be illustrated through the story of Bob. Bob, a student with a learning disability and with significant reading and writing disabilities, transitioned from high school to an apprenticeship program in plumbing as a part of his transition plan. Bob was an industrious young man and was very committed to being successful in his plumbing apprenticeship. As Bob prepared for graduation, there was much concern regarding Bob's ability to read and write effectively and the ultimate effect that would have on Bob's ability to pass the written examinations to become a practicing journeyman plumber. Bob was a tactile and kinesthetic learner. As such he learned best through hands-on learning. An apprenticeship program offered an excellent match between Bob's learning style and his career goal of becoming a plumber. As Bob worked as an apprentice, he was very successful developing the knowledge and skills necessary to be a plumber. Bob learned the tools and vocabulary of his craft as he did the job. By doing the job, Bob's ability to read the vocabulary involved in the plumbing profession grew rapidly. When it came time for written exams involved in his plumbing apprenticeship, Bob passed the written examinations to the surprise of many who knew his reading and writing skills in high school. In less than ten years later, Bob has moved from "apprentice plumber" to "journeyman plumber," and is currently a "master plumber." He lives in Iowa. He recently changed jobs into a more supervisory capacity and has apprentice and journeyman plumbers under his supervision. The ability to get this job was based not only on his attitude and work history, but also on his license as a master plumber.

Bob was a success because of many of the reasons we have discussed in earlier chapters. Bob was industrious and committed to a career plan, and he demonstrated the components of career maturity. Also, however, Bob found a career that allowed him to learn in a preferred manner. As a tactile and kinesthetic learner, Bob learned the knowledge and skills of plumbing by touching and manipulating concrete objects. As he learned the vocabulary and the specific skills, he applied that knowledge to reading the vocabulary. His reading was made easier by his experience. Too often middle school and high school curriculum is over-reliant on visual and auditory presentation of information at the expense of tactile and kinesthetic and multisensory learning styles. Many students with disabilities learn best by **doing**, which is an underutilized method of teaching in many schools. Research supports that for all learners, the percentage of information retained increases as the learner moves from being a passive recipient of information to being actively involved in the learning process. Learning retention rates are found to be the highest as students practice doing learning activities or immediately apply the learning to real situations. Remember, identifying the learning style of a student is useless if it does not lead to changes in methods of instruction and changes in the curriculum and learning environment to address student needs.

The evaluation case study of Joe Site found earlier in this chapter and in Appendix D is another example of the possible importance of learning style with the delivery of curriculum. Did you note Joe's clear preference for "hands-on" learning? The IEP team might well hypothesize that increasing the use of tactile/kinesthetic learning opportunities may improve Joe's constructive involvement and participation in his educational program.

Using Learning Style Assessment Information to Identify and Address Learning Preferences and Needed Academic Accommodations

Sarah Jones is a sixteen-year-old junior with a learning disability. Sarah's career goal is to attend a technical/community college and become an occupational therapist assistant after graduation from high school. As part of her ongoing transition assessment and in preparation for her senior year IEP meeting, Sarah completed the C.I.T.E. Learning Styles Instrument (Babich, et al., 1976) to identify and update her learning style and learning preferences (see Appendix B, part 4 (B-4) for complete test results). The C.I.T.E. Learning Styles Instrument is a public domain instrument and as such, may be used by anyone. A clean copy of the C.I.T.E. Learning Styles Instrument is included in Appendix A for your use. This instrument is also available on the web at http:wvabe.org/cite.htm. At this web address, you can download additional copies of the C.I.T.E. With the use of this information, the IEP team may be better prepared to identify the methods and materials that will assist Sarah to learn best in her academic classes in high school and beyond. The results of the C.I.T.E. indicate the following:

- Sarah's learning style preferences include strong preferences for oral expressive and auditory, visual, and kinesthetic learning.
- Sarah learns best by working on an individual basis as opposed to working with a group.
- Sarah does not enjoy written assignments. It is difficult for her to complete written assignments and to demonstrate her level of understanding of academic materials

using written expression. She is much more likely to demonstrate her true skill level either by demonstrating (doing) the activity or by discussing (oral communication) the assignment.

- Information presented through auditory learning methods (speaking and listening) are preferable to the presentation of materials through the visual learning mode (reading and seeing materials)
- As a kinesthetic/tactile learner, providing Sarah with opportunities to immediately apply information that is presented orally to hands-on activities is likely to increase the likelihood that Sarah will learn and remember the information presented in the academic class.

Figure 5.3 includes a summary of C.I.T.E. test results for major learning styles, minor learning styles, and learning styles of negligible use for Sarah.

Success in the academic setting is critical to Sarah's goal of attending a technical/community college to major in an occupational therapy assistant program after high school. Sarah needs to understand and be able to articulate how she learns best. First, Sarah will need to practice use of her learning preferences to develop competence in these learning styles. Second, Sarah will need to be able to articulate her learning preferences to maximize her opportunity for reasonable accommodation at the technical/community college. After high school, Sarah will not receive accommodations unless she can articulate what accommodations she needs and unless she can request the specific accommodations. Third, identification of learning style preferences is critical to the IEP team as they identify and select reasonable accommodations for her to use in her academic classes while in high school. Anything that can be done in the academic setting during high school to maximize her ability to learn while maintaining the academic rigor of the class is an important consideration for the IEP team and is of great significance in planning the transition from high school to life after high school.

Summary of C.I.T.E. Learning Style Assessment Results for Sarah (Age 16)

Major Learning Styles	**Raw Score**
Expressive oral	40
Auditory–Visual–Kinesthetic	38
Social–individual	34
Minor Learning Styles	
Auditory language	30
Auditory number	28
Social—group	22
Negligible Use	
Visual number	20
Visual language	18
Expressive written	10

Score: 34–40 = Major learning style
20–32 = Minor learning style
10–18 = Negligible use

Figure 5.3

CHAPTER SUMMARY

Chapter 5 explored the relationship between academic and behavioral assessment information and transition planning. We found that:

- academic and behavioral assessment information are critical to a comprehensive transition assessment.
- ongoing collection of assessment information provides fresh assessment data that may be critical to assisting the IEP team to stay focused on student need interests, and preferences.
- academic and behavioral goals must be included, if warranted, based on assessment results.
- assessment of learning styles and preferences is an important component of the transition assessment of academic skills for planning in high school and beyond.
- the student must be involved in the learning style assessment process.

CHAPTER ACTIVITIES

1. Carefully review the emotional/social/behavioral assessment information in this chapter and Appendix D. The results of Joe Site's 9th grade educational reevaluation in this assessment area will dramatically impact Joe's ability to be successful in school and in life after high school. The IEP team will want to address the emotional/social/ behavioral area as the next IEP is developed. This fresh evaluation information should assist the IEP team in developing IEP goals to assist Joe with needed behavioral control and social skills. Based on the information provided in the reevaluation as included in this chapter and Appendix D, please do the following activities:

   1. Develop for Joe Site one behavioral goal and four short-term objectives that address the emotional/behavior information provided in this chapter and Appendix D.
   2. Based on the reevaluation, what strategies or accommodations would you suggest to increase Joe's success in his general education classes?
   3. As Joe's teacher, what methods would you use to address Joe's work refusal in the general education or special education setting?

2. Carefully review the C.I.T.E. Learning Style assessment results in this chapter and in Appendix B, part 4 (B-4). Pay particular attention to the results of the specific test questions in Appendix B. The results of Sarah's learning style assessment will impact Sarah's ability to be successful in school and in life after high school. The IEP team will want to address learning preferences and possible learning accommodations as the next IEP is developed. Based on the information provided in this chapter and Appendix B, part 4, please do the following activities:

   1. Identify six methods, materials, or strategies related to learning style that will help Sarah be successful in the academic high school setting.
   2. Identify three methods, materials, or strategies related to learning style that should be minimized to enhance Sarah's academic success.
   3. As Sarah's special education teacher, what learning accommodations would you and Sarah request of Sarah's general education teachers to maximize Sarah's opportunity to learn in the general education classroom?

DISCUSSION QUESTIONS

How does high stakes testing impact students with disabilities in the secondary school setting? Discuss the range of accommodations that students with disabilities have in the general education setting and any impact these accommodations may have on their future goals.

CHAPTER REFERENCES

Advanogy.com. (2003). *Overview of learning styles*. Retrieved March 17, 2005 from http//www.learning-styles-online.com/overview

Apling, R. N., & Jones, N. L. (January 5, 2005). *CRS report for congress. Individuals with disabilities education act (IDEA): Analysis of changes made by P. L. 108–446*. Washington, DC: Congressional Research Service, The Library of Congress.

Babich, A. M., Burdine, P., Albright, L., & Randol, P. (1976). *C.I.T.E. learning styles instrument*. Retrieved July 26, 2005 from http:// wvabe.org/cite.htm

Blackorby, J., & Wagner, M. (1996). Longitudinal postschool outcomes of youth with disabilities: Findings from the National Longitudinal Transition Study. *Exceptional Children, 62*(5), 399–413.

Brigance, A. H. (1999). *Brigance Comprehensive Inventory of Basic Skills (CIBS-R)*. North Billerica, MA: Curriculum Associates.

Dietel, R. J., Herman, J. L., & Knuth, R. A. (1991). *What does research say about assessment*? North Central Regional Education Laboratory. Retrieved February 12, 2005 from http.//www.ncrel.org/sdrs/areas/stw-esys14assesss.htm

Dunn, K., & Dunn, R. (1978). *Teaching students through their individual learning styles: A practical approach*. Reston, VA: Reston.

Finn, J.D. (1993). *School engagement and students at risk*. Buffalo, NY: State University. (ERIC Document Reproduction Service No. 362 322).

Janisch, K. A., & Schreifels, R. T. (2001). Strategies for a successful (litigation-free) school year. *Legal Notes for Education, XV*(7), 1, 11.

McMillian, J. H. (2000). Fundamental assessment principles for teachers and school administrators. *Practical Assessment, Research and Evaluation, 7*(8). Retrieved January 30, 2005 from http://PAREonline.net/getvn.asp?v=7&N=8

McLoughlin, J. A. & Lewis R. B. (2001). *Assessing students with special needs* (5th ed.). Upper Saddle River, NJ: Prentice Hall.

Sitlington, P. L, & Clark, G. M. (2006). *Transition education and services for students with disabilities* (4th ed). Boston, MA: Pearson Education Inc.

Thurlow, M. L., & Johnson, D. R. (2000). High-stakes testing of students with disabilities. *Journal of Teacher Education, 51*(4), 305–314.

Wechsler, D. (1991). *Wechsler Intelligence Scale for Children, Third Edition (WISC-III)*. San Antonio, TX: Harcourt Assessments.

Woodcock, R., McGrew, K., & Mather, N. C. (2001). *Woodcock Johnson III Test of Achievement (WJIII ACH)*. Itasca, IL: Riverside Publishing Company.

CHAPTER 6

Functional Life Skills Assessment

Functional life skills assessment is integral to a comprehensive transition evaluation. Research and follow-up studies confirm that broad arrays of life skills are necessary for students with mild disabilities to be successful in adult life. What are these life skills? How do we assess students to find out whether they need instruction to develop these skills? In Chapter 1, the transition model for effective transition planning depicts Life Skills Assessment as a necessary component of a comprehensive transition assessment. This chapter will describe how data gathered from functional life skills assessment can contribute meaningful information for a transition plan (see Figure 6.1).

Knowles (1990) organized adult life skills into the six domains of (1) home and family living, (2) leisure pursuits, (3) personal responsibility and relationships, (4) physical/ emotional health, (5) community involvement, and (6) employment/education. These domains were related to the ways we organize our lives. Clearly, all facets of adult living require a wide range of these skills to be exercised across multiple environments. Even though life skills are essential for young adults with mild disabilities, these skills are often not directly taught to students. The assumption may be that students with mild disabilities have a need only to acquire academic and vocational skills. This is just not true! Haring, Lovett, and Smith (1990) conducted a student follow-up study that found that 79% of young adults with learning disabilities live at home after graduation from high school. Fifty-seven% of parents of the youth in the study preferred to have their sons or daughters living independently.

For students with mild cognitive disabilities their outcomes for independent living may require short-term supports in the community. However, West, et al. (1996) noted that while support planning should occur, no specific list of supports currently exists. The need for supports is derived from the transition assessment of functional life skills. The IEP team must plan for and prepare the student for linkage to supports for: housing options, shopping, transportation, financial, social and recreational activities, and health and safety. More specifically, the area of transportation could include the following options that may require varying levels of support: public transportation, bike, parents, friends, taxi, walking, etc.

Many theorists have described the secondary special education curriculum as being composed of four domains including academic skills, vocational skills, social skills, and independent living skills. Successful transition from school to adult living may depend on skill mastery in all domains (Michaels, 1994). For most students with mild disabilities, the reality of No Child Left Behind legislation and standards-based education has put a major focus on the academic skills portion of their secondary education. However, IDEA 2004 continues to mandate transition planning for students with IEPs with a focus on future goal attainment. Functional life skills are critical to successful outcomes since without these necessary skills the desired goals of employment and postsecondary education can be jeopardized.

Life skills cover a broad area of daily living and social adjustment. Mary Cronin (1996) conducted a review of literature related to life skills and used the following definition: Life skills are those skills or tasks that contribute to the successful independent functioning of

Transition Assessment Model

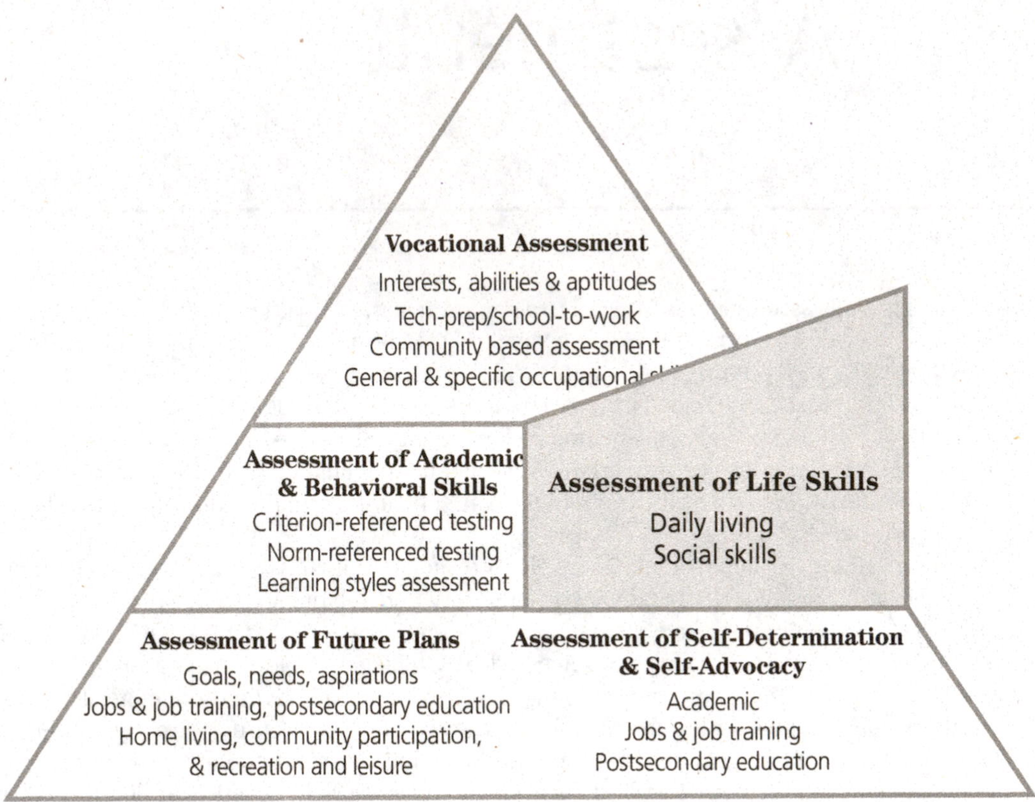

Figure 6.1

an individual in adulthood. In a review of literature regarding life skills, Cronin (1996) identified the following terminology that has been used to describe life skills:

- career education
- functional curriculum
- functional literacy
- functional academics
- survival skills
- daily living skills
- life skills
- independent living skills
- functional skills

Literature review findings by Cronin (1996) suggest:

1. Life skills are appropriate for ALL students.
2. Life skills should be part of the ongoing curriculum.
3. Vocational training is an important life skill.
4. Life skills are best taught in natural settings.
5. Life skills should be addressed daily.
6. Parental understanding of life skills instruction can be advantageous.

7. Challenges to teaching life skills do exist.
8. Transition planning is important to overall quality of life.

In 1990, the Minnesota Department of Education developed a resource guide for transition planning entitled, "Teaching the Possibilities: Home Living." In this guide, learner outcomes were identified and instructional strategies were described for the transition area of home living. The following independent living skills areas were described:

- housing alternatives
- money and finances
- consumer awareness
- food preparation
- personal development
- safety
- clothing care
- personal care
- medical and dental services
- housekeeping

Each of these independent living skill areas was further divided into learner outcomes. For example, in the independent skill area of "money and finances" the following learner outcomes were identified as necessary for independent living:

1. Distinguish between earned income and financial assistance program.
2. Identify the types of information necessary when applying for assistance services.
3. List the various financial assistance programs that are applicable to me.
4. Describe the difference between fixed and flexible expenses.
5. Plan a basic monthly budget.
6. Describe checking and savings accounts and give advantages and disadvantages of each account.
7. Define credit, credit cards, bankcards, and loans. Give examples of each.
8. Other outcomes per individual needs.

This guide also addressed the individual considerations that should be taken into account in the above learner outcomes. Included in these considerations are sources of income, math skills, and accessibility to banks, employment/wages, credit eligibility, transportation needs, living expenses and budget requirements. As demonstrated in this example, life skills represent a multifaceted, interdependent, and complex set of skills necessary for all youth to function independently in life after high school. Functional skills assessment is needed in order to identify goals and develop programming to meet an individual student's specific needs.

Zetlin, Turner, and Wenik (1987) found that individuals with mild disabilities who adjust well to the demands of independence come from homes in which parents were supportive and developed the individual's self-confidence. Parents allowed the individual to take risks and assume responsibilities. Poorly adjusted individuals with mild disabilities came from homes that reinforced dependence and compliance. Individuals with mild disabilities need to overcome barriers to independence on many fronts and the lack of access to direct instruction in the area of life skills is often related to the lack of assessment and identification of needs early on in their educational program. Based on need, life skills instruction is appropriate for all students.

Parents of young adults with mild disabilities usually expect their child to grow up and live independently after high school or post high school training. However, parents are not always aware that independent living skills are lacking in their child. Parents may see their young adult as manifesting their disability characteristics in the academic arena (school) and may not think other areas, such as life skills, are impacted by the disability. A reason for this is that parents often take care of many of the life skills tasks for their young adult. They make their doctor appointments, complete the student's income taxes, handle maintenance of their wardrobe, and manage some or all of the student's personal finances. For many students with mild disabilities, the importance of functional life skills is often times not considered until the student stumbles or even fails in post high school environments such as employment and post secondary education.

Parents may also be confused by the mixed messages provided to them during the time of transition planning. Educators often tell parents to "get involved" with the transition planning of their young adult. At the time of planning for transition, parents are also told to "let go" and allow the student to make his or her own choices. While both these messages are correct, these messages may confuse parents under considerable stress during the transition planning years of junior high school, high school, and beyond. Clearly, a steady, increasing exchange or hand-off of responsibilities from parents to the students in the area of life skills is necessary for the young adult to transition to the adult world. Parents/guardians are not always going to be there to complete a loan application, purchase groceries, and handle consumer disagreements. The pace of the "hand-off" of life skills responsibilities to the young adult with mild disabilities will be considered as the IEP team develop the IEP goals in this important transition planning area and will be significantly impacted based on life skills assessment information. Gajar, Goodman, & McAfee (1993) concluded that overprotection and inefficient or neglected curricula and methodology are responsible for many problems. Many of these problems can be avoided or alleviated with systematic assessment of life skills and the resulting direct instruction in the skills needed.

Social Skills

Social skills are fundamental to the acquisition of functional life skills and an integral component of the comprehensive model for transition assessment described in Chapter 1. Michaels (1994) identified four approaches for assessing social skills. These four approaches include:

1. behavior checklist—observer checks whether or not an individual can perform a task in a specific kind of situation;
2. behavioral observation codes—involves asking an individual to complete an interactive task;
3. sociometric assessment—involves the use of sociograms that identify students who are the most and least liked within their classes; and
4. behavioral rating scales—a list of behaviors or descriptive items that a respondent is asked to rate on a Likert-type scale of 1–5 regarding how well the person fits a given description or emits a particular behavior.

Elksnin and Elksnin (1998) discussed the importance of occupational social skills necessary for an individual to be successful in the workplace. Numerous assessments were employed to determine who would benefit from occupational social skills instruction and to identify social skills needed for specific vocational training in a specific occupational setting. The various approaches that the Elksnins used were rating scales, interviews, observations, role-play, and curriculum-based vocational assessment (CBVA)(see Chapter 7 for an in-depth discussion of CBVA).

Social Competence

Garjar, Goodman, and McAfee (1993) list social skills deficits associated with people with mild disabilities as: (a) making friends; (b) dissatisfaction with family relationship; (c) restricted range of social contacts; and (d) a variety of emotional and psychological problems. The purpose of assessing social skills for transition planning is to determine if the individual is socially competent, that is, does the individual effectively use social skills across environments (work, home, school, and community). Hazel, et al. (1985) describe social competence as the ability to:

- discriminate situations in which social behavior is appropriate;
- determine appropriate verbal and nonverbal behaviors;
- perform these skills smoothly, in appropriate combinations, according to social norms; and
- exhibit the flexibility to adjust to feedback.

For example, Gardner, Beatty, and Gardner (1984) found the following work-related social problems exhibited by individuals with mild disabilities often lead to dissatisfaction and job loss. These work-related social problems included:

- inability to get along with coworkers or boss;
- inability to accept responsibility for one's own life and career;
- tendency to blame others for one's own failures;
- lack of understanding of self-related work problems; and
- inappropriate work attitudes.

There are hidden rules regarding how people act, and these rules are difficult for many people both with and without disabilities to discern (Brown, 2000). These social skills need to be assessed and directly taught for students with mild disabilities and especially for students with emotional disabilities who qualify for special education services due to behaviors that interfere with not only their learning but also their social interactions. Numerous rating scales and assessment instruments that assess components of life skills acquisition including social competence are available. The following assessments will assist the students, educators, families, and other transition-related personnel in pinpointing specific life-skill deficits that require direct instruction at home, at school, and in the community.

Comprehensive Transition Assessments

The following instruments are examples of comprehensive transition assessment instruments. As such, each deserves special consideration in the transition assessment process, since each instrument gathers a broad array of information for transition planning. These instruments include the Enderle-Severson Transition Rating Scale, the Life Centered Career Education Assessments, and the Transition Planning Inventory.

Enderle-Severson Transition Rating Scale (ESTR)

One scale to use for assessing functional life skills for students with disabilities is the Enderle-Severson Transition Rating Scale (ESTR). This scale was first released in 1991, then updated in 1996 and again in 2003. A modified version, more appropriate to learners with mild disabilities (ESTR-J), was introduced in 1996. This version eliminated the lower-level items such as toileting, eating, and dressing—skills that students with mild disabilities usually demonstrate at the age of transition planning. In the 1996 edition, the items within each subscale were rearranged to reflect difficulty level.

The ESTR-J assesses five transition planning areas including employment, recreation and leisure, home living, community participation, and postsecondary education. Both home living and community participation encompass the life skills area. The 2003 version has fifteen probes in the home living area on topics such as: telephone use, household maintenance, sexual awareness, medical problems, meal planning, financial, and parenting skills. There are seven probes in the community participation area including: community resources, social behaviors in the community, understanding of cost-saving techniques, getting around in the community, planning for and securing housing, purchasing large items, and understanding and purchasing insurance coverage.

Each probe is scored based on a "yes" or "no" response. A "yes" (yes = 1) means the learner is performing the skill(s) independently and consistently. A "no" response (no = 0) means the learner is not performing the skill(s) or does not have the skill at the level of independence or consistence. The ESTR-J revised, Parent Form can be given to the parent for completion or it may be completed collaboratively with the special educator, guidance counselor, or social worker. If the parent form is sent home to the parent/guardian to complete, then information regarding how to complete the form must also be sent.

Enderle and Severson (2003) have included in their protocol a section entitled Future Outcomes/Goals Assessment. The purpose of this portion of the assessment is to determine the student's interests and preferences. For example, the home living future outcomes/goals page has the student fill in the blank, "I plan to move away from home when I'm ___ (age)." This component provides a basis for identifying the student's preferences and interests in relation to post school outcomes.

Young adults with mild disabilities may have "splinter skills" in the life skills area. A splinter skill is mastery by a student of some, but not all the skills in a skill sequence. For example, a student may know some aspects of a functional life skill such as how to subtract the checks from the ledger on the checkbook, but not be able to complete the entire skill such as reconcile the bank statement with the amount of money in the checkbook or even correctly and independently write a check. One of the purposes of life skills assessment is to document that students have all the skills necessary to successfully use the functional skill. It is easy for a teacher to assume that a skill is present in the student's behavioral repertoire simply because a student has a similar or more complex skill. A complete functional life skills assessment will identify the gaps in skills and provide the special educator and entire IEP team with the needed information for transition planning.

In Figure 6.2 you will find a completed Home Living section of the ESTR-J for Tenisha. Tenisha is a sixteen-year-old female student with a learning disability and attention deficit hyperactivity disorder (ADHD). The information found in Figure 6.2 represents the rating scales results as completed by Tenisha's teacher, with input from Tenisha's parents.

Based on the Enderle-Severson assessment, Tenisha is able to independently:

- perform written correspondence;
- treat minor medical problems;
- dress appropriately for specific situations;
- use the telephone; and
- perform household cleaning/laundry.

Results from the Enderle-Severson suggest Tenisha is currently unable to independently and consistently:

- use a checking and savings account;
- demonstrate the qualities of a good citizen;
- practice preventive health care;
- handle household emergencies;
- plan balanced meals;
- manage her money responsibly;
- demonstrate an understanding of parenting skills;

Enderle-Severson Transition Rating Scale (ESTR-J-Revised)

Results for Tenisha

Home Living

1. The learner demonstrates the ability to use the telephone	**[Yes]**	No
2. The learner dresses appropriately for specific situations • Weather conditions • Various activities	**[Yes]**	No
3. The learner performs household cleaning/laundry	**[Yes]**	No
4. The learner is able to safely perform light household maintenance • Uses basic appliances and tools • Performs basic home care tasks	**[Yes]**	No
5. The learner demonstrates the qualities of a good citizen • Obeys rules and laws • Shows consideration for others • Respects the environment • Knows how to vote • Knows about state and federal governments	Yes	**[No]**
6. The learner has an acceptable understanding of concepts related to • Sexual awareness • Awareness of physical self • Understands the reproductive process • Understands dating, relationships, marriage	Yes	**[No]**
7. The learner treats minor medical problems, performs basic first aid, and knows how and when to seek medical assistance	Yes	**[No]**
8. The learner understands checking and savings accounts • Could open a checking/savings account • Check writing, making deposits, and recording checking transactions • Making deposits and withdrawals and recording savings transactions • Understanding interest • Can use ATM	Yes	**[No]**
9. The learner has the skills necessary to perform written correspondence • Notes • Letters • Phone messages • E-mails	**[Yes]**	No
10. The learner practices preventive health care • Manages body weight • Gets sufficient sleep • Does not abuse alcohol/drugs • Makes and keeps routine medical/dental appointments	Yes	**[No]**
11. The learner knows how to respond to household emergency situations • Plumbing problems • Heating problems • Fire • Accidents • Poisoning	Yes	**[No]**
12. The learner understands nutrition and is able to plan balanced meals • Understands basic food groups • Plans meals within a budget	Yes	**[No]**

(continued)

13. The learner manages his/her own money responsibly • Knows how to develop a budget • Understands the importance of financial records • Pays bills on time • Understands taxes	Yes	No
14. The learner demonstrates an understanding of basic parenting skills	Yes	No
15. The learner is able to prepare and serve foods that require a variety of cooking procedures • Proper food storage • Personal hygiene • Kitchen safety procedures • Food preparation	Yes	No

From *Enderle-Severson Transition Rating Scale*. Published by ESTR Publications. Copyright © 2003. Reprinted with permission.

Figure 6.2

- understand concepts related to sexual awareness;
- perform light household maintenance; and
- prepare and serve food that requires a variety of cooking procedures.

Based on the Enderle-Severson assessment result, Tenisha is currently not independent and consistent in some aspects of the home living area. The IEP team could design transition services around Tenisha's needs by developing goals and objectives, designing a course of study that addresses her needs through general education classes, and/or identifying activities that parents or community services/agencies could address outside of the school setting.

Life Centered Career Education Assessment Instruments

The Life Centered Career Education (LCCE) assessment system consists of several components including the LCCE Knowledge Battery and the LCCE Performance Battery. The Knowledge Battery (Brolin, 1996) is designed to assess the career education knowledge of students with special education needs, especially those with both mild cognitive disabilities and severe learning disabilities in Grades 7–12 (Clark, 1996). The instrument is a criterion-referenced assessment and contains 200 multiple-choice questions with ten questions covering each of the first twenty competencies of the LCCE Mild Curriculum (Brolin & Lloyd, 2004). The LCCE Performance Battery is a nonstandardized, criterion-referenced instrument that accompanies the Knowledge Battery. It assesses critical life skills and includes five performance-based measures for each of twenty of the twenty-two LCCE competency areas. Figure 6.3 depicts the twenty-two LCCE competencies grouped into the three curriculum areas identified by Donn Brolin.

The LCCE Performance Battery includes a combination of role-playing scenarios, open-ended questions, and hands-on activities such as use of a telephone directory and filling out a credit application (Brolin & Lloyd 2004). The Life Centered Career Education Curriculum is a framework for presenting functional curriculum for transition in three categories: Daily Living Skills, Occupational Guidance and Preparation, and Personal-Social Skills. Academic skills are infused into each of these areas. Each competency is comprised of sub-competencies.

Life-Centered Career Education Competencies	
Daily Living Skills	
	1. Managing personal finances
	2. Selecting & managing a household
	3. Caring for personal needs
	4. Raising children & meeting marriage responsibilities
	5. Buying, preparing, & consuming food
	6. Buying & caring for clothing
	7. Exhibiting responsible citizenship
	8. Utilizing recreational facilities & engaging in leisure
	9. Getting around the community
Personal-Social Skills	
	10. Achieving self-awareness
	11. Acquiring self-confidence
	12. Achieving socially responsible behavior
	13. Maintaining good interpersonal skills
	14. Achieving independence
	15. Making adequate decisions
	16. Communicating with others
Occupational Guidance and Preparation	
	17. Knowing & exploring occupational possibilities
	18. Selecting & planning occupational choices
	19. Exhibiting appropriate work habits & behavior
	20. Seeking, securing & maintaining employment
	21. Exhibiting sufficient physical-manual skills
	22. Obtaining specific occupational skills

Figure 6.3

In the area of Daily Living Skills the sub-competencies are:

- Managing personal finances;
- Selecting and managing a household;
- Caring for personal needs;
- Raising children and meeting marriage responsibilities;
- Buying, preparing, and consuming food;
- Buying and caring for clothing;
- Exhibiting responsible citizenship;
- Utilizing recreational facilities and engaging in leisure; and
- Getting around in community.

The competencies and sub-competencies are well aligned for assessment and subsequent IEP/transition goal development. For example, the competency of Managing Personal Finances could lead to the following IEP/transition goals based on the subcompetencies and assessment results:

The student will be able to:

1. Count money and make correct change;
2. Make responsible expenditures;
3. Keep basic financial records;
4. Calculate and pay taxes;
5. Use credit responsibly;
6. Use banking services.

A Daily Living Skills, Competency Rating Scale is used to rate the student according to his or her mastery of each sub-competency using the rating key: 0 = not competent; 1 = partially competent; 2 = competent; NR = not rated. A check mark in the *yes* or *no* column is used to indicate the student's ability to perform the sub-competency with assistance from the community. LCCE has extensive materials that include Competency Assessment Knowledge Batteries, Competency Assessment Performance Batteries, IEP Planner for LCCE Transition Skills, LCCE Demonstration Video, Modified Curriculum for Individuals with Moderate Disabilities, and separate lesson plan books for Daily Living Skills, Personal-Social Skills, and Occupational Guidance and Preparation.

According to Donn Brolin (1997), career education provides the opportunity for children to learn, in the least restrictive environment possible, the academic, daily living, personal-social, and occupational knowledge and the specific vocational skills necessary for attaining their highest levels of economic, personal, and social fulfillment. As such, Brolin's LCCE assessment system is a comprehensive assessment system in the area of career/transition education.

Figure 6.4 represents a summary of the assessment results of the Daily Living Skills domain for our sixteen-year-old student, Tenisha. Based on this assessment testing, Tenisha is able to identify and make change and buy clothes and food independently. She also exhibits proper grooming and hygiene and dresses appropriately. She is partially competent in making responsible expenditures, using banking services, keeping financial records, using credit responsibly and calculating and paying taxes. She needs to become competent in using appliances and tools, selecting adequate housing, and setting up a household and maintaining home grounds. Other areas in which Tenisha needs knowledge include: physical fitness, nutrition and weight, and acquiring knowledge of common illness, prevention, and treatment, and practice of personal safety. She is only partially competent in washing, ironing, mending, and storing clothes. In the area of food preparation she needs additional

LCCE Daily Living Skills Domain Assessment Summary for Tenisha

Managing personal finances: Based on assessment results, Tenisha demonstrated she can Independently (scored 2 = competent) identify money and make correct change. Tenisha has knowledge, but is not independent (scored 1 = partially competent), at making responsible expenditures, keeping financial records, using credit responsibly, and using banking services. In the area of managing personal finances, Tenisha is not competent (score = 0) in calculating and paying taxes.

Managing home exterior/interior: Tenisha is not totally competent in this area of life skills as documented with the assessment results (scored 1 = partially competent) in each of the following skill areas: use of basic appliances and tools, selecting adequate housing, setting up household, and maintaining home grounds.

Caring for personal needs: The assessment results suggest that Tenisha is independent (scored 2 = competent) in grooming, hygiene, and dressing appropriately. However, she is not independent or fully competent (scored 1 = partially competent) in her knowledge of physical fitness, nutrition, and weight, knowledge of common illness, prevention and treatment, and practicing personal safety.

Buying and caring for clothes: While the test results showed that Tenisha is independent (scored 2 = competent) in buying clothes, she still needs additional competence (scored 1 = partially competent) in washing/cleaning clothes, ironing, mending, and storing clothes.

Buying and preparing and consuming food: Tenisha is independent in buying food (scored 2 = competent) but needs further skills in storing food, preparing meals, demonstrating appropriate eating habits, and planning and eating balanced meals (scored 1= partially competent).

Figure 6.4

skills in storing food, preparing meals, demonstrating appropriate eating habits, and planning and eating balanced meals.

Transition Planning Inventory (TPI)

The Transition Planning Inventory (TPI) (Clark & Patton, 1997) consists of forty-six transition planning statements, organized according to planning areas: employment, further education/training, daily living, leisure activities, community participation, health, self-determination, communication, and interpersonal relationships. The TPI is composed of four forms: a student form; a home form; a school form; and a profile and further assessment recommendation form. The student, the student's parent/guardian, and one or more school personnel participate in the assessment. Each individual participating in the assessment evaluates the student on the forty-six transition statements with the use of a Likert-type scale. Ratings are based on the level of agreement with the item as stated with 0 representing "strongly disagree" to 5 "strongly agree" with each statement. The rater may also rate an item as DK (don't know) or NA (not appropriate). This assessment is designed for students with disabilities age fourteen and older. The test will take from 15 to 30 minutes to administer for each participant (student, home, school). Each TPI item is evaluated for agreement that reflects the student's present level of performance in each of the nine transition planning areas as reviewed by each of the raters. The student form requests information about the student's preferences and interests in likely postschool settings (employment, further education/training, and living arrangements).

Profile and Further Assessment Recommendation Form

The TPI is a three level assessment tool. The responses from all three sources (school, home, and student forms) are transferred to the profile form. If an item received a rating that indicates disagreement with any of the forty-six transition competency statements, (rating of 0, 1, or 2) it should be examined in more depth. Based on need for additional assessment, the TPI provides a second level of assessment entitled *Informal Assessments for Transition Planning* (Clark, Patton, & Moulton, 2000). This assessment instrument provides from seven to twenty-nine additional in-depth transition statements for each of the forty-six general statements. The TPI also offers forty-seven additional informal assessment instruments (Level Three Assessment) based on the need for additional assessment information.

Life Skills Assessments

Brigance Assessment System: The Inventory of Essential Skills

The Inventory of Essential Skills assesses the academic and survival skills of secondary-level special education students or adult learners. The Inventory of Essential Skills, as well as all Brigance assessment tools, uses a color-coding system to develop an ongoing, graphic record for developing IEPs. The following academic skills are assessed: reading and language arts (word recognition, oral reading, reading comprehension, word analysis, writing, and spelling), math (numbers, number facts, computation of whole numbers, fractions, decimals, percents, measurement, metrics, math vocabulary), and study skills (reference skills, schedules, and graphics).

The life skills assessments include: food and clothing, money and finance, travel and transportation, and communication and telephone skills. Applied skills are measured with rating scales for: health and attitude, responsibility and self-discipline, job interview preparation, communication, and auto safety.

As in other Brigance System assessments there is a student record book which records competency levels and helps define instructional objectives. The student record book also provides a visual of student progress for teachers and parents.

Brigance Assessment System: The Employability Skills Inventory

The Employability Skills Inventory is a criterion-referenced tool that assesses basic skills and employability skills in the context of job-seeking or employment situations. It includes reading grade placement, rating scales, career awareness and self-understanding, reading skills, speaking and listening, job-seeking skills and knowledge, preemployment writing, and math skills and concepts.

Brigance Assessment System: The Life Skills Inventory

This is a companion assessment to the Employability Skills Inventory (1995). The inventory is appropriate to be used with students of high school age with all disabilities and students with mild cognitive disabilities reading at grades 2–8. It is criterion-referenced and composed of subscales including: speaking and listening, functional writing, words on common signs and warning labels, telephone skills, money and finance, food, clothing, health, and travel and transportation. It can be administered individually or in groups, and either in oral or written format. A Learner Record Book is color-coded and provides performance and instructional objectives generated from the results.

A quick-screen feature contains a sampling of items from each skill area and helps identify areas where more detailed assessment is needed. The feature also verifies the results of other assessments and determines the learner's level of functioning. Rating scales assist with evaluating subjective items such as aptitude or attitude. Assessment results are recorded in the Learner Record Book, which is used as an ongoing record of assessments, objectives, and progress, as well as a communication tool with learners, staff, and families.

Use of the Future Planning System (FPS) to Gather Life Skills Assessment Information

The interview method can best be exemplified in the Future Planning System (FPS) described in Chapter 3. The interviewer uses similar forms to illicit responses from parents/guardians and the student. With the interview format, additional probes can further clarify responses and lead to follow-up questioning. A copy of the FPS is included in Appendix A for your use.

Figure 6.5 is the home living section of the Future Planning System. It was completed using the results from interviewing Tenisha's parents.

Home Living Options: Parent Response

A. Where do you think your son or daughter will likely live after graduation?

____ Large urban What city? ____
_X_ Urban What city? Minneapolis
____ Rural What town?____
____ Farm

B. Please check one from the list.
____ Live independently in apartment or home
_X_ With family member (who?) Parents
____ With support
____ Supervised apartment (which one?) ____________________
____ Group home (which one?) ____________________
____ College dormitory (where?) ____________________
____ Other, please describe ____________________

V. Financial Support

A. Does your son or daughter need financial assistance in any of the following areas to reach his or her long-range goals?

1. Postsecondary education _X_ Yes ____ No

If yes, please check all of the following for which you would like information.
_X_ a. Rehabilitation Services
_X_ b. Pell Grants
_X_ c. Scholarships
_X_ d. Work study
_X_ e. Study loans
_____ f. Supplemental Security Income (SSI)
_____ g. Social Security Disability Insurance (SSDI), (i.e., PASS)

2. Employment Assistance _X_ Yes _____No

If yes, please check all of the following for which you would like information.
_X_ a. Rehabilitation Services
_X_ b. Local Job Training Agency and State Job Services
_X_ c. State Job Services—Targeted Job Tax Credits (TJTC)
_X_ d. Supplemental Security Income (SSI)
_____ e. County social services
_____ f. Rehabilitation Centers

3. Home Living Assistance _____ Yes _X_ No

If yes, please check all of the following for which you would like information.
_____ a. County social services
_____ b. Supplemental Security Income (SSI/medical assistance)
_____ c. Housing assistance—city government
_____ d. Independent living center services

VI. Health–related Needs

When was the last physical examination completed for your son or daughter?
Date: March 28, 20-

Does your son or daughter have any of the following needs?
_X_ medical _____ counseling
_____ other ____________________

Figure 6.5

Summary of Future Planning System for Tenisha

Through the interview process, Tenisha's parents have provided information about their desires for her future, her present situation, and what information is necessary for transition planning. What is known about Tenisha from this parent interview using the FPS includes:

- Tenisha lives in an urban area of Minneapolis with her parents.
- Her parents are seeking information specific to financial assistance for Tenisha's postsecondary education from Rehabilitation Services, Pell grants, scholarships, work study, and student loans.
- They are looking for assistance with employment from Rehabilitation Services, JTPA, and state job services.
- No assistance for housing is needed at this time.
- Tenisha has health related needs due to ADHD and had her last physical examination on March 28, 20–.

This assessment data would be incorporated into a comprehensive transition evaluation from which transition needs would be generated and transition planning would ensue.

Evaluation Report: Tenisha's Functional Life Skills

The evaluation report is a compilation of the battery of assessments that were conducted on Tenisha. This portion of the comprehensive transition evaluation has addressed only the

Present Levels of Performance: Functional Life Skills for Transition

Tenisha has great strength in the area of daily living. She is able to identify money and make change, and buy her own clothes and food independently. She exhibits proper grooming and hygiene, and dresses appropriately. She is partially competent in making expenditures, using banking services, keeping financial records, using credit responsibly, and calculating and paying taxes. She uses the phone, performs household cleaning and laundry, and treats minor medical problems. She is able to perform written correspondence.

Although she has these skills she is still lacking sufficient skills for a successful transition in the area of daily living. She needs to develop the following functional life skills:

Food preparation: preparing and serving food that requires a variety of cooking procedures, planning balanced meals, storing foods, preparing meals, demonstrating good eating habits.

Budgeting: using a checking and savings account.

Personal health care: physical fitness and nutrition and weight, practice preventive health care—last physical exam was March 28, 20–, understanding concepts related to sexual awareness, practicing personal safety.

Housekeeping: handling household emergencies, ironing, mending and storing clothes, performing light household maintenance, using appliances and tools, selecting adequate housing and setting up a household, maintaining home grounds.

Employment and training: seeking postsecondary financial assistance, seeking employment assistance, contacting Rehabilitation Services.

Personal development: demonstrating parenting skills, demonstrating the qualities of a good citizen.

IEP/Transition Planning

Home Living

Future Goal After graduation, I (Tenisha) plan to live with a roommate in an apartment in the city. (*Tenisha and her IEP team agree that her future goal is attainable; however, she will need additional specialized instruction in functional life skills during her senior year in order to transition to independent living in her community.*)

Transition Needs Tenisha needs to develop skills in food preparation, budgeting, personal health care, housekeeping, and personal development (*specifics are described in the present levels of performance*). She needs to know how to locate and lease an apartment.

Transition Services/Activities

1. Tenisha will visit an apartment leasing agency and conduct an informational interview to determine the steps for leasing an apartment.
2. Tenisha will contact the local Center for Independent Living (*an adult service provider*) to find out what resources/services are available to support her future goal.
3. Tenisha will register for family/life sciences as an elective course for one semester during her senior year. (*The course syllabus covers parenting and some areas of personal health care.*)

IEP Annual Goal

Tenisha will increase her home living skills from partial competence to competent. Instructional objectives/benchmarks include:

1. Tenisha will reconcile her checkbook two months in a row with minimal assistance and no errors as recorded by her special education teacher.
2. Tenisha will plan and prepare a balanced lunch without assistance as observed by her IEP manager by her next annual IEP meeting.
3. When given six common household appliances, Tenisha will name the appliance and demonstrate their use correctly four out of five times as measured by her classroom teacher by the next annual IEP meeting.
4. Tenisha will develop a six-month apartment budget with all required components as evaluated by her teacher by the next annual IEP meeting.
5. Given a list of five household emergencies, Tenisha will identify the steps to take to respond to the emergency in each of the five situations as measured by the special education teacher.
6. Tenisha will keep a weekly personal health journal that includes physical fitness activities, diet, weight, health care activities, and personal safety awareness reflections, and share new insights with peers during a weekly social group as measured by the school social worker.

functional life skills aspect of her transition needs. In this case study, the IEP team selected the following transition assessment tools/instruments to gather information about Tenisha's life skills:

- Transition Planning Inventory (TPI)
- Life Centered Career Education (LCCE) Knowledge Battery
- Enderle-Severson Transition Rating Scale—Form J—Revised (ESTR-J-Revised)
- Future Planning System (FPS)

This summary integrates the data gathered from all the assessment tools and summarizes strengths and needs which would serve as the basis for IEP/transition planning.

CHAPTER SUMMARY

Chapter 6 described functional life skills assessments and the role these assessments play in gathering data for transition planning in the IEP process. We found that

- Functional life skills are integral to conducting a comprehensive transition assessment for students with mild disabilities.
- Gathering life skills assessment data from multiple sources (students, parents, and school staff) ensures quality information for planning.
- Students with mild disabilities often have splinter skills (competent in some areas and lacking skills in other areas) in the area of functional life skills.
- Criterion-referenced life skills assessments assist the IEP team in transition planning and IEP development.
- Social skills are fundamental to the acquisition of functional life skills.

CHAPTER ACTIVITIES

Please review the assessment data for Juan Rodrigiez found in Appendix B, part 5 (B-5). These data were gathered with use of the Transition Planning Inventory (Clark & Patton, 1997). Based on this assessment information answer the following questions:

1. What are two transition goals and corresponding objectives that you would recommend to the IEP team for Juan for his junior year?
2. You will note that there is a discrepancy between the parent/guardian and student rating in the assessment results. How would you address this discrepancy?
3. What are three transition-planning activities that Juan, his parents, or his special education teacher could do to assist Juan to develop money skills? How would you build on Juan's areas of strength?
4. How could Juan work on his money skills within the general education curriculum?
5. How could Juan's transition plan for his junior and senior years include community-based instruction?

DISCUSSION QUESTIONS

Discuss an array of options for teaching functional life skills within the context of the general education curricula.

CHAPTER REFERENCES

Brigance, A.H. (1981) *Inventory of Essential Skills*. North Billerica, MA: Curriculum Associates.

Brigance, A. H. (1995). *The Employability Skills Inventory.* North Billerica, MA: Curriculum Associates.

Brigance, A.H. (1995). *The Life Skills Inventory.* North Billerica, MA: Curriculum Associates.

Brolin, D. E (1997). *Life centered career education: A competency based approach.* Reston, VA: Council for Exceptional Children.

Brolin, D.E. (1992). *Competency assessment knowledge batteries: Life centered career education*. Reston, VA: Council for Exceptional Children.

Brolin, D.E. (1996). *Life centered career education. Professional development activity book: Using LCCE assessments*. Reston, VA: Council for Exceptional Children.

Brolin, D. E., & Lloyd, R. J. (2004). *Career development and transition services: A functional life skills approach, (4th ed.).* Upper Saddle River, NJ: Pearson, Merrill, and Prentice Hall.

Brown, D. S. (2000). Learning a living: A guide to planning your career and finding a job for people with learning disabilities, attention deficit disorder, and dyslexia. Bethesda, MD: Woodbine House.

Clark, G. M. (1996). Transition planning assessment for secondary-level students with learning disabilities. *Journal of Learning Disabilities, 29* (1), 79–92.

Clark, G. M. & Patton, J. (1997). *Transition planning inventory: Administration and resource guide.* Austin, TX: PRO-ED.

Clark, G. M., Patton, J. R., & Moulton, R. (2000). *Informal assessments in transition planning.* Austin, TX: PRO-ED.

Cronin, M. (1996). Life skills curricula for students with learning disabilities: A review of the literature. In Patton, J. & Blalock, G. (Eds)., *Transition and students with learning disabilities: Facilitating the movement from school to adult life.* (pp. 85–112) Austin, Texas: PRO-ED.

Cronin, M. E., & Patton, J. R. (1993). *Life skills instruction for all students with special needs: A practical guide for integrating real-life content into the curriculum.* Austin, Texas: PRO-ED.

Enderle, J., & Severson, S., (2003). *Enderle-Severson transition rating scale form J—revised.* Moorhead, MN: ESTR Publications.

Elksnin, N., & Elksnin, L. (1998). *Teaching occupational social skills.* Austin, TX: PRO-ED.

Gajar, A., Goodman, L., & McAfee. (Eds.). (1993). *Secondary schools and beyond: Transition of individuals with mild disabilities.* Upper Saddle River, NJ: Merrill/Prentice Hall.

Gardner, D. C., Beatty, G. J., & Gardner, P. L. (1984). *Career and vocational education for mild handicapped and disadvantaged youth.* Springfield, IL: Thomas.

Haring, K. A., Lovett, D.L., & Smith, D.D., (1990). A follow-up of recent special education graduates of learning disabilities programs. *Journal of Learning Disabilities, 23 (2),* 108–113.

Hazel, J.S., Sherman, J.A., Schumaker, J.B., & Sheldon, J. (1985). Group social skills training with adolescents: A critical review. In D. Upper and S. Ross (Eds.), *Handbook of behavioral group therapy* (pp. 203–246). New York: Plenum Publishing.

Knowles, M. (1990). *The adult learner: The neglected species.* Houston, TX: Gulf Publishing.

Michaels, C. A. (Ed.). (1994). *Transition strategies for persons with learning disabilities.* San Diego, CA: Singular Publishing Group, Inc.

Miller, R. J. & Corbey, S. A. (1993). Future Planning Inventories. In S. Corbey, R. Miller, S. Severson, and J. Enderle (Eds.), *Teaching the Possibilities: Identifying Individual Transition Needs* (pp. 17–31). St. Paul, MN: Minnesota Educational Services.

Minnesota Department of Education. (1990). *Home living: Resource guide for transition planning.* St. Paul, MN: Minnesota Department of Education.

Patton, J.R. & Blalock, G., (Eds.). (1996). *Transition and students with learning disabilities: Facilitating the movement from school to adult life.* Austin, TX: PRO-ED.

West, M.D., Gibson, K., Unger, D., & Kane, K. (1996). Independent living. In P. Wehman, (Ed.), *Life beyond the classroom: Transition strategies for young people with disabilities* (pp. 231–246). York, PA: Paul Brookes.

Zetlin, A. G., Turner, J., & Wenik, L., (1987). *Socialization effects on the community adaptation of adults who have mild mental retardation* (pp. 293–313). Washington, DC: American Association on Mental Retardation.

CHAPTER

Vocational Assessment

Federal legislation clearly links vocational assessment to formal transition planning efforts. Comprehensive transition planning cannot occur without the collection and utilization of vocational assessment information. Vocational assessment information is a key component of the five types of assessment information required in the Transition Assessment Model suggested in this text (see Figure 7.1). Vocational assessment data are relatively meaningless unless they contribute to and result in formal transitional planning. Placing students with disabilities into vocational programs and courses that prepare them for future training and/or employment is a fundamental function of vocational assessment procedures (McMahan & Baer, 2001). Vocational assessment has been defined by Sarkees and Scott (1995) as "a comprehensive process conducted over a period of time, involving a multidisciplinary team. . . with the purpose of identifying individual characteristics, education, and training needs which provide educators with the basis for planning an individual's career pathway" (p. 211). Vocational assessment procedures can have maximum impact only if a full range of academic and/or vocational planning options are made available as a result of assessment activities (Harvey, 2002). Ongoing documentation of vocational assessment information can be conducted by completing a Vocational Assessment Profile (VAP) for each student with special needs (Sitlington, et al., 1996).

Vocational Assessment Assumptions

According to Lombard (1991), development of a vocational assessment profile must be based on seven basic assumptions:

1. Vocational assessment will have maximum benefit if it occurs within the context of a comprehensive K–12 career development curriculum.
2. Vocational assessment is an integral component of transition assessment and educational programming.
3. Responsibility for vocational assessment and use of results must be shared across and throughout educational programs.
4. Vocational assessment is not an isolated event; rather it is an integral component of the ongoing collection of assessment data.
5. The validity of vocational assessment procedures can be judged according to transition planning and postsecondary placement outcomes.
6. Vocational assessment should focus on student strengths, interests, preferences, and future goals.
7. The vast majority of vocational assessment data are obtained through formal and informal procedures that represent the best educational practices for all students.

Vocational assessment procedures that will accommodate these assumptions must differ in scope and purpose from the evaluation model common to the field of vocational rehabilitation. In most cases, rehabilitation evaluations are conducted to assist adults with disabilities in determining the appropriate match between their pool of interests, experiences,

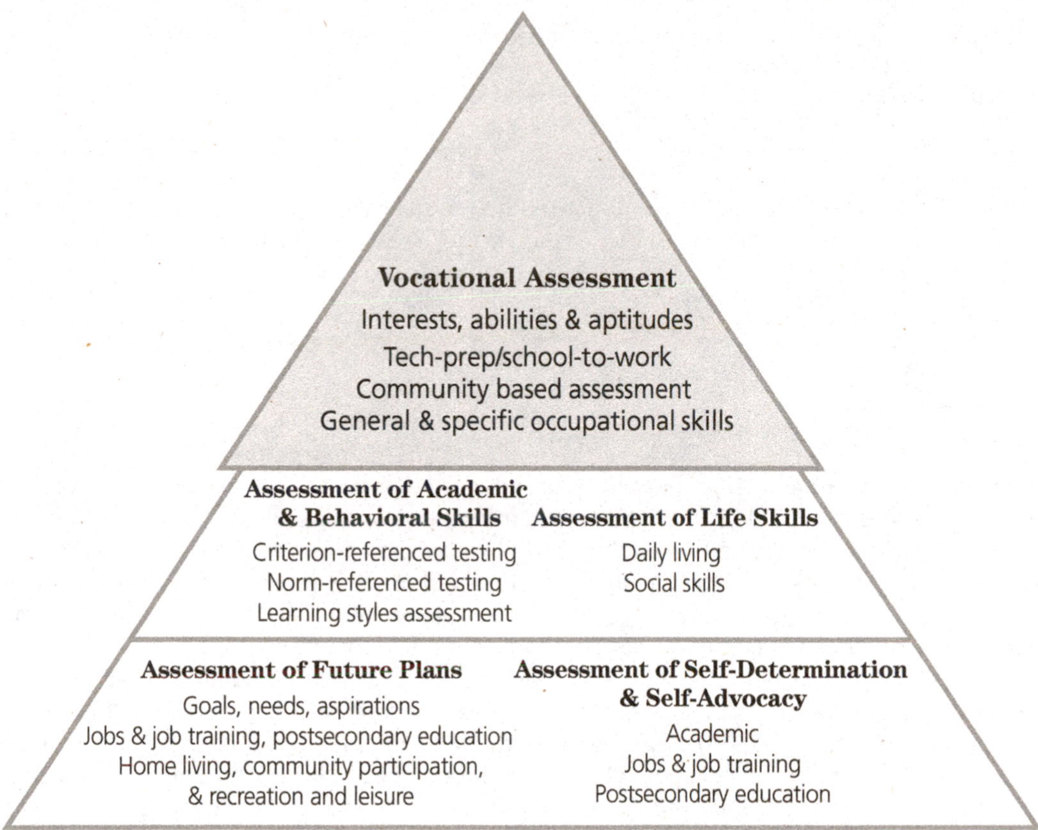

Figure 7.1

and aptitudes with potential training or employment opportunities. Data collection procedures including work samples, simulated job tryouts, and an array of psychometric instruments are typically administered to adult clients receiving rehabilitation services often as a result of traumatic injury or a developmental delay. Although the evaluation procedures common to vocational rehabilitation continue to provide an invaluable service to adult clients in need of training, retraining, and/or employment counseling, the rehabilitation model is not always useful in public school settings for the following reasons:

1. Many psychometric instruments used by rehabilitation personnel to evaluate occupational interest and vocational aptitude may not be standardized on school-age persons.
2. Many instruments commonly used by rehabilitation professionals have not been standardized on persons with disabilities.
3. The time constraints of the rehabilitation evaluation model (a limited number of days) do not accommodate the programming demands of high school vocational courses that are usually one or two semesters long. Consequently, the rehabilitation model is unable to generate assessment data that are related to the curricular and/or instructional features of a particular middle school or high school vocational program.

Given the limitations of the rehabilitation evaluation model, an integrated approach to vocational assessment is necessary in order to accommodate the various transition needs of students with disabilities. Collaborative career development planning is designed to provide a structure within which meaningful vocational assessment activities can be implemented.

Seven-Step Vocational Assessment Model

Step 1: Identify information that must be examined before the student enters a vocational education program.
Step 2: Develop collection and exchange procedures for Entry Phase data.
Step 3: Use Entry Phase data for program planning.
Step 4: Identify information that must be examined to monitor student performance in vocational education.
Step 5: Develop collection and exchange procedures for Monitor Phase data.
Step 6: Identify information that must be reviewed to plan the student's transition from school to postschool settings.
Step 7: Conduct an exit school-to-postschool transition meeting.

Figure 7.2

When vocational assessment information is integrated with the assessment information gathered over the longitudinal transition evaluation process, the ability of the student to weigh personal strengths and limitations and make sound career decisions is dramatically enhanced. The seven-step assessment model that will now be presented incorporates the critical elements of comprehensive vocational assessment including curriculum-based vocational assessment (CBVA) and formal psychometric assessments. In addition, this process takes into account the need for IEP development that is based on student abilities, preferences, and needs. (Figure 7.2 depicts the Seven-Step Vocational Assessment Model.)

Albright and Cobb (1988) have designed the curriculum-based vocational assessment model that is central to this chapter. Curriculum-based vocational assessment is an ongoing attempt to match the student, the curriculum, and the training environment and to collect continuous data to assess both current and subsequent vocational placements or training sites. This vocational assessment model is much more than just testing. CBVA should be viewed as a continuous process of gathering information regarding a student's interests, aptitudes, and capacities (Albright & Cobb, 1988). The Albright and Cobb CBVA approach is based on three phases of assessment. The first phase pertains to information that must be collected prior to a student entering a vocational course of study. This stage is known as the **Entry Phase** and it focuses upon the types of information that must be collected and examined in order to place a student into a vocational course of study for which they have both interest and aptitude. The second stage, known as the **Monitor Phase**, focuses on the types of information that must be collected and examined during the time a student is enrolled in a vocational course of study. The third stage, known as the **Transition Phase**, focuses on the types of information that must be collected and examined during the time a student is planning to make the transition from secondary school to postsecondary settings. The initial three steps of the seven-step assessment model each pertain to the Entry Phase of the Albright and Cobb CBVA approach.

Step One: Identifying Essential Information That Must Be Collected Prior to Vocational Program Entry

A primary goal of the entry phase of CBVA is to identify both student-centered information as well as information pertaining to the vocational curriculum. The intent is to collect as much pertinent data as needed to ensure that students with disabilities are (a) placed in the most appropriate vocational program; (b) given an opportunity to acquire entry-level vocational skills prior to entry, and (c) provided with adequate instructional support once placement has taken place.

To accomplish this goal, the assessment team must identify a list of student-centered skills that can be documented on a Vocational Assessment Profile (VAP). (See Appendix A, part 8 [A-8] for a copy of the Vocational Assessment Profile.) Information on the VAP represents these four categorical domains:

1. Student identification information including demographic, medical, and behavior data.
2. Family information.
3. Summary of student skills information including academic, life skills, work skills.
4. Recommendations including future work and/or education predictions.

In addition to the student-centered data specified above, important aspects of the vocational curriculum must also be identified. Curricular features to be reviewed during the Entry Phase of CBVA include the following:

- entry-level skills required to be successful in the vocational course or program (e.g. academic, behavior/safety, manipulative/physical).
- evaluation options (e.g. oral exams, written exams, class projects).
- grading criteria (e.g. quizzes, exams, projects, attitude, attendance, cooperative learning, progress toward exit-level skills, effort).
- Instructional support available to the student to maximize the student's likelihood of success in the course or program (e.g. support in general education classrooms, vocational classrooms, resource rooms, and community work settings).

In addition to the vocational curriculum, CBVA is a process that can be used to gather data about community-based vocational programming. Community-based vocational programming options such as work experience, job try outs, and apprenticeships are often used to provide opportunities for students to apply the vocational competencies acquired in the classroom to authentic employment settings. Once again, placement of students in community work settings should be done after a careful assessment of the students' interests and abilities has taken place.

An assessment of the student's occupational interests can be achieved in a number of ways. One of the most common methods is to administer an occupational interest inventory that determines interest levels in multiple career clusters. Student interests can also be determined through student interviews, parent interviews, situational job tryouts, and observation of student performance in a variety of community settings.

In order to place a student in appropriate community work settings, an examination of his or her occupational interests is vital. It is also necessary to assess the student's vocational aptitude as it pertains to various career clusters and related community work options. Vocational aptitude can be assessed using commercial vocational aptitude batteries or inventories. Additional approaches may be used to determine vocational aptitude, including work sample assessment, situational job tryouts, student self-reports, and work-site observations. During this phase of assessment, questions to be answered through the use of formal or informal interest and aptitude assessment include:

- In which career cluster and vocational program is the student most interested?
- Which community job experience option is most consistent with the student's interests and aptitude?
- What accommodations or special supports are needed to ensure the student can successfully participate in community-based job sites?

The following activities can be conducted by school personnel to clarify the types of information that should be collected before placing students in school and community vocational programs:

- Develop a list of psychometric student data (e.g. interests, abilities, learning styles) that will be needed.
- Develop a list of student behavioral data that will be needed (e.g. safety skills).
- Develop a list of student medical/physical data that will be needed (e.g. strength, any physical limitations that should be noted prior to placement in the vocational course or at the community-based work experience).
- Develop a list of general education curriculum data that will be needed (e.g. entry-level skills in math, reading, oral communication, writing, etc.).
- Develop a list of general education instructional data that will be needed (e.g. testing options).

After assessment personnel have generated a list of student, curriculum, and community-based information to be collected during the Entry Phase of CBVA, the team can determine how to collect and exchange the information.

Step Two: Develop Data Collection and Exchange Procedures for the Entry Phase

In order for data collection to proceed in an efficient manner, it may be helpful to identify the range of student information that is already available. Data related to achievement scores, academic history, medical and behavioral issues, etc. are usually documented in a student's cumulative folder and can be accessed without conducting further assessment. Other student data can be documented on the VAP as soon as formal and/or informal assessment practices have been completed.

Psychometric Assessment

Formal or psychometric assessment is an important aspect of data collection activities during this phase of the model. Psychometric assessment refers to the administration of standardized instruments such as occupational interest surveys, vocational aptitude batteries, and learning style inventories. While the majority of psychometric instruments are only valid when used with an adult population, there are a limited number of existing or relatively new instruments that were normed with individuals of school age.

Examining student preferred learning styles is another type of psychometric assessment that should occur at this phase. Again, there is a growing list of formal learning style instruments available on the commercial market due in large part to the increase in national interest in this topic. One of the most popular public domain instruments is known as the C.I.T.E. Learning Style Instrument which is discussed in Chapter 5. This inventory is designed to identify a variety of learning preferences related to information processing. Types of learning preferences include information input (receiving), information integration (synthesis), and information output (expressive). A copy of the C.I.T.E. can be reviewed in Appendix A, part 4 (A-4). A relatively new learning style instrument, published by Piney Mountain Press, is the Learning and Working Learning Styles Inventory (see Appendix B, part 7 [B-7], form 3). It measures the same information processing domains as the C.I.T.E. plus two additional domains—climate and work characteristics. While information-processing data can be useful with respect to educational planning, program placement, and the provision of instructional support within general education classes, climate and work characteristics preferences can be of additional help in planning transition services from school to the world of work. Like aptitude and interest assessment, collecting learning-style data should occur prior to vocational program placement and in concert with educational planning procedures. (See Appendix E for a list of Transition Assessment Instruments that may be used to gather transition assessment information across the five areas that are included in the Transition Assessment Model.)

In addition to gathering pertinent data from existing files and conducting formal psychometric assessment procedures to identify occupational interest, vocational aptitude, and learning style characteristics, the IEP team should determine individual student goals and parental expectations. These issues can readily be addressed by conducting informal interviews with individual students and their parents.

Student Interview Student interviews are an important link in the data collection process. It is often most productive to interview the student in an uninterrupted one-on-one situation. Establishing rapport with each student in the early stages of the interview will increase the likelihood that information obtained by the interviewer is a fair representation of the student's beliefs, interests, attitude, and goals. To ensure accurate recording of data, it is suggested that student responses be documented on a predesigned questionnaire or recorded on a tape recorder. In either case, the student should be made aware of the recording procedure being used.

Although the student interview is intended to be a free flowing exchange of information, there are eight specific issues that need to be addressed in this forum. They include:

- Student attitude toward disability or special needs
- Self-perception of abilities/strengths
- Occupational interests/activities
- Career awareness/experience
- Work and classroom preferences
- Educational interests/goals
- Functional skill abilities/needs
- Family/parental concerns

(Please see Appendix A, part 6 [A-6] for a sample student interview format.)

Parent Interview There is often a discrepancy between individual student goals and the expectations of his or her parents. This discrepancy can be a source of confusion, resentment, and mistrust within the family. To help understand and resolve this conflict, it is essential to communicate with the parent(s) as part of the vocational assessment process. Parent feedback will also assist the team develop realistic educational and transitional plans for individual students. Their input at the middle school level, combined with other available data, will also help the team to develop a four-year educational plan. The four-year plan is basically a suggested sequence of coursework which will enable the student to acquire prerequisite skills for postschool training and/or employment. Parental feedback at the high school level will enable the team to make appropriate recommendations regarding postschool training/employment options, independent living arrangements, support from adult agencies, financial support, etc.

Vocational Curriculum Data After the Vocational Assessment Profile has been completed (see Appendix A, part 8 [A-8]), it will be necessary to obtain information related to the vocational program or courses offered within the district. Due to the competency-based orientation of vocational programs, it is critical that vocational educators participate in this process. Again, collaboration between special educators and vocational educators is the most effective mechanism for collecting this data.

Community Work Experience Data Because community work experience is often a vital component of a student's total vocational program, information regarding community work options must also be obtained. Employment surveys or employer interviews may be conducted to determine essential job readiness skills, job-shadowing options, needed supported-employment services, etc.

Vocational Program Inventory One collaborative strategy is to conduct a vocational program inventory (see Appendix A, part 7 [A-7] for a vocational program inventory). This procedure allows the assessment team to identify a variety of concerns related to the vocational program. Instructional approaches used by the instructor of a class and needed by the student can be determined and may include:

- Information sources (textbooks, lectures, discussion)
- Classroom/lab structure (small group, independent, large group)
- Test format
- Assignments
- Academic skills needed
- Behavioral skills needed
- Attendance policy
- Entry-level skills

Yet another collaboration assessment procedure is to identify the continuum of entry-level skills related to specific vocational courses and/or community based vocational work settings. Identifying entry-level skills prior to vocational program entry or community work experience participation will enable the IEP team to evaluate student readiness for each program. By comparing entry-level skills against the Vocational Assessment Profile, the IEP team can determine the most critical skills not yet in command of the student. As a result, instructional content can be prioritized to ensure that students have every opportunity to acquire entry-level skills before being placed in a vocational program or participating in a community work setting. This procedure will also help prescribe the type and intensity of instructional and/or workplace accommodations each student may need to successfully participate in the school- or community-based vocational program.

Exit-Level Skills While the determination of entry-level skills will assist in making appropriate placement decisions, identification of exit-level criteria will prove to be invaluable once the student has been enrolled. Knowledge of exit-level criteria will enable the IEP team to monitor student progress during program placement.

The following activities are designed to help school personnel to determine various formal and informal procedures to use to collect and exchange vocational assessment information:

1. Identify formal assessment instruments that will generate essential student information (e.g. Occupational Aptitude Survey and Interest Schedule (OASIS – III), Career Decision Making System, Interest Determination, Exploration and Assessment System (IDEAS).
2. Identify informal assessment approaches that will generate essential student information (e.g. observations, student interview).
3. Develop informal strategies to obtain the general education curriculum data (e.g. teacher interview).
4. Develop informal strategies to obtain the general education instructional data (e.g. teacher observation).
5. Develop informal approaches to obtain information about community-based work options (e.g. employer interview).
6. Develop procedures to ensure the assessment information is shared with each assessment stakeholders (e.g. student, parent, teachers).

Step Three: Utilize Assessment Information to Plan the Student's Vocational Education Program

Unfortunately, when vocational assessment information is collected, it often is under-used. Like academic/achievement testing, vocational assessment data can provide a firmer rationale for instructional planning, program placement, and overall curricular development. Once collected, student, parent, and vocational curriculum information can be valuable in a number of ways. This data can provide a basis for the following activities:

- Identification of career/vocational goals for IEP
- Determination of student aptitude for school and community program options
- Determination of student interest in school and community program options
- Prioritization of instruction prior to program entry
- Placement of students into appropriate school and community programs
- Development of instructional and workplace accommodations

The following activities can be used by school personnel to plan the student's vocational education program:

1. Use assessment information to reflect the following IEP elements: statement of needed transition services, present level of performance statement, future goal statement, instructional objectives, and statement of interagency linkage.
2. Use assessment information for program placement outcomes such as the following: placing students in programs that are consistent with interests and abilities, providing community work experiences that are consistent with interests and abilities, and involving students in apprenticeship opportunities that are related to high school coursework.
3. Use assessment information to ensure that appropriate curricular accommodations are made within the general education setting.
4. Use assessment information to ensure that appropriate instructional accommodations are made within the general education setting.

Step Four: Identify Essential Information That Must Be Collected to Monitor Each Student's Progress in the Vocational/ Community-Based Education Program

Once the placement decision has been made and the student is enrolled in a particular vocational course of study, the Monitor Phase of CBVA should be initiated (Albright & Cobb, 1988). The primary goal of this phase is to monitor student performance within the vocational education classroom and/or community setting. By monitoring student performance in each vocational setting, potential problems are often identified before a failure situation has arisen. Consequently, if problems do surface, the student, vocational educator, employer, and special needs staff can work cooperatively to modify instructional and workplace accommodations and/or program requirements. If, however, it is determined that the student cannot successfully complete the program in question in spite of school and/or workplace accommodations, alternative program options must be cooperatively explored by the IEP team.

Student information that must be collected during this phase falls into three categories: (1) behavioral, (2) academic, and (3) progress toward exit-level criteria. As a result of prior assessment activities, each program or course of study should have a list of exit-level criteria. To identify essential data for monitoring, the assessment team simply examines curriculum data and uses this as a guide or reference. If, for example, working in groups was determined to be an entry-level academic skill, as documented by a vocational program inventory, this skill would then be evaluated throughout program participation. The sample procedure holds true for behavior skills and skills needed to meet exit-level criteria.

Monitoring student performance in community work sites should also be conducted during this phase of the assessment model. As the student participates on the community-based job site, assessment should focus on the information gathered during the course of the student's employment. During this phase of the assessment process, questions to be answered may include the following:

- How is the student performing on the job site?
- What modifications or accommodations can be made to make this experience more successful?
- What changes or modifications in work behavior can the student make to increase the likelihood that the community-based experience will be more successful?

The following activities can be used by school personnel to determine the information that must be collected while a student is participating in school and/or community programs:

1. Identify student behaviors that must be monitored (e.g. safety).
2. Identify student academic progress areas that must be monitored (e.g. reading, math, etc.).
3. Identify exit-level criteria in general education classes that must be monitored (e.g. project completion).
4. Determine the curricular accommodations that must be monitored (e.g. textbooks on tape).
5. Determine the instructional accommodations that must be monitored (e.g. classroom simulations).
6. Determine community work related skills that must be monitored (e.g. customer relations).
7. Determine community workplace accommodations that must be monitored (e.g. job coach).

Step Five: Develop Data Collection and Data Exchange Procedures for Information That Is Monitored in School and Community Settings

After performance checklists have been developed for academic, behavioral, and exit-level skill categories, data collection and exchange procedures must be identified. Although the variety of recording documents and formats is virtually limitless, a number of questions must be resolved to facilitate efficient and strategic use of data collection and exchange procedures. They include the following:

- How frequently will performance data be collected?
- Who will be responsible for evaluating student performance?
- Who will receive the data after it is collected?

- Who will be responsible for modifying instructional and workplace accommodations if required?
- Who will be responsible for making alternative program recommendations if required?

After the IEP team has made these procedural decisions, data collection and exchange strategies can be implemented. Monitor Phase data collection formats include the following:

- competency-based checklists;
- task performance checklists;
- student progress charts;
- behavioral rating scales; and,
- academic achievement scales.

The following activities can be used by school personnel to help create methods to monitor student performance in school and in community settings:

1. Develop data collection procedures for monitoring student behavior in general education.
2. Develop data collection procedures for monitoring academic performance in general education.
3. Develop data collection procedures for monitoring student progress toward exit-level course criteria.
4. Develop data collection procedures to monitor the success of curricular accommodations in general education classes.
5. Develop data collection procedures to monitor the success of instructional accommodations in general education classes.
6. Develop data collection procedures to monitor work related skills in the community.
7. Develop data collection procedures to monitor the success of workplace accommodations in the community.

Step Six: Identify Essential Information That Must Be Reviewed Prior to the Student's Transition into Future Training or Employment Settings

Just prior to a student's completion of a secondary vocational education program, it will be necessary to begin preparations for the final exit transition meeting that will take place three or four months before high school departure. The primary goal of this specific CBVA phase is to conduct an exit transition meeting to review information related to the student's school to postschool transition. Some of the issues to be reviewed at this exit transition meeting include:

- student mastery of exit-level criteria in current programs;
- postsecondary training options;
- postsecondary employment options;
- availability of adult support services;
- current occupational interests of student;
- current vocational aptitude of student;
- adult living and community mobility options;
- final clarification of transition roles/responsibilities for student, parents, adult service providers, employer, teachers, and other stakeholders.

The following activities can be used by school personnel to help a student prepare for his or her transition into future training or employment settings:

1. Review the most recent IEP to determine if the postsecondary transition goals are still relevant.
2. Review a list of postsecondary education options.
3. Review a list of postsecondary employment options.
4. Review a list of adult support services that offer assistance to individuals with disabilities.
5. Determine the range of independent living options in the community.
6. Determine the range of transportation options that exist in the community.

Step Seven: Conduct a School-Exit-to-Postschool Transition Meeting

At least four months prior to high school departure, a formal exit transition meeting should be convened. This meeting represents the culminating process for all previous vocational assessment activity and should be a review of student interests and abilities. The exit transition meeting should include: (a) public school personnel, (b) adult service representatives, (c) postsecondary training/employer representatives, (d) student, and (e) parents. The primary goal of this meeting is to *review* and make final decisions regarding the roles and responsibilities of key stakeholders in the student's school-to-adult-life transition process. The IDEA legislation of 2004 requires that post-high school adult service needs and responsibilities are to be identified prior to high school departure. To do so, the IEP/transition team must review all pertinent data and determine if all existing transition information is still current and relevant.

A transition exit form such as the one in Appendix A, part 5 (A-5), will provide a format for determining school-to-adult-life concerns and potential problem areas as well as identify adult agencies that will continue to work with the student after graduation from high school. A completed copy of this document can be found in Appendix B, part 6 (B-6). In that example, a high school student named Heidi Camper is planning to attend a technical college following high school departure. As this student makes the transition to the technical college and to the complexities of adult life, a variety of issues must be planned for. Issues such as financial need, insurance, community mobility, living arrangements, and medical concerns have been identified, and the specific responsibilities of the student, parent, school, and adult support agencies have been outlined with regard to Heidi's transition to postsecondary settings.

In order to determine the extent to which Heidi has made a successful transition to adulthood, implementation of postschool follow-up procedures should be conducted. Public school personnel such as guidance counselors or special education staff may coordinate postschool follow-up procedures (see Appendix C, part 5 [C-5] for an example of the Burnsville-Eagan-Savage Independent School District Post High School Follow-Up Survey). The use of a postschool follow-up on a one-year and three-year basis is strongly recommended to provide school staff with meaningful, quantifiable, and concrete information regarding the effectiveness of transition services in preparing students for life after high school. Without this information, it would be difficult for schools to gauge their success in preparing students with disabilities for life after high school or to address appropriate curricular changes as warranted.

If, however, the district does not have a routine procedure to determine the postschool outcomes of former students with disabilities, specific responsibilities for follow-up must be delineated on the formal transition plan. Moreover, all roles and responsibilities for responding to problem areas, should they surface as a result of follow-up, could also be prescribed on the Statement of Interagency Responsibilities and Linkages Transition document.

The following activities can be used by school personnel to help clarify stakeholder responsibilities for student, parents, school personnel, adult service providers, employers, etc.:

1. Develop an exit transition form to document the roles and responsibilities of the student, family members, support services personnel, and other participants of the school-to-postschool transition process.
2. Develop a list of key stakeholders who should participate in the school-to-postschool exit transition planning process.
3. Develop a timeline for holding the final school-to-postschool exit transition meeting.
4. Develop a follow-up survey to be completed by former students at least one year after high school departure.

CHAPTER SUMMARY

Vocational assessment is a critical component of a comprehensive transition evaluation. Vocational assessment is a longitudinal process that must be addressed by the IEP team on an ongoing basis. A variety of vocational assessment approaches have been described in this chapter. Due to the multiple uses of vocational assessment data, it is clear that the IEP team can rely on no single vocational assessment approach to address all the important school to postschool transition issues. Information gathered as a result of psychometric assessment, curriculum-based vocational assessment, student and parent interviews, and existing cumulative data can all contribute to vocational assessment and the transition planning process. Comprehensive vocational assessment information can be used for the following:

- Promotion of appropriate program placement;
- Development of instructional and curricular accommodations;
- Development of workplace accommodations;
- Monitoring of student performance in both vocational and community settings;
- IEP development for students of transition age.

It is recommended that school personnel conduct an annual review of vocational assessment practices. An example of one school's model to gather transition assessment information over time can be found in Appendix C, part 1 (C-1). In this example, the school district has developed a plan to systematically gather assessment information in grades 8, 9, 10, 11, and 12. Through this systematic and ongoing process, the IEP team will be provided with the types and depth of information to make transition planning meaningful. An in-depth analysis of postschool follow-up reports will enable school personnel to identify the extent to which comprehensive vocational assessment activities have impacted the postschool outcomes of former students (Harvey, 2002).

DISCUSSION QUESTIONS

What are the responsibilities of special education teachers to collaborate with vocational education professionals regarding the placement and support of students with disabilities?

CHAPTER ACTIVITIES

Activity One: Statements of Interagency Responsibilities and Linkages for Transition for Heidi Camper

Please review the Transition Exit Form for Heidi Camper found in Appendix B, part 6 and answer the following questions.

1. Who were the IEP team participants who attended the June 10, 2005 IEP transition exit meeting?
2. What were the eight recommendations for placement, services, or other options made by the IEP team at the time of the completion of this transition exit form?

3. What were the five responsibilities assigned to the parents and student (Heidi Camper) at this IEP meeting?
4. What were the three responsibilities assigned to high school personnel prior to graduation as a part of this exit process?
5. What were the identified responsibilities of adult service providers as outlined in the transition exit form?
6. Why is the identification of specific responsibilities of all members of the IEP team, including adult service providers, critical to the successful transition of Heidi Camper from high school to post high school life?
7. Why is it critical that a formal transition exit meeting be held at least four months prior to graduation?

Activity Two: Performance Assessment: So . . . Sue wants to be a Carpenter

One relatively simple and informal method of assessing a student's strengths, limitations, and skill level in preparation to participate in either in-school vocational programming or a community based work experience is through the use of a performance assessment. According to Dietel, Herman, and Knuth (1991), **performance assessment** is an evaluation in which a student is asked to engage in a complex task which often involves the creation of a product. Many performance assessments emulate real-life skill application that requires higher-order processing skills, and student performance is rated based on the item produced, the task completed, or the process in which the student engages. For example, Sue wants to be a carpenter. She wants to participate in the high school based carpenter training program. Prior to placing Sue in the carpenter training class, it would be very important to assess her skill level. To do this, the teacher designs the following activity to take place in the shop area.

Activity

A. Materials: hammer, nails, saw, tape measure, square.
B. Sue is provided with four **written directions** including

   1. Cut the six foot 2 × 4 board into two boards. Make one board 2 feet 4 inches in length, and make the other 2 feet 1 and 3/8 inches.
   2. Cut the end of the board that is 2 feet 4 inches at a 45-degree angle.
   3. Cut the end of the board that is 2 feet 1 and 3/8 inches at a 45-degree angle.
   4. Nail the two boards together where the 45-degree angles meet, to form a square.

This simple activity can help the evaluator find out many things regarding the student's strengths, limitations, and skill level in the carpentry area. For example,

- Can the student independently use hand tools?
- Can the student correctly measure boards?
- Can the student independently follow four-step written directions?
- Can the student independently complete the performance sample?
- How much time did the performance sample take the student to complete?
- How does the amount of time this student required to complete this activity compare to the time required by other students?

This activity could be modified and repeated with oral directions to again assess the student's strengths, limitations, and skills. In this manner, the evaluator could compare Sue's ability to follow a four-step oral direction sequence to her ability to follow four-step written directions.

Results

Based on the scenario performance sample in entry-level carpentry skills, you (the vocational evaluator) found the following assessment results:

- Sue could identify all the tools as needed for the activity.
- Sue was able to independently cut each board with a handsaw.
- Sue measured one board correctly and one board incorrectly. Sue correctly measured the board measuring 2 feet and 4 inches. Sue incorrectly measured the second board. She measured the second board at 2 feet 1 and 3/4 inches.
- Sue asked for assistance with cutting each board at a 45-degree angle.
- Sue was able to independently nail the boards together and form a square.
- When comparing the time it took Sue to complete the activity to three other students registered for the class (n = 4), Sue completed the activity in the slowest time. Sue completed the activity in twice the amount of time as the next slowest student (two male, one female).
- When given the performance activity with different specific directions (e.g. cut boards

to different lengths) Sue made the same set of errors when following oral directions. In addition, Sue did not remember the fourth oral direction.

Given these assessment results, please write one annual goal and three short term objectives to assist Sue in participating in her carpentry class and work toward developing the vocational skills to be more successful in her area of career interest.

CHAPTER REFERENCES

Albright, L. & Cobb, B. (1988). curriculum-based vocational assessment: A concept whose time has come. *The Journal for Vocational Special Needs Education*. American Vocational Association. pp. 13–16.

Dietel, R. J., Herman, J. L., & Knuth, R. A. (1991). *What does research say about assessment?* Oak Brook, IL: North Central Regional Educational Laboratory. Retrieved January 30, 2005 from http://www.ncrel.org/ sdrs/ area/ stw_esys/4assess.htm

Harrington, T. F. & O'Shea, A. J. (2003). *CDM: The Harrington-O'Shea career decision-making system*. Circle Pines, MN: American Guidance Service, Inc.

Harvey, M.W. (2002). Comparison of postsecondary transitional outcomes between students with and without disabilities by secondary vocational education participation: Findings from the national longitudinal study. *Career Development for Exceptional Individuals, 25* (2), 99–122.

Johansson, C. B. (1996). *Interest determination, exploration and assessment system*. Bloomington, MN: NCS Pearson Inc.

Lombard, R.C. (1995). *Vocational assessment: Prevention vs. treatment model. In designated vocational instruction handbook*. Madison, WI: Wisconsin Department of Public Instruction.

McMahan, R. & Baer, R. (2001). IDEA transition policy compliance and practice: Perceptions of transition stakeholders. *Career Development for Exceptional Individuals, 24* (2), 169–184.

Parker, R. M. (2002). *Occupational aptitude survey and interest schedule-third edition*. Austin, TX: PRO-ED.

Sarkees-Wircenski, M. & Scott, J. L. (1995). *Vocational special needs*. Homewood, IL: American Technical Publishers.

Sitlington, P. L., Neubert, D. A., Begun, W., Lombard, R. C., & Leconte, P. J. (1996). *Assess for success: Handbook on transition assessment*. Reston, VA: Council for Exceptional Children.

CHAPTER 8

The MAGIC Model: How to Integrate Formal and Curriculum-Based Assessment for Career Planning

The concept of future planning has been discussed elsewhere in this book. One approach that integrates a combination of formal or psychometric assessment procedures with informal data collection procedures is known as the MAGIC Model (Lombard, Larson, & Westphal, 1993). This approach consists of five sequential steps that are designed to take full advantage of data that are generated through formal and informal assessment activities (see Figure 8.1).

The five components of the MAGIC Model (see Figure 8.2) include the following:

- **M**ake a prediction about future settings
- **A**ssess the entry-level skills of future settings
- **G**uide student acquisition of entry-level skills
- **I**nstruct students to generalize skills to future settings
- **C**oordinate maintenance checks to monitor student outcomes

Component One: Make a Prediction about Future Settings

Making a tentative prediction regarding a student's academic, employment, or vocational future is the initial step in the MAGIC Model. As noted earlier, formal assessment of student interests, academic and vocational abilities, and learning styles and preferences will provide a basis for making these tentative predictions. According to McMahan and Baer (2001), the implementation of functional vocational evaluations is consistent with "best practices" in comprehensive transition planning. Moreover, the IDEA legislation of 2004 requires that transition planning be conducted with the student's interests, abilities, and preferences in mind. In order to make a prediction about a student's academic/vocational future, the following information must be collected and reviewed: occupational interest data, vocational aptitude data, academic ability data, and learning style preferences. In most cases, information about a student's academic history will be readily available in the student's cumulative file. In order to determine a student's occupational interests, vocational aptitude, and learning style preferences, school personnel will need to administer formal psychometric instruments. When choosing formal standardized instruments, one must be sure to examine the extent to which the tool was standardized on students of

Transition Assessment Model

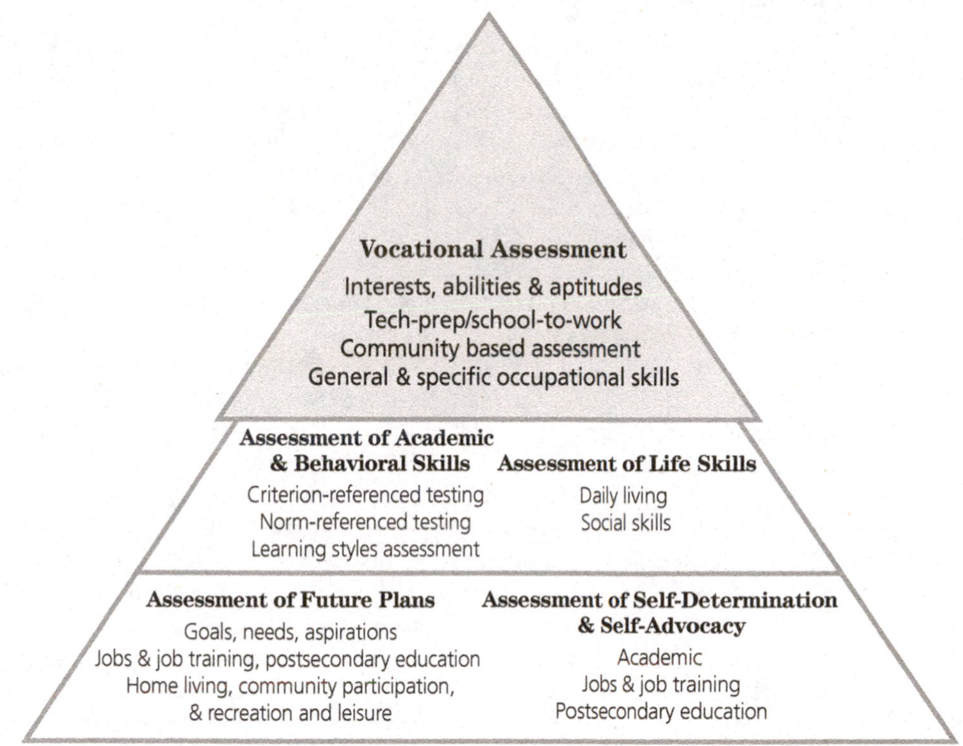

Figure 8.1

MAGIC Model

M Make a Prediction for Student's Future
Assess: (1) interests, (2) aptitude, and (3) learning styles, and (4) map vocational congruence.

A Assess Entry-level
(1) Skills review course related print material, (2) interview the teacher, and (3) complete a program inventory form.

G Guide IEP Development and Skill Acquisition
(1) conduct discrepancy analysis, (2) objectify discrepant skills for IEP, and (3) identify curricular and instructional supports needed.

I Instruct for Generalization
Teach student to use: (1) skill rehearsal, (2) orientation techniques, and (3) skill activation methods.

C Conduct Maintenance Checks
Consult with: (1) teachers, (2) family members, and (3) student.

Figure 8.2

school age and if the population sample included students with disabilities. Although the following descriptions of assessment instruments are not an exhaustive compilation of commercially available assessments, those that are included here have been reported by special education personnel to be highly appropriate for students with disabilities.

Commercially-Available Occupational Interest Assessments

The California Occupational Preference Survey (COPS) (Knapp & Knapp, 2004b) is an example of an occupational interest instrument with versions that were standardized on middle school, secondary, and postsecondary college students. This instrument measures an individual's interest in fourteen career clusters that are plotted on a matrix chart. After interest scores have been plotted on the matrix, the student can use reference material to investigate the career clusters for which he or she scored the highest level of interest. The entire COPS system is published by EDITS in San Diego, California.

The Reading-Free Vocational Interest Inventory: 2 (R-FV11-2) measures interest patterns in eleven areas including automotive, building trades, clerical, animal care, food service, patient care, horticulture, housekeeping, personal service, laundry service, and materials handling. This instrument was designed to evaluate the occupational interests of students with limited reading ability. This instrument is published by Elbern Publications (Becker, 2000).

The Self-Directed Search (Holland, Powell, & Fritzche, 1997) is based on Holland's theory of career choice that states there are six occupational personality types: realistic, investigative, artistic, social, enterprising, and conventional. This instrument is designed to help individuals to identify their personality type in relationship to the occupations that are related to that personality type. It is published by Psychological Assessment Resources Inc. in Odessa, Florida.

The Interest Determination, Exploration and Assessment System (IDEAS) is published by National Computer Systems, Inc. in Minneapolis, Minnesota. This instrument provides information regarding a student's current career preference by evaluating vocational likes and dislikes in sixteen vocational areas including: mechanical/fixing, protective services, nature/outdoors, mathematics, science, medical, creative arts, writing, community service, educating, child care, public speaking, business, sales, office practices, and food service. There are three scoring profiles available including one for grades 7, 8, and 9; another for grades 10, 11, and 12, and one for adults.

Commercially-Available Occupational and Vocational Aptitude Assessments

The OASIS-3: Occupational Aptitude Survey and Interest Schedule was developed by Randall M. Parker and is published by PRO-ED in Austin, Texas. This instrument is designed to assist students in grades 8–12 with career exploration, vocational exploration, and career development. OASIS scores should be used to help students to organize their search for occupational information that is related to their interest and ability areas.

The Career Ability Placement Survey (CAPS), created by Knapp and Knapp, is a timed instrument that measures student ability in eight vocational domains including: mechanical reasoning, spatial relations, verbal reasoning, numerical ability, language usage, word knowledge, perceptual speed and accuracy, and manual speed and dexterity. Like the COPS, the CAPS scores can be plotted on a matrix chart that will demonstrate a student's skill level in relationship to fourteen career clusters. This instrument is published by EDITS in San Diego, California.

The Harrington-O'Shea Career Decision-Making System–Revised (CDM) is a self-assessment inventory that allows individuals to assess their abilities, work values, school subject preferences, and occupational interests. After matching abilities, interests, and work values to career options, individuals can then use reference material to investigate specific details about education and training requirements needed to pursue related career options. CDM Level 1 is designed for middle school students and CDM Level 2 is appropriate for high school students and college students. This instrument is published by AGS Publishing, in Circle Pines, Minnesota.

Once the formal data have been collected, the relationship between a student's interests and aptitude can be examined. The relationship between interest and aptitude, known as **vocational congruence** (Holland, 1985), can be mapped in pencil to provide the student with a visual representation of where their interests and abilities do or do not correspond. If this process were being used in a middle school setting for example, first year high school courses of study would be selected (predicted) based on the occupational areas for which the student expressed interest and requisite aptitude. If this process were being used at the secondary level, a determination of postsecondary goals in educational and/or employment settings would be based on the occupational areas in which the student has demonstrated a strong relationship between interest and ability. It is highly recommended that the compilation of student data required for phase one be documented on a student vocational assessment profile form (see Appendix A, part 8 [A-8]).

Vocational Congruence Mapping Activity

According to Holland's (1985) theory of vocational congruence, an individual must exhibit both interest and aptitude for a training program or an occupation in order for that person to be both successful and intrinsically satisfied. It follows therefore, that in order to ensure that students are making the transition into training programs and/or occupations for which they have interest and ability, an examination of student's vocational congruence must take place.

In order to map the relationship between a student's occupational interests and his or her vocational aptitude, school personnel must administer an interest inventory and a vocational aptitude instrument that measure similar career clusters. The California Occupational Preference System (Knapp & Knapp, 2004) for example, consists of both an occupational interest inventory and a vocational aptitude battery. Both instruments measure interest and ability dimensions according to fourteen career clusters. These career clusters include the following: science professional, science skilled, technology professional, technology skilled, consumer economics, outdoor, business professional, business skilled, clerical, communication, arts professional, arts skilled, service professional, and service skilled. Following the administration of the occupational interest inventory, school personnel can plot percentile scores for each of the fourteen career clusters. Given the variability of human interests in occupations, the plotting procedure typically takes on a "peak and valley" appearance as the individual scores are mapped across the career cluster profile matrix. Once the occupational interests have been mapped, the vocational aptitude battery can now be administered. Because the vocational aptitude data provide information about the student's ability level in relationship to the same fourteen career clusters identified above, the percentile ability scores can now be plotted on the same career cluster profile matrix as the interest scores. It is recommended that the interest scores are mapped using a different color maker than the ability scores so the student can easily see the differences and similarities between their interests and abilities on the profile matrix.

Once the relationship between an individual's occupational interests and vocational abilities have been mapped, school personnel must review the results with the student. The objective of this activity is to determine the occupational clusters where the student has exhibited a significant degree of interest and ability. Once the highly congruent clusters have been identified, an examination of the following should take place:

1. the various occupations that are consistent with each highly congruent career cluster,
2. the skills needed to perform these occupations,
3. the courses available (secondary or postsecondary) where these skills can be learned, and
4. the availability of these occupations in the community.

MAGIC Case Study: Spencer McGillacutty

Phase One: Making a Prediction for Spencer

As indicated earlier in this chapter, documentation of student assessment information can be achieved by using a vocational assessment profile (VAP). In Appendix B, part 7 (B-7), a completed VAP can be reviewed for a high school student named Spencer McGillacutty. Spencer is a seventeen-year-old student with learning disabilities and ADHD. Spencer also has oral and written communication difficulties and a slight visual disorder that has been corrected with glasses. An assessment of Spencer's occupational interests indicates that he is highly interested in computers, electronic technology, and graphic design. He has work experience as a grocery store food stocker and he enjoys leisure and recreational hobbies such as playing soccer and playing computer games on the Internet.

With respect to job seeking skills, Spencer is able to express his work related interests and skills by referring to his resume. He can also independently complete a job application form and describe his previous work experience. Spencer would benefit from a job tryout where he would be able to practice his job interviewing skills. His work history shows that he is able to make corrections to his own work, follows company rules and procedures, and always notifies his employer when he is unable to work due to illness. In addition, Spencer has shown that he can perform the following work related behaviors: follow directions, ask for help when needed, work well with others, and interact well with customers.

Spencer possesses very strong personal self-care skills and his travel/community mobility skills are good although he does not yet have a driver's license. He is able to independently take medication, plan and prepare meals with visual cues, and manage his money with some budgeting assistance. His academic strengths pertain to simple math, computer usage, and written expression. Although Spencer speaks very good English, he does have difficulty expressing his feelings.

Based upon the information presented in the vocational assessment profile and a review of other pertinent transition assessment information, it is predicted that Spencer will enroll in a computer-programming course of study at Regional Technical College after graduation from high school. A future goal can now be developed for the IEP that reflects Spencer's intention to make the transition to this post-high school setting.

Spencer's Future Goal After graduation, I plan to attend the Computer Programming Associate Degree Program at Regional Technical College.

Transition services/activities that support Spencer's future goal are:

1. Spencer will participate on a walking tour of Regional Technical College.
2. Spencer will attend an orientation meeting at Regional Technical College where issues related to financial assistance, application procedures, student assistance, and community housing will be addressed.
3. Spencer will log on to a computer job locator program to determine the employment prospects and earning potential for computer programmers in his state.

Component Two: Assess Entry-Level Skills of Predicted Settings

Remember, after a tentative course of study and/or occupation has been predicted, an informal assessment process known as curriculum-based vocational assessment (CBVA) can be implemented. Curriculum-based vocational assessment is a data collection process that focuses on (a) the entry-level skills of a particular course of study and/or occupation and

(b) the instructional design of a particular course of study (see Chapter 7). Albright and Cobb (1988) have incorporated three specific phases or levels into their CBVA approach. The first phase, known as the "entry" phase, is primarily concerned with data collection that takes place prior to a student being placed in a vocational program or course of study. A fundamental purpose of collecting information during this phase is to ensure that students are placed in vocational programs that are consistent with their expressed interests and abilities. The second phase, known as the "monitor" phase, involves the monitoring of student performance during program participation. A primary objective of collecting information during this phase is to determine if students are being successful in the vocational program and if a change in the level of instructional support is needed. The third or "transition" phase is related to data that are collected as students complete the vocational program and prepare to make the transition to postsecondary training or employment. A basic purpose of this phase is to ensure that students are prepared to make a successful transition from the secondary school setting to a postschool environment that is consistent with their interests and abilities.

A fundamental goal of the MAGIC Model is to ensure students have acquired the requisite skills of their predicted course of study or occupation well before they actually enter that setting. If, for example, assessment personnel determine the entry-level skills of a predicted course of study a year or two before the student enrolls in the program, that time can be used to assist the student to acquire the necessary skills prior to program placement. The entry-level skills to be assessed would include but not be limited to the following: following directions, staying on task, verbal expression, written expression, spelling, note-taking, keyboarding, punctuality, following safety rules, problem solving, technology usage, reading skills, and organizational skills.

Another important goal of the MAGIC Model is to determine the curricular and instructional accommodations a student must receive in order to successfully complete the program of interest. In order to plan these accommodations, information about the instructional design of the course in question must be collected. Instructional design elements to be assessed would include but not be limited to the following teacher preferences: formal or informal classroom design, instructional preferences, testing methods, assignment and project timelines, homework and makeup policies, extra credit options, technology usage, extent of group activities, and grading procedures.

An instrument that can be used to obtain and record the information listed above is known as a program inventory (see Appendix A, part 7 [A-7] for a sample program inventory). It is recommended that the program inventory be completed collaboratively between special educators and general educators.

Program Inventory Activity

In order for high school personnel to learn about the entry-level skill requirements of postsecondary settings such as technical colleges, it will be helpful to use the program inventory included in Appendix A (A-7). It is highly recommended that the program inventories be completed in a face-to-face meeting so that all concerned parties have an opportunity to discuss how this information can be used to the benefit of all stakeholders. As mentioned earlier, the purpose of the program inventory activity is to answer two basic questions about the general education program. The first part of the program inventory is designed to determine how the general educator prefers to teach. Items related to classroom design, testing approaches, instructional methods, and grading procedures are identified in this process. Information of this nature will enable school personnel to develop, curricular and instructional accommodations that take into account the general educator's teaching preferences and the learning style preferences of his or her future student.

The second objective of this activity is to determine the entry-level skills a student must possess in order to be successful in this program. This part of the program inventory activity will enable the general educator to identify the most essential skills a student needs upon entry to this program. Once this information has been identified, school personnel can provide instruction to ensure entry-level skills are learned prior to the student attending this program.

MAGIC Case Study: Spencer McGillacutty

Phase Two: Assessing Entry-Level Skills for Introduction to Computer Programming

Now that the IEP/transition team has reviewed the vocational assessment profile and other pertinent data and has made a tentative post high school prediction for Spencer based upon that information, it is necessary to conduct an inventory of that program. A completed program inventory for the "Introduction to Computer Programming" course is included in Appendix B (B-7, Form 2).

Special education staff from Spencer's high school completed the program inventory. In this example, high school special education staff met with Mr. Jenson, the instructor of the Introduction to Computer Programming course at Regional Technical College. The completed program inventory indicates that Mr. Jenson relies heavily upon lecture, audiotapes, and simulations for his instructional preferences. The course assignments he uses daily include oral reports, demonstrations, written reports, and portfolios. Mr. Jenson also prefers to use either large group or teacher directed instructional activities. Although Mr. Jenson uses multiple test formats, he prefers to use oral examinations or student demonstrations to evaluate skill development. When grading students he usually uses the traditional A–F format, and he allows two extra credit options per semester. There are weekly homework assignments and students must attend at least 95% of classes.

An examination of the most important skills a student should possess to successfully enter the computer programming course reveals that oral expression, written expression, working in groups, and keyboarding are the most critical skills. According to the program inventory, there is limited instructional support from technical college support staff available. Instructional support from the Disability Services Office includes textbooks on tape, test preparation support, assignment assistance, and computer-assisted instruction.

At this point in the MAGIC Model, two data pools have been created. The student data regarding Spencer have been documented on the vocational assessment profile and the curriculum data regarding the Introduction to Computer Programming course have been documented on the program inventory. The transition assessment team is now prepared to compare the information on the VAP (that describes what skills Spencer currently possesses and how he learns) with the program inventory (that describes what skills he will need in the future as well as the instructional preferences of his future teacher).

Component Three: Guide Student's Acquisition of Discrepant Skills

At this stage in the process, assessment personnel have two data pools to review. First, as a result of the formal assessment activities that were undertaken in the first stage of the model, information regarding the student's interests, aptitude, and learning styles and preferences has been documented. In addition, information about the curricular and instructional elements of the predicted course of study has been documented on the program inventory in stage two. Assessment personnel are now able to conduct a review of the two data pools in an effort to determine if any of the skills needed in the predicted course of study are or are not currently possessed by the student. This review, known as a **discrepancy analysis**, will enable the assessment team to determine precisely what skills the student needs to learn prior to being placed in the predicted course of study. Moreover, the identification of discrepant skills will enable the IEP team to develop goals and objectives that are directly linked to individual student preferences and abilities as required by the IDEA. The IEP team will also be able to pinpoint specific curricular and instructional accommodations needed by the student due to the assessment data that are now available. By involving general educators throughout this process, the accommodations can be developed collaboratively and well in advance of program placement. This preenrollment planning will allow students to learn the entry-level skills before they actually attend the course of study.

Transition IEP Activity

The purpose of the transition IEP activity is to ensure that the formal transition assessment information collected during the first phase of the MAGIC Model and the curriculum based data collected during the second phase of the model are both used to develop appropriate transition goals and objectives for the IEP. In addition, specific instructional and curricular accommodations can be developed as a result of data collection activities.

For this activity, school personnel will need the student vocational assessment profile form and the vocational congruence map that were completed in the first phase of the MAGIC Model. With this information, school personnel can predict a future course of study or an occupation that is consistent with the student's interests and abilities. After a future course of study or future occupation has been identified, school personnel can develop a future goal statement that can be included in the IEP.

In order to develop objectives that pertain to the future goal statement, school personnel must have the student profile form and the vocational congruence map developed in phase one of MAGIC. The program inventory completed in phase two of MAGIC is also needed at this time. At this stage of the process, school personnel must conduct a discrepancy analysis between the student information collected in phase one and the curricular/instructional information collected in phase two. The purpose of this activity is to determine the most essential skills the student will need in order to make the successful transition from the current program into the future program/occupation. By examining the data collected in phases one and two of MAGIC, school personnel can identify (1) the essential entry-level skills needed for the future program and (2) the degree to which the student currently possesses these entry-level skills. If a student possesses some of the skills needed for the future program, these need not be objectified for the IEP. If, however, the student does not currently possess some of the critical skills needed for the future program, these discrepant skills can be turned into goals or objectives for the IEP.

Another important element of the IEP pertains to instructional and curricular accommodations. To identify specific accommodations needed by the student, school personnel must have the students learning style preference information collected during phase one of MAGIC. They will also need the program inventory form that was completed in phase two of MAGIC. By comparing the students learning style preferences with the instructional preferences of the future teacher, school personnel can develop specific instructional and/or curricular accommodations that will enable the student to succeed even though there may be differences between the learning preferences of the student and the instructional preferences of the future teacher. After instructional and curricular accommodations have been specified, they can be included in the IEP.

MAGIC Case Study: Spencer McGillacutty

Phase Three: Guiding Spencer's Acquisition of Entry-Level Skills

In this phase of the MAGIC Model, the transition assessment team will help Spencer acquire the skills he needs to successfully enter his future course of study at the technical college. A review of the VAP and the program inventory suggests that Spencer currently possesses a number of important entry-level skills for the Introduction to Computer Programming course. However, there are several skills that will be needed in the future that Spencer currently does not possess. Although the VAP indicates that Spencer has some difficulty with respect to oral and written expression, the program inventory reveals that oral and written reports are primary instructional approaches used for class assignments and tests by the instructor of the Introduction to Computer Programming course.

In this case study example, oral expression is considered a "discrepant" skill. It is discrepant because Spencer will need this skill in the future, but he does not currently possess the skill. Before the IEP team can help Spencer acquire this discrepant skill, oral expression should become an annual goal in the IEP.

Transition Needs Based upon the discrepancy analysis, it has been determined that Mr. Jenson, the instructor for Introduction of Computer Programming, uses the following instructional techniques most often: written reports, oral reports, demonstrations, and portfolios. Based on Spencer's vocational assessment profile, it has been determined that Spencer has the following strengths and limitations related to participation in the Introduction to Computer Programming course.

> *Strengths:* classroom demonstrations, participation in simulations, and following directions.
> *Limitations:* oral expression, written expression, and participation in small group activities.

Based on these transition needs, the following annual goal was developed to address his successful participation in the Introduction to Computer Programming course that is consistent with his future goal of becoming a computer programmer.

Annual goal Spencer will move from rarely expressing his opinion orally on a predetermined topic in the general education classroom to consistently expressing his opinion orally on predetermined topics in the general education classroom.

1. Spencer will demonstrate oral skill development by asking his teachers for clarification of instructions in 90% of his general education classes.
2. Spencer will orally express two future goals during his annual IEP meeting.
3. Spencer will orally request instructional support from special education staff on two occasions during his annual IEP meeting.
4. Spencer will orally express differences of opinion (on two occasions) during his annual IEP meeting.
5. Spencer will participate in four simulated job interviews where he responds orally to employer questions with 100% accuracy.

In addition to instructional objectives, a discrepancy analysis can result in the development of meaningful instructional accommodations. As a part of his assessment, Spencer McGillacutty completed the Learning/Working Styles Inventory that is published by Piney Mountain Press Inc. Based on these learning and working styles assessment results, the IEP/transition team was able to document how Spencer preferred to receive, organize, and express his information. As a result of the program inventory, the team also has documented how Spencer's future instructor, Mr. Jenson, prefers to teach, grade, test, etc.

The completed Learning/Working Style Inventory for Spencer (B-7, Form 3) and the completed Program Inventory from Mr. Jenson (B-7, Form 2) are included in Appendix B. One of the important findings for Spencer was that, based on the use of the Learning/Working Styles

(continued)

MAGIC Case Study: Spencer McGillacutty (continued)

Inventory, he shows a low tolerance or low preference for sedentary activities (sedentary score = 6—a very low score on this instrument). In other words, Spencer prefers classroom activities where he is able to move about the room, change activities frequently, and be physically active (nonsedentary score = 22—a major learning and working style). On the other hand, his future teacher, Mr. Jenson, uses a traditional classroom structure where students are to remain seated most of the time. He also requires students to closely follow classroom rules and to remain focused and on task for the majority of each class period. In this example, an instructional accommodation can be developed to ensure that Spencer has an opportunity to experience non-sedentary activities while in the classroom.

Instructional Accommodation Spencer will be given the opportunity to provide hands-on physical demonstrations of computer/Internet related projects, assignments, and tests.

Component Four: Instruct for Generalization

Assessing and teaching discrepant skills will have little value for students with disabilities unless those skills are transferred into the predicted setting. There is ample support in the literature to indicate that students with disabilities have difficulty generalizing skills from the setting in which the skills are learned to the settings where skills may be applied (Deshler, Ellis, & Lenz, 1996). Research has shown that in addition to being strategy-deficient with respect to skill generalization, students with disabilities can acquire generalization skills if given specific strategy instruction. Although vocational and school-to-work programs typically provide opportunities for students to apply new skills in a community setting, additional efforts must be made by special needs personnel to equip students with specific strategies for transferring skills from the setting where skills are learned to the setting where skills must be applied. Examples of instructional approaches which may promote skill generalization include but are not limited to the following:

- verbal rehearsal (verbal repetition of information that must be committed to memory)
- auditory rehearsal (auditory repetition of information that must be committed to memory)
- visual rehearsal (visual repetition of information that must be committed to memory)
- haptic rehearsal (combining visual repetition with motoric repetition such as rereading and rewriting information that must be committed to memory)
- verbal orientation to applied settings (discussing the various school, community, and home settings where skills can be generalized)
- physical orientation to applied settings (personal visitation to the various school, community, or home settings where skills can be generalized)
- activation of skills in proximity within one setting (school)
- activation of skills in proximity within two settings (school and home)
- activation of skills in proximity within three settings (school, home, and community)

Generalization Activity

School personnel often assume that students know how to transfer skills learned in the classroom to other school and community settings. Because students with disabilities tend to be strategy-deficient with respect to skill generalization, it is important for teachers to assess the degree to which students know how to generalize. To develop baseline data regarding student comprehension and use of generalization behavior, teachers can implement the following procedures:

1. observation of in-class behavior;
2. observation of behavior within general education classes;
3. student interview;
4. parent interview;
5. general educator interview;
6. employer interview; and
7. community observations.

After baseline data have been collected, school personnel will be able to develop instructional approaches to assist students with disabilities to acquire and use generalization strategies. If, for example, students learn how to use visual or auditory rehearsal techniques within the context of a special education resource room, the students must then be oriented to the various school and community settings where the newly acquired skill may be independently applied. Once the students have an understanding of the various settings where new skills can be used, the students should be required to use or activate this skill in other settings. For this activity, it is suggested that students use newly acquired skills to successfully generalize in school settings before they are asked to generalize them in community settings. This will ensure that students have ample opportunity to be successful in a controlled setting, such as school, before they transfer skills to an uncontrolled setting, such as the community.

MAGIC Case Study: Spencer McGillacutty

Phase Four: Instructing Spencer for Generalization

As a result of the initial three phases of the MAGIC Model, discrepant skills, such as oral expression, have been integrated into Spencer's IEP and into the curriculum design at his high school. To ensure that important entry-level skills are eventually generalized into post-high school settings such as Regional Technical College, Spencer must be taught explicitly how to transfer skills for one setting into another. There are a number of generalization strategies that Spencer could learn while in high school that would enable him to transfer his oral expression skills into post-high school settings. In this example, Spencer will be taught how to generalize using three specific approaches.

First, Spencer will be taught how to use rehearsal techniques.

Visual rehearsal: Spencer will learn to use visual cues, such as written outlines, that will help him organize and sequence his oral presentations.

Auditory rehearsal: Spencer will listen to audio recordings of his oral presentations. This technique will enable him to critique his oral expression skills by hearing himself the way others hear him.

Haptic rehearsal: Spencer will combine written motor activity with oral expression. In this example, Spencer will be asked to make written notations as he speaks. This activity will enable Spencer to keep a running record of his oral skills as they are expressed. Following his oral performance, Spencer will review the running record to evaluate the extent to which he accurately described what he communicated orally.

Component Five: Conduct Maintenance Checks

After a student has exited a particular grade level, it is often difficult to determine the extent to which he or she is being successful in the next setting. Although a teacher may work diligently to prepare a student to enter and be successful in a future school or postschool environment, the teacher may never receive feedback about the performance of former students (Test, et al., 2004). As a result, teachers seldom appreciate the extent to which their instructional approaches have been effective. Without this feedback, teachers also cannot fully evaluate the quality of the curriculum they teach. In the fifth and final phase of the MAGIC Model, a series of maintenance checks will be implemented. These maintenance checks are designed to provide feedback to teachers so they are able to evaluate important elements of their instruction and the quality of the curriculum they use.

After a student has entered the future setting, it will be necessary to determine if previously learned skills have generalized to the new setting. It will also be important to determine the extent to which these skills are being maintained. Special education personnel must work collaboratively with the general education instructors to evaluate the extent to which students are applying the skills in question. Strategies that my be used to conduct these maintenance checks include but are not limited to the following:

- former student self reports/interviews;
- classroom observation;
- periodic interviews with new teachers;
- periodic written feedback from new teachers;
- written feedback from former students; and
- instructor feedback

Maintenance Check Activity

The purpose of this activity is to solicit feedback about former students in order to determine the degree to which they are being successful in current settings. To accomplish this, teachers must create a roster of former students for the past three-year period. Teachers can randomly select a sample of five to seven students for each of the past three years. After the final student list has been randomly selected, teachers must determine the school or postschool settings (classes or occupations) where the students are either enrolled or employed. Once this has been determined, teachers can create a list of seven to ten questions that will generate feedback about their instructional approaches. Teachers can then generate a list of seven to ten questions that will generate feedback about their curriculum content. After the questions have been developed, teachers can either send the questions to former students or they can arrange to interview former students.

After the instructional and curricular feedback has been compiled, teachers can evaluate the extent to which they need to modify any instructional and/or curricular aspects of their program.

MAGIC Case Study: Spencer McGillacutty

Phase Five: Conducting Maintenance Checks

Now that Spencer has been taught how to use rehearsal techniques, he is ready to generalize his oral expression skills into various settings. His long-term goal is to transfer oral expression skills into his computer programming studies after high school graduation. It is essential, however, that Spencer practice the art of skill generalization while he is still in high school. In order for the IEP team to evaluate the extent to which Spencer is generalizing oral expression skills into high school, home, and community settings, they must conduct maintenance checks in each of those settings.

(continued)

MAGIC Case Study: Spencer McGillacutty (continued)

The IEP team can conduct maintenance checks using the following techniques:

Self reports: The student provides written and/or oral feedback to the IEP team regarding his ability to generalize oral expression skills in general education classes, in the home, and in the community.
Teacher reports: General education teachers provide written and/or oral feedback concerning the extent to which the student is using oral expression skills in the classroom setting.
Parent/family reports: Parents and family members provide written and/or oral feedback to the IEP team regarding the extent to which oral expression skills are being used at home.
Employer reports: Employers provide written and/or oral feedback to the IEP team regarding the extent to which oral expression skills are used successfully on the job.

Based on the information gathered as a result of the MAGIC Model process, the following transition goal was included on Spencer's IEP.

Spencer McGillacutty: Transition Goal for Postsecondary Education

Spencer's Future Goal After graduation, I plan to attend the Computer Programming Associate Degree Program at Regional Technical College.

Transition Needs Based on the discrepancy analysis, it has been determined that Mr. Jenson, instructor for Introduction of Computer Programming, uses the following instructional techniques most often: written reports, oral reports, demonstrations, and portfolios. Based on Spencer's vocational assessment profile, it has been determined that Spencer has the following strengths and limitations related to participation in the Introduction to Computer Programming course.

Strengths: classroom demonstrations, participation in simulations, and following directions.
Limitations: oral expression, written expression, and participation in small group activities.

Transition services/activities

1. Spencer will participate on a walking tour of Regional Technical College.
2. Spencer will attend an orientation meeting at Regional Technical College where issues related to financial assistance, application procedures, student assistance, and community housing will be addressed.
3. Spencer will log on to a computer job locator program to determine the employment prospects and earning potential for computer programmers in his state.

Annual Goal

1. Spencer will demonstrate oral skill development by asking his teachers for clarification of instructions in 90% of his general education classes.
2. Spencer will orally express two future goals during his annual IEP meeting.
3. Spencer will orally request instructional support from special education staff on two occasions during his annual IEP meeting.

4. Spencer will orally express differences of opinion on two occasions during his annual IEP meeting.
5. Spencer will participate in four simulated job interviews where he orally responds to employer questions with 100% accuracy.

Based upon the information gathered in the MAGIC Model process, the following accommodation is recommended for Spencer.

Instructional Accommodation Spencer will be given the opportunity to provide hands on physical demonstrations of computer/Internet related projects, assignments, and tests.

CHAPTER SUMMARY

This chapter discussed the MAGIC Model—a five-step process that uses multiple forms of formal and informal assessment procedures. As a result of comprehensive data collection activities, transition assessment personnel can develop meaningful goals and objectives for inclusion in the IEP. Assessment of a student's preferred learning styles allows for development of appropriate curricular and instructional accommodations for use in general education classrooms. This chapter also highlighted the importance of teaching specific generalization strategies to students with disabilities. Transferring skills from setting to setting is essential to the success of all transition planning efforts. Finally, procedures to conduct maintenance checks were presented in order to monitor the extent to which students are using generalized skills over time and in various conditions and multiple settings.

DISCUSSION QUESTIONS

In a national study of teacher attitudes and practices regarding the inclusion of students with disabilities in school-to-work and technical preparation programs, Miller, Lombard, and Hazelkorn (2000) reported that nearly six out of ten (58%) vocational educators reported no assistance was provided by special education staff in designing course modification and accommodations. Further, fewer than four in ten (38%) school-to-work and technical preparation teachers were confident that career interest and abilities determined the placement of students with disabilities in their courses.

1. How might these data affect the working relationship between vocational education personnel and special education personnel in high schools?
2. How might these data affect students with disabilities placed in vocational coursework?
3. How will the MAGIC Model assist to address these concerns?

CHAPTER ACTIVITIES

In Chapter 8 we discussed Spencer McGillacutty's preference for non-sedentary activities and we identified an instructional accommodation based on this learning preference. Please review the results of the Learning/Working Styles Inventory for Spencer McGillacutty found in Appendix B, part 8, Form 3.

1. Please identify Spencer's top eight learning and working preferences. Based on a review of test questions, what information does this test provide you regarding Spencer's learning and working preferences?
2. Please identify the eight methods of learning and working that Spencer least prefers. Based on your review of test questions, what information does this test provide you regarding the types of learning activities and work activities in which Spencer does not choose to work or enjoy learning?

3. Based on these findings, identify three additional instructional accommodations that you would suggest for Spencer in an English, Social Studies or Computer Keyboarding class.
4. Based on the results of this test, can you think of an additional career that Spencer should explore in order to maximize this learning and working style?

CHAPTER REFERENCES

Albright, L. & Cobb, B. (1988). Curriculum based vocational assessment: A concept whose time has come. *The Journal for Vocational Special Needs Education*. American Vocational Association, pp. 13–16.

Becker, R.L. (2000). *Reading-free vocational interest inventory: 2*. Columbus, OH: Elbern Publications.

Deshler, D.D., Ellis, E.S., & Lenz, B.K. (1996). *Teaching adolescents with learning disabilities*. Denver, CO: Love Publishing Company.

Harrington, T.F. & O'Shea, A.J. (2003). *The Harrington-O'Shea career decision-making system–revised*. Circle Pines, MN: AGS Publications.

Holland, J.L., Powell, A. & Fritzche, B. (1997). *Self-Directed Search*. Odessa, FL: Psychological Assessment Resources, Inc.

Holland, J.L. (1985). *Making vocational choices: A theory of vocational personalities and work environments* (2nded.) Englewood Cliffs, NJ: Prentice Hall.

Johansson, C.B. (1996). *Interest determination, exploration, and assessment system*. Minneapolis, MN: NCS Pearson, Inc.

Knapp, R.R. & Knapp, L.F. (2004a) *Career ability placement survey*. Technical Manual. San Diego, CA: EDITS.

Knapp, R.R., & Knapp, L.F. (2004b). *California occupational preference system: Technical manual*. San Diego, CA: EDITS.

Lombard, R.C., Larson, K.A., & Westphal, S.E. (1993). Validation of vocational assessment services for special populations in tech-prep. A model for translating the Perkins assurances into practice. *The Journal for Vocational and Special Needs Education, 16* (1), 14–22.

McMahan, R. & Baer, R. (2001). IDEA transition policy compliance and best practice: Perceptions of transition stakeholders. *Career Development for Exceptional Individuals, 24* (2), 169–184.

Miller, R. J., Lombard, R., & Hazelkorn, M. (2000). Teacher attitudes and practices regarding the inclusion of students with disabilities in school-to-work and technical preparation programs: Strategies for inclusion and policy implications. In D. R. Johnson & E. J. Emanuel (Eds.), *Issues influencing the future of transition programs and services in the United States* (pp. 127–136). Minneapolis, MN: University of Minnesota National Transition Network.

Parker, R.M. (2002). *Occupational aptitude survey and interest schedule-3*. Austin, TX: PRO-ED.

Test, D.W., Eddy, S.E., Neale, M. & Wood, W.M. (2004). A survey of the types of data collected by transition teachers. *Career Development for Exceptional Individuals, 27* (1), 87–100.

CHAPTER

9 Using Transition Assessment Information to Design an Effective Transition Plan

Ultimately, the purpose of transition assessment is to use the information gathered to design and implement an effective and meaningful transition plan that engages the student and family in planning for high school and life after high school. For the purposes of this book, the terms transition assessment and transition evaluation may be used interchangeably. Flexer, et al. (2001) suggest four characteristics of a comprehensive transition evaluation.

1. The transition evaluation should be continuous and ongoing. Effective transition planning is a dynamic and longitudinal process. Between the time the student enters adolescence (thirteen years of age) and the time the student graduates from high school, most young adults change dramatically—physically, emotionally, intellectually, and with regard to their career maturity. Over this timeframe, most young adults move toward crystallizing their aspirations, interests, and preferences. Most young adults move from a fantasy vision to a more realistic vision of their life after high school. This is a developmental process and can only be captured with continuous transition evaluation.

2. The transition evaluation should clearly identify the areas in which the IEP team needs information to develop a transition plan. The transition evaluation must have a clear and specific purpose.

3. The transition evaluation must be individualized. To this end, transition assessment tools must be chosen that are relevant and appropriate for the student.

4. Transition evaluation information must be effectively summarized and integrated into a comprehensive and accurate profile of the student's transition strengths, interests, and needs. The results must then be used to design an individualized educational program that addresses both the academic and behavioral needs of the student as well as the student's transition needs. To this end, transition assessment results must be functional and relevant, and provide appropriate recommendations and decisions for transition planning (Johnson, Corbey, & Hoff, 2004).

Transition planning requires choice making and problem solving by the student as well as by other members of the IEP team. The information gathered during the transition evaluation process assists the student and IEP team in weighing curricular decisions during high school and choosing life direction after high school. Every decision made during this important developmental timeframe has an "opportunity cost." Put another way, there are "X" hours in the school day, how do you want to spend them? As such, effective and longitudinal transition assessment information is *the* critical component of developing and implementing an effective and meaningful transition plan.

Joe Site—Longitudinal Transition Planning

In this chapter, you will find a three-year longitudinal transition plan for Joe Site. Joe is a student with a mild disability. He has been diagnosed with attention deficit hyperactivity disorder (ADHD) and oppositional defiance disorder. He is provided special education services under the disability category of "other health disability" (OHD). Together, we will follow the design, implementation, and results of Joe's IEP and transition plan from Joe's ninth grade reevaluation summary report and initial transition assessment through graduation from high school. During this three-year transition planning process, you will have the opportunity to see how transition assessment information is woven into the IEP process with the goal of making the individual educational program a more meaningful and student-driven process.

The changes in IDEA brought about by P. L. 108–446 (IDEA 2004) went into effect on July 1, 2005. A notable change in IDEA 2004 is the elimination of the requirements for benchmarks and short term objectives for all children with disabilities except those who are the most severely cognitively disabled (Section 614(d)(1)(A)(i)(I)(cc)) (Apling & Jones, 2005). Clearly, the population of students with mild disabilities for whom this text was written will be students for whom benchmarks and short-term objectives will no longer be required. However, it is our strong belief that best practice requires the inclusion of short term objectives to identify how components of annual goals will be measured and to assure that each student's educational program is individualized to address the student's educational needs, interests, and preferences.

A complete three-year reevaluation of Joe Site completed in spring of his 9th grade year (age fifteen) can be found in Appendix D. You should review this reevaluation to gather baseline evaluation summary information as the transition process begins (see Appendix D). The entire reevaluation summary report is important in the design of the IEP for Joe's high school career.

Summary of Transition Assessment Information from 9th Grade Evaluation

IDEA 2004 requires postsecondary goals for appropriate education, training, employment, and independent living skills (Section 614(d)(1)(A)(i)(VII)(aa)). IDEA 2004 mandates that transition planning begin *no later than* the first IEP to be in effect when the child is sixteen years of age, and is updated annually thereafter (Section 614(d)(1)(A)(i)(VIII)) (Apling & Jones, 2005). As a result, assessment of transition needs should begin when the student is fifteen years of age or younger. Based on career development concerns for students with disabilities, best practice would suggest transition assessment and transition planning begin with the movement of the young adult from junior high school to high school. As a part of the 9th grade educational reevaluation, the following assessment tools were used to gather transition assessment information.

1. Future Planning Inventory (assessment of future planning needs and goals) (Miller & Corbey, 1993),
2. Interest Determination Exploration and Assessment System (IDEAS) (career interest inventory) (Johansson, 1996),
3. Steps to Self-Determination (STEPS): Self-Determination Knowledge Scale (assessment of level of self-determination and self-advocacy) (Hoffman, Field, & Sawilowksy, 1995), and
4. Brigance Life Skills Inventory (Brigance, 1995).

Future Planning Inventory

In spring of 9th grade year, Joe (student), his parents, and his special education teacher completed the **Future Planning Inventory**. Student completed his assessment with assistance from school counselor. The compilation of results from the transition planning team are as follows:

Vocational Interest/Vocational Goals Results indicate student is unsure of career interest after high school. Parties agree that student needs to explore career options.

Postsecondary Education Interest/Goals Student is currently uninterested in exploring postsecondary education.

Home Living At this time, student and parents anticipate student will live at home during the year after high school.

Recreation and Leisure Options Results indicate student is involved in numerous leisure activities including swimming, fishing, canoeing, softball, and bike riding. Student attends movies and sporting events. Student listens to music, watches TV, participates in shopping and lawn care, and plays video games. Student would like to participate in football or soccer (fall high school sport) and baseball (spring) as extracurricular activities during high school.

Transportation Options Student currently gets around the community by walking, riding bike, and depending on others. Student, parent, and educator agree that student needs to learn to drive vehicle and needs to get learner's permit when possible.

Financial/Agency Support Student and parents do not see need for financial support or the assistance of adult support services in postsecondary education, getting a job, or home living at this time.

Health Related Needs Last physical examination was in February of this school year. Student takes medication as noted in the evaluation summary report.

Greatest Concern Student's greatest concern for 10th grade is "Getting along with my teachers in my classes in high school."

Interest Determination Exploration and Assessment System (IDEAS)

An interest inventory was given to student during English class in spring of 9th grade year. Student areas of high interest included the following three career areas: (a) mechanical/fixing careers, (b) nature and outdoor careers, and (c) protective services.

Steps to Self-Determination (STEPS)

Student completed **Self-Determination Knowledge Scale—Form A** in spring of 9th grade year. Based on the results of this criterion referenced test:

- Student appears unclear regarding how to set goals and how to work toward attaining those goals.
- Student indicates weakness in career planning skills.
- Student is unclear regarding process of "active listening." He is also unclear regarding effective communication strategies including passive, assertive, and aggressive communication styles.
- Student identified three of five components of self-determination model. Student perceived compliance (follow the leader and avoid conflict) as components of the

model. He did not include important components (know yourself or value yourself). Suggests external locus of control and a desire to be compliant.

Brigance Life Skills Inventory

Results of this criterion referenced assessment instrument indicate that Student currently lacks skills in (a) basic banking skills including checking skills, (b) use of credit and credit cards, (c) budgeting for expenses, and (d) independent living after high school (e.g. apartment living and roommates).

As a result of the evaluation summary report, Student's IEP team designed and agreed to the following sophomore year IEP. (see Sophomore Year IEP, pages 116–120). The sophomore year IEP addresses the transition areas of employment, postsecondary education, recreation and leisure, community participation, home living, and the Student's behavioral needs.

Sophomore Year IEP for Joe Site

Transition Planning IEP (Age 16)

TRANSITION AREA

_X_Employment
____Home living
____Postsecondary education
____Recreation and Leisure
____Community participation

Future Adult Goals (What I Want After High School): I am not sure what job I want to do after high school.

Present Level of Performance: Joe, his parents, and the special education teacher have completed the Future Planning Inventories and brought them to Joe's IEP conference. Joe completed his form with the help of the school counselor. Joe's parents and special educator completed the FPI separately. As a result of this initial assessment, Joe, his parents, and educators are unsure of the employment goals of the student. IDEAS interest inventory suggests Joe has interest in mechanical/fixing careers, nature and outdoor careers, and protective services. Results from the Self-Determination Knowledge Scale – Form A suggest Joe is unclear regarding how to set and attain goals, and is weak in career planning skills.

Transition Needs (What I Still Need to Do and Learn): I need to explore different careers and work to decide my future career direction. I need to participate in community based job-shadowing and I need to complete career exploration activities in school.

Transition Services/Activities (Student, Parent, and Professional)

1. Joe will complete the OASIS – 3 Interest inventory during his sophomore year in high school. Joe will also complete the aptitude component of the OASIS – 3.
2. Joe, his parent(s) and the teacher will complete the Transition Planning Inventory during sophomore year in high school.
3. Special educator will provide Joe and his parents with information regarding community resources. This information can be found on a website developed by a local transition advisory committee (TAC) (for example see a CTIC website at www.hennepinCTIC.com or www.isd917.k12.mn.us/ctic.htm)
4. Special educator will provide Joe's parents with a copy of *Transition Tips and Tools for Parents*, published by X Advocacy Group. This publication includes transition tips and resources for families.

(continued)

Annual Goal (1 of 1 Goals): Joe will participate in four half-day job-shadowing experiences in the community during the sophomore school year. During each of these four job experiences, Joe will use a checklist of general employability skills to document the skills needed to maintain the job. Joe will complete each checklist (100% completion) regarding skills needed to maintain the job. Checklists will be discussed with the special education teacher.

Objectives (Measurable Steps)

1. Joe will write a two-page typewritten paper outlining the job skills he observed at each of the four job-shadowing experiences, and what he liked and disliked about each job.
2. Joe will answer the following questions regarding each of his job-shadowing experiences.
   (A) Was the job skilled, semi-skilled, or unskilled employment?
   (B) What kind of training is needed to obtain this type of employment?
   (C) Where could I get this training?
   (D) Will there be more or less need for employees in this area of employment in the future?
3. Joe will choose one job observed during the four separate job-shadowing experiences and will independently identify and write a five-step plan he would implement to achieve this career after high school (choose a long-term goal and break the long-term goal into several short-term goals).

TRANSITION AREA

____Employment
____Home living
_X_ Postsecondary education
____Recreation and Leisure
____Community participation

Future Adult Goals (What I Want After High School): At this time, I do not want to participate in postsecondary education after high school.

Present Level of Performance: Joe, his parents, and the special education teacher have completed the Future Planning Inventories and brought them to Joe's IEP conference. As a result of this initial assessment, Joe and his parents do not believe that Joe will participate in postsecondary education after high school. Assessment results from the Self-Determination Knowledge Scale – Form A suggest Student lacks self-advocacy and self-determination skills. Student scored 18 of 37 correct on this pretest for the STEPS to Self-Determination curriculum pretest.

Transition Needs (What I Still Need to Do and Learn): I need to learn the skills of self-advocacy and self-determination so I can say what I need and get what I want.

Transition Services/Activities (Student, Parent, and Professional)

1. Completed Future Planning Inventories.
2. Joe will complete the Arc's Self-Determination Scale during sophomore year.
3. This area will be re-examined at end of the sophomore year. Participation in postsecondary education is not a concern at this time.

Annual Goal (1 of 1 Goals): By the end of the year, Joe will demonstrate the ability to advocate for his own academic needs in secondary school. He will demonstrate this by identifying and using at least three academic accommodations in each of his general education classes.

(continued)

Sophomore Year IEP for Joe Site (continued)

Objectives (Measurable Steps)

1. After reviewing his IEP and cumulative folder, Joe will identify his disability out loud and discuss three specific strengths and three specific limitations.
2. From a list of possible academic accommodations, Joe, his parents, and the special education teacher will identify and agree on three strategies that Joe will practice throughout his sophomore year. Joe will practice and become familiar with these three accommodations. At the end of each quarter during the academic year, Joe will write a paper outlining what accommodations are working and which accommodations need to be changed or adjusted. Changes will be made based on student input regarding effectiveness of the accommodations.
3. Joe will request, out loud, appropriate accommodations from each of his general education teachers during the last three quarters of the school year. Each general education teacher will complete an evaluation of Joe's ability to describe his needed accommodations. Given a rating scale including excellent (5), above average (4), adequate (3), below expectation (2), and much below expectation (1), Joe will receive a rating of adequate or better from three out of five of his general education teachers in this activity.
4. Joe will be able to identify and state at least five rights that he has under IDEA and section 504 of the Rehabilitation act of 1973.

TRANSITION AREA

____Employment
____Home living
____Postsecondary education
__X__ Recreation and Leisure
__X__ Community participation

Future Adult Goals (What I Want After High School): I would like to participate in high school soccer and high school baseball. I would also like to gather more information about community based recreation activities.

Present Level of Performance: Joe is involved in numerous leisure activities including swimming, fishing, canoeing, softball, and bike riding. He attends movies and sporting events. Joe listens to music, watches TV, participates in shopping and lawn care, and plays video games. He would like to participate in football or soccer (fall high school sport) and baseball (spring) as extracurricular activities during high school. During his freshman year of high school, Joe participated as a member of the C-squad soccer team.

Transition Needs (What I Still Need to Do and Learn): I need to explore community based recreation and leisure activities, and I need to try out for high school soccer and high school baseball.

Transition Services/Activities (Student, Parent, and Professional)

1. Joe, his family, and the teacher will explore community based recreation activities offered by the YMCA.
2. Joe will participate in after school weight lifting activities.
3. Joe will try out for the soccer team (no cut policy) and will participate as a member of the soccer team.
4. Joe will try out for the baseball team.

Annual Goal (1 of 1 Goals): Based on personal evaluations gathered during try outs at soccer and baseball, Joe will establish and list three individual goals for the season in each sport. With the help of the special education teacher and coaches, Joe will monitor his progress toward these goals over the academic year. At the end of the academic year, Joe will write a four-page

(continued)

typewritten paper listing his goals and summarizing his progress toward each goal. Joe will write this paper independently. Joe will also explore recreation activities offered by the YMCA.

Objectives (Measurable Steps)

1. Joe will participate in the preseason evaluation process for soccer. The evaluation process will provide Joe with an individual score in (a) dribbling, (b) trapping, (c) heading, (d) shooting location and pace, (e) shot quality, (f) speed in 40-yard dash, (g) juggling, and (h) field play. Joe will examine his individual score in each segment of the evaluation and will compare his scores to the average high school player, the minimum score for players trying out for the team, and the maximum score for players trying out for the team. Based on the evaluation of his performance, Joe will establish three individual goals for improving his soccer skills over the season. At the end of the season, the coach and Joe will evaluate whether Joe has accomplished his three goals. Joe will meet two of the three individual goals he has established for the soccer season. At the end of the year, Joe will decide whether he will try out for soccer again during the next academic year.
2. Joe will participate in spring try outs for the high school baseball teams. There are three competitive teams for baseball. These are: Varsity, Jr. Varsity (B-squad), and C-squad. Joe will try out for the team with the personal goal of making one of the competitive squads. After the try out, Joe will review his evaluation results from the try out. The evaluation process will provide Joe with and individual score in (a) fielding ground balls, (b) fielding fly balls, (c) hitting the ball, (d) bunting the ball, (e) throwing for accuracy and velocity, and (f) 40-yard dash speed. Joe will examine his individual scores in each segment of the evaluation and will compare his scores to the average for high school players, the minimum score for players attempting to make the team, and the maximum score for players attempting to make the team. Joe will also identify the minimum score for players to make the team in each area. Based on these results Joe will establish three individual goals to improve his baseball skills regardless of whether he makes any of the competitive baseball teams as a sophomore. At the end of the year, Joe will decide whether he plans to try out for baseball again next year.
3. Joe will independently contact the YMCA and will identify three after-school recreational activities offered by the organization in which he could participate as a sophomore in high school. For each activity Joe will identify (a) the name of the activity, (b) the beginning and end of the season, (c) the cost, and (d) the sign-up period. He will do this with 100% accuracy as measured by conversation with the special education teacher.
4. Joe will participate in weight lifting after school at least two times per week for half an hour. Joe will document his participation by bringing a copy of the sign-in log for weight lifting to the special education teacher at least two times per month.
5. Joe will establish three goals for weight lifting for the academic year. With the assistance of the special education teacher, Joe will monitor his progress toward reaching these goals in weight lifting. At the end of the year, Joe will orally summarize his accomplishments and establish new goals for next year.

TRANSITION AREA

____Employment
__X__Home living
____Postsecondary education
____Recreation and Leisure
____Community participation

Future Adult Goals (What I Want After High School): I plan on living at home with my parents in the year after high school.

Present Level of Performance: While Joe and his parents anticipate Joe will live at home in the year after high school, Brigance assessment results indicate he currently lacks independent

(continued)

Sophomore Year IEP for Joe Site (continued)

living skills in (a) basic banking and checking, (b) use of credit and credit cards, (c) budgeting for expenses, and (d) independent living after high school (e.g. apartment living and roommates).

Transition Needs (What I Still Need to Do and Learn): I need to develop basic banking skills including the ability to operate my own checking account.

Transition Services/Activities (Student, Parent, and Professional)

1. During his sophomore year of high school, Joe and his family will open a savings account for Joe at a bank or credit union of their choice.
2. Joe and his special education teacher will visit a bank and gather information regarding the scope and types of services offered by a full service bank.
3. Joe and an adult (aide or teacher) will visit a credit union to gather information regarding the scope and types of services offered by a credit union.

Annual Goal (1 of 1 Goals): In sophomore math class, Joe will learn to independently operate both a savings and checking account with 90% accuracy as measured by the math teacher.

Objectives (Measurable Steps)

1. In a simulated in-class activity, Joe will independently complete a savings deposit slip with 100% accuracy on three of three attempts.
2. Joe will independently write five checks to predetermined businesses for a predetermined amount of money with 100% accuracy on three of three attempts.
3. During an examination in math, when given a check register with a predetermined amount of money, five cancelled checks, and one deposit amount, Joe will independently balance the account with 90% accuracy on three of three attempts.
4. Given a monthly bank statement with ten cancelled checks, three deposits, and two ATM withdrawals, Joe will independently reconcile the checkbook and monthly statement with 100% accuracy.
5. Joe will identify three ways in which a full service bank and a credit union are alike and three ways they are different.

Behavior Goal 10th Grade

Present Level of Performance: Joe becomes disrespectful and defiant in school on occasion during the school day. He becomes angry and may threaten others with verbal aggression or violent behavior.

Needs (What I Still Need to Do and Learn): I need to improve my self-control skills in the academic classroom and increase the amount of time I am working in the classroom without disrupting others.

Annual Goal: Joe will increase his level of self-control from a level of poor self-control to a level of effective self-control.

Objectives (Measurable Steps)

1. During daily work and listening activities in the general classroom, Joe will use learned techniques to redirect and control distractibility and remain on task for a fifteen-minute period

(continued)

in four of five daily opportunities over a two-week period as measured by data collected from teacher logs and teacher observation.

2. When assigned daily group tasks, Joe will comply with established group procedures without negative comment or emotional outburst. He will do this in three of four consecutive opportunities over a two-week period as measured by data collected from teacher log and teacher observation.
3. After complying with tasks and behavioral expectations, Joe will wait for reward and reinforcement without negative comments or emotional outburst in five of five situations as measured by teacher log and teacher observation.

Based on Evaluation Summary results, the IEP team decided to enroll Joe in a program of study which was non-college bound, with a focus on classes that provide an opportunity for "hands-on activities" during his sophomore year of high school. Course selection was made to maximize his interest in each class and to enhance his likelihood of success in each class. Joe's right to be included in the general classroom to the maximum extent appropriate (34 C.F.R. 300. 550, (b)) was weighed *with* his right to an individually designed educational program. As a result, the IEP team decided on the following class schedule: (1) Art, (2) Social Studies, (3) General English, (4) General Math, (5) General Science, and (6) a "pull out" class in special education focusing on self-advocacy and self-determination skills, life skills, and a provision for tutoring support with a focus on development of compensatory strategies for use in general education classes.

Note that Joe Site's sophomore year IEP includes one behavior goal. This goal could have been included under the areas of employment or postsecondary education in the transition plan or these behavior goals could stand alone in addition to the transition plan areas addressed in the IEP. Either approach would be appropriate for including the behavior goal in the IEP. Some families, teachers, and IEP members will want the academic and behavior goals to be integrated under the transition umbrella. Other IEP teams will choose to list academic and behavior goals as separate goal areas. Both decisions are appropriate and the location of these goals is an IEP team decision.

Summary of Transition Assessment Information from 10th Grade Evaluation

As a part of the ongoing assessment of Joe's transition needs in 10th grade, the following assessment tools were used to gather transition assessment information.

1. Transition Planning Inventory (TPI) (a global transition assessment instrument) (Clark & Patton, 1997),
2. Occupational Aptitude Survey and Interest Schedule (OASIS –3) (vocational interest and aptitude test) (Parker, 2002),
3. Arc Self-Determination Scale (Wehmeyer & Kelchner, 1995) and Post-test results of Steps to Self-Determination Knowledge Scale-Form B (Hoffman, Field, & Sawilowksy, 1995),
4. Review of academic progress and testing results as well as progress on behavioral IEP goals, and
5. Learning Styles Inventory (LSI) (Dunn, Dunn, & Price, 2003).

Transition Planning Inventory

In the 10th grade year, student, parents, and special education teacher completed the **Transition Planning Inventory**. The compilation of results from the transition planning team are as follows:

Employment Results indicate that parents and teacher strongly believe (student moderately believes) that student does not have the work habits and attitudes to keep a job and could be promoted with or without assistance.

Further Education and Training Results indicate that student, parents, and teacher all registered concern regarding student's knowledge of vocational/technical education.

Daily Living Results indicate concern regarding student's ability to manage money and live independently. Results are consistent with Brigance assessment findings (see Brigance assessment results in Appendix D).

Community Participation Parties agree that student does not know basic legal rights and responsibilities. Nor does student have ability to find and use community services and resources.

Self Determination Parties registered concern regarding student's ability to set personal goals, make personal decisions, and express feelings and ideas to others in a constructive way with confidence.

Communication Student needs to work toward improving listening skills.

Interpersonal Relationships Student, parents, and teacher register concern regarding student's ability to get along with adults in a school setting. Parents and teacher register similar concern regarding student's current capacity to get along with adults on the job. Student registers more confidence in his ability to get along on the job.

OASIS – 3

Results from the **OASIS – 3** for Joe Site indicate strong preference for employment in industrial careers (high interest—Stanine 7) and mechanical careers (high interest—Stanine 7). Student demonstrated moderate interest in physical performance careers (Stanine 5). Areas of low career interest included artistic, scientific, nature, selling, accommodating, humanitarian, and leading-influencing career areas (all Stanine 2).

Arc Self-Determination Scales

Results from the **Arc Self-Determination Scales** indicated student scores in self-realization subtest were high. Student scored in lower quartile compared to norm group in autonomy subtest.

Learning Styles Inventory (LSI)

The LSI and review of academic testing results and academic progress suggest student has strong preference for tactile (learning by doing) and visual learning styles. Auditory (listening) learning style is not area of preference.

Academic and Behavioral Results of Sophomore School Year

Joe continues to struggle with poor grades in his academic courses and has trouble relating to the importance of much academic coursework to his future. During sophomore year, Joe received a D− grade in his General Science course and got a D grade for each semester of General English. He has made some progress regarding his level of disrespect and defiance in class. He has demonstrated some gains in self-control and accepting feedback from adults. Additional work in these areas is warranted in the junior year IEP.

As a result of the evaluation of the student's accomplishments during the sophomore year, and with the additional transition assessment information and evaluation summary report, the student's IEP team designed and agreed to the following junior year IEP (see Junior Year IEP on pages 123–129).

As a result of the IEP, the IEP team decided on the following class schedule for Joe's junior year: (1) Auto Mechanics, (periods 2 and 3) community-based Technical Preparation (vocational placement), (4) General Social Studies, (5) General English, (6) General Math,

Junior Year IEP for Joe Site

Transition Planning IEP

TRANSITION AREA

____Employment
____Home living
_X_ Postsecondary education
____Recreation and Leisure
____Community participation

Future Adult Goals (What I Want After High School): I have decided that I want to be an auto repair technician.

Present Level of Performance: Joe participated in four job-shadowing experiences and, as a result of these and his summer work experience, he has developed an interest in becoming an auto repair technician. One of his job-shadowing experiences during his sophomore year was auto repair technician. Parents concur that this is a good career for Joe to explore.

Joe, his parents, and the special education teacher completed the Transition Planning Inventory (TPI). Results indicate that Joe has a lack of knowledge regarding vocational/technical education, which will be required for a career as an auto repair technician. Concern was registered regarding Joe's ability to set personal goals, make personal decisions, and express feelings and ideas to others in a constructive way.

OASIS-3 interest testing was completed in fall of sophomore year. Instrument identified mechanical careers, industrial careers, and physical performance careers as high and moderate interest. Auto careers are consistent with high career interest area according to test.

Results from Transition Planning Inventory assessment indicate concern regarding Joe's ability to set goals and make personal decisions. Post-test results from STEPS curriculum suggest Joe has better understanding of how to set goals but continues to have weak career planning skills. Goal setting remains an area of concern.

Transition Needs (What I Still Need to Do and Learn): I need to explore careers in auto repair and other related fields. I need to participate in community-based work exploration and I need to complete career exploration activities in school. I need to participate in vocational education classes to assist me in exploring this interest area. I need to explore what training I need to reach this career goal. I need to explore postsecondary education training sites and begin to establish career goals for myself.

Transition Services/Activities (Student, Parent, and Professional)

1. Joe and his parents will tour West Side Technical College and visit the auto repair program.
2. While visiting West Side Technical College, Joe will visit with the special needs coordinator. Joe will identify himself as a person with a disability during that visit and discuss disability-related services available to him at the technical college.

(continued)

Junior Year IEP for Joe Site (continued)

3. During his visit to the technical college, Joe will identify and list three accommodations offered at the technical college that are similar to those he is using in his high school classes.
4. In preparation for his senior year planning meeting, Joe (with help of school social worker), parents, and special education teacher will each complete the FPI.
5. Joe will take the Armed Services Vocational Aptitude Battery (ASVAB) during the junior year. Joe may study for this aptitude and interest test. (See website: www.march2success.com.)
6. With the assistance of the special education teacher, Joe will complete the C.I.T.E. Learning Styles Instrument in preparation for senior year planning meeting.

Annual Goal (1 of 2 Goals): Joe will participate in the high school auto repair program. Joe's knowledge and skills in the area of auto repair will move from little specific knowledge in the career area to moderate knowledge and improved skill in the career area.

Objectives (Measurable Steps)

1. Given twenty tools used in auto mechanics, Joe will correctly and verbally identify and explain the use of each tool with 100% accuracy to his auto mechanics teacher during an exam at the end of the first semester.
2. Given a twenty-step task analysis regarding changing oil in an automobile, Joe will independently change the oil in the vehicle with 100% accuracy on three of three attempts.
3. Joe will demonstrate the ability to remove a flat tire from an automobile and replace that flat tire with a new tire independently and with 100% accuracy on three of three attempts.

Annual Goal (2 of 2 Goals): In a general education English course in 11th grade, Joe will improve his ability and willingness to complete written assignments from unwilling to moderate willingness.

Objectives (Measurable Steps)

1. There are five major writing assignments in this English course. Joe will independently complete four of five writing assignments with minimal assistance from staff. Each assignment will be at least four double-spaced typewritten pages in length and will include no more than five punctuation mistakes. At least two of these papers will discuss auto related career issues.
2. Joe will independently run a spelling and grammar check on each for the five major papers turned in during 11th grade English. Each paper will include no more than three grammar or spelling mistakes.
3. Joe will independently use the Internet to identify at least three sources for each of the five major papers for 11th grade English.

TRANSITION AREA

_X_ Employment
____Home living
____Postsecondary education
____Recreation and Leisure
____Community participation

Future Adult Goals (What I Want After High School): I have decided that I want to be an auto repair technician.

Present Level of Performance: Joe participated in four job-shadowing experiences and as a result of these and his summer work experience, he has developed an interest in becoming an auto repair technician. One of his jobs shadowing experiences during his sophomore year was auto repair technician. He did not like his work experience in retail sales. Joe passed his basic standards test in reading and math. Parents concur that auto repair is a good career for Joe to explore.

(continued)

OASIS-3 interest inventory completed in fall of sophomore year. Instrument identified mechanical careers, industrial careers, and physical performance careers as high and moderate interest. Auto careers are consistent with high career interest area according to test.

Transition Planning Inventory results indicate that the IEP team has concerns regarding Joe's work habits and attitudes, and his ability to keep a job and get along with adults on a job site or in the school setting.

Transition Needs (What I Still Need to Do and Learn): I need to explore careers in auto repair and other automotive related fields. I need to participate in community based work exploration and I need to complete career exploration activities in school. I need to participate in vocational education classes to assist me in exploring this interest area.

Transition Services/Activities (Student, Parent, and Professional)

1. For his senior year, Joe (with the help of the school counselor), his parents, and the special education teacher will each complete a Future Planning Inventory to begin to identify Joe's transition needs in each transition area.
2. Joe will submit application to Rehabilitation Services and will complete the intake process.
3. Joe and his family will submit application to the Social Security Supplemental Security Income Program (SSI) and complete the intake process.

Annual Goal (1 of 1 Goals): Joe will participate in two nonpaid work exploration placements during the school year, with each lasting approximately ten weeks for two hours per day and four days per week. One of the ten-week explorations will be in the area of auto repair technician. The second will be in an additional auto related service area. At the end of each ten-week exploration, Joe's work performance will be evaluated by the site supervisor and Joe will receive ratings of 2.5 or better on the employer's rating scale (2.5 of possible 4).

Objectives (Measurable Steps)

1. Joe will answer the following questions regarding each of the two ten-week job explorations with 100% accuracy.
   (a) What is the entry-level training required of this job?
   (b) Do you have to have references to get this job?
   (c) Is there a dress code for the job?
   (d) Is insurance coverage provided to full-time employees? (If so, what kinds?)
   (e) How often are employees paid?
   (f) Can employees eat or drink on the job?
   (g) What is the policy regarding use of the telephone for personal reasons?
   (h) Are employees required to punch in or sign in?
   (i) Is there a policy regarding excused or unexcused absence from work?
2. Joe will discuss with two employees at each job site what they like and dislike about their current employment. Joe will submit to his instructor a written list of at least five likes and five dislikes for each of the two employees at each job site.
3. Joe will interview his direct supervisor on each job site. Based on an interview with the supervior, Joe will list ten general employment expectations of each supervisor.

TRANSITION AREA

____Employment
____Home living
____Postsecondary education
__X__ Recreation and Leisure
____Community participation

(continued)

Junior Year IEP for Joe Site (continued)

Future Adult Goals (What I Want After High School): I would like to participate in high school soccer and high school baseball. I would also like to gather more information about community-based recreation activities.

Present Level of Performance: Joe is involved in numerous leisure activities including swimming, fishing, canoeing, softball, and bike riding. He attends movies and sporting events. He listens to music, watches TV, participates in shopping and lawn care, and plays video games. Joe tried out for and made the C-level soccer squad for high school. Joe tried out for and made the C-level baseball squad for high school.

Joe established three personal goals for soccer during the year and successfully made progress toward all three goals. Joe's main goal was to win a starting position on the C-squad. Joe split time as a starter at outside mid-field. Joe's goals of increasing his speed and skill at dribbling and increasing his juggling skills were somewhat met. Joe did increase his skill level in each area but not to the level of skills identified in his goal.

Joe established three personal goals for the C-level baseball team. Joe was back-up third baseman for the squad and did play in many games. His personal goals were (a) to start on the ball team (played but did not start), (b) improve his hitting (some improvement noted), and (c) increase fielding of ground balls (Joe not satisfied with progress in fielding).

Transition Activities (What I Still Need to Do and Learn): I need to explore community based recreation and leisure activities. I need to improve my soccer and baseball skills and make the B-squad of each unit.

Transition Services/Activities (Student, Parent, and Professional)

1. Joe and his family will explore the costs, benefits, and locations of summer soccer camps.
2. Joe will try out for summer traveling community-wide soccer team.
3. Joe will sign up and participate in youth summer softball through the YMCA.
4. Joe will participate in after-school weight lifting activities.
5. Joe will try out for Junior Varsity Soccer team (B-squad)
6. Joe will try out for Junior Varsity Baseball team (B-squad)

Annual Goal (1 of 1 Goals): Based on personal evaluations gathered during try outs at soccer and baseball, Joe will establish and list three individual goals for the season in each sport. With the help of the special education teacher and coaches, Joe will monitor his progress toward these goals over the academic year. At the end of the academic year, Joe will write a four-page type-written paper listing his goals and summarizing his progress toward each goal. Joe will write this paper independently.

Objectives (Measurable Steps)

1. Joe will participate in the preseason evaluation process for soccer with the goal of making the Junior Varsity (B-Squad) team. The evaluation process will provide Joe with and individual score in (a) dribbling, (b) trapping, (c) heading, (d) shooting location and pace, (e) shot quality, (f) speed in forty-yard dash, (g) juggling, and (h) field play. Joe will examine his individual scores in each segment of the evaluation and will compare his scores to the average high school player, the minimum score for players trying out for the team, and the maximum score for players trying out for the team. Based on the evaluation of his performance, Joe will establish three individual goals for improving his soccer skill over the season. At the end of the season, the coach and Joe will evaluate whether Joe has accomplished his three goals. Joe will meet two of the three individual goals he has established for the soccer season. At the end of the year, Joe will decide whether he will try out for soccer again next academic year.

(continued)

2. Joe will participate in spring try outs for the high school baseball teams. There are three competitive teams for baseball. These are the Varsity baseball team, the Jr. Varsity (B-squad), and the C-squad. Joe will try out for the team with the personal goal of making the B Squad competitive squad. After the try out, Joe will review his evaluation results from the try out. The evaluation process will provide Joe with an individual score in (a) fielding ground balls, (b) fielding fly balls, (c) hitting the ball, (d) bunting the ball, (e) throwing for accuracy and velocity, and (f) forty-yard dash speed. Joe will examine his individual scores in each segment of the evaluation and will compare his scores to the average for high school players, the minimum score for players attempting to make the team, and the maximum score for players attempting to make the team. Joe will also identify the minimum scores for players to make the team in each area. Based on these results Joe will establish three individual goals to improve his baseball skills regardless of whether he makes any of the competitive baseball teams as a junior.
3. Joe will independently contact the YMCA and the community competitive summer soccer organization. Joe will visit each organization to find the answers to these questions. Joe will identify (a) the number and kinds of soccer team opportunities in which Joe might participate, (b) the beginning and end of the season, (c) the cost, (d) the sign-up period (e) whether there are any scholarships to defray the costs of participating. He will do this with 100% accuracy as measured by conversation with the special education teacher.
4. Joe will participate in weight lifting after school at least two times per week for half an hour. Joe will document his participation by bringing a copy of the sign-in log for weight lifting to the special education teacher at least two times per month.
5. Joe will establish three goals for weight lifting for the academic year. With the assistance of the special education teacher, Joe will monitor his progress toward reaching these goals in weight lifting. At the end of the year, Joe will orally summarize his accomplishments and will establish new goals for next year.

TRANSITION AREA

____Employment
__X__Home living
____Postsecondary education
____Recreation and Leisure
____Community participation

Future Adult Goals (What I Want After High School): I plan on living at home with my parents in the year after high school.

Present Level of Performance: Joe and his parents anticipate Joe will live at home in the year after high school. During sophomore year, Joe made great progress in banking and checking skills. He has demonstrated the ability to operate a checking account and write checks independently.

Brigance assessment results indicate Joe currently lacks independent living skills in (a) use of credit and credit cards, (b) budgeting for expenses, and (c) independent living after high school (e.g. apartment living and roommates). TPI assessment results from this year support concern of family, student, and teacher regarding Joe's abiltiy to manage money and live independently.

Transition Needs (What I Still Need to Do and Learn): I need to develop the knowledge and skill to use credit wisely.

Transition Services/Activities (Student, Parent, and Professional)

1. Joe and his special education teacher will visit a personal banker to discuss the process of applying for a credit card and how one might establish good credit.

(continued)

Junior Year IEP for Joe Site (continued)

2. In preparation for his senior year planning meeting, Joe will complete the component of the Brigance Assessment (home living and adaptive behavior test section) regarding independent living skills.

Annual Goal (1 of 1 Goals): Joe will demonstrate the knowledge and skills to apply for credit and use credit wisely.

Objectives (Measurable Steps)

1. On a test, when given twelve reasons for using credit, Joe will correctly identify five of six good reasons for using credit and five of six inappropriate reasons for using credit, as measured by the instructor.
2. In a simulated in-class activity, Joe will independently complete a simulated credit card application with 100% accuracy on three of three attempts.
3. Given a credit card bill, Joe will independently identify (a) the annual percentage rate of the card for both purchases and cash advances, (b) the minimum payment amount due, (c) the total credit card bill amount due, (d) the date the bill is due, and (e) the customer services number with 100% accuracy on three of three attempts.
4. In a simulated activity, when given a credit card bill that is incorrect, Joe will contact the credit card company and lodge a complaint with 100% accuracy.
5. On an exam, Joe will list four ramifications of losing your credit card or giving your credit card number to an irresponsible person.

TRANSITION AREA

____Employment
____Home Living
____Postsecondary education
____Recreation and Leisure
_X_Community participation

Future Adult Goals (What I Want After High School): I plan on having a driver's license and owning my own car after high school.

Present Level of Performance: Transition Planning Inventory (TPI) results indicate Joe does not have the ability to find and use community services and resources independently. Joe does not have a driver's license but both he and his parents want him to accomplish that goal. Joe needs to work toward improving listening skills.

Transition Needs (What I Still Need to Do and Learn): I need to take a community-based driver's education training program and pass my driver's education test.

Transition Services/Activities (Student, Parent, and Professional)

1. Joe and his special education teacher will contact three private driver's education training programs to find out cost and availability.
2. Joe will gather information by phone regarding driver's education.
3. Joe will contact the state to find out the location and times that the driver's permit test is given.
4. Joe, his parents, and his teacher will complete the Self-Determination and Self-Advocacy Skills Questionnaire in preparation for senior year planning meeting.

Annual Goal (1 of 2 Goals): Based on his parent's approval and support, Joe will participate in a community based private driver's education program and will pass the course. This will be measured by receipt of his certificate that documents that he has passed the course.

(continued)

Annual Goal (2 of 2 Goals): Joe will independently complete the driver's permit licensure examination at the community driver's license station and will receive a passing score. He will demonstrate this by receiving his driver's permit.

Behavior Goal 11th Grade

Present Level of Performance: All parties, including Joe, continue to register concern regarding Joe's ability to get along with adults in the school setting. While progress is being made, Joe continues to become somewhat disrespectful and defiant in school on occasion during the school day. Self-control and effective listening are areas of concern.

Needs (What I Still Need to Do and Learn): I need to improve my self-control skills in the academic classroom and increase the amount of time I am working in the classroom without becoming angry or disruptive.

Annual Goal (1 of 1 Goal): In the general education classroom, Joe will demonstrate improvement in the skill of handling frustration and anger by remaining under emotional control and by choosing a way to resolve a situation that demonstrates regard for the feelings of others and is staying engaged in the learning environment as measured by reducing the number of incidences related to these behaviors from three or four per month to one to zero per month.

Objectives (Measurable Steps)

1. Through direct teaching, role-play, and practice modeling, at the request of a teacher, Joe will verbally identify the six behaviors needed to demonstrate the skill of handling anger with 100% accuracy on three of three occasions.
2. Given redirection and a verbal reminder regarding how to handle anger, Joe will respond to redirection by remaining calm and verbalizing a plan to be respectful to the teacher and class without the need for further adult intervention on three of four consecutive occasions.
3. When Joe's behavior requires separation from the learning environment due to unsafe behavior demonstrated when angry, he will be able to verbalize alternative safe behavior choices and demonstrate specifically what a selected choice would have looked like in that situation without further behavioral escalation in 4 of 5 events.
4. When assigned daily group tasks, Joe will comply with established group procedures without negative comment or emotional outburst. He will do this in three of four consecutive opportunities as measured by data collected from teacher log and teacher observation.
5. After complying with tasks and behavioral expectations, Joe will wait for reward and reinforcement without negative comments or emotional outburst in five of five situations as measured by teacher log and teacher observation.

(7) a "pull out" class in special education focusing on self-advocacy and self-determination skills and life skills, and with provision for tutoring support with a focus on compensatory strategies for independence in learning environments.

Transition Planning for the Senior Year

As student gets closer to graduation, it is increasingly important to identify the adult services and agency support that student will need in life after high school. A critical and federally-required segment of transition planning is that the IEP identify the transition services needed by the student to succeed in life after high school. The IEP planning team must intensify their focus on needed transition services and address those needed services in the IEP. Again, to be effective, transition planning is a longitudinal process and the IEP results from the sophomore and junior years, as well as additional transition assessment information, are critical for the IEP team to be able to design an effective and appropriate IEP with the student for the senior year.

Since the student's last three-year reevaluation was completed in 9th grade (age fifteen), it is now time to complete another three-year reevaluation. The importance of the three-year reevaluation late in high school (junior or senior year) may be underestimated by the IEP planning team. For example, on occasion school psychologists are hesitant to repeat IQ testing on students at this late stage of their high school careers. This is especially true if the IQ testing has been relatively consistent over recent IQ testing. Often there are many competing needs for the school psychologist's time. Unfortunately, this IQ testing during the junior or senior school year is of critical importance. Some adult service providers will accept only "recent" IQ testing when considering whether students meet the criteria for their services. For some adult service providers, "recent" testing may be defined as within three years or less. Given the realities of shrinking adult service budgets and the need to prioritize who will receive services from adult providers, IEP teams need to make sure that a full three–year reevaluation is completed during the junior or senior school year. The student's disability and individual strengths and limitations need to be fully and recently documented as a part of the transition process.

Summary of Transition Assessment Information from 11th Grade Evaluation

As part of the ongoing assessment of transition needs and services in 11th grade, the following assessment tools were used to gather transition assessment information for the senior year.

1. Future Planning Inventory (assessment of future planning needs and goals) (see Appendix A [A-2]) (Miller & Corbey, 1993),
2. Armed Services Vocational Aptitude Battery (ASVAB)—Interest and Aptitude test) (U.S. Department of Defense, 1997),
3. Self-Determination and Self-Advocacy Skills Questionnaire (Appendix A [A-3]),
4. C.I.T.E. Learning Styles Inventory (Babich, et al., 1976) (Appendix A [A-4]),
5. Brigance Life Skills Inventory (home living and adaptive behavior test section) (Brigance, 1995), and
6. Review of academic progress and testing results as well as progress regarding behavioral IEP goals.

Future Planning Inventory

In spring of 11th grade year, student, parents, and special education teacher completed the **Future Planning Inventory**. Student completed his assessment with assistance from the school counselor. The compellation of results from the transition planning team are as follows:

Vocational Interest/Vocational Goals Student continues to narrow his career goal for after high school. Based on test results, student is now interested in becoming an auto body repair technician after high school.

Postsecondary Education Interest/Goals Student is interested in exploring postsecondary education/training as an auto body repair technician.

Home Living At this time, student and parents anticipate student will live at home in the year after high school. Student plans to move into his own apartment with friends as soon as he can afford it.

Recreation and Leisure Options Results indicate student is involved in numerous leisure activities including swimming, fishing, canoeing, softball and bike riding. Student attends movies and sporting events. Student listens to music, watches TV, participates in shopping and lawn care, and plays video games. Student participates in soccer (fall high school sport) and has participated in baseball (spring) as extracurricular activities during high school. Student has chosen to continue in soccer but not try out for baseball in his senior year.

Transportation Options Student currently gets around the community by walking, riding bike, and depending on others. Student has a driver's license at this time. He has access to his parent's car on occasion. Student would like to get his own vehicle.

Financial/Agency Support Student and parents would like to explore scholarships, Pell Grants, and loans for college.

Health Related Needs Last physical examination was in November of this school year. Student continues to take medication as discussed in the 9th grade Evaluation Summary Report.

Greatest Concern Student's greatest concern for 11th grade is "Getting trained as an auto body repair technician and getting my own car and place to live."

ASVAB Aptitude and Interest Survey Results

Student studied for and took the ASVAB test in March of his junior year. His Armed Forces Qualifying Test (AFQT) score was 45%. This score was 5% below the current 50% cut-off score for consideration of army recruitment. At this time, student is not interested in military as career. (NOTE: current medication and recent history of medication would negatively impact his capacity to enter military.) Interest section of ASVAB is consistent with student's chosen career. Strong interest and strong aptitude in mechanical and artistic career areas.

Self Determination and Self-Advocacy Questionnaire

Questionnaire was completed by student, parents, and teachers in 11th grade year. Based on the results of this criterion-referenced test:

- Student, parents, and teacher all register concern regarding student's ability to independently contact adult services providers and discuss needs and goals.
- Parents and teacher (to a lesser degree student) are concerned regarding student's ability and willingness to identify self as a person with a disability in order to get the support services needed on the job or in postsecondary education.
- Student does not lead own IEP team meetings.

C.I.T.E. Learning Style Inventory

Results indicate strengths in (a) visual language and visual numerical and (b) kinesthetic and tactile learning styles. Areas of least strength were (a) auditory learning styles (language and numerical) and (b) expressive learning styles (oral and written).

Brigance Life Skills Inventory

Results of this criterion-referenced assessment instrument given in 11th grade indicate that student currently lacks skills in (a) budgeting for expenses and (b) independent living after high school (e.g. apartment living and roommates). Results indicate student now understands and can use basic banking and checking skills, and understands and can use credit and credit cards.

Academic and Behavioral Results of Junior School Year

Student has made progress in understanding the importance of academic grades and the importance of acceptable behavior in general education classes. During his junior year, he received a C+ in Auto Mechanics, a B− in community based Technical Preparation coursework, a D+ in General Social Studies, a C− in General English and a C− in General Math. He continues to struggle with marginal grades in his academic courses and he has trouble relating to the importance of many academic courses to his future. Student has made some progress regarding his level of disrespect and defiance in class. He has demonstrated some gains in self-control and accepting feedback from adults. Additional work in these areas is warranted in the senior IEP.

As a result of the evaluation of the student's accomplishments during the junior year and with the additional transition assessment information and evaluation summary report, the student's IEP team designed and agreed to the following senior year IEP (see Senior Year IEP, pages 132-138).

Senior Year IEP for Joe Site

Transition Planning IEP

TRANSITION AREA

__X__ Employment
____ Home living
____ Postsecondary education
____ Recreation and Leisure
____ Community participation

Future Adult Goals (What I Want After High School): I have decided that I want to be an auto body repair technician. I am committed to becoming an auto body repair technician. I am no longer interested in auto mechanic training or auto repair technician.

Present Level of Performance: Joe, his parents, and the special education teacher have completed the future planning inventories and brought them to Joe's junior IEP conference. Joe participated in an auto mechanics training course in the technical preparation (tech-prep) strand of the high school's school-to-work program. With accommodations, Joe received a grade of C+ in

(continued)

the course but has decided that a different career in the automotive field is more to his liking. Joe and his parents believe that auto body repair technician may be a good career match for Joe to explore. Joe was accepted as a client of Rehabilitation Services (RS) at the end of his junior school year. Joe was not accepted for SSI services.

Student studied for and took the ASVAB test in March of his junior year. Armed Forces Qualifying Test (AFQT) score was 45%, or 5% below the current 50% cut-off score for consideration of army recruitment. At this time, Joe is not interested in military as career. Interest section of ASVAB is consistent with Joe's chosen career. Strong interest and strong aptitude in mechanical and artistic career areas.

Transition Needs (What I Still Need to Do and Learn): I need to continue to explore careers in auto related fields and particularly in auto body repair. Through the school-to-work program I would like to explore paid employment in an automotive related field.

Transition Services/Activities (Student, Parent, and Professional)

1. Joe and his parents will apply to the local Job Training Support Agency for assistance in finding and maintaining a job in the automotive field through the local school-to-work partnership.
2. Joe will complete the intake process at the local Job Training Support Agency.
3. Joe will develop a resume of work exploration and paid work experience along with a list of references for employment.
4. School staff will assist Joe in updating his entire academic and IQ testing so that all tests are current as he transitions from high school to adult life.
5. Joe will identify and list all the accommodations that he may need to be successful in paid work.

Annual Goal (1 of 2 Goals): If available, Joe will participate in a part-time job in the community. He will receive ratings of 2.5 or better on the employer's rating scale (2.5 of possible 4). Joe will do this with bi-weekly visits to the job site from a job coach, work experience coordinator, or school-to-work coordinator.

Objectives (Measurable Steps)

1. On a monthly basis, Joe will be evaluated by the employer/supervisor. As a result of these monthly evaluations, Joe will identify and write two work improvement goals. With the assistance of the work coordinator, Joe will monitor his personal progress toward his monthly goal.
2. Joe will independently evaluate his progress toward his monthly work goals and will independently write out a progress report each month.
3. Based on conversations with the school work coordinator, when provided with five strengths and five areas of needed improvement, Joe will listen to the conversation regarding strengths and limitations on the job site and will independently list four of five strengths and four of five areas needing improvement on a written form within ten minutes after completing the conversation.

Annual Goal (2 of 2 Goals): Given three work samples consisting of ten problems each, Joe will independently measure fractions, mixed numbers, and decimals at the 1/2, 1/3, 1/4, 1/8, 1/16, and 1/32 (or corresponding decimal levels) three of three times with 90% accuracy.

TRANSITION AREA

____Employment
____Home living
__X__ Postsecondary education
____Recreation and Leisure
____Community participation

(continued)

Senior Year IEP for Joe Site (continued)

Future Adult Goals (What I Want After High School): I have decided that I want to be an auto body repair technician. I am no longer interested in auto mechanic or auto repair technician training.

Present Level of Performance: Joe, his parents, and the special education teacher have completed the future planning inventories and brought them to Joe's senior IEP conference. Joe participated in an auto mechanics training course in the technical preparation (tech-prep) strand of the high schools school-to-work program. With accommodations, Joe received a grade of C+ in the course but has decided that a different career in the automotive field is more to his liking. Joe and his parents believe that auto body repair technician may be a good career match for Joe to explore. Joe was accepted as a client of Rehabilitation Services (RS) at the end of his junior school year. Joe was not accepted for SSI services. Joe is now interested in attending a technical college to be trained as an auto body repair technician.

OASIS – 3 interest inventory scores suggest strong interest in auto related careers as well as strong interest in artistic occupations.

Transition Needs (What I Still Need to Do and Learn): I need to continue to explore careers in auto related fields and particularly in auto body repair. Through the school-to-work program I would like to explore paid employment in a automotive related field. I need to explore postsecondary education training options in auto body repair.

Transition Services/Activities (Student, Parent, and Professional)

1. Joe and his parents will visit two technical colleges offering programs in auto body repair.
2. No later than December of senior year, Joe will apply for admission to technical college in an auto body repair program of choice.
3. The special education teacher will confirm the application for admission has been received.
4. Joe will take the admission test for the chosen technical college program.
5. Special education teacher will monitor admission into auto body program.
6. Joe and his family will set up an appointment with the special needs coordinator at technical college and will deliver his material to college to confirm his status as person with a disability at college.
7. Joe and special needs coordinator will identify and list accommodations that Joe will be using in his auto body program.
8. Joe will visit with his Rehabilitation Services (RS) counselor to discuss his Employment Plan and the support services he can expect to receive from RS when attending the technical college auto body program (e.g. transportation, RS assistance, support for tools and uniforms, etc.).
9. The special education teacher will obtain a copy of the first semester textbooks from the technical college auto body program and will teach needed auto body vocabulary to Joe.
10. Joe will organize a file of recent IEPs and test results to take with him to his technical college.

Annual Goal (1 of 2 Goals): Given a catalog of automotive parts, and a list of twenty parts to order, Joe will read the catalog independently (with the use of technological accomodations as needed) and, in a mock exercise, he will place an order for the correct twenty parts five of five times with 100% accuracy. He will also correctly calculate the cost of those parts, including state tax, five of five times with 100% accuracy.

Annual Goal (2 of 2 Goals): In a general education English activity, when given a list of fifty commonly-used auto body terms, Joe will orally read all fifty terms and will demonstrate the ability to orally define forty-five of the fifty (90%) accurately to the teacher.

(continued)

TRANSITION AREA

____Employment
____Home living
____Postsecondary education
_X_ Recreation and Leisure
____Community participation

Future Adult Goals (What I Want After High School): I would like to participate as a member of the varsity high school soccer team during my senior year. I am no longer interested in participating in high school baseball. I would like to play in a community soccer league after I graduate from high school.

Present Level of Performance: Joe is involved in numerous leisure activities including swimming, fishing, canoeing, softball, and bike riding. Joe attends movies and sporting events. He listens to music, watches TV, participates in shopping and lawn care, and plays video games. Joe tried out for and made the B-level soccer squad for high school. Joe tried out for and made the B-level baseball squad for high school.

Joe established three personal goals for soccer during the year and successfully made progress toward all three goals. Joe's main goal was to win a starting position on the B-squad. Joe split time as a starter and outside mid-field. Joe's goals of increasing his speed and skill at dribbling and increasing his juggling skills were somewhat met. Joe did increase his skill level in each area but not to the level of skills identified in his goal.

Joe established three personal goals for the B-level baseball team. Joe was back-up third baseman for the squad and did not play in many games. His personal goals were (a) to start on the ball team (played but did not start), (b) improve his hitting (some improvement noted), and (c) increase fielding of ground balls (Joe not satisfied with progress in fielding). During his senior year, Joe has chosen to focus on soccer and stop playing baseball.

Transition Needs (What I Still Need to Do and Learn): I need to explore community based recreation and leisure activities in soccer after high school. I need to improve my soccer skills and participate on the varsity soccer team.

Transition Services/Activities (Student, Parent, and Professional)

1. Joe will try out for the varsity soccer team with the goal of winning a starting position.
2. Joe will contact three community agencies and gather information regarding opportunities to play adult soccer after high school.

Annual Goal (1 of 1 Goals): Based on personal evaluations gathered during soccer try outs. Joe will establish and list three individual goals for the season. With the help of the special education teacher and coaches, Joe will monitor his progress toward these goals over the academic year. At the end of the academic year, Joe will write a four-page typewritten paper listing his goals and summarizing his progress toward each goal. Joe will write this paper independently.

Objectives (Measurable Steps)

1. Joe will participate in the preseason evaluation process for soccer with the goal of making the varsity (A-Squad) team. The evaluation process will provide Joe with an individual score in (a) dribbling, (b) trapping, (c) heading, (d) shooting location and pace, (e) shot quality, (f) speed in forty-yard dash, (g) juggling, and (h) field play. Joe will examine his individual scores in each segment of the evaluation and will compare his scores to the average high school player, the minimum score for players trying out for the team, and the maximum score for players trying out for the team. Based on the evaluation of his performance, Joe will establish

(continued)

Senior Year IEP for Joe Site (continued)

three individual goals for improving his soccer skill over the season. At the end of the season, the coach and Joe will evaluate whether Joe has accomplished his three goals. Joe will meet two of the three individual goals he has established for soccer season.

2. With the use of the Transition Advisory Committee website, Joe will independently identify and contact three community recreation and leisure organizations that have some level of participation with community soccer. Joe will identify himself as a young adult with a disability and will gather information regarding (a) the kinds of soccer activities provided by the organization, (b) whether there is an adult soccer opportunity through the organization, and (c) the costs of participating in soccer activities. Joe will gather this information with 90% accuracy as measured by the special education teacher.
3. Joe will participate in weight lifting after school at least two times per week for half an hour. Joe will document his participation by bringing a copy of the sign-in log for weight lifting to the special education teacher at least two times per month.
4. Joe will establish three goals for weight lifting for the senior academic year. With the assistance of the special education teacher, Joe will monitor his progress toward reaching these goals in weight lifting. At the end of the year, Joe will orally summarize his accomplishments and will establish new goals for the next year.

TRANSITION AREA

____Employment
_X_ Home living
____Postsecondary education
____Recreation and Leisure
____Community participation

Future Adult Goals (What I Want After High School): I plan on living at home with my parents in the year after high school, but I would like to consider moving into my own apartment when I can afford it.

Present Level of Performance: Joe and his parents anticipate Joe will live at home in the year after high school. During junior year, Joe made great progress in using credit and credit cards wisely and effectively.

Brigance assessment results in 11th grade indicate Joe currently lacks independent living skills in budgeting for expenses and independent living after high school (e.g. apartment living and roommates).

TPI assessment results from this year support concern of family, student, and teacher regarding Joe's ability to manage money and live independently.

Transition Needs (What I Still Need to Do and Learn): I need to develop the knowledge and skill to live independently in an apartment.

Transition Services/Activities (Student, Parent, and Professional)

1. With the use of the newspaper, Joe will identify three possible apartments that he and a roommate would find acceptable.
2. Joe and his parents will visit two apartments in the community. Joe will gather information regarding costs of renting an apartment (e.g. monthly rent cost, utility costs, deposit costs and lease features.)

Annual Goal (1 of 1 Goals): Joe will demonstrate the knowledge and skills of independent living.

(continued)

Objectives (Measurable Steps)

1. When asked the costs of renting an apartment, Joe will list at least five realistic costs of renting an apartment on three of three occasions.
2. On a test regarding independent living, Joe will list three positive and three negative consequences associated with having a roommate.
3. Given a lease contract for an apartment, Joe will independently read the contract and will answer six of six questions with 100% accuracy.

   Are utilities included in the cost of the apartment per month?

   If not, what utilities am I required to pay each month?

   What is the deposit required to rent the apartment?

   How and when do I get my deposit back after I leave the apartment?

   How and why can I break the lease?

   Can I be evicted from the apartment for parties or noise?

TRANSITION AREA

____Employment
____Home living
____Postsecondary education
____Recreation and Leisure
_X_ Community participation

Future Adult Goals (What I Want After High School): I plan to participate as a member of the community after graduation. I plan to use community resources and advocate for my own goals.

Present Level of Performance: Student has received a driver's license at this time. He uses his parents' car as available for transportation.

TPI results indicate Joe needs to work toward improving listening skills.

Self-Determination and Self-Advocacy Questionnaire results indicate (a) parties are concerned regarding Joe's ability to independently contact adult service providers and discuss his needs and goals, (b) parties are concerned regarding Joe's ability and willingness to self-identify as a person with a disability in order to get the support services needed in life after high school. Joe does not lead own IEP team meeting at this time.

CITE Learning Style Inventory results indicate Joe is a visual and kinesthetic-tactile learner. Weakest learning styles include auditory and expressive.

Transition Needs (What I Still Need to Do and Learn): I need to improve my ability to gather information from community agencies and improve my self-advocacy skills.

Transition Services/Activities (Student, Parent, and Professional)

1. Joe will contact the Center for Independent Living. He will independently find out three services offered to adults with disabilities by this community agency.
2. Joe will visit the website of community resources and will identify two additional adult agencies that offer self-support groups for persons with disabilities.

Annual Goal (1 of 1 Goals): Joe will attend and lead his senior year IEP meeting.

(continued)

Senior Year IEP for Joe Site (continued)

Objectives (Measurable Steps)

1. During the IEP meeting, Joe will introduce all the team participants.
2. During the IEP meeting, Joe will discuss two personal strengths and two limitations.
3. During the IEP meeting, Joe will identify at least three goals for the academic year, and he will state his vocational and educational goals for after high school.
4. During the IEP meeting, Joe will identify at least three academic accommodations he will use during the upcoming academic year.
5. During the IEP meeting, Joe will use SHARE behaviors (S—sit up straight, H—have a pleasant voice, A—activate his listening, R—relax during the meeting, and E—engage in appropriate eye contact. (See discussion of the Self Advocacy Strategy [Van Reusen, et al., 1994] in Chapter 3).
6. On a Likert scale with five being "excellent" and 1 being "poor" demonstration of these SHARE behaviors, Joe and his special educator will rate Joe's performance as four or above during three of three simulated IEP meetings.

Behavior Goal 12th Grade

Present Level of Performance: All parties, including Joe, continue to register concern regarding Joe's ability to get along with adults in the school setting. While progress is being made, Joe continues to become somewhat disrespectful and defiant in school on occasion during the school day. Self-control and effective listening are areas of concern.

Needs (What I Still Need to Do and Learn): I need to improve my self-control skills in the academic classroom and increase the amount of time I am working in the classroom without becoming angry or disruptive.

Annual Goal (1 of 1 Goals): Provided with direct instruction, Joe will demonstrate improvement in the skill of accepting feedback and direction from adults. He will do this by listening calmly to what the adult says, asking questions or verbalizing his point of view appropriately when he does not understand, and accepting the decision of the adult without arguing or opposition, as measured by reducing the number of incedents related to these behaviors from his current range of one to two per week to one or no incedents per week over a month-long period of time.

Objectives (Measurable Steps)

1. When discussing a problem with an adult, Joe will face the adult and allow the adult to finish what they are saying without interrupting, arguing, or opposition before replying at least 75% of the time as measured by teacher log.
2. Given the opportunity to state his account of a problem, Joe will speak calmly, using school appropriate language without name-calling or threatening, then listen to the adult's feedback and accept the decision of the adult without argument at least 75% of the time as measured by teacher log.
3. When assigned consequences from an adult as a result of a poor behavioral choice, Joe will accept the follow-through with the consequences without argument or opposition in 75% of situations as measured by teacher log.
4. Joe will, independent of additional intervention, accept constructive feedback or decisions from all adult authority figures in the school environment without arguing, refusal, or further behavioral escalation in 85% of situations based on teacher report and administrative records.

Summary of Joe Site's Transition Plan

When summarizing transition assessment information and completing longitudinal transition evaluation, Johnson, et al., (2004) suggest that the IEP team:

- Focus on the student's postschool goals in each transition area.
- Look at information across all transition planning areas and interpret the data.
- Review the student's present levels of interest and preferences in each transition area and focus on the relationship between the student's current skill levels and postschool goals.
- Consider how the student's disability will affect the student's goals in adult life.
- Consider what the student will need to learn to meet his or her post-high school goals.

Also, we suggest you are careful to conduct a thorough and comprehensive transition assessment in each of the identified transition assessment model components.

In the case of Joe Site, we have attempted to integrate these concepts into Joe Site's longitudinal plan. First, you will note that the transition evaluation included a broad array of twelve transition assessment tools over the freshman, sophomore, junior, and senior school years. The following transition assessment tools were used to evaluate Joe Site's transition needs, interests, preferences, and goals:

1. Future Planning Inventory (Miller & Corbey, 1993) (See Appendix A [A-2]) (future planning assessment)
2. Interest Determination Exploration and Assessment System (IDEAS) (Johansson, 1996) (vocational assessment)
3. Steps to Self-Determination (STEPS): Self-Determination Knowledge Scale—Form A (Hoffman, Field, & Sawilowksy, 1995) (self-determination and self-advocacy assessment)
4. Brigance Life Skills Inventory (Brigance, 1995) (life skills assessment)
5. Transition Planning Inventory (TPI) (Clark & Patton, 1997) (comprehensive transition assessment)
6. Occupational Aptitude Survey and Interest Inventory (OASIS – 3) (Parker, 2002) (vocational assessment)
7. Arc Self-Determination Scales (Wehmeyer & Kelchner, 1995) (self-determination and self-advocacy assessment)
8. Steps to Self-Determination (STEPS): Self-Determination Knowledge Scale—Form B (Hoffman, Field, & Sawilowksy, 2005) (self-determination and self-advocacy assessment)
9. Learning Styles Inventory (LSI) (Dunn, Dunn, & Price, 2003) (learning styles assessment)
10. Armed Services Vocational Aptitude Battery (ASVAB) (U.S. Department of Defense, 1997) (vocational assessment)
11. Self-Determination and Self-Advocacy Skills Questionnaire (Appendix A [A-3]) (self-determination and self-advocacy assessment) and,
12. C. I. T. E. Learning Styles Inventory (Babich, et al., 1976) (Appendix A [A-4]) (learning styles assessment)

These tools were used along with an ongoing review of progress in meeting annual goals and short term objectives, an ongoing review of academic progress and testing, as well as an ongoing review of progress regarding behavioral IEP goals to assist the IEP team in designing an individual education program that will engage the student in the process of preparation for life after high school.

Over the three-year transition planning process, the student, family, and educators worked as a team to organize and complete many activities and to apply for adult services. Over the three-year period, activities in the IEP included:

1. involving student and family in use of websites including the community resource websites (e.g. www.hennepinCTIC.com).
2. exploration of services through the YMCA.
3. participation in school-based extracurricular activities.
4. visitation with full-service bank and credit union.
5. tour of two technical colleges.
6. visitation with special needs coordinators of technical colleges.
7. visitation with military recruiter (to take ASVAB test).
8. contact with private driver's education program.
9. gathering of information regarding driver's license examination.
10. updating of IQ and academic testing.
11. admission testing for a specific technical college/auto body repair program.
12. organization of file including recent IEPs/ test results for transfer to technical college.
13. exploration of community resources related to self-advocacy.

Specific agencies that the student applied to for services as a part of transition planning included:

1. application to Rehabilitation Services (RS) (student accepted).
2. application for Social Security Services (denied).
3. application for local Job Training Support Agency (student accepted).
4. application to technical college auto repair program (student ultimately accepted).

Based on the successful transition plan and the effective use of transition assessment information,

- student remained engaged in his high school experience.
- student graduated with a plan to succeed in life after high school.
- student had communicated with and become the client of adult agencies necessary for him to be successful in life after high school.
- student believed he belonged in post-high school education.

As noted in Chapter 1, the transition plan is the engine of the IEP process for secondary-aged students. The transition plan drives all curricular decisions as well as helps the IEP team to define instructional goals and objectives.

CHAPTER ACTIVITIES

Designing an IEP and developing a longitudinal transition plan is a team process. The IEP team is always left with the choice of including some goals but not others in the IEP for each student. For this activity, review the sophomore and junior year transition plans for Joe Site as included in this chapter. Based on the assessment information and the interests and preferences of the student, please write two additional transition goals and at least three short-term objectives for each transition goal for the senior year IEP for Joe Site.

DISCUSSION QUESTIONS

What are the implications of No Child Left Behind (NCLB) in secondary schools? How can transition assessment data be used for planning high school IEPs within this context?

CHAPTER REFERENCES

Apling, R. N. & Jones, N. L. (January 5, 2005). *CRS report for congress—Individuals with disabilities education act (IDEA): Analysis of changes made by P. L. 108–446*. Washington; DC. Congressional Research Service, The Library of Congress.

Babich, A. M., Burdine, P., Albright, L., & Randol, P. (1976). *C.I.T.E. learning styles instrument*. Retrieved July 26, 2005 from http:wvabe.org/cite.htm

Brigance, A. H. (1995). *Life skills inventory*. North Billerica, MA: Curriculum Associates.

Clark, G. M. & Patton, J. R. (1997). *Transition planning inventory*. Austin, TX: PRO-ED.

Corbey, S., Miller, R. J., Severson, S. & Enderle, J. (1993). *Teaching the possibilities: Identifying individual transition needs.* St. Paul, MN: Minnesota Department of Education.

Dunn, R., Dunn, K., & Price, G. E. (2003). *Learning styles inventory.* Lawrence, KS: Price Systems, Inc.

Flexer, R. W., Simmons, T. J., Luft, P., & Baer, R. M. (2001). *Transition planning for secondary students with disabilities.* Upper Saddle River, NJ: Merrill and Prentice Hall.

Field, S. & Hoffman, A. (2005). *Steps to self-determination: A curriculum to help adolescents learn to achieve their goals (2nd ed.)*. Austin, TX: PRO-ED.

Hoffman, A., Field, S., & Sawilowsky, S. (1995). *Self-determination knowledge scale.* Austin, TX: PRO-ED.

Johansson, C. B. (1996). *Interest determination, exploration and assessment system*. Bloomington, MN: NCS Pearson, Inc.

Johnson, D., Corbey, S., & Hoff, M. (2004). Transition. In M. Hoff (Ed.). *Burnsville–Eagan–Savage school district: Special education due process manual* (pp. 112–144). Burnsville, MN: Burnsville–Eagan–Savage School District.

Miller, R. J. & Corbey, S. A. (1993). Future planning inventories. In S. A. Corbey, R. J. Miller, S. Severson, & J. Enderle (Eds.). *Teaching the possibilities: Identifying individual transition needs*. St. Paul, MN: Minnesota Educational Services. pp. 17–31.

Parker, R. M. (2002). *Occupational aptitude survey and interest schedule-third edition.* Austin, TX: PRO-Ed.

U.S. Department of Defense. (1997). *Armed services vocational aptitude battery (ASVAB).* Washington, DC: Author.

Van Reusen, A. K., Bos, C. S., Schumaker, J. B., & De Shler, D. D. (1994). *Self-advocacy strategy for education and transition planning*. Lawrence, KS: Edge Enterprises.

Wehmeyer, M. L., & Kelchner, K. (1995). *The Arc self-determination scale*. Arlington, TX: The ARC of the United States.

CHAPTER 10

The Collaborative Transition Model: An Interdisciplinary Approach to District-Wide Transition Planning

The Collaborative Transition Model is a systematic approach that addresses the active recruitment and collaboration of school and community members, including students with disabilities, teachers, support personnel, school administrators, adult service providers, parents, postsecondary educators, and employers. Figure 10.1 presents a six-stage interdisciplinary model designed to address the collaborative involvement of key stakeholders in the transition planning process.

Since schools have both a legal and ethical obligation to prepare students for the challenges of adult life, the primary responsibility for coordinating district wide transition services is often assumed by the local educational agency (LEA). Accordingly, the initial planning for implementing the Collaborative Transition Model can be conducted by school personnel. A fundamental goal of this model is to facilitate the cooperative planning required for successful transitions between grade levels and from school to postschool settings. These planning procedures can be outlined in the early stages of the model by an internal steering committee.

Step One: Internal Steering Committee

The collaborative transition process begins with the development of an internal steering committee. Ideally, this change team is comprised of a small but highly motivated group of stakeholders who share a common belief about the need for district wide transition planning procedures. Vortruba (1981) suggests that organizing a change effort around a small team often generates the desired outcomes and overall influence more efficiently than a large, more cumbersome committee. The primary objective of the internal steering committee is to obtain the support and cooperation of school district administrators, local agency representatives, employers, parents, educators, and students. The collective support of these interest groups is vital to the success of all future transition planning efforts. It is critical, therefore, that their commitment to the transition planning initiative be established during the beginning stages of the process. Once the steering committee has established a nucleus of community support, an interdisciplinary core team can be developed to plan and execute the remaining phases of the model.

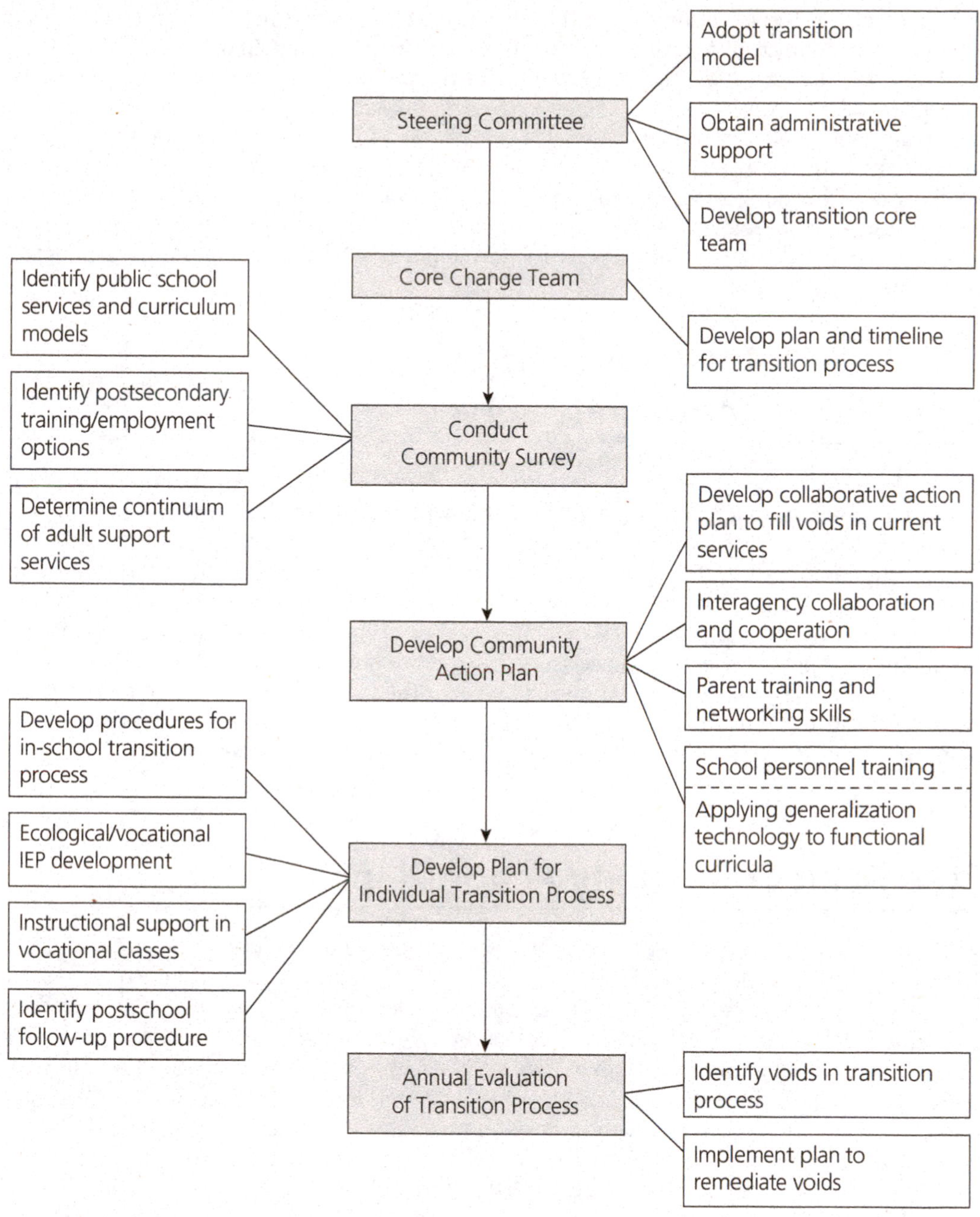

Figure 10.1

Step Two: Transition Core Team

Once the steering committee has established a nucleus of community support for implementing the Collaborative Transition Model, a transition core team must be established to plan and implement the remaining phases of the process. Composition of the core team is dependent upon the continuum of service providers within the school district, local agencies, postsecondary educators, and employers. In this regard, rural districts will often have fewer service providers within the community, and therefore the size of the transition core team will be smaller when compared to a school district located in an urban area. In one rural area in central Wisconsin, several districts formed a cooperative that increased the pool of core team representatives and also reduced the degree of service replication between the districts. Ideally, core team membership should include but not be limited to the following: students with special education needs, parents, school administrators, teachers/support personnel, employers, adult service providers, and postsecondary educators/support staff. At this juncture, the internal steering committee merges with the transition core team and assumes the complexities of community-wide transition planning and the development of a timeline for completion of the remaining phases of the model.

Step Three: Community Survey

The initial responsibility of the transition core team is to evaluate the continuum of transition services and program options currently available within the school district and community. Formal and/or informal assessment of public school services and curriculum models will enable the core team to determine if voids exist in relationship to in-school transition programming. In addition, this needs assessment will examine the availability of local postschool training options and employment opportunities as they pertain to individuals with disabilities. Local adult support services also need to be assessed to determine the extent to which they are being utilized by special populations as they exit the local school system and enter postsecondary settings. Information from the community surveys will enable the transition core team to address the most critical barriers to district-wide transition planning.

Step Four: Community Action Plan

After completing the school and community needs assessment, the transition core team can analyze the data to determine where voids in the continuum of services currently exist. Once the voids are determined, the transition core team develops an action plan to rectify the most critical voids in the district and community. The needs assessment may reveal, for example, that local vocational rehabilitation services are readily available to individuals with learning disabilities but less available to individuals with emotional disabilities. In this scenario, the transition core team would develop an action plan to expand the availability of vocational rehabilitation services to individuals with emotional disabilities. In yet another example, the needs assessment may reveal that high school students with disabilities routinely have their occupational interests and vocational aptitudes assessed, while middle school students with disabilities do not receive similar evaluations. In this situation, the transition core team would develop an action plan to integrate the use of occupational interest and vocational aptitude assessments within the local middle schools, if the team considered this an important element in the transition process.

The transition core team can also use the action plan concept to provide public awareness activities about district-wide transition planning. Awareness activities such as parent workshops, self-determination training for students with disabilities, staff development for school personnel, and interagency and employer workshops can all be provided to ensure that key stakeholders have the awareness and the skills to participate in related planning activities. The fundamental purpose of the community action plan is to ensure that existing voids are addressed and that key stakeholders in the transition process have an opportunity to acquire the skills needed to successfully participate as the transition process is being implemented.

In numerous school districts where the Collaborative Transition Model has been implemented, several topics have emerged as priorities with respect to community action planning. These include: (a) interagency collaboration; (b) parent training for the transition process; (c) student training for participation in the IEP process; and (d) staff development for school personnel.

Interagency Collaboration

Sitlington, et al. (1996) outlined the need for cooperative transition planning between educational and community service providers in order for students with disabilities to experience a seamless transition from secondary schools to postschool adult life. According to the IDEA 2004 legislation, interagency linkages must be established and documented on the IEP prior to a student's departure from the public school setting. Moreover, improved collaboration between secondary schools and postsecondary educational programs, including technical colleges and universities, will increase the likelihood that students are properly prepared for the academic, vocational, and personal/social demands of adult training programs.

Parent Training

Parent involvement in the transition planning process is another vital concern of the transition core team. Parent education activities can be successful in preparing parents to be effective advocates for services and knowledgeable consumers of the various adult services to which their children may be entitled. There are four fundamental outcomes associated with parent training activities. First, parents should become oriented to the continuum of adult service providers that assist individuals with disabilities. Second, parents should become familiar with the specific roles and responsibilities of key service providers including special educators, vocational educators, rehabilitation personnel, guidance counselors, etc. Third, parents must become aware of their roles and responsibilities with respect to the transition planning process and, lastly, parents need to understand why students with disabilities need to achieve self-determination skills such as full participation in the IEP planning process.

Parents have a critical role to play in the transition planning process. If parents are given an opportunity to learn about the roles and responsibilities of each stakeholder and service provider associated with their child, they will be able to provide invaluable input as a member of the transition planning team.

Student Training

According to Field, et al. (1998), students with disabilities need to be involved in all aspects of the transition planning process. Student participation in the IEP/transition meetings is vital to the successful implementation of district-wide transition procedures. In order for students with disabilities to fully participate in the IEP/transition process, they must be prepared to assume the role of an active IEP team member. The action plan that addresses this important consideration can be oriented around three phases: pre-planning phase, planning phase, and the plan implementation phase (Sitlington, et al., 1996).

Pre-Planning Phase To promote student involvement in the IEP/transition planning process, the transition core team can use the following instructional approaches during the preplanning phase and prior to the IEP meeting:

Discuss the purpose of the IEP/transition meeting.
Show video of an IEP/transition meeting.
Discuss roles of IEP meeting participants.

Review student's assessment information.
Conduct role-play simulations of an IEP meeting.
Introduce student to IEP team members.
Assist student with developing a list of questions to ask during IEP meeting.
Assist student with developing a list of personal goals to share at meeting.
Discuss effective nonverbal communication skills.
Discuss effective verbal communication skills.
Review previous IEP goals and objectives.
Develop a list of instructional accommodations needed.
Develop a list of curricular accommodations needed.

Planning Phase Once the pre-planning activities have been implemented by the transition core team, students may become active members of the IEP transition team. During the meeting, students should be encouraged to engage in meaningful discussions with other team members. A sample of behaviors that can be demonstrated during the IEP meeting include the following:

Introduce team members.
Express interests and abilities.
Review special needs and/or limitations.
Review educational goals.
Ask for feedback from team members.
Express personal goals.
Request reasonable accommodations and support.
Express personal responsibility for goal setting.
Express personal responsibility for goal attainment.
Review new planning goals and objectives.
Thank members for attending the meeting.

Plan Implementation Phase After students have successfully participated in their individualized IEP meeting, they must now be prepared by the core team to carry out the transition goals and objectives indicated on the IEP. As an outcome of the planning process, students should have a complete understanding of their individual role in implementing the goals and objectives stated within the plan. Additional self-determination activities that can be implemented by students with disabilities during this phase include the following:

Attend class on time.
Request instructional accommodations when needed.
Request testing accommodations when needed.
Exhibit appropriate nonverbal behavior.
Exhibit appropriate verbal behavior.
Organize study habits and study schedule.
Investigate postschool educational options.
Investigate postschool employment options.
Explore adult support services and eligibility requirements.
Participate in all school-to-adult life transition meetings.

School Personnel Training

Another major effort to be undertaken by the core team concerns the training of school personnel. In order for school personnel to fully participate in transition planning procedures, they must be given an opportunity to learn about their roles and responsibilities within the process. Sitlington, et al. (1996) identified key stakeholders within the school that must become involved in the transition planning process. These include the following: special educators, guidance personnel, secondary and postsecondary educators, work experience staff, job coaches, support services personnel, students, parents, and adult service providers.

In addition to learning about the formal transition process, school personnel must also become aware of their role in providing career development opportunities for students with special education needs. School personnel must equip students with the academic, daily living, social, and occupational skills needed to be successfully independent after high school. Educational forums such as staff development seminars, district in-services, online courses, and conferences can be used to acquaint teachers with effective strategies for integrating career development content into existing curricula.

Step Five: Individualized Transition Process

Individualizing the transition process to schools serving students with disabilities is another important responsibility of the transition core team. During this phase of the model, the core team must collaborate with school personnel to resolve the following issues: (a) identification of students to be targeted for transition services during the initial stages of the process, and (b) development of systematic procedures for in-school transition planning.

Identification of Students for Transition Planning

Formal transition planning procedures must be established throughout the school district. Best practice in transition planning would suggest that transition assessment begin no later than age fifteen, and preferably earlier. IDEA 2004 requires that transition planning begin for each student with a disability at sixteen years of age. Students who are sixteen years of age and in their final years of high school are in critical need of immediate planning. To ensure successful postsecondary outcomes for these high-priority students, they must receive information about postsecondary educational opportunities, employment options, and adult support services at least one full year before completing high school. This process is often more complex for students who are living in rural communities. Students from rural areas must often be prepared to pursue postsecondary education or employment some distance from their home community. Issues such as transportation, independent living, community mobility, and financial considerations need to be resolved in advance of high school graduation.

Another important period that requires formal planning is the middle school to high school juncture. Studies have shown that students with mild disabilities often do not participate in the full range of secondary vocational programs (Lombard, Hazelkorn, & Neubert, 1992). Formal transition planning may occur at the middle school to high school juncture to ensure students are placed in secondary school courses that are in line with their interests, abilities, preferences, and personal goals. Students with disabilities who are given the opportunity to enroll in academic and/or vocational programs of choice will be better prepared to make appropriate choices with respect to postsecondary education and/or employment.

In-School Transitional Planning Procedures

The next programmatic concern for the core team is the identification, development, and implementation of a viable in-school transition process. When possible, this process should take full advantage of existing procedures to reduce the degree of service replication. The primary components of in-school transition planning include: (a) transition assessment procedures, (b) IEP development, (c) instructional support for students enrolled in academic and vocational classes, and (d) postschool follow-up procedures.

Transition Assessment Procedures

Transition assessment has been defined as an individualized, ongoing process that assists students with disabilities and their families to define goals to be included in their individualized education programs (IEPs) as they prepare for adult roles. Adult roles can include employment, postsecondary education or training programs, independent living, community involvement, and social/personal relationships. Valid assessment data serve as the common thread in the transition process and form the basis for planning and placement decisions regarding adult roles (Sitlington, et al., 1996). The use of both formal and informal assessment approaches has been illustrated elsewhere in this text. According to Sitlington, et al. (1996), the broad purposes for conducting transition assessment include the following:

1. To determine students' level of career development when planning transition assessment activities.

2. To assist students with disabilities to identify their interests, preferences, strengths, and abilities in relation to postsecondary goals, including employment opportunities, postsecondary education and training opportunities, independent living situations, community involvement, and personal/social goals.

3. To determine appropriate placements within educational, vocational, and community settings that facilitate the attainment of these postsecondary goals.

4. To determine and facilitate students' self-determination skills.

5. To determine the accommodations, supports, and services individuals with disabilities will need to attain and maintain their postsecondary goals related to employment, postsecondary education/training programs, independent living, community involvement, and social/personal roles/relationships.

IEP Procedures

A fundamental purpose of transition assessment activities is the development of outcome-oriented transition goals and related objectives for the student's IEP. When formal and informal assessment data are available, the IEP/transition team will be able to develop a plan that takes into account the student's future or postsecondary goals, the skills needed to succeed in the future setting, and the assistance needed from support staff and/or adult service providers. With the benefit of both formal and informal transition assessment data, team members will be able to include the following elements within the IEP: (a) outcome-oriented goal statements that describe where the student is going with respect to future school or postsecondary settings; (b) short-term objectives that describe the entry-level skills needed to successfully enter the future settings; (c) instructional strategies that describe what educators will do to promote the student's acquisition of needed entry-level skills; (d) generalization strategies that describe how the student can learn to transfer skills from their current setting to future settings; (e) maintenance strategies that describe how the student can be monitored to determine if skills are being generalized into settings outside the classroom, and (f) interagency linkage statements that indicate what role(s) agencies may play in the school-to-postsecondary transition process.

Instructional Support

The next procedural concern of the transition core team is to determine the level of instructional support students with disabilities must receive while enrolled in general education classes. According to the IDEA 2004, students must be placed in secondary courses that prepare them for their postsecondary goals. If students are to have access to the full range of academic and vocational program options, general educators must receive instructional support from special education staff to ensure student success. Although traditional programming may provide support to students in the context of a resource room, it is often necessary for special education staff to offer support within the general education classroom itself.

Instructional support can be broken down into two categories, direct instructional support and indirect instructional support. Direct instructional support generally refers to face-to-face classroom interactions between a special educator and students with special education needs or face-to-face interactions between a special education teacher and vocational or academic instructors. Indirect instructional support refers to activities that are carried out by a special educator that help build a foundation for inclusion of special populations in either vocational and/or academic courses of study. Indirect instructional support activities do not typically include classroom interactions but do include supportive activities such as staff development/inservice, vocational assessment, administrative support, and interdisciplinary planning.

Direct Instructional Support Providing direct instructional support is the component of the Collaborative Transition Model which impacts students with disabilities and their general education instructors most directly. These face-to-face interactions typically occur in three settings: academic vocational labs, special education resource rooms, or work experience/apprenticeship community sites. One fundamental purpose of providing direct support is to ensure that students with special education needs are given the assistance they need to complete their courses of study successfully. Another goal is to help general educators provide effective instruction to all students within their lab or classroom settings. If special populations are to succeed within the regular vocational or academic classrooms, then those students and their instructors must receive meaningful support from special education personnel. Direct instructional support activities can be categorized into four areas: instructional accommodations, materials and equipment modification, testing options, and grading options.

Instructional Accommodations As indicated earlier, special education personnel typically receive substantial training in effective instructional approaches. These approaches or strategies are designed to accommodate the information-processing difficulties often experienced by students with disabilities. In effect, these strategies represent "best practices" and are, therefore, beneficial to all students in the general education classroom. To provide quality instruction in general education settings, it is often necessary to understand the unique abilities and learning-style preferences of each and every student. (Procedures to assess student ability and learning styles were discussed in Chapter 5). A fundamental role of the special educator is to assist general education staff in the development of instructional approaches that will accommodate the abilities and preferences of each student. It is clear that some instructional approaches work better for certain students than others. What follows, however, is a sample of instructional approaches that special educators may use to provide instructional accommodations:

multi-sensory approaches (video, slides, demonstration, etc.)
cooperative learning groups
computer assisted instruction and training
advance organizers (study guides, lecture outlines, etc.)
verbal rehearsal of essential information to increase recall
haptic rehearsal (physical practice of essential competencies)
peer tutoring

Special education personnel can collaborate with general education staff to design and implement instructional innovations within the regular vocational or academic setting. Collaboration is also the key to identifying the degree to which curriculum materials and equipment need modification.

Modification of Curriculum Materials/Equipment Special educators can offer assistance to vocational and academic instructors if and when curriculum materials or lab equipment needs to be modified for special populations. Again, redesigning curriculum materials for purposes of readability, clarity, and accessibility will ultimately benefit all students, not just those with special education needs. A sample of curriculum modification activities that are often useful are provided below:

redesigning handouts
outlining chapter questions
highlighting and color-coding texts
organizing class notes
developing study guides
identifying assistive technology devices
labeling equipment parts
putting textbooks on tape
video taping of classroom demonstrations for review

Testing Options It is not unusual for teachers to rely on one, or possibly two, testing formats to determine student comprehension of course material. When testing formats are limited, some students will be unable to demonstrate their "true" understanding of the material. Again, this is a result of differences in learning styles that pertain, in this instance, to mode of expression preferences. To increase the likelihood that students are tested in a manner that evaluates their "true" understanding, a variety of testing options can be presented to general educators for adoption in their lab or classroom setting. Testing options which can be used in vocational and academic courses include the following:

online examinations/projects
oral examinations
written examinations
physical demonstrations
cooperative group testing
competency-based testing
teacher-student interviews
rapid-fire testing (questions are asked randomly to class)
oral and written reports
individual or group presentations

Grading Options Another instructional support category that promotes student success in the general education setting pertains to student grading. Like testing, general education teachers may use a single approach to student grading although there are numerous options available. It is critical, however, that instructional support staff discuss the grading options with general educators before the academic semester begins so decisions about student grading can be made prior to the student's placement in that program. If decisions are made before and not during the grading period, the integrity of the program will not be jeopardized. A sample of grading options available to general education instructors include the following:

pass/fail
traditional letter grades
competency checklists
subscript grading (grades for motivation, cooperation, behavior, etc.)
teacher-student contracts
individual performance grades
cooperative grading (student, instructor)
self reports

This section provided a variety of direct instructional support activities that were categorized under four separate headings including: instructional accomodations, modification of curriculum materials/equipment, testing options, and grading options. The activity lists are by no means exhaustive but they do represent what special educators have found to be useful when supporting special populations in vocational and academic courses. It is highly recommended that implementers of the Collaborative Transition Model expand the list of options under each category by engaging in meaningful collaboration with general education staff and students with disabilities.

Indirect Instructional Support Although direct instructional support activities are vital to the success of special populations enrolled in general education courses, special education personnel must also be engaged in indirect activities that promote positive perceptions of special populations and the importance of comprehensive transition planning. Additional indirect instructional support activities will now be addressed. Indirect instructional support activities will be categorized as they are in the "special populations assurances" section of the Carl D. Perkins Vocational Education and Applied Technology Act of 1998 (P.L. 105–332). The categories include early notification, equal assess, and formal transition planning.

Early Notification Activities To ensure that students with disabilities have a full understanding of the vocational/academic options available to them, special education personnel must provide information to students and their parents one full year before the student can enroll in such options. A middle school student, for example, must be given information about ninth grade vocational education options a year before entering the ninth grade. A high school student must be informed about postsecondary vocational opportunities at least one year before leaving the secondary setting. It is important that both students and their parents be given early notification of the vocational options. Informing both students **and** parents will increase the likelihood that program placement decisions are based on the best interests of the student and his or her family. The list of activities that promote early notification are endless. The following activities represent a sample of indirect instructional support strategies that can be used to inform students and parents about vocational and academic education opportunities:

disseminate informational brochures
hold informational meetings/workshops
have student and parents visit/observe courses in progress
invite teachers to speak to students/parents about their courses
discuss options during IEP or other educational planning meetings
invite students who have completed programs to share experiences
invite employers to discuss necessary skills for employment
provide information in primary language of student/parents
provide a glossary of vocational education terms and acronyms
direct students and parents to related Internet websites

Equal Access Activities After students and parents have been fully informed about the vocational and academic options available, it will be necessary to ensure equal access to those options. A variety of indirect instructional support activities can be used at this juncture to assist students with disabilities to enter programs which are consistent with their interests, abilities, and preferences. Activities that will promote access to appropriate vocational and academic courses of study include the following:

invite counseling staff to discuss enrollment procedures
indicate placement decision or other educational plans on IEP
help student acquire entry-level skills for program before placement
discuss student support services that are available
use assessment data when making placement decision

provide enrollment assistance and counseling
discuss instructional preferences of program instructors
discuss curricular aspects of program (testing, grading options, etc.)

Formal Transition Activities The third category of indirect instructional support pertains to activities that take place once the student is enrolled in a particular course of study and in preparation for the transition to postsecondary education or employment. If early notification and equal access activities have been carried out, transition planning strategies can be efficiently implemented. Indirect instructional support activities which support formal transition planning include the following:

formal and informal vocational assessment
counseling with qualified guidance personnel
collaborative planning for support services
identification of postsecondary goals/interests
identification of adult support agencies and services
identification of postsecondary education options
identification of employment opportunities
completion of individual transition plan by interdisciplinary team
discussion of student role in transition process
implementation of follow-up surveys

The direct and indirect strategies presented in this chapter represent a sample of the activities that can be implemented to improve total service delivery for students with disabilities. Incorporating a variety of innovative strategies will require a good deal of time and effort for general and special education personnel. Ideally, the strategies presented here will assist in the prevention of serious learning problems that often result in student failure and/or low motivation. The question isn't whether or not time and effort will be spent because it certainly will—either in the prevention of learning difficulties before they occur, or in the treatment of problems after a failure situation has arisen. The provision of instructional support, both indirect and direct, is designed to be preventative in nature. A primary goal of the Collaborative Transition Model is to provide students with disabilities with every opportunity to be included in courses, activities, and student organizations which best prepare them for a meaningful and productive adult life. To accomplish this objective, it will be necessary for general and special education personnel and other stakeholders to assume a "prevention" rather than "treatment" posture.

Postschool Follow-Up Procedures

The development of formal postschool follow-up procedures represents another responsibility of the transition core team. Specific steps should be taken to ensure that high school graduates are performing successfully in postsecondary environments. Accordingly, core team members must work cooperatively with other school personnel to evaluate the extent to which former students are adapting to social, educational, employment and community settings (see Appendix C, part 5 [C-5] for a post-high school follow-up survey sample).

Step Six: Annual Evaluation

Following the implementation of the first five phases of the Collaborative Transition Model, the transition core team must conduct a formal evaluation to determine whether the primary goals of the model have been achieved. In addition to reviewing the in-school transition procedures, follow-up data should be examined to determine the number of students who have been successfully placed in appropriate postsecondary settings. A formal review of the availability of adult support services is an integral component of the annual evaluation.

CHAPTER SUMMARY

The Collaborative Transition Model is an interdisciplinary planning approach that is designed to promote a systematic transition process throughout a school district. The intent of this model is to ensure that students with disabilities engage in a formal process as they make the transition through critical junctures within the school as well as the school-to-postsecondary period. There are many stakeholders in collaborative transition planning, including students with disabilities. This model attempts to provide a forum whereby all stakeholders have an opportunity to achieve a sense of ownership for improving the postschool outcomes for individuals with disabilities.

DISCUSSION QUESTIONS

1. What strategies has your school district used to systematically integrate transition assessment and transition planning as critical components for middle school and high school students with disabilities?
2. Visit with your local or regional Transition Advisory Committee (TAC) or Community Transition Interagency Committee (CTIC). What are the goals of this group of key area transition stakeholders for the upcoming year? How do these goals assist you, the city, or the region in addressing transition assessment and transition planning for students with disabilities?

CHAPTER REFERENCES

Carl D. Perkins Vocational and Technical Education Act of 1998, P.L. 105–332 (1998). Congressional Information Services [online], 112, 3076. Available: Lexis-Nexis Database: P.L. 105–332 [1999, May 21].

Field, S., Martin, J., Miller, R., Ward, M., & Wehmeyer, M. (1998). *A practical guide for teaching self-determination.* Reston, VA: The Council for Exceptional Children.

Lombard, R.C., Hazelkorn, M.N., & Neubert, D.A. (1992). A survey of accessibility to secondary vocational education programs and transition services for students with disabilities in Wisconsin. *Career Development for Exceptional Individuals, 15*, 179–188.

Sitlington, P.L., Neubert, D.A., Begun, W., Lombard, R. C., & Leconte, P.J. (1996). *Assess for success: Handbook on transition assessment.* Reston, VA: The Council for Exceptional Children.

The Individuals with Disabilities Education Act of 2004, P.L. 108–466 [online]. Retrieved March 28, 2005 from http:// thomas.loc.gov/cgi-bin/ querry/z?c108h.1350.enr:

Vortruba, J. C. (1981). Strategies for organizational change. *New Directions for Continuing Education, 9*, 13–27.

APPENDIX

A Informal Transition Assessment Instruments

Questions to Ask to Gauge Career Maturity of Student

1. Can I (student) name two jobs that I (student) am interested in finding out more information about for a career after high school? (Career decidedness and reality orientation)

2. Can I (student) list three reasons (rational) why I (student) am interested in each of the two jobs listed above? (Information regarding career interests, maturity of choice)

3. Can I (student) list two reasons why I believe I would be good at the job I am interested in? Do I have any limitations that I would need to address or accommodations I would need to request to get and keep a job in this area? (Strengths and limitations, reality orientation)

4. I (student) got a "C-" on English assignment that I thought I had done really well on. What are two questions I might ask my English teacher to improve my grade on the next assignment? (Willingness and ability to ask questions and seek solutions)

5. A friend asks you (student) to go to the lake for the weekend with his or her family. The friend says you will have a great time fishing and boating. What are five questions you need to ask your friend in order to get the information necessary for your parents and you to decide if you will go? (Willingness and ability to ask questions, planning for near and distant futures)

6. Pick out one of the careers from question one (e.g. plumber or cosmetologist). If you had the opportunity to talk to someone in this field, (e.g. plumber or cosmetologist), what are five questions you would ask that professional to find out if that job were right for you? (gathering information, understanding goal attainment, willingness to ask questions and seek solutions)

7. Would you like to spend one afternoon in the business community watching this professional work and asking him or her questions about the career? If yes, why? If no, why not? (Ability and willingness to explore careers, willingness to ask questions, willingness to seek out resources and use resources, willingness to participate in community-based activity)

Future Planning Inventory

Student Form

What are your plans during high school and after graduation? Please complete this future planning document and bring it to your next Individual Educational Planning conference.

General Student Information

Student's name: ____
first middle last

Social Security number: ____________________ Birthdate: ____________________

Anticipated graduation date: ____________________ Grade: ____________________

Current address: ____________________ Phone number: ____________________

Parent's name: ____________________ Parent's business phone: ____________________

What kind of courses do you want to take during high school? (Be sure you choose the kind of coursework that will meet your future planning goals!)

_________ College preparatory _________ General education (Minimum graduation requirements)

_________ Vocational _________ I don't know

I. Vocational/Postsecondary Education Options

A. Upon graduation, I want to go on for future education or training.

_________ Yes _________ No

If yes, please check each kind of postsecondary education or training that interests you.

_________ Four-year college/university _________ Private occupational training program

_________ Community college _________ Military service

_________ Technical college _________ Adult education program

What do you want to study or train to be? ______________________________

My level of motivation to succeed in the academic setting:

_________ high _________ medium _________ low

The level of control I have over decision making and my individual success:

_________ high _________ medium _________ low

My ability to identify what I need and how to get it:

_________ high _________ medium _________ low

B. Upon graduation, I am going to get a job right away.

_________ Yes _________ No

If yes, please check the kind of job you expect to have.

_________ Competitive employment: _________ Full-time _________ Part-time

_________ Self-employment

_________ Supported employment: _________ Full-time _________ Part-time

_________ Sheltered employment: _________ Full-time _________ Part-time

C. In what type of job/occupation will you be working one year after graduation?

____

D. In what type of job/occupation will you be working in five years after graduation?

____

E. What courses do you need to take in high school this year that will help you attain your employment or postsecondary education goals?

_____________________ _____________________

_____________________ _____________________

F. Do you want information on tests required to get into post-secondary education (e.g. ASVAB, SAT, ACT, PSAT)?

G. What chores do you have at home and how much do you like to do them?

Activity (e.g. make bed, carry out trash: mow lawn.)	Degree of Independence: Do it independently	Need some help
1. _______________		
2. _______________		
3. _______________		
4. _______________		
5. _______________		

H. List jobs you do now and really enjoy.

____

I. What jobs or work experience have you had in your community?

_____________________ _____________________

_____________________ _____________________

J. List any jobs you really dislike.

_____________________ _____________________

_____________________ _____________________

II. Home Living Options

A. Where do you plan on living after graduation?. (Please check one from this list.)

_________ Large urban (100,000 population plus) What city? _______________

_________ Urban (30,000 to 100,000 population) What city? _______________

_________ Rural (under 30,000 population) What town? _______________

_________ Farm

B. (Please check one from this list)

_________ Live independently in apartment or home

_________ With family member (who?) _______________

_________ With support _______________

_________ Supervised apartment (which one?) _______________

    _________ Group home (which one?) _______________

    _________ College dormitory (where?) _______________

_________ Other, please describe _______________

III. Recreational and Leisure Options

A. Leisure Interest Inventory

Check any of the following leisure activity resources that are available in the community where you think you will live following graduation.

Athletic/Sports Activities

_____ swimming _____ lifting weights _____ skiing
_____ running _____ aerobics _____ canoeing
_____ softball _____ basketball _____ riding motorcycle
_____ walking _____ fishing _____ camping
_____ riding bike _____ bowling _____ riding horses
_____ other _____

Large Group Events

_____ movies _____ car races
_____ sporting events _____ horse, dog, car shows
_____ music events _____ community education classes
_____ other _____

Individual Activities

_____ sewing _____ listening to music _____ playing pool/billiards
_____ handcrafts _____ cooking _____ video games
_____ reading _____ playing instrument _____ shopping
_____ caring for pets _____ writing letters _____ caring for lawn
_____ talking on phone _____ watching TV _____ cleaning/repairing car
_____ playing cards or board games _____ Internet _____ other

Social Activities

_____ dating _____ entertaining at home
_____ picnicking _____ dancing
_____ eating out _____ driving around
_____ attending church _____ spending time with family or friends
_____ belonging to social club _____ volunteering
_____ other _____

B. In which extracurricular activities would you like to participate during this year of high school?

_____

_____

Do you need any extra supports to participate in this/these extracurricular activities?

_____ Yes _____ No

If yes, please describe: _____

C. Future Leisure Activities

Check any of the following leisure activity resources that are available in the community where you think you will live following graduation:

_____ YMCA or YWCA _____ bowling leagues _____ movie
_____ recreation clubs, classes _____ city/county/state parks _____ sports arenas
_____ other _____

Please list all the community leisure activities in which you plan to participate after high school.

____

____

____

Do you need any extra supports to participate in these leisure activities?

_________ Yes _________ No

If yes, please describe: ____

IV. Transportation Options

How will you get around the community and to work?

	I Do Now	I Need to Learn
_________ drive own vehicle	_________	_________
_________ drive family vehicle	_________	_________
_________ use city bus transportation	_________	_________
_________ take taxi	_________	_________
_________ ride bicycle	_________	_________
_________ walk	_________	_________
_________ use special regional transportation system (i.e., bus between towns)	_________	_________
_________ depend on others	_________	_________
_________ other _____________________________		

V. Financial Support

A. Do you need financial help in any of the following areas to reach your long-range goals?

1. Postsecondary education _________ Yes _________ No

If yes, please check all of the following for which you would like information.

_________ a. Division of Rehabilitation Services (DRS)

_________ b. Pell Grants

_________ c. Scholarships

_________ d. Work study

_________ e. Student loans

_________ f. Supplemental Security Income (SSI)

2. Help getting the right job _________ Yes _________ No

If yes, please check all of the following for which you would like information.

_________ a. Division of Rehabilitation Services (DRS)

_________ b. Local Job Training Agency

_________ c. State Job Service

_________ d. Supplemental Security Income (SSI)

3. Home living assistance _________ Yes _________ No

If yes, please check all of the following for which you would like information.

_________ a. County Social Services

_________ b. Supplemental Security Income (SSI)/ medical assistance

_________ c. Housing assistance—city government

_________ d. Independent Living Center services

B. Have you contacted any of the following agencies regarding financial help?

_________ Yes _________ No

(Please check all that apply.)

_________ Not applicable _________ Social Security Office

_________ Division of Rehabilitation Services (DRS) _________ County Social Services

_________ Local Job Training Agency

_________ Other, please describe ____

VI. Health-related Needs

A. When was your last physical examination?

(date) ________________________________

B. Do you have any of the following needs?

_________ medical (i.e., medications) _________ yes* _________ no

_________ counseling _________ yes* _________ no

_________ other ____

*Please explain ____

C. What are some possible supports you may require in the future?

____

____

VII. Currently, what is your greatest concern for your future?

____

____

____

About the Future Planning Inventory for Parents/Guardians

The following inventory has been designed to assist your son or daughter plan for his or her future after high school. For this planning to be successful, your son or daughter will need your help. Please fill out this inventory based on your own thoughts. Your son or daughter will complete his or her own Future Planning Inventory, as will his or her special education teacher.

Bring your completed inventory to the next Individual Education Planning (IEP) meeting scheduled on ___________. At that time we will discuss your young adult's future plans and discuss how we can work together to make sure he or she attains these goals. Depending on the age of your child, some questions may be more timely than others. If you have any question when you are filling out this form, leave the item blank and this item will be discussed at the meeting. If you completed this form last year, your previous form will be attached to this blank form for your reference when completing this year's inventory.

Future Planning Inventory

Parent/Guardian Form

Please complete this future planning document and bring it to the upcoming Individual Education Planning conference scheduled for your son/daughter.

General Student Information

Student's name: ____
first middle last

Social Security number: ____________________ Birthdate: ____________________

Anticipated graduation date: ____________________ Grade: ____________________

Current address: ____________________ Phone number: ____________________

Parent's name: ____________________ Parent's business phone: ____________________

What kind of secondary curriculum do you feel best meets the needs of your son or daughter?

_________ College preparatory

_________ General education

_________ Vocational

I. Vocational/Postsecondary Education Options

A. Upon graduation, what do you see your son/daughter doing for future education or training? (Please check all that apply)

_________ Four-Year college/university _________ Private occupational training program

_________ Community college _________ Military service

_________ Technical college _________ Community education program

What will your son/daughter be studying or training to be?

____

My son's/daughter's level of motivation to succeed in the academic setting:

_________ high _________ medium _________ low

The level of control my son/daughter believes he or she has over decision making and his/her individual success:

_________ high _________ medium _________ low

My son's/daughter's ability to identify what he she needs and how to get it:

_________ high _________ medium _________ low

B. Upon graduation, in what kind of employment setting do you see your son/daughter engaged in?

_________ Competitive employment: _________ Full-time _________ Part-time

_________ Self-employment

_________ Supported employment: _________ Full-time _________ Part-time

_________ Sheltered employment: _________ Full-time _________ Part-time

C. What type of job/occupation do you see your son/daughter working in one year after graduation?

____

D. What type of job/occupation do you see your son/daughter working in five years after graduation?

____

E. What work-related demands are being placed on your son or daughter at home, and what is his or her reaction to them?

Activity (For example makes bed, carries out trash, mows lawn.)	Degree of Independence: Does Independently	Needs Guidance	Unwilling to Perform Task
1. ______			
2. ______			
3. ______			
4. ______			
5. ______			

F. List any jobs or chores your son/daughter does now and enjoys.

____

____

G. What jobs or work experience has your son/daughter had in your community?

______________________ ______________________

______________________ ______________________

H. List any jobs your son/daughter seems to really dislike.

______________________ ______________________

______________________ ______________________

II. Home Living Options

A. Where do you think your son/daughter will likely live after graduation? (Please check one from this list.)

______ Large urban (100,000 population plus) What city? ______

______ Urban (30,000 to 100,000 population) What city? ______

______ Rural (under 30,000 population) What town? ______

______ Farm

B. (Please check one from this list.)

______ Live independently in apartment or home ______

______ With family member (who?) ______

______ With support

  ______ Supervised apartment (which one?) ______

  ______ Group home (which one?) ______

______ College dormitory (where?) ______

______ Other, please describe ______

III. Recreational and Leisure Options

A. Leisure Interest Inventory

Check all of the following leisure activities in which your son or daughter currently spends free time.

Athletic/Sports Activities

_________ swimming _________ liftingweights _________ skiing
_________ running _________ aerobics _________ canoeing
_________ softball _________ basketball _________ riding motorcycle
_________ walking _________ fishing _________ camping
_________ riding bike _________ bowling _________ riding horses
_________ other ____

Large Group Events

_________ movies _________ car races
_________ ball games _________ horse, dog, car shows
_________ music events _________ community education classes
_________ other ____

Individual Activities

_________ sewing _________ listening to music _________ Internet
_________ handcrafts _________ cooking _________ shopping
_________ reading _________ playing instrument _________ playing pool/billiards
_________ caring for pets _________ writing letters _________ caring for lawn
_________ talking on phone _________ watching TV _________ playing video games
_________ clean/repair car _________ playing cards or board games
_________ other ____

Social Activities

_________ dating _________ entertaining at home _________ attending church
_________ picnicking _________ volunteering _________ belonging to a social club
_________ eating out _________ driving around _________ spending time with family or friends
_________ dancing _________ other ____

B. In which extracurricular activities would you like your son/daughter to participate during high school?

____

____

____

Does your son/daughter need any specific supports or accommodations to participate in this/these extracurricular activities? _________ Yes _________ No

If yes, please describe: ____

C. Future Leisure Activities

Check any of the following leisure activity resources that are available in the community where you think your son/daughter will live following graduation:

_________ YMCA or YWCA _________ bowling leagues _________ recreation clubs, classes
_________ city/county/state parks _________ movie _________ sports arenas
_________ city recreation facilities _________ church groups _________ community education center
_________ other ____

Please list all the community leisure activities in which you hope your son/daughter will choose to participate after high school.

____

____

____

Does your son/daughter need any specific supports or accommodations to participate in these leisure activities? ________ Yes ________ No

If yes, please describe: ______________________________

IV. Transportation Options

How will your son/daughter get around the community and to work?

	Does Now	Needs to Learn
________ drive own vehicle		
________ drive family vehicle		
________ use city bus transportation		
________ take taxi		
________ ride bicycle		
________ walk		
________ use special regional transportation system (i.e., bus between towns)		
________ depend on others		
________ other ____________		

Are you willing to drive your son/daugher to work? ________ Yes ________ No

How many miles? ______________________________

V. Financial Support

A. Does your son/daughter need financial assistance in any of the following areas to reach his/her long-range goals?

1. Postsecondary education ________ Yes ________ No
   If yes, please check all of the following for which you would like information.
   ________ a. Division of Rehabilitation Services (DRS)
   ________ b. Pell Grants
   ________ c. Scholarships
   ________ d. Work study
   ________ e. Student loans
   ________ f. Supplemental Security Income (SSI)
   ________ g. Social Security Disability Insurance (SSDI)

2. Employment assistance ________ Yes ________ No
   If yes, please check all of the following for which you would like information.
   ________ a. Division of Rehabilitation Services (DRS)
   ________ b. Local Job Training Agency
   ________ c. State Job Service
   ________ d. Supplemental Security Income (SSI)

__________ e. County social services
__________ f. Rehabilitation centers

3. Home living assistance __________ Yes __________ No
   If yes, please check all of the following for which you would like information.
   __________ a. County Social Services
   __________ b. Supplemental Security Income (SSI)/ medical assistance
   __________ c. Housing assistance—city government
   __________ d. Independent Living Center services

B. Which of the following agencies have you contacted with regard to financial support for your son or daughter?
__________ Not applicable
__________ Division of Rehabilitation Services (DRS)
__________ Local Job Training Agency
__________ Social Security Office
__________ County Social Services
__________ Other, please describe ______________________________

VI. Health-Related Needs

A. When was the last physical examination completed for your son or daughter?
(date) __________________

B. Does your son/daughter currently have any of the following needs?
__________ medical (i.e., medications) __________ yes* __________ no
__________ counseling __________ yes* __________ no
__________ other ______________________________
*Please explain ______________________________

C. What are some supports your son/daughter may require in the future?

____

____

____

VII. Currently, what is your greatest concern for your son/daughter's future?

____

____

____

Future Planning Inventory

Educator Form

Please complete this future planning document and bring it to the upcoming Individual Education Planning conference scheduled for your student.

General Student Information

Student's name: ____
first middle last

Student's Social Security number: ____________ Birthdate: ____________

Anticipated graduation date: ____________ Grade: ____________

Current address: ____________ Phone number: ____________

Parent's name: ____________ Business phone: ____________

What kind of secondary curriculum do you feel best meets the needs of your student?

_______ College preparatory

_______ General education

_______ Vocational

I. Vocational/Postsecondary Education Options

A. Upon graduation, where do you see your student participating in future education or training? (Please check all that apply)

_______ Four-year college/university

_______ Community college

_______ Technical college

_______ Private occupational training program

_______ Military service

_______ Community education program

B. What kind of employment do you see your student participating in after graduation? (Check all that apply).

_______ Competitive employment: _______ Full-time _______ Part-time

_______ Supported employment: _______ Full-time _______ Part-time

_______ Sheltered employment: _______ Full-time _______ Part-time

C. Academic and life skills assessment

1. Current reading recognition score:

_______________ Test _______________ Date given _______ Grade level

2. Current reading comprehension score:

_______________ Test _______________ Date given _______ Grade level

Reading strengths ____

____

Reading concerns ____

____

3. Current math score:

_______ Test _______ Date given _______ Grade level

Math strengths ____

____

Math concerns ____

____

4. Life skills curricula:

   Areas of strength ____

   ____

   Areas of concern ____

   ____

5. Student level of motivation ________ high ________ medium ________ low

   Student locus of control ________ high ________ medium ________ low

   Ability of student to self-advocate ________ high ________ medium ________ low

II. Home Living Options

A. Where do you think the student will likely live after graduation?

________ Live independently in apartment or home

________ With family member (who?) ____________________

________ With support

   ________ Supervised apartment (which one?) ____________________

   ________ Group home (which one?) ____________________

________ College dormitory (where?) ____________________

________ Other, please describe ____________________

III. Recreational and Leisure Options

A. In which extracurricular activities would you like to see the student participate during high school?

____

____

____

Does your student need any specific supports or accommodations to participate in this/these extracurricular activities? ________ Yes ________ No

If yes, please describe: ____

____

B. Future Leisure Activities

Please list all the community leisure activities in which you hope your student will choose to participate after high school.

____

____

____

Does your student need any specific supports or accommodations to participate in this/these leisure activities?

________ Yes ________ No

If yes, please describe: ____

IV. Transportation Options

How will your student get around the community and to work?

	Does Now	Needs to Learn
________ drive own vehicle		
________ drive family vehicle		
________ use city bus transportation		
________ take taxi		
________ ride bicycle		
________ walk		
________ use special regional transportation system (i.e., bus between towns)		
________ depends on others		
________ other ________________		

V. Financial Support

A. Which of the following agencies need to be contacted regarding transition planning and financial assistance for your student?

________ Not applicable

________ Division of Rehabilitation Services (DRS)

________ Local Job Training Agency

________ Social Security office

________ County social services

________ Other, please describe ____

VI. Currently, what is your greatest concern for future of your student?

____

____

____

Self-Determination and Self-Advocacy Skills Questionnaire

Student Form

Name: ______________________ Today's Date: ______________________

Grade: ______________________

Age: ______________________ Anticipated Graduation Date: ______________

Disability (please be specific): ______________________

The following questionnaire was developed to identify your level of knowledge and skill in issues related to self-determination and self-advocacy. After reading each of the following sixteen skill statements, please circle the **one number** that best describes your level of skill.

1. I can list and discuss the academic accommodations I need to be successful in high school.

   1 Not at all 2 3 4 5 6 All the time

2. I can list and discuss the support services I need on the job in order to be successful.

   1 Not at all 2 3 4 5 6 All the time

3. I am able to independently contact the adult service providers that I will need to help me reach my employment goals.

   1 Not at all 2 3 4 5 6 All the time

4. I can independently request and effectively use academic accommodations in all my classes.

   1 Not at all 2 3 4 5 6 All the time

5. I can list and discuss the accommodations I will use to be successful in my job.

   1 Not at all 2 3 4 5 6 All the time

6. I can list and discuss my rights for reasonable academic accommodation under the law.

   1 Not at all 2 3 4 5 6 All the time

7. I identify myself as a person with a disability in order to get the support services I deserve in postsecondary education.

   1 Not at all 2 3 4 5 6 All the time

8. I can list and discuss the support services I will need in postsecondary education in order to be successful.

   1 Not at all 2 3 4 5 6 All the time

9. I can state accommodations I need in the workplace that are guaranteed to me by law.

   1 Not at all 2 3 4 5 6 All the time

10. I identify myself as a person with a disability in order to get the support services I deserve from my employer.

    1 Not at all 2 3 4 5 6 All the time

11. I am able to independently contact the adult service providers that will help me reach my postsecondary education goals.

    1 Not at all 2 3 4 5 6 All the time

12. I lead my own IEP team meetings.

1	2	3	4	5	6
Not at all					All the time

13. I state my goals and aspirations for each school year during the annual IEP team meeting.

1	2	3	4	5	6
Not at all					All the time

14. I can independently request and effectively use accommodations on the job.

1	2	3	4	5	6
Not at all					All the time

15. I have identified my long-term employment goals for after high school and I can state and discuss these long-term goals.

1	2	3	4	5	6
Not at all					All the time

16. I am able to identify and discuss the amount and type of postsecondary education or training I will need to reach my long-term employment goals.

1	2	3	4	5	6
Not at all					All the time

Self-Determination and Self-Advocacy Skills Questionnaire

Parent Form

Parent Name: ______________________ Today's Date: ________________

Student Name: ______________________ Grade: ____________________

Student Age: ____________ Anticipated Graduation Date: ____________________

Student Disability (please be specific): ____

The following questionnaire was developed to identify the level of knowledge and skill in issues related to self-determination and self-advocacy of your young adult. After reading each of the following sixteen skill statements, please circle the **one number** that best describes her/his level of skill.

1. My young adult can list and discuss the academic accommodations he/she needs to be successful in high school.

   1 Not at all — 2 — 3 — 4 — 5 — 6 All the time

   ________ I am not aware of my son's/daughter's skills in this area. (Please check only if applicable.)

2. My young adult can list and discuss the support services he/she needs on the job in order to be successful.

   1 Not at all — 2 — 3 — 4 — 5 — 6 All the time

   ________ I am not aware of my son's/daughter's skills in this area. (Please check only if applicable.)

3. My young adult is able to independently contact the adult service providers that he/she will need to help reach his/her employment goals.

   1 Not at all — 2 — 3 — 4 — 5 — 6 All the time

   ________ I am not aware of my son's/daughter's skills in this area. (Please check only if applicable.)

4. My young adult can independently request and effectively use academic accommodations in all his/her classes.

   1 Not at all — 2 — 3 — 4 — 5 — 6 All the time

   ________ I am not aware of my son's/daughter's skills in this area. (Please check only if applicable.)

5. My young adult can list and discuss the accommodations he/she will use to be successful in a job.

   1 Not at all — 2 — 3 — 4 — 5 — 6 All the time

   ________ I am not aware of my son's/daughter's skills in this area. (Please check only if applicable.)

6. My young adult can list and discuss his/her rights for reasonable academic accommodations under the law.

   1 Not at all — 2 — 3 — 4 — 5 — 6 All the time

   ________ I am not aware of my son's/daughter's skills in this area. (Please check only if applicable.)

7. My young adult can identify himself/herself as a person with a disability in order to get the support services that he/she deserves in postsecondary education.

1	2	3	4	5	6
Not at all					All the time

__________ I am not aware of my son's/daughter's skills in this area. (Please check only if applicable.)

8. My young adult can list and discuss the support services that he/she will need in postsecondary education in order to be successful.

1	2	3	4	5	6
Not at all					All the time

__________ I am not aware of my son's/daughter's skills in this area. (Please check only if applicable.)

9. My young adult can state accommodations that he/she needs in the workplace that are guaranteed by law.

1	2	3	4	5	6
Not at all					All the time

__________ I am not aware of my son's/daughter's skills in this area. (Please check only if applicable.)

10. My young adult can identify himself/herself as a person with a disability in order to get the support services that he/she deserves from an employer.

1	2	3	4	5	6
Not at all					All the time

__________ I am not aware of my son's/daughter's skills in this area. (Please check only if applicable.)

11. My young adult is able to independently contact the adult service providers that will help her/him reach his/her postsecondary education goals.

1	2	3	4	5	6
Not at all					All the time

__________ I am not aware of my son's/daughter's skills in this area. (Please check only if applicable.)

12. My young adult leads his/her own IEP meetings.

1	2	3	4	5	6
Not at all					All the time

__________ I am not aware of my son's/daughter's skills in this area.

13. My young adult states goals and aspirations for each school year at her/his annual IEP meeting.

1	2	3	4	5	6
Not at all					All the time

__________ I am not aware of my son's/daughter's skills in this area. (Please check only if applicable.)

14. My young adult can independently request and effectively use accommodations on the job.

1	2	3	4	5	6
Not at all					All the time

__________ I am not aware of my son's/daughter's skills in this area. (Please check only if applicable.)

15. My young adult has identified long-term employment goals for after high school and can state and discuss his/her long-term goals.

1	2	3	4	5	6
Not at all					All the time

__________ I am not aware of my son's/daughter's skills in this area. (Please check only if applicable.)

16. My young adult is able to identify and discuss the amount and type of postsecondary education or training that he/she will need to reach their long-term employment goals.

1	2	3	4	5	6
Not at all					All the time

__________ I am not aware of my son's/daughter's skills in this area. (Please check only if applicable.)

Self-Determination and Self-Advocacy Skills Questionnaire

Teacher Forms A and B

Today's Date: ______________________________
Student Name: ______________________________
Grade: ______________________________
Anticipated Graduation Date: ______________________________
Student Disability: ______________________________
Teacher Name: ______________________________

Unlike the student and parent instruments, the teacher form of this instrument is divided into Form A and Form B. Form A includes only those foils regarding accommodations relating to academic needs in secondary school and future postsecondary education. Form B includes all foils regarding employment related issues. These forms may be used in a number of manners. A case manager/teacher may choose to complete both Form A and B if appropriate. The case manager/teacher may choose to request that Form B of the instrument be completed by a teacher who works with the student directly in a tech-prep, school-to-work, or career/vocational area of education. The case manager/teacher may choose to complete only Form A or only Form B of the instrument as appropriate based on their observations of the student in either an academic or vocational setting.

Form A includes eight foils (numbers 1, 4, 6, 7, 8, 11, 12, and 13) related to academic skills and postsecondary education. Form B includes eight foils (numbers 2, 3, 5, 9, 10, 14, 15, and 16) related to employment skills. These numbers correspond with the numbered foils found on the student and parent forms to simplify the graphing and presentation of all data.

A-3, Form 3

Self-Determination and Self-Advocacy Skills Questionnaire

Teacher Form A: Academic Skills

Student Name: ______________________ Date: ______________________

Teacher Name: ______________________

Please circle the one number that best describes the above student's knowledge and skill level related to each of the statements below.

1. The student can list and discuss the academic accommodations needed to be successful in high school classes.

1	2	3	4	5	6
Not at all					All the time

4. The student can independently request and effectively use academic accommodations in the class that I teach.

1	2	3	4	5	6
Not at all					All the time

6. The student can list and discuss her/his rights for reasonable academic accommodations under the law.

1	2	3	4	5	6
Not at all					All the time

7. The student identifies him/herself as a person with a disability in order to get the support services she/he is entitled to in postsecondary education.

1	2	3	4	5	6
Not at all					All the time

8. The student can list and discuss the support services needed in postsecondary education in order to be successful.

1	2	3	4	5	6
Not at all					All the time

11. The student is able to independently contact the adult service providers that will help him/her reach postsecondary education goals.

1	2	3	4	5	6
Not at all					All the time

12. The student leads his/her own IEP team meetings.

1	2	3	4	5	6
Not at all					All the time

13. The student states goals and aspirations for each school year at her/his annual IEP team meeting.

1	2	3	4	5	6
Not at all					All the time

Self-Determination and Self-Advocacy Skills Questionnaire

Teacher Form B: Employment Skills

Student Name: ______________________ Date: ______________________

Teacher Name: ______________________

Please circle the one number that best describes the above student's knowledge and skill level related to each of the statements below.

2. The student can list and discuss the support services he/she will need on the job to be successful.
   1 2 3 4 5 6
   Not at all All the time

3. The student is able to independently contact the adult service providers that he/she will need to reach his/her employment goals.
   1 2 3 4 5 6
   Not at all All the time

5. The student can list and discuss the accommodations he/she will use to be successful on a job.
   1 2 3 4 5 6
   Not at all All the time

9. The student can state accommodations needed in the workplace that are guaranteed under the law.
   1 2 3 4 5 6
   Not at all All the time

10. The student can identify himself/herself as a person with a disability in order to get the support services guaranteed under law.
    1 2 3 4 5 6
    Not at all All the time

14. The student can independently request and effectively use needed accommodations on the job.
    1 2 3 4 5 6
    Not at all All the time

15. The student has identified his/her long-term employment goals for after high school and can state and discuss his/her long-term goals.
    1 2 3 4 5 6
    Not at all All the time

16. The student is able to identify and discuss the amount and type of postsecondary education or training needed to reach his/her long-term employment goals.
    1 2 3 4 5 6
    Not at all All the time

Self-Determination and Self-Advocacy Skills Questionnaire

Student and Teacher Interview: Performance Battery

1. Please list and discuss the academic accommodations you use in high school classes.
   a. Student did not identify any academic accommodations he/she is using. ____________
   b. Student identified some, but not all, academic accommodations he/she is using. ____________
   c. Student provided a comprehensive list of academic accommodations, as identified on the student's IEP. ____________
   d. Academic accommodations discussed by the student included:
      1. ____________
      2. ____________
      3. ____________

2. Please list and discuss support services you need on the job to be successful.
   a. Student did not identify any support services that he/she will need on the job. ____________
   b. Student identified support services that he/she will need on the job. ____________
   c. Support services discussed by the student included:
      1. ____________
      2. ____________
      3. ____________

3. Please list and discuss the adult service providers with whom you have communicated over the past two years to assist you in reaching your employment goals.
   a. Student did not identify any adult service providers that he/she had contacted over the past two years. ____________
   b. Student identified adult service providers with whom he/she had contact over the past two years. ____________
   c. Adult service providers discussed by the student included:
      1. ____________
      2. ____________
      3. ____________

4a. You are starting a new academic class. Let's pretend I am the teacher of that class and I don't know you. Give me an example of how you would request accommodations in that class.
   a. Student was *not able* to role-play an adequate request for accommodations. ____________
   b. Student was *able* to role-play an adequate request for accommodations. ____________

4b. In the first question in this interview, you listed academic accommodations you use in high school. Please explain how you effectively use those accommodations in your classes.
   a. Student did not discuss the effective use of accommodations. ____________
   b. Student was able to discuss the use of some, but not all, accommodations. ____________
   c. Student discussed the effective use of all accommodations. ____________

5. Please list and discuss the accommodations you use on your job.
   a. Student did not identify any accommodations he/she is using on the job. ____________
   b. Student identified some, but not all, accommodations he/she is using on the job. ____________
   c. Student provided a comprehensive list of accommodations as identified on the student's IEP. ____________

d. Accommodations focused on the job discussed by the student included:

1. ______________________________

2. ______________________________

3. ______________________________

6. Please tell me what your rights are for reasonable accommodation under federal law.
   a. Student did not identify any specific rights, under IDEA, Section 504, or ADA. ____________
   b. Student identified a few rights under IDEA, Section 504, or ADA. ____________
   c. Student provided a substantial list of rights under IDEA, Section 504, or ADA. ____________
   d. Rights identified by the student included:

      1. ______________________________

      2. ______________________________

      3. ______________________________

7. Let's pretend that I am a college disabilities coordinator and that you are applying for support services from my university. Give me an example of how you would identify yourself as a person with a disability to get support services.
   a. Student was *not able* to adequately role-play identification of self as a person with a disability. ____________
   b. Student was *able* to adequately role-play identification of self as a person with a disability. ____________

8. Please list and discuss the support services you will use in postsecondary education in order to be successful.
   a. Student did not identify any support services he/she will use in postsecondary education. ____________
   b. Student identified some support services he/she will be using in postsecondary education. ____________
   c. Support services discussed by the student included:

      1. ______________________________

      2. ______________________________

      3. ______________________________

9. Please identify accommodations you need in the workplace that are guaranteed to you by law.
   a. Student was not able to identify accommodations in the workplace guaranteed by law. ____________
   b. Student was able to identify accommodations in the workplace guaranteed by law. ____________
   c. Accommodations listed by the student included:

      1. ______________________________

      2. ______________________________

      3. ______________________________

10. Let's pretend you were just hired for a new job and I am your new employer. Give me an example of how you would identify yourself to me as a person with a disability.
    a. Student was *not able* to adequately role-play identification of self as a person with a disability in an employment situation. ____________
    b. Student was *able* to adequately role-play identification of self as a person with a disability in an employment situation. ____________

11. (Give the student access to a phone in a private location.) Please call and contact one adult service provider with whom you are currently working in preparation for high school graduation.
    a. Student was *not able* to independently contact an adult service provider. ____________
    b. Student was *able* to independently contact an adult service provider. ____________

12. Student can lead own IEP meeting.
    a. Student does not participate in IEP meetings. ________________
    b. Student attends and participates in IEP meetings. ________________
    c. Student assumes a leadership role in own IEP meetings. ________________

13. Let's pretend you are currently at an IEP meeting. Please state your goals and aspirations for the next academic school year.
    a. Student could not identify goals and aspirations for next academic school year. ________________
    b. Student identified goals and aspirations for next academic school year. ________________

14a. You are starting a new job in the community. Give me an example of how you would request accommodations on the job site.
    a. Student was *not able* to role-play an adequate request for accommodations on the job. ________________
    b. Student was *able* to role play an adequate request for accommodations on the job. ________________

14b. In question 5 in this interview, you identified accommodations you would use on the job. Please explain how you use those accommodations on the job effectively.
    a. Student did not discuss the effective use of accommodations. ________________
    b. Student was able to discuss the use of some, but not all, accommodations. ________________
    c. Student discussed the effective use of all accommodations. ________________

15. Please discuss your long-term employment goals after high school.
    a. Student could not identify and discuss long-term employment goals. ________________
    b. Student identified long-term employment goals and discussed those long-term goals. ________________

16. Please identify and discuss the amount and type of postsecondary education or training you will need to reach your long-term employment goals.
    a. Student was *not able to realistically discuss* the amount of postsecondary education or training needed to reach long-term employment goals. ________________
    b. Student was *able to realistically discuss* the amount of postsecondary education or training needed to reach long-term employment goals. ________________

A-3, Form 5

Scoring Summary

For the Self-Determination and Self-Advocacy Skills Questionnaire

Student Name: ______________________ **Testing Date:** ______________________

Academic Skills

Question #	1	4	6	7	8	11	12	13	Average
Parent (Likert score)									
Student (Likert score)									
Teacher (Likert score)									
Need area									X
SD/SA Skills Questionnaire: Performance Battery									

Employment Skills

Question #	2	3	5	9	10	14	15	16	Average
Parent (Likert score)									
Student (Likert score)									
Teacher (Likert score)									
Need area									X
SD/SA Skills Questionnaire: Performance Battery									

Scoring Key
Need Area:
K—Knowledge and skills needed in this area (rankings of two of three raters [Parent, Student, Teacher]) 4 or less.
O—Team member scores are dissimilar (two or more points discrepant)
KO—Both

SD/SA Skills Questionnaire: Performance Battery
A—student demonstrated ***adequate*** knowledge and skill
L—student demonstrated ***limited*** knowledge and skill
N—student demonstrated ***significant discrepancy*** in knowledge and skill

C.I.T.E. Learning Styles Instrument

The *C.I.T.E.* Instrument (Babich, Burdine, Albright, and Randol, 1976) was formulated at the Murdoch Teachers Center in Wichita, Kansas to help teachers determine the learning styles preferred by their students. It is divided into three main areas:

- **Information gathering** includes auditory language, visual language, auditory numerical, visual numerical, and auditory-visual language, auditory numerical, visual numerical, and auditory-visual-kinesthetic combination.
- **Work conditions** focus on whether a student works better alone or in a group.
- **Expressiveness** considers if a student is better at oral or written communication.

Scores on the Learning Styles Inventory fall into one of three categories: major, minor, and negligible. These categories may be defined as follows:

Major: The student prefers this mode of learning, feels comfortable with it, and uses it for important (to the student) learning. A student does not necessarily have one and only one preferred style.

Minor: The student uses this mode but usually as a second choice or in conjunction with other learning styles.

Negligible: The student prefers not to use this if other choices are available. The student does not feel comfortable with this style.

Frank B. Mann, III, Wyoming County, West Virginia, programmed a computer application system for the ***C.I.T.E. Learning Styles Inventory*** so that students may respond to the questions through use of the computer. The computer will tally the scores automatically. Teachers may obtain copies by contacting Louise Miller at 1-800-766-7372 email: lbmiller@access.k12.wv.us

Definitions and Teaching Techniques for Major Learning Styles

The following are descriptions of learning styles found in every learner to a major, minor, or negligible extent and teaching suggestions related to each learning style.

Learning Style	Teaching Techniques
Visual-Language: This is the student who learns well from seeing words in books or workbooks, on the chalkboard or charts. He/she may write down words that are delivered orally in order to learn by seeing them on paper. He or she remembers and uses information better if it has been read.	This student will benefit from a variety of books, pamphlets, and written materials on several levels of difficulty. Given some time alone with a book, he or she may learn more than in class. Make sure important information has been given on paper, or that he or she takes notes if you want this student to remember specific information.
Visual-Numerical: This student has to see numbers on the board, in a book, or on paper in order to work with them. He or she is more likely to remember and understand math facts if he or she has seen them. He or she does not seem to need as much oral explanation.	This student will benefit from worksheets, workbooks, and texts. Give a variety of written materials and allow time to study it. In playing games and being involved in activities with numbers and number problems, make sure they are visible, printed numbers, not oral games and activities. Important data should be given on paper.
Auditory-Language: This is the student who learns from hearing words spoken. You may hear him or her vocalizing or see the lips or throat move as he or she reads, particularly when striving to understand new material. He or she will be more capable of understanding and remembering words or facts that have been learned by hearing.	This student will benefit from hearing audio tapes, rote oral practice, lecture, or a class discussion. He or she may benefit from using a tape recorder to make tapes to listen to later, by teaching another student, or conversing with the teacher. Groups of two or more, games, or interaction activities provide the sounds of words being spoken that is so important to this student.

Learning Style	Teaching Techniques
Auditory-Numerical: This student learns from hearing numbers and oral explanations. He or she may remember phone and locker numbers with ease, be successful with oral numbers, games, and puzzles. He or she may do just about as well without a math book, for written materials are not as important. He or she can probably work problems in his or her head. You may hear this student saying the numbers aloud or see the lips move as a problem is read.	This student will benefit from math sound tapes or from working with other people, talking about a problem. Even reading written explanations aloud will help. and Games or activities in which the number problems are spoken will help. This student will benefit from tutoring another or delivering an explanation to his or her study group or to the teacher. Make sure important facts are spoken.
Auditory-Visual-Kinesthetic: The A/V/K student learns best by experience and self-involvement. He or she definitely needs a combination of stimuli. The manipulation of material along with the accompanying sights and sounds (words and numbers seen and spoken) will make a big difference to him or her. This student may not seem able to understand or keep his or her mind on work unless he or she is totally involved. He or she seeks to handle, touch, and work with what is being learned. Sometimes just writing or a symbolic wriggling of the fingers is a symptom of the A/V/K learner.	This student must be given more than just a reading or math assignment. Involve him or her with at least one other student and give him or her an activity to relate to the assignment. Accompany an audiotape with pictures, objects, and an activity such as drawing or writing, or following directions with physical involvement.
Social-Individual: This student gets more work done alone. He or she thinks best and remembers more when he or she has learned alone. He or she cares more for his or her own opinions than for the ideas of others. You will not have much trouble keeping this student from over-socializing during class.	This student needs to be allowed to do important learning alone. If you feel he or she needs socialization, save it for a non-learning situation. Let him or her go to the library or back in a corner of the room to be alone. Do not force group work on him or her when it will make the student irritable to be held back or distracted by others. Some great thinkers are loners.
Social-Group: This student strives to study with at least one other student and he or she will not get as much done alone. He or she values others' ideas and preferences. Group interaction increases his or her learning and later recognition of facts. Socializing is important to this student.	This student needs to do important learning with someone else. The stimulation of the group may be more important at certain times in the learning process than at others and you may be able to facilitate the timing for this student.
Expressive Oral: This student prefers to tell what he or she knows. He or she talks fluently, comfortably, and clearly. The teacher may find that this learner knows more than written tests show. He or she is probably less shy than others about giving reports or talking to the teacher or classmates. The muscular coordination involved in writing may be difficult for this learner. Organizing and putting thoughts on paper may be too slow and tedious a task for this student.	Allow this student to make oral reports instead of written ones. Whether in conference, small group or large, evaluate him or her more by what is said than by what is written. Reports can be on tape, to save class time. Demand a minimum of written work, but demand good quality so he or she will not be ignorant of the basics of composition and legibility. Grammar can be corrected orally but is best done at another time.
Expressiveness-Written: This student can write fluent essays and good answers on tests to show what he or she knows. He or she feels less comfortable, perhaps even stupid, when oral answers are required. His or her thoughts are better organized on paper than when they are given orally.	This student needs to be allowed to write reports, keep notebooks and journals for credit, and take written tests for evaluation. Oral transactions should be under non-pressured conditions, perhaps even in a one-to-one conference.

C.I.T.E. Learning Styles Instrument

Name: ______________________ Date: ______________________

Instructions: Read each statement carefully and decide which of the four responses agrees with how you feel about the statement. Put an X on the number of your response.

Questions	Most Like Me			Least Like Me
1. When I make things for my studies, I remember what I have learned better.	4	3	2	1
2. Written assignments are easy for me.	4	3	2	1
3. I learn better if someone reads a book to me than if I read silently to myself.	4	3	2	1
4. I learn best when I study alone.	4	3	2	1
5. Having assignment directions written on the board makes them easier to understand.	4	3	2	1
6. It's harder for me to do a written assignment than an oral one.	4	3	2	1
7. When I do math problems in my head, I say the numbers to myself.	4	3	2	1
8. If I need help in the subject, I will ask a classmate for help.	4	3	2	1
9. I understand a math problem that is written down better than one I hear.	4	3	2	1
10. I don't mind doing written assignments.	4	3	2	1
11. I remember things I hear better than I read.	4	3	2	1
12. I remember more of what I learn if I learn it when I am alone.	4	3	2	1
13. I would rather read a story than listen to it read.	4	3	2	1
14. I feel like I talk smarter than I write.	4	3	2	1
15. If someone tells me three numbers to add I can usually get the right answer without writing them down.	4	3	2	1
16. I like to work in a group because I learn from the others in the group.	4	3	2	1
17. Written math problems are easier for me to do than oral ones.	4	3	2	1
18. Writing a spelling word several times helps me remember it better.	4	3	2	1
19. I find it easier to remember what I have heard than what I have read.	4	3	2	1
20. It is more fun to learn with classmates at first, but it is hard to study with them.	4	3	2	1
21. I like written directions better than spoken ones.	4	3	2	1
22. If homework were oral, I would do it all.	4	3	2	1

A-4, Form 2

Questions	Most Like Me			Least Like Me
23. When I hear a phone number, I can remember it without writing it down.	4	3	2	1
24. I get more work done when I work with someone.	4	3	2	1
25. Seeing a number makes more sense to me than hearing a number.	4	3	2	1
26. I like to do things like simple repairs or crafts with my hands.	4	3	2	1
27. The things I write on paper sound better than when I say them.	4	3	2	1
28. I study best when no one is around to talk or listen to.	4	3	2	1
29. I would rather read things in a book than have the teacher tell me about them.	4	3	2	1
30. Speaking is a better way than writing if you want someone to understand it better.	4	3	2	1
31. When I have a written math problem to do, I say it to myself to understand it better.	4	3	2	1
32. I can learn more about a subject if I am with a small group of students.	4	3	2	1
33. Seeing the price of something written down is easier for me to understand than having someone tell me the price.	4	3	2	1
34. I like to make things with my hands.	4	3	2	1
35. I like tests that call for sentence completion or written answers.	4	3	2	1
36. I understand more from a class discussion than from reading about a subject.	4	3	2	1
37. I remember the spelling of a word better if I see it written down than if someone spells it out loud.	4	3	2	1
38. Spelling and grammar rules make it hard for me to say what I want to in writing.	4	3	2	1
39. It makes it easier when I say the numbers of a problem to myself as I work it out.	4	3	2	1
40. I like to study with other people.	4	3	2	1
41. When the teachers say a number, I really don't understand it until I see it written down.	4	3	2	1
42. I understand what I have learned better when I am involved in making something for the subject.	4	3	2	1
43. Sometimes I say dumb things, but writing gives me time to correct myself.	4	3	2	1
44. I do well on tests if they are about things I hear in class.	4	3	2	1
45. I can't think as well when I work with someone else as when I work alone.	4	3	2	1

C.I.T.E. Learning Styles Instrument Worksheet

Name: ______________________ Date: ______________

Directions: Look at each statement number on the worksheet below. Find the statement number on the Learning Styles Inventory and get the "most like/least like" number of the response you selected for each statement. Write the number (1–4) in the blank provided. Total the numbers under each heading. Multiply the total by two. Look at the scores to decide if this is major, minor, or negligible.

Visual-Language
5 ______
13 ______
21 ______
29 ______
37 ______
Total ______ × 2 = 16 (Score)

Visual-Numerical
9 ______
17 ______
25 ______
33 ______
41 ______
Total ______ × 2 = 20 (Score)

Auditory-Language
3 ______
11 ______
19 ______
36 ______
44 ______
Total ______ × 2 = 40 (Score)

Auditory-Numerical
7 ______
15 ______
23 ______
31 ______
39 ______
Total ______ × 2 = 30 (Score)

Auditory-Visual-Kinesthetic
1 ______
18 ______
26 ______
34 ______
42 ______

22

Social-Individual
4 ______
12 ______
20 ______
28 ______
45 ______
Total ______ × 2 = 22 (Score)

Social-Group
8 ______
16 ______
24 ______
32 ______
40 ______
Total ______ × 2 = 26 (Score)

Expressiveness-Oral
6 ______
14 ______
22 ______
30 ______
38 ______
Total ______ × 2 = 18 (Score)

Expressiveness-Written
2 ______
10 ______
27 ______
35 ______
43 ______
Total ______ × 2 = 34 (Score)

Score: 34–40 = Major Learning Style
20–32 = Minor Learning Style
10–18 = Negligible Use

Transition Exit Form: Interagency Responsibilities

Student Name: ______________________ Date of IEP: __________

School: ______________________ Soc. Sec. No.: __________

Projected Date of Graduation or Program Completion: __________ Date of Birth: __________

IEP Committee Members: __________ __________ __________ __________

Teacher *Parent* *Student* *Admin. Rep.*

__________ __________ __________

Name *Agency* *Name* *Agency* *Name* *Agency*

		Responsibilities					
		Parent/Guardian/Student		**School**		**List Community Agency**	
Transition Needs	Recommendations for Placements, Services, or Other Options	Action	Time Line	Action	Time Line	Action	Time Line
1. Financial/ Income Security							
2. Voc. Train./ Job Placement/ Postsec. Ed.							
3. Secure Living Arrangements							

A-5, Form 1

		Responsibilities					
		Parent/Guardian/Student		***School***		***List Community Agency***	
Transition Needs	Recommendations for Placements, Services, or Other Options	Action	Time Line	Action	Time Line	Action	Time Line
4. Adequate Personal Management							
5. Access to and Enjoyment of Leisure/Recreation Activities							
6. Efficient Transportation System							
7. Provision of Medical Services							

		Responsibilities					
		Parent/Guardian/Student		***School***		***List Community Agency***	
Transition Needs	Recommendations for Placements, Services, or Other Options	Action	Time Line	Action	Time Line	Action	Time Line
8. Link age to and Use of Advocacy/ Legal Services							
9. Appropriate Personal/Family Relationships							
10. Other Instructional Support While Attending College							

Student-Centered Data/Student Interview Format

(Modify questions—choose questions that pertain to ability.)

Name: ______________________________ Date: ______________________

Address: ______________________________ Grade: __________ Age: __________

I. Attitudes Toward Special Needs

1. Do you have any sort of disability or special needs?
2. Are you limited in any way by your disability or special needs?
3. Are you in a special needs program? Which one? Why?
4. How do you feel about being in this program?
5. How do your family and friends feel about it?

II. Abilities/Strengths

6. What do you like to do?
7. What do you do well?
8. What do people compliment you on?

III. Interests and Activities

9. What do you do in your leisure time? Sports? Hobbies? Church?
10. Do you have any jobs at home? What?
11. What job do you think you would like to do and be good at?
12. What job(s) do you really think you would not like? Why?
13. What do you spend your money on?

IV. Occupational and Career Awareness

14. What have you done to earn money?
15. What do you see yourself doing in five years?
16. Name three jobs available in the field you're interested in
17. What are ways to find out about job openings?
18. What do employers look for when they hire someone?
19. What are some reasons people get fired from jobs?
20. What would an employer like about you? Not like?

V. Work and Classroom Preferences

21. How do you learn best?
22. What teachers do you like best? Why?
23. Do you like to work by yourself or with a group?
24. On a job, would you rather sit most of the time or move around a lot?
25. Would you rather work outside or inside, or both?
26. How would you feel about working where it is cold? Hot? Wet? Where there are dangerous things about?
27. How do you feel about jobs that use math skills, such as counting money?
28. What kinds of people do you *not* like to work with?

VI. Educational Interests

29. What courses would you like to take? Which do you not like to take?
30. Would you like to enroll in vocational training now or later? What kind?
31. What classes, here at ________, would help you train for (job interest area)?

VII. Functional Skills

32. If you lived by yourself and had a job, what are some of the things you would *have* to spend your money on each month?
33. Can you use a telephone? How do you dial emergency?
34. If you had a job, how would you get to work? Can you drive?
35. Do you go shopping by yourself? What do you buy?
36. If you save money, how do you do it?

VIII. Family

37. How do your parents feel about you working?
38. Do they trust you?
39. What kinds of responsibilities does your family assign you?
40. What do your parents say they want you to do?

Program Inventory

Person(s) Requesting Inventory Completion: ____________________ Date: ____________

Program Title: ________________________ Instructor: ____________

Text Title: ________________________ Reading Level: ____________

Teaching Preferences of Instructor

Indicate the frequency of teaching methods used below:
1 = Used daily; 2 = Used occasionally; 3 = Never used

Information Input (Instructional Methods)

(Information Sources)

____ textbooks
____ worksheets
____ lecture
____ discussion
____ Internet
____ video
____ computer
____ compact disc
____ audio tapes
____ slides
____ simulations
____ other ________________________

(Structure of Instruction)

____ teacher-directed
____ independent
____ small group
____ peer tutoring
____ one-to-one adult
____ large group
____ other ________________________

Information Output

(Assignments)

____ worksheets
____ short papers
____ term papers
____ oral reports
____ group discussions
____ demonstration
____ written reports
____ portfolio
____ panel presentation
____ word problems/math
____ artistic expression
____ other ________________________

(Test Formats)

____ short answer
____ essay
____ multiple choice
____ oral exam
____ true/false
____ demonstration
____ matching
____ online
____ word problems/math
____ other ________________________

Grading Options ____
____

Extra Credit Options ____
____

Homework Requirements ____
____

Make-up Policy ____

____

____

Attendance Policy ____

____

Behavior Policy ____

____

Curricular Requirements for Program

Put a check next to the most important skills a student should possess upon entry to this program.

Entry-Level Skills

__________ following directions
__________ safety skills
__________ paying attention
__________ staying on task
__________ working independently
__________ oral expression
__________ written expression
__________ social skills
__________ working in groups
__________ spelling
__________ math/calculation skills
__________ note taking
__________ keyboarding
__________ artistic/drawing
__________ measuring
__________ independent research
__________ problem solving
__________ other __________________

Instructional Support Options

(within classroom)

__________ special education teacher
__________ classroom aide

(in resource room)

__________ taped textbooks
__________ assistive technology
__________ alternative testing
__________ note taker
__________ outlining
__________ test preparation
__________ assignment assistance
__________ computer assisted instruction
__________ research assistance
__________ study guides
__________ other __________________

Vocational Assessment Profile

Date(s) of profile completion: ______________________________

Compiled by: ______________________________

I. Identification information

A. Name: ______________________________

B. Date of birth: ______________________________

C. Social Security #: ______________________________

D. Address: ______________________________

E. Phone: ______________________________

F. School district: ______________________________

G. Primary school contact: ______________________________

H. Year of expected graduation/exit: ______________________________

I. Disability (check all that apply):

( ) Mental/Cognitive disability
( ) Mild
( ) Moderate
( ) Brain injury
( ) Autism
( ) Deafness or hearing impairment
( ) Other ____________
( ) Behavioral disability
( ) Speech and language impairment
( ) Physical impairment
( ) Other health disabilities
( ) Learning disability
( ) Visual impairment

J. Vision/hearing screening (check all that apply):

Does individual use assisted devices such as:

( ) Hearing aid
( ) Glasses
( ) Braille reader
( ) Other ____________

K. Physical/health restrictions:

List additional information regarding medications, allergies, recurring health problems, physical restrictions, or limitations.

____

L. SSDI Application (check all that apply):

( ) Receives: amount per month ____________
( ) Completed, awaiting determination
( ) Not applied

Other sources of income and amounts:

____________________ amount ____________ /mo.
____________________ amount ____________ /mo.
____________________ amount ____________ /mo.

M. Additional Information (check all that apply):

( ) Physical exam date: ______________
( ) Psychological exam date: ______________
( ) Most recent IEP/transition plan date: ______________
( ) Most recent resume date: ______________

II. Residential/Domestic Information

A. Family (parent or guardian) address (if different from student's)

____

B. Phone Number: ____

C. Names, ages, and relationships of family members:

1.	Age:	Relation:
2.	Age:	Relation:
3.	Age:	Relation:
4.	Age:	Relation:
5.	Age:	Relation:

D. Residential status (check all that apply)

( ) Lives at home with natural parent(s)
( ) Lives with guardian
( ) Lives in residential facility
( ) Lives with spouse
( ) Other (specify) ____________________________

E. Family supports

Estimate the extent to which this student's family can assist him/her with respect to the following areas:
Rate the following areas (1) none or minimal support, (2) some support, (3) full support

( ) Finances ( ) Housing ( ) Transportation
( ) Education ( ) Work/Education

F. Description of neighborhood and location in community:

G. General types of employment near home:

H. Transportation available:

I. Potential employers among family or friends:

III. Summary of student skills (attach resume)

A. Describe work related abilities:

B. Describe occupational interests:

C. Describe work related experiences:

D. Describe leisure/recreational interests/hobbies:

E. Quality considerations: Rate the following items as to the importance for the student/family on a scale of:
(1) not important, (2) somewhat important, (3) very important

( ) Opportunity for interaction with nondisabled coworkers
( ) Opportunity for high wages
( ) Opportunity to receive health benefits
( ) Opportunity to receive vacation and sick pay
( ) Potential for long-term employment
( ) Opportunity for supported employment
( ) Proximity to transportation

Comments: ____

____

F. Job-seeking skills (check all that apply):

( ) Describes own job interests and skills ( ) Needs assistance
( ) Uses resume during interview ( ) Needs assistance
( ) Initiates job-seeking tasks ( ) Needs assistance
( ) Demonstrates job interview skills and can interview independently ( ) Needs assistance
( ) Describes past work experience ( ) Needs assistance
( ) Completes application forms ( ) Needs assistance
( ) Prepares a resume ( ) Needs assistance
( ) Other: be specific ______________________________
______________________________ ( ) Needs assistance

Describe the Supports Needed in each area of Job-Seeking Skills in which the student needs assistance.

____
____
____

G. Work-performance skills (check all that apply):

( ) Arrives, takes breaks, leaves at right times ( ) Needs assistance
( ) Obtains more work when needed ( ) Needs assistance
( ) Modification of job demands ( ) Needs assistance
( ) Adjusts to job demands ( ) Needs assistance
( ) Completes assignments and tasks within timelines ( ) Needs assistance
( ) Travels independently to job ( ) Needs assistance
( ) Makes transitions smoothly from old to new tasks ( ) Needs assistance
( ) Checks and corrects own work ( ) Needs assistance
( ) Follows company rules/procedures ( ) Needs assistance
( ) Calls in when sick ( ) Needs assistance
( ) Follows written work schedule ( ) Needs assistance
( ) Other: be specific ______________________________
______________________________ ( ) Needs assistance

Describe the Supports Needed in each area of Work Performance Skills in which the student needs assistance.

____
____
____

H. Working with others (check all that apply):

( ) Follows directions ( ) Needs assistance
( ) Asks for help ( ) Needs assistance
( ) Works well with others ( ) Needs assistance
( ) Self-care skills at independent level ( ) Needs assistance
( ) Interacts well with customers ( ) Needs assistance
( ) Other: be specific ______________________________
______________________________ ( ) Needs assistance

Describe the Supports Needed in each area of Working with Others in which the student needs assistance.

____
____
____

I. What additional support/adaptations will be necessary for a job:

____

____

J. Travel skills (check all that apply):

( ) Can use mass transit ( ) Needs assistance
( ) Uses taxi ( ) Needs assistance
( ) Drives automobile ( ) Needs assistance
( ) Uses maps or bus schedules ( ) Needs assistance
( ) Reaches destinations on time ( ) Needs assistance
( ) Other: be specific ____________________
____________________ ( ) Needs assistance

Describe the Supports Needed in each area of Travel Skills in which the student needs assistance.

____

____

____

K. Health and safety skills (check all that apply):

( ) Recognizes safety and warning symbols ( ) Needs assistance
( ) Monitors own medications/takes medication appropriately ( ) Needs assistance
( ) Follows safety practices ( ) Needs assistance
( ) Responds to emergencies ( ) Needs assistance
( ) Schedules and attends medical/dental care ( ) Needs assistance
( ) Other: be specific ____________________
____________________ ( ) Needs assistance

Describe the Supports Needed in each area of Health and Safety skills in which the student needs assistance.

____

____

____

L. Meal planning (check all that apply):

( ) Displays manners ( ) Needs assistance
( ) Obtains prepared foods ( ) Needs assistance
( ) Prepares nutritious meals ( ) Needs assistance
( ) Purchases groceries ( ) Needs assistance
( ) Other: be specific ____________________
____________________ ( ) Needs assistance

Describe the Supports Needed in each area of Meal Planning in which the student needs assistance.

____

____

____

M. Money management (check all that apply):

( ) Can identify "best buy" consistently ( ) Needs assistance
( ) Can accurately exchange money for goods ( ) Needs assistance
( ) Uses checking and savings services ( ) Needs assistance

( ) Writes checks correctly ( ) Needs assistance
( ) Balances checkbook ( ) Needs assistance
( ) Can independently use an ATM machine ( ) Needs assistance
( ) Other: be specific ____________________
____________________ ( ) Needs assistance

Describe the Supports Needed in each area of Money Management in which the student needs assistance.

____
____
____

N. Recreation/Leisure Activities

List recreation and leisure activities in which the student routinely participates.

____
____
____

List recreation and leisure activities in which the student would like to participate.

____
____
____

O. Academic skills (reading, writing, mathematics) (check all that apply)

( ) Uses simple mathematics independently ( ) Needs assistance
( ) Uses mathematics for problem solving ( ) Needs assistance
( ) Uses computers/software ( ) Needs assistance
( ) Can keyboard effectively ( ) Needs assistance
( ) Writes in complete sentences ( ) Needs assistance
( ) Uses phone book independently ( ) Needs assistance
( ) Uses study skills independently ( ) Needs assistance
( ) Reads newspapers, books ( ) Needs assistance
( ) Reads with understanding ( ) Needs assistance
( ) Other: be specific ____________________
____________________ ( ) Needs assistance

Describe the Supports Needed in each area of Academic Skills in which the student needs assistance.

____
____
____

P. Telling time (check all that apply):

( ) Tells time accurately ( ) Needs assistance
( ) Can follow his/her own schedule ( ) Needs assistance
( ) Needs to follow prompts ( ) Needs assistance
( ) Other: be specific ____________________
____________________ ( ) Needs assistance

Describe the Supports Needed in each area of Money Management in which the student needs assistance.

____
____
____

Q. Communication skills (check all that apply):

( ) Speaks English clearly ( ) Needs assistance
( ) Speaks language other than English clearly ( ) Needs assistance
( ) Other: be specific ______________________________
____ ( ) Needs assistance

Describe the Supports Needed in each area of Communication Skills in which the student needs assistance.

____
____
____

R. Social interaction skills (check all that apply):

( ) Communicates basic needs ( ) Needs assistance
( ) Listens and follows directions ( ) Needs assistance
( ) Resists negative peer pressure ( ) Needs assistance
( ) Initiates, maintains, and ends conversation ( ) Needs assistance
( ) Effectively deals with teasing or negative comments ( ) Needs assistance
( ) Uses telephone effectively ( ) Needs assistance
( ) Expresses feelings in appropriate manner ( ) Needs assistance
( ) Cooperates and shares in group activities ( ) Needs assistance
( ) Respects others' property and privacy ( ) Needs assistance
( ) Recognizes and deals with interpersonal issues ( ) Needs assistance
( ) Makes appropriate decisions ( ) Needs assistance
( ) Assists others when needed ( ) Needs assistance
( ) Follows through on plans and decisions ( ) Needs assistance
( ) Manages own anger and frustration ( ) Needs assistance
( ) Adapts to changing situations ( ) Needs assistance
( ) Functions appropriately under pressure ( ) Needs assistance
( ) Responds appropriately to affection ( ) Needs assistance
( ) Takes part in recreation/leisure activities ( ) Needs assistance
( ) Interacts appropriately with authority figures ( ) Needs assistance
( ) Writes letters to friends and family ( ) Needs assistance
( ) Other: be specific______________________________
____ ( ) Needs assistance

Describe the Supports Needed in each area of Social Interaction Skills in which the student needs assistance.

____
____

IV. Predictions/Recommendations

Make a tentative prediction regarding this student's future course(s) of study or future employment.

____
____
____

APPENDIX B

Completed Informal Assessment Information for Activities

IDEA 1997: Critical Part 300 Regulations Regarding Transition Planning

Section 300.29 Transition services

(11) As used in this part, ***transition services*** means a coordinated set of activities for a student with a disability that

(1) Is designed within an outcome-oriented process, that promotes movement from school to postschool activities, including postsecondary education, vocational training, integrated employment (including supported employment), continuing and adult education, adult services, independent living, or community participation;

(2) Is based on the individual student's needs taking into account the student's preferences and interests; and

(3) Includes

(i) Instruction;

(ii) Related services;

(iii) Community experiences;

(iv) The development of employment and other postschool adult living objectives; and

(v) If appropriate, acquisition of daily living skills and functional vocational evaluation.

(12) Transition services for students with disabilities may be special education, if provided as specifically designed instruction, or related services, if required to assist a student with a disability to benefit from special education.

(Authority: 20 U.S.C. 1401(30))

Section 300.347 Content of IEP

(b) ***Transition services.*** The IEP must include

(1) For each student with a disability beginning at age 14 (or younger if determined appropriate by the IEP team), and updated annually, a statement of the transition service needs of the student under the applicable components of the student's IEP that focuses on the student's courses of study (such as participation in advanced-placement courses or a vocational program); and

(2) For each student beginning at age 16 (or younger, if determined appropriate by the IEP team), a statement of needed transition services for the student, including, if appropriate, a statement of the interagency responsibilities or any needed linkages.

(13) ***Transfer of rights.*** In a State that transfers rights at the age of majority, beginning at least one year before a student reaches the age of majority under State law, the student's IEP must include a statement that the student has been informed of his or her rights under Part B of the Act, if any, that will transfer to the student on reaching the age of majority, consistent with Section 300.517.

(Authority: 20 U.S.C. 1414(d)(1)(A) and (d)(6)(A)(vii))

Section 300.348 Agency responsible for transition services

(a) If a participating agency, other than the public agency, fails to provide that transition services described in the IEP in accordance with Section 300.347(b)(1), the public agency shall reconvene the IEP team to identify alternative strategies to meet the transition objectives for the student set out in the IEP.

(b) Nothing in this part relieves any participating agency, including a State vocational rehabilitation agency, of the responsibility to provide or pay for any transition service that the agency would otherwise provide to students with disabilities who meet that eligibility criteria of that agency.
(Authority 20 U.S.C. 1414(d)(5); 1414(d)(1)(A)(vii))

Future Planning Inventory

Student Form

What are your plans during high school and after graduation? Please complete this future planning document and bring it to your next Individual Educational Planning conference.

General Student Information

Student's name: Susan (first) P (middle) McMillin (last)

Social Security number: 543-00-0000 Birthdate: ______

Anticipated graduation date: ______ Grade: 9th

Current address: 444 West 7th Phone number: ______

Parent's name: Jim and Ruth McMillin Parent's business phone: ______

What kind of courses do you want to take during high school? (Be sure you choose the kind of coursework that will meet your future planning goals!)

_____ College preparatory   __X__ General education (Minimum graduation requirements)

_____ Vocational   _____ I don't know

I. Vocational/Postsecondary Education Options

A. Upon graduation, I want to go on for future education or training.

__X__ Yes   _____ No

If yes, please check each kind of postsecondary education or training that interests you.

__X__ Four-year college/university   _____ Private occupational training program

_____ Community college   _____ Military service

_____ Technical college   _____ Adult education program

What do you want to study or train to be? business manager

My level of motivation to succeed in the academic setting:

_____ high   __X__ medium   _____ low

The level of control I have over decision making and my individual success:

_____ high   __X__ medium   _____ low

My ability to identify what I need and how to get it:

_____ high   __X__ medium   _____ low

B. Upon graduation, I am going to get a job right away.

_____ Yes   __X__ No

If yes, please check the kind of job you expect to have.

_____ Competitive employment: _____ Full-time   _____ Part-time

_____ Self-employment

_____ Supported employment: _____ Full-time   _____ Part-time

_____ Sheltered employment: _____ Full-time   _____ Part-time

C. In what type of job/occupation will you be working one year after graduation?

business manager

D. In what type of job/occupation will you be working in five years after graduation?

business manager

E. What courses do you need to take in high school this year that will help you attain your employment or postsecondary education goals?

Art | English/Communication
Computers | Math

F. Do you want information on tests required to get into post-secondary education (e.g. ASVAB, SAT, ACT, PSAT)? No

G. What chores do you have at home and how much do you like to do them?

Activity (e.g. make bed, carry out trash: mow lawn.)	Degree of Independence: Do it independently	Need some help
1. clean room	✓	
2. do dishes	✓	
3. trash	✓	
4. dog	✓	
5.		

H. List jobs you do now and really enjoy.

I like working on Computers

I. What jobs or work experience have you had in your community?

Baby sitting

J. List any jobs you really dislike.

cleaning room

II. Home Living Options

A. Where do you plan on living after graduation?. (Please check one from this list.)

_____ Large urban (100,000 population plus) What city? _____
X Urban (30,000 to 100,000 population) What city? Our Town
_____ Rural (under 30,000 population) What town? _____
_____ Farm

B. (Please check one from this list)

X Live independently in apartment or home
_____ With family member (who?) _____
_____ With support _____
_____ Supervised apartment (which one?) _____
_____ Group home (which one?) _____
_____ College dormitory (where?) _____
_____ Other, please describe _____

III. Recreational and Leisure Options

A. Leisure Interest Inventory

Check any of the following leisure activity resources that are available in the community where you think you will live following graduation.

Athletic/Sports Activities

✓	swimming	____	lifting weights	____	skiing
____	running	____	aerobics	____	canoeing
____	softball	____	basketball	____	riding motorcycle
✓	walking	____	fishing	✓	camping
✓	riding bike	____	bowling	____	riding horses
____	other ____________				

Large Group Events

✓	movies	____	car races
____	sporting events	____	horse, dog, car shows
✓	music events	____	community education classes
____	other ____________		

Individual Activities

____	sewing	✓	listening to music	____	playing pool/billiards
____	handcrafts	____	cooking	✓	video games
____	reading	____	playing instrument	✓	shopping
✓	caring for pets	____	writing letters	____	caring for lawn
✓	talking on phone	✓	watching TV	____	cleaning/repairing car
____	playing cards or board games	____	Internet	____	other

Social Activities

____	dating	____	entertaining at home
____	picnicking	____	dancing
✓	eating out	____	driving around
____	attending church	____	spending time with family or friends
____	belonging to social club	____	volunteering
____	other ____________		

B. In which extracurricular activities would you like to participate during this year of high school?

None

Do you need any extra supports to participate in this/these extracurricular activities?

____ Yes X No

If yes, please describe: ____________

C. Future Leisure Activities

Check any of the following leisure activity resources that are available in the community where you think you will live following graduation:

✓	YMCA or YWCA	____	bowling leagues	✓	movie
____	recreation clubs, classes	____	city/county/state parks	____	sports arenas
____	other ____________				

Please list all the community leisure activities in which you plan to participate after high school.

go to park

go to mall and shop

____

Do you need any extra supports to participate in these leisure activities?

________ Yes ___X___ No

If yes, please describe: ______________________________

IV. Transportation Options

How will you get around the community and to work?

		I Do Now	I Need to Learn
X	drive own vehicle		✓
	drive family vehicle		
	use city bus transportation		
	take taxi		
	ride bicycle		
	walk		
	use special regional transportation system (i.e., bus between towns)		
	depend on others		
	other ______________		

V. Financial Support

A. Do you need financial help in any of the following areas to reach your long-range goals?

1. Postsecondary education ________ Yes ___X___ No
   If yes, please check all of the following for which you would like information.
   ________ a. Division of Rehabilitation Services (DRS)
   ________ b. Pell Grants
   ________ c. Scholarships
   ________ d. Work study
   ________ e. Student loans
   ________ f. Supplemental Security Income (SSI)

2. Help getting the right job ________ Yes ___X___ No
   If yes, please check all of the following for which you would like information.
   ________ a. Division of Rehabilitation Services (DRS)
   ________ b. Local Job Training Agency
   ________ c. State Job Service
   ________ d. Supplemental Security Income (SSI)

3. Home living assistance ________ Yes ___X___ No
   If yes, please check all of the following for which you would like information.
   ________ a. County Social Services
   ________ b. Supplemental Security Income (SSI)/ medical assistance
   ________ c. Housing assistance—city government
   ________ d. Independent Living Center Services

B. Have you contacted any of the following agencies regarding financial help?

_____ Yes __X__ No

(Please check all that apply.)

_____ Not applicable _____ Social Security Office

_____ Division of Rehabilitation Services (DRS) _____ County Social Services

_____ Local Job Training Agency

_____ Other, please describe _____

VI. Health-related Needs

A. When was your last physical examination?

(date) last year

B. Do you have any of the following needs?

_____ medical (i.e., medications) _____ yes* __X__ no

_____ counseling __X__ yes* _____ no

_____ other _____

*Please explain eating – I don't eat enough

C. What are some possible supports you may require in the future?

none

VII. Currently, what is your greatest concern for your future?

How do I get in college?

What business will I work in?

B-2, Form 2

About the Future Planning Inventory for Parents/Guardians

The following inventory has been designed to assist your son or daughter plan for his or her future after high school. For this planning to be successful, your son or daughter will need your help. Please fill out this inventory based on your own thoughts. Your son or daughter will complete his or her own Future Planning Inventory as will his or her special education teacher.

Bring your completed inventory to the next Individual Education Planning (IEP) meeting scheduled on _________. At that time we will discuss your young adult's future plans and discuss how we can work together to make sure he or she attains these goals. Depending on the age of your child, some questions may be more timely than others. If you have any questions when you are filling out this form, leave the item blank and this item will be discussed at the meeting. If you completed this form last year, your previous form will be attached to this blank form for your reference when completing this year's inventory.

Future Planning Inventory

Parent/Guardian Form

Please complete this future planning document and bring it to the upcoming Individual Education Planning conference scheduled for your son/daughter.

General Student Information

Student's name: susan (first) P (middle) McMillin (last)

Social Security number: 543-00-0000 Birthdate: ______

Anticipated graduation date: ______ Grade: 9th grade

Current address: 444 West 7th Phone number: 567 142 0000

Parent's name: Jim and Ruth McMillin Parent's business phone: 567 142 0000

What kind of secondary curriculum do you feel best meets the needs of your son or daughter?

__X__ College preparatory
______ General education
______ Vocational

I. Vocational/Postsecondary Education Options

A. Upon graduation, what do you see your son/daughter doing for future education or training? (Please check all that apply)

______ Four-Year college/university ______ Private occupational training program
__X__ Community college ______ Military service
__X__ Technical college ______ Community education program

What will your son/daughter be studying or training to be?

health related technical training

My son's/daughter's level of motivation to succeed in the academic setting:

______ high ______ medium __X__ low

The level of control my son/daughter believes he or she has over decision making and his/her individual success:

__X__ high ______ medium ______ low

My son's/daughter's ability to identify what he she needs and how to get it:

______ high ______ medium __X__ low

B. Upon graduation, in what kind of employment setting do you see your son/daughter engaged in?

__X__ Competitive employment: ______ Full-time __X__ Part-time
______ Self-employment
______ Supported employment: ______ Full-time ______ Part-time
______ Sheltered employment: ______ Full-time ______ Part-time

C. What type of job/occupation do you see your son/daughter working in one year after graduation?

food service

D. What type of job/occupation do you see your son/daughter working in five years after graduation?
LPN or Health Technician

E. What work-related demands are being placed on your son or daughter at home, and what is his or her reaction to them?

Activity (For example makes bed, carries out trash, mows lawn.)	Degree of Independence: Does Independently	Needs Guidance	Unwilling to Perform Task
1. clean room		✓	
2. make bed	✓		
3. wash dishes			✓
4. take care of dog		✓	
5.			

F. List any jobs or chores your son/daughter does now and enjoys.
doesn't like to clean
likes to walk dog

G. What jobs or work experience has your son/daughter had in your community?
baby sitting

H. List any jobs your son/daughter seems to really dislike.
cleaning room
washing dishes

II. Home Living Options

A. Where do you think your son/daughter will likely live after graduation? (Please check one from this list.)

- ______ Large urban (100,000 population plus) What city? ______
- X Urban (30,000 to 100,000 population) What city? our town
- ______ Rural (under 30,000 population) What town? ______
- ______ Farm

B. (Please check one from this list.)

- ______ Live independently in apartment or home ______
- X With family member (who?) mother & father
- ______ With support
  - ______ Supervised apartment (which one?) ______
  - ______ Group home (which one?) ______
- ______ College dormitory (where?) ______
- ______ Other, please describe ______

III. Recreational and Leisure Options

A. Leisure Interest Inventory

Check all of the following leisure activities in which your son or daughter currently spends free time.

Athletic/Sports Activities

✓	swimming		liftingweights		skiing
	running		aerobics		canoeing
	softball		basketball		riding motorcycle
✓	walking	✓	fishing	✓	camping
✓	riding bike		bowling		riding horses
	other ______				

Large Group Events

✓	movies		car races
	ball games		horse, dog, car shows
✓	music events		community education classes
	other ______		

Individual Activities

	sewing	✓	listening to music		Internet
	handcrafts		cooking	✓	shopping
	reading		playing instrument		playing pool/billiards
✓	caring for pets		writing letters		caring for lawn
✓	talking on phone	✓	watching TV	✓	playing video games
	clean/repair car				playing cards or board games
	other ______				

Social Activities

	dating		entertaining at home	✓	attending church
	picnicking		volunteering		belonging to a social club
✓	eating out		driving around		spending time with family or friends
	dancing		other ______		

B. In which extracurricular activities would you like your son/daughter to participate during high school?

cheer leading

Does your son/daughter need any specific supports or accommodations to participate in this/these extracurricular activities? X Yes ______ No

If yes, please describe: just help getting going

C. Future Leisure Activities

Check any of the following leisure activity resources that are available in the community where you think your son/daughter will live following graduation:

✓	YMCA or YWCA		bowling leagues	✓	recreation clubs, classes
	city/county/state parks	✓	movie		sports arenas
✓	city recreation facilities	✓	church groups		community education center
	other ______				

Please list all the community leisure activities in which you hope your son/daughter will choose to participate after high school.

Church group

she needs to take up a community activity to

stay in shape -maybe raquetball

Does your son/daughter need any specific supports or accommodations to participate in these leisure activities? ______ Yes ___X___ No

If yes, please describe: ____________________

IV. Transportation Options

How will your son/daughter get around the community and to work?

	Does Now	Needs to Learn
______ drive own vehicle		
___X___ drive family vehicle		✓
___X___ use city bus transportation		✓
______ take taxi		
______ ride bicycle		
______ walk		
______ use special regional transportation system (i.e., bus between towns)		
______ depend on others		
______ other ____________		

Are you willing to drive your son/daugher to work? ___X___ Yes ______ No

How many miles? wherever necessary

V. Financial Support

A. Does your son/daughter need financial assistance in any of the following areas to reach his/her long-range goals?

1. Postsecondary education ___X___ Yes ______ No
   If yes, please check all of the following for which you would like information.
   - ______ a. Division of Rehabilitation Services (DRS)
   - ___X___ b. Pell Grants
   - ___X___ c. Scholarships
   - ______ d. Work study
   - ______ e. Student loans
   - ______ f. Supplemental Security Income (SSI)
   - ______ g. Social Security Disability Insurance (SSDI)
2. Employment assistance ___X___ Yes ______ No
   If yes, please check all of the following for which you would like information.
   - ______ a. Division of Rehabilitation Services (DRS)
   - ___X___ b. Local Job Training Agency
   - ______ c. State Job Service
   - ______ d. Supplemental Security Income (SSI)

_________ e. County social services
_________ f. Rehabilitation centers

3. Home living assistance _________ Yes ____X____ No
   If yes, please check all of the following for which you would like information.
   _________ a. County Social Services
   _________ b. Supplemental Security Income (SSI)/ medical assistance
   _________ c. Housing assistance—city government
   ____✓____ d. Independent Living Center services

B. Which of the following agencies have you contacted with regard to financial support for your son or daughter?
____X____ Not applicable *none*
_________ Division of Rehabilitation Services (DRS)
_________ Local Job Training Agency
_________ Social Security Office
_________ County Social Services
_________ Other, please describe _________________________

VI. Health-Related Needs

A. When was the last physical examination completed for your son or daughter?
(date) *last year*

B. Does your son/daughter currently have any of the following needs?
_________ medical (i.e., medications) _________ yes* _________ no
_________ counseling ____X____ yes* _________ no
_________ other _________________________
*Please explain *eating disorder*

C. What are some supports your son/daughter may require in the future?
counseling

VII. Currently, what is your greatest concern for your son/daughter's future?
concerned about her lack of interest in food
no real understanding of careers and what it takes to get one.

Future Planning Inventory

Educator Form

Please complete this future planning document and bring it to the upcoming Individual Education Planning conference scheduled for your student.

General Student Information

Student's name: Susan (first) P (middle) McMillin (last)

Student's Social Security number: ______ Birthdate: ______

Anticipated graduation date: 4+ years Grade: 9th grade

Current address: 444 West 7th Phone number: 567 142 0000

Parent's name: Ruth and Jim McMillin Business phone: ______

What kind of secondary curriculum do you feel best meets the needs of your student?

- ______ College preparatory
- ______ General education
- X Vocational

I. Vocational/Postsecondary Education Options

A. Upon graduation, where do you see your student participating in future education or training? (Please check all that apply)

______	Four-year college/university	X	Private occupational training program
X	Community college	______	Military service
X	Technical college	______	Community education program

B. What kind of employment do you see your student participating in after graduation? (Check all that apply).

X	Competitive employment:	______	Full-time	X	Part-time
______	Supported employment:	______	Full-time	______	Part-time
______	Sheltered employment:	______	Full-time	______	Part-time

C. Academic and life skills assessment

1. Current reading recognition score:
   Woodcock Reading Mastery Test last year Sept. Date given 6.1 Grade level
2. Current reading comprehension score:
   Woodcock Reading Mastery Test last year Sept. Date given 5.6 Grade level

   Reading strengths Strong interest in reading

   Reading concerns Susan has problem with comprehension of written material
3. Current math score:
   key math Test last Sept. Date given 8.2 Grade level

   Math strengths average math skills this is strength area

   Math concerns needs to work on Algebra skills

4. Life skills curricula:

   Areas of strength strong social skills

   Areas of concern budgeting and use of credit

5. Student level of motivation ______ high ______ medium __X__ low

   Student locus of control ______ high __X__ medium ______ low

   Ability of student to self-advocate ______ high ______ medium __X__ low

II. Home Living Options

A. Where do you think the student will likely live after graduation?

__X__ Live independently in apartment or home

______ With family member (who?) ______

______ With support

______ Supervised apartment (which one?) ______

______ Group home (which one?) ______

______ College dormitory (where?) ______

______ Other, please describe ______

III. Recreational and Leisure Options

A. In which extracurricular activities would you like to see the student participate during high school?

Susan needs to participate in extra curricular activities to stay engaged in school

Does your student need any specific supports or accommodations to participate in this/these extracurricular activities? ______ Yes __X__ No

If yes, please describe: ______

B. Future Leisure Activities

Please list all the community leisure activities in which you hope your student will choose to participate after high school.

I believe the team should identify community-based leisure activities and work to develop skills and interest.

Does your student need any specific supports or accommodations to participate in this/these leisure activities?

______ Yes __X__ No

If yes, please describe: ______

IV. Transportation Options

How will your student get around the community and to work?

		Does Now	Needs to Learn
X	drive own vehicle		✓
X	drive family vehicle		✓
______	use city bus transportation		
______	take taxi		
______	ride bicycle		
______	walk		
______	use special regional transportation system (i.e., bus between towns)		
______	depends on others		
______	other ______		

V. Financial Support

A. Which of the following agencies need to be contacted regarding transition planning and financial assistance for your student?

______ Not applicable
__X__ Division of Rehabilitation Services (DRS)
__X__ Local Job Training Agency
______ Social Security office
______ County social services
______ Other, please describe ______

VI. Currently, what is your greatest concern for future of your student?

• eating disorder

• needs to develop clear career interest

Self-Determination and Self-Advocacy Skills Questionnaire

Student Form

Name: Sara P Today's Date: March 1, 20--

Grade: 10 th

Age: 16 Anticipated Graduation Date: two years +

Disability (please be specific): learning disability

The following questionnaire was developed to identify your level of knowledge and skill in issues related to self-determination and self-advocacy. After reading each of the following sixteen skill statements, please circle the **one number** that best describes your level of skill.

1. I can list and discuss the academic accommodations I need to be successful in high school.
   1 Not at all 2 3 4 5 (6) All the time
2. I can list and discuss the support services I need on the job in order to be successful.
   1 Not at all 2 3 4 (5) 6 All the time
3. I am able to independently contact the adult service providers that I will need to help me reach my employment goals.
   1 Not at all (2) 3 4 5 6 All the time
4. I can independently request and effectively use academic accommodations in all my classes.
   1 Not at all 2 3 (4) 5 6 All the time
5. I can list and discuss the accommodations I will use to be successful in my job.
   1 Not at all 2 (3) 4 5 6 All the time
6. I can list and discuss my rights for reasonable academic accommodation under the law.
   1 Not at all 2 3 4 5 (6) All the time
7. I identify myself as a person with a disability in order to get the support services I deserve in postsecondary education.
   1 Not at all 2 3 4 5 (6) All the time
8. I can list and discuss the support services I will need in postsecondary education in order to be successful.
   1 Not at all 2 3 4 (5) 6 All the time
9. I can state accommodations I need in the workplace that are guaranteed to me by law.
   1 Not at all 2 (3) 4 5 6 All the time
10. I identify myself as a person with a disability in order to get the support services I deserve from my employer.
    1 Not at all 2 3 4 5 (6) All the time
11. I am able to independently contact the adult service providers that will help me reach my postsecondary education goals.
    1 Not at all (2) 3 4 5 6 All the time

12. I lead my own IEP team meetings.

1	2	3	4	5	(6)
Not at all					All the time

13. I state my goals and aspirations for each school year during the annual IEP team meeting.

1	2	3	4	5	(6)
Not at all					All the time

14. I can independently request and effectively use accommodations on the job.

1	2	(3)	4	5	6
Not at all					All the time

15. I have identified my long-term employment goals for after high school and I can state and discuss these long-term goals.

1	2	3	4	5	(6)
Not at all					All the time

16. I am able to identify and discuss the amount and type of postsecondary education or training I will need to reach my long-term employment goals.

1	2	3	4	5	(6)
Not at all					All the time

Self-Determination and Self-Advocacy Skills Questionnaire

Parent Form

Name: Sara P Today's Date: ____________

Grade: 10th

Age: 16 Anticipated Graduation Date: 2+ years

Disability (please be specific): learning disability

The following questionnaire was developed to identify the level of knowledge and skill in issues related to self-determination and self-advocacy of your young adult. After reading each of the following sixteen skill statements, please circle the **one number** that best describes her/his level of skill.

1. My young adult can list and discuss the academic accommodations he/she needs to be successful in high school.

   1 Not at all 2 3 4 (5) 6 All the time

   ________ I am not aware of my son's/daughter's skills in this area. (Please check only if applicable.)

2. My young adult can list and discuss the support services he/she needs on the job in order to be successful.

   1 Not at all 2 3 4 5 6 All the time

   ___X___ I am not aware of my son's/daughter's skills in this area. (Please check only if applicable.)

3. My young adult is able to independently contact the adult service providers that he/she will need to help him/her reach his/her employment goals.

   1 Not at all (2) 3 4 5 6 All the time

   ________ I am not aware of my son's/daughter's skills in this area. (Please check only if applicable.)

4. My young adult can independently request and effectively use academic accommodations in all his/her classes.

   1 Not at all (2) 3 4 5 6 All the time

   ________ I am not aware of my son's/daughter's skills in this area. (Please check only if applicable.)

5. My young adult can list and discuss the accommodations he/she will use to be successful in a job.

   1 Not at all (2) 3 4 5 6 All the time

   ________ I am not aware of my son's/daughter's skills in this area. (Please check only if applicable.)

6. My young adult can list and discuss his/her rights for reasonable academic accommodation under the law.

   1 Not at all 2 3 4 5 (6) All the time

   ________ I am not aware of my son's/daughter's skills in this area. (Please check only if applicable.)

7. My young adult can identifies himself/herself as a person with a disability in order to get the support services that he/she deserves in postsecondary education.

   1 Not at all 2 3 4 5 (6) All the time

   ________ I am not aware of my son's/daughter's skills in this area. (Please check only if applicable.)

8. My young adult can list and discuss the support services that he/she will need in postsecondary education in order to be successful.
   1 Not at all   2   (3)   4   5   6 All the time

   ________ I am not aware of my son's/daughter's skills in this area. (Please check only if applicable.)

9. My young adult can state accommodations he/she needs in the workplace that are guaranteed by law.
   1 Not at all   (2)   3   4   5   6 All the time

   ________ I am not aware of my son's/daughter's skills in this area. (Please check only if applicable.)

10. My young adult can identify himself/herself as a person with a disability in order to get the support services that he/she deserves from an employer.
   1 Not at all   2   3   4   5   (6) All the time

   ________ I am not aware of my son's/daughter's skills in this area. (Please check only if applicable.)

11. My young adult is able to independently contact the adult service providers that will help her/him reach his/her postsecondary education goals.
   1 Not at all   (2)   3   4   5   6 All the time

   ________ I am not aware of my son's/daughter's skills in this area. (Please check only if applicable.)

12. My young adult leads his/her own IEP meetings.
   1 Not at all   2   3   (4)   5   6 All the time

13. My young adult states goals and aspirations for each school year at her/his annual IEP meeting.
   1 Not at all   2   3   4   5   (6) All the time

   ________ I am not aware of my son's/daughter's skills in this area. (Please check only if applicable.)

14. My young adult can independently request and effectively use accommodations on the job.
   1 Not at all   2   3   4   5   6 All the time

   ___X___ I am not aware of my son's/daughter's skills in this area. (Please check only if applicable.)

15. My young adult has identified long-term employment goals for after high school and can state and discuss his/her long-term goals.
   1 Not at all   2   3   4   5   (6) All the time

   ________ I am not aware of my son's/daughter's skills in this area. (Please check only if applicable.)

16. My young adult is able to identify and discuss the amount and type of postsecondary education or training that he/she will need to reach his/her long-term employment goals.
   1 Not at all   2   3   4   (5)   6 All the time

   ________ I am not aware of my son's/daughter's skills in this area. (Please check only if applicable.)

Self-Determination and Self-Advocacy Skills Questionnaire

Teacher Forms A and B

Today's Date: ______________________
Student Name: ______________________
Grade: ______________________
Anticipated Graduation Date: ______________________
Student Disability: ______________________
Teacher Name: ______________________

Unlike the student and parent instruments, the teacher form of this instrument is divided into Form A and Form B. Form A includes only those foils regarding accommodations relating to academic needs in secondary school and future postsecondary education. Form B includes all foils regarding employment related issues. These forms may be used in a number of manners. A case manager/teacher may choose to complete both Form A and B if appropriate. The case manager/teacher may choose to request that Form B of the instrument be completed by a teacher who works with the student directly in a tech-prep, school-to-work, or career/vocational area of education. The case manager/teacher may choose to complete only Form A or only Form B of the instrument as appropriate based on their observations of the student in either an academic or vocational setting.

Form A includes eight foils (numbers 1, 4, 6, 7, 8, 11, 12, and 13) related to academic skills and postsecondary education. Form B includes eight foils (numbers 2, 3, 5, 9, 10, 14, 15, and 16) related to employment skills. These numbers correspond with the numbered foils found on the student and parent forms to simplify the graphing and presentation of all data.

B-3, Form 3

Self-Determination and Self-Advocacy Skills Questionnaire

Teacher Form A: Academic Skills

Student Name: Sara P Date: March 1, 20--

Teacher Name: Mr. Smith

Please circle the one number that best describes the above student's knowledge and skill level related to each of the statements below.

1. The student can list and discuss the academic accommodations needed to be successful in high school classes.
   1 Not at all 2 3 4 (5) 6 All the time

4. The student can independently request and effectively use academic accommodations in the class that I teach.
   1 Not at all (2) 3 4 5 6 All the time

6. The student can list and discuss her/his rights for reasonable academic accommodations under the law.
   1 Not at all 2 3 4 (5) 6 All the time

7. The student identifies him/herself as a person with a disability in order to get the support services she/he is entitled to in postsecondary education.
   1 Not at all 2 3 4 5 (6) All the time

8. The student can list and discuss the support services needed in postsecondary education in order to be successful.
   1 Not at all (2) 3 4 5 6 All the time

11. The student is able to independently contact the adult service providers that will help him/her reach postsecondary education goals.
   1 Not at all (2) 3 4 5 6 All the time

12. The student leads his/her own IEP team meetings.
   1 Not at all 2 3 (4) 5 6 All the time

13. The student states goals and aspirations for each school year at her/his annual IEP team meeting.
   1 Not at all 2 3 4 5 (6) All the time

Self-Determination and Self-Advocacy Skills Questionnaire

Teacher Form B: Employment Skills

Student Name: ______________________ Date: ______________________

Teacher Name: ______________________

Please circle the one number that best describes the above student's knowledge and skill level related to each of the statements below.

2. The student can list and discuss the support services he/she will need on the job to be successful.

1	2	3	4	5	6
Not at all					All the time

3. The student is able to independently contact the adult service providers that he/she will need to reach his/her employment goals.

1	2	3	4	5	6
Not at all					All the time

5. The student can list and discuss the accommodations he/she will use to be successful on a job.

1	2	3	4	5	6
Not at all					All the time

9. The student can state accommodations needed in the workplace that are guaranteed under the law.

1	2	3	4	5	6
Not at all					All the time

10. The student can identify himself/herself as a person with a disability in order to get the support services guaranteed under law.

1	2	3	4	5	6
Not at all					All the time

14. The student can independently request and effectively use needed accommodations on the job.

1	2	3	4	5	6
Not at all					All the time

15. The student has identified his/her long-term employment goals for after high school and can state and discuss his/her long-term goals.

1	2	3	4	5	6
Not at all					All the time

16. The student is able to identify and discuss the amount and type of postsecondary education or training needed to reach his/her long-term employment goals.

1	2	3	4	5	6
Not at all					All the time

Scoring Summary

For the Self-Determination and Self-Advocacy Skills Questionnaire

Student Name: Sara P **Testing Date:** March 1, 20--

Academic Skills

Question #	1	4	6	7	8	11	12	13	Average
Parent (Likert score)	5	2	6	6	3	2	4	6	34 / 4.25
Student (Likert score)	6	4	6	6	5	2	6	6	41 / 5.12
Teacher (Likert score)	5	2	5	6	2	2	4	6	32 / 4.0
Need area		KO			KO	K	KO		
SD/SA Skills Questionnaire: Performance Battery									

Employment Skills

Question #	2	3	5	9	10	14	15	16	Average
Parent (Likert score)	not scored	2	2	2	6	not scored	6	5	23 / 3.83
Student (Likert score)	5	2	3	3	6	3	6	6	34 / 4.25
Teacher (Likert score)	-	-	-	-	-	-	-	-	
Need area		K	K	K		K			
SD/SA Skills Questionnaire: Performance Battery									

Scoring Key

Need Area:

K—Knowledge and skills needed in this area (rankings of two of three raters [Parent, Student, Teacher]) 4 or less.

O—Teammember scores are dissimilar (two or more points discrepant)

KO—Both

SD/SA Skills Questionnaire: Performance Battery

A—student demonstrated ***adequate*** knowledge and skill

L—student demonstrated ***limited*** knowledge and skill

N—student demonstrated ***significant discrepancy*** in knowledge and skill

C.I.T.E. Learning Styles Instrument

The *C.I.T.E.* Instrument (Babich, Burdine, Albright, and Randol, 1976) was formulated at the Murdoch Teachers Center in Wichita, Kansas to help teachers determine the learning styles preferred by their students. It is divided into three main areas:

- **Information gathering** includes auditory language, visual language, auditory numerical, visual numerical, and auditory-visual language, auditory numerical, visual numerical, and auditory-visual-kinesthetic combination.
- **Work conditions** focus on whether a student works better alone or in a group.
- **Expressiveness** considers if a student is better at oral or written communication.

Scores on the Learning Styles Inventory fall into one of three categories: major, minor, and negligible. These categories may be defined as follows:

Major: The student prefers this mode of learning, feels comfortable with it, and uses it for important (to the student) learning. A student does not necessarily have one and only one preferred style.

Minor: The student uses this mode but usually as a second choice or in conjunction with other learning styles.

Negligible: The student prefers not to use this if other choices are available. The student does not feel comfortable with this style.

Frank B. Mann, III, Wyoming County, West Virginia, programmed a computer application system for the ***C.I.T.E. Learning Styles Inventory*** so that students may respond to the questions through use of the computer. The computer will tally the scores automatically. Teachers may obtain copies by contacting Louise Miller at 1-800-766-7372 email: lbmiller@access.k12.wv.us

Definitions and Teaching Techniques for Major Learning Styles

The following are descriptions of learning styles found in every learner to a major, minor, or negligible extent and teaching suggestions related to each learning style.

Learning Style	Teaching Techniques
Visual-Language: This is the student who learns well from seeing words in books or workbooks, on the chalkboard or charts. He/she may write down words that are delivered orally in order to learn by seeing them on paper. He or she remembers and uses information better if it has been read.	This student will benefit from a variety of books, pamphlets, and written materials on several levels of difficulty. Given some time alone with a book, he or she may learn more than in class. Make sure important information has been given on paper, or that he or she takes notes if you want this student to remember specific information.
Visual-Numerical: This student has to see numbers on the board, in a book, or on paper in order to work with them. He or she is more likely to remember and understand math facts if he or she has seen them. He or she does not seem to need as much oral explanation.	This student will benefit from worksheets, workbooks, and texts. Give a variety of written materials and allow time to study it. In playing games and being involved in activities with numbers and number problems, make sure they are visible, printed numbers, not oral games and activities. Important data should be given on paper.
Auditory-Language: This is the student who learns from hearing words spoken. You may hear him or her vocalizing or see the lips or throat move as he or she reads, particularly when striving to understand new material. He or she will be more capable of understanding and remembering words or facts that have been learned by hearing.	This student will benefit from hearing audio tapes, rote oral practice, lecture, or a class discussion. He or she may benefit from using a tape recorder to make tapes to listen to later, by teaching another student, or conversing with the teacher. Groups of two or more, games, or interaction activities provide the sounds of words being spoken that is so important to this student.

Learning Style	Teaching Techniques
Auditory-Numerical: This student learns from hearing numbers and oral explanations. He or she may remember phone and locker numbers with ease, be successful with oral numbers, games, and puzzles. He or she may do just about as well without a math book, for written materials are not as important. He or she can probably work problems in his or her head. You may hear this student saying the numbers aloud or see the lips move as a problem is read.	This student will benefit from math sound tapes or from working with other people, talking about a problem. Even reading written explanations aloud will help. and Games or activities in which the number problems are spoken will help. This student will benefit from tutoring another or delivering an explanation to his or her study group or to the teacher. Make sure important facts are spoken.
Auditory-Visual-Kinesthetic: The A/V/K student learns best by experience and self-involvement. He or she definitely needs a combination of stimuli. The manipulation of material along with the accompanying sights and sounds (words and numbers seen and spoken) will make a big difference to him or her. This student may not seem able to understand or keep his or her mind on work unless he or she is totally involved. He or she seeks to handle, touch, and work with what is being learned. Sometimes just writing or a symbolic wriggling of the fingers is a symptom of the A/V/K learner.	This student must be given more than just a reading or math assignment. Involve him or her with at least one other student and give him or her an activity to relate to the assignment. Accompany an audiotape with pictures, objects, and an activity such as drawing or writing, or following directions with physical involvement.
Social-Individual: This student gets more work done alone. He or she thinks best and remembers more when he or she has learned alone. He or she cares more for his or her own opinions than for the ideas of others. You will not have much trouble keeping this student from over-socializing during class.	This student needs to be allowed to do important learning alone. If you feel he or she needs socialization, save it for a non-learning situation. Let him or her go to the library or back in a corner of the room to be alone. Do not force group work on him or her when it will make the student irritable to be held back or distracted by others. Some great thinkers are loners.
Social-Group: This student strives to study with at least one other student and he or she will not get as much done alone. He or she values others' ideas and preferences. Group interaction increases his or her learning and later recognition of facts. Socializing is important to this student.	This student needs to do important learning with someone else. The stimulation of the group may be more important at certain times in the learning process than at others and you may be able to facilitate the timing for this student.
Expressive Oral: This student prefers to tell what he or she knows. He or she talks fluently, comfortably, and clearly. The teacher may find that this learner knows more than written tests show. He or she is probably less shy than others about giving reports or talking to the teacher or classmates. The muscular coordination involved in writing may be difficult for this learner. Organizing and putting thoughts on paper may be too slow and tedious a task for this student.	Allow this student to make oral reports instead of written ones. Whether in conference, small group or large, evaluate him or her more by what is said than by what is written. Reports can be on tape, to save class time. Demand a minimum of written work, but demand good quality so he or she will not be ignorant of the basics of composition and legibility. Grammar can be corrected orally but is best done at another time.
Expressiveness-Written: This student can write fluent essays and good answers on tests to show what he or she knows. He or she feels less comfortable, perhaps even stupid, when oral answers are required. His or her thoughts are better organized on paper than when they are given orally.	This student needs to be allowed to write reports, keep notebooks and journals for credit, and take written tests for evaluation. Oral transactions should be under non-pressured conditions, perhaps even in a one-to-one conference.

C.I.T.E. Learning Styles Instrument

Name: Sara Jones, age 16 Date: ______________

Instructions: Read each statement carefully and decide which of the four responses agrees with how you feel about the statement. Put an X on the number of your response.

Questions	Most Like Me			Least Like Me
1. When I make things for my studies, I remember what I have learned better.	X	3	2	1
2. Written assignments are easy for me.	4	3	2	X
3. I learn better if someone reads a book to me than if I read silently to myself.	4	X	2	1
4. I learn best when I study alone.	4	X	2	1
5. Having assignment directions written on the board makes them easier to understand.	4	X	2	1
6. It's harder for me to do a written assignment than an oral one.	X	3	2	1
7. When I do math problems in my head, I say the numbers to myself.	X	3	2	1
8. If I need help in the subject, I will ask a classmate for help.	4	3	2	X
9. I understand a math problem that is written down better than one I hear.	X	3	2	1
10. I don't mind doing written assignments.	4	3	2	X
11. I remember things I hear better than I read.	4	3	2	X
12. I remember more of what I learn if I learn it when I am alone.	4	3	X	1
13. I would rather read a story than listen to it read.	4	3	2	X
14. I feel like I talk smarter than I write.	X	3	2	1
15. If someone tells me three numbers to add I can usually get the right answer without writing them down.	4	3	2	X
16. I like to work in a group because I learn from the others in the group.	X	3	2	1
17. Written math problems are easier for me to do than oral ones.	4	3	2	X
18. Writing a spelling word several times helps me remember it better.	4	X	2	1
19. I find it easier to remember what I have heard than what I have read.	X	3	2	1
20. It is more fun to learn with classmates at first, but it is hard to study with them.	X	3	2	1
21. I like written directions better than spoken ones.	4	X	2	1
22. If homework were oral, I would do it all.	X	3	2	1

Questions	Most Like Me			Least Like Me
23. When I hear a phone number, I can remember it without writing it down.	4	3	2	1
24. I get more work done when I work with someone.	4	3	2	1
25. Seeing a number makes more sense to me than hearing a number.	4	3	2	1
26. I like to do things like simple repairs or crafts with my hands.	4	3	2	1
27. The things I write on paper sound better than when I say them.	4	3	2	1
28. I study best when no one is around to talk or listen to.	4	3	2	1
29. I would rather read things in a book than have the teacher tell me about them.	4	3	2	1
30. Speaking is a better way than writing if you want someone to understand it better.	4	3	2	1
31. When I have a written math problem to do, I say it to myself to understand it better.	4	3	2	1
32. I can learn more about a subject if I am with a small group of students.	4	3	2	1
33. Seeing the price of something written down is easier for me to understand than having someone tell me the price.	4	3	2	1
34. I like to make things with my hands.	4	3	2	1
35. I like tests that call for sentence completion or written answers.	4	3	2	1
36. I understand more from a class discussion than from reading about a subject.	4	3	2	1
37. I remember the spelling of a word better if I see it written down than if someone spells it out loud.	4	3	2	1
38. Spelling and grammar rules make it hard for me to say what I want to in writing.	4	3	2	1
39. It makes it easier when I say the numbers of a problem to myself as I work it out.	4	3	2	1
40. I like to study with other people.	4	3	2	1
41. When the teachers say a number, I really don't understand it until I see it written down.	4	3	2	1
42. I understand what I have learned better when I am involved in making something for the subject.	4	3	2	1
43. Sometimes I say dumb things, but writing gives me time to correct myself.	4	3	2	1
44. I do well on tests if they are about things I hear in class.	4	3	2	1
45. I can't think as well when I work with someone else as when I work alone.	4	3	2	1

C.I.T.E. Learning Styles Instrument Worksheet

Name: Sara Jones Date:__________

Directions: Look at each statement number on the worksheet below. Find the statement number on the Learning Styles Inventory and get the "most like/least like" number of the response you selected for each statement. Write the number (1–4) in the blank provided. Total the numbers under each heading. Multiply the total by two. Look at the scores to decide if this is major, minor, or negligible.

Visual-Language
5 3
13 1
21 3
29 1
37 1
Total 9 × 2 = 18 (Score)

Visual-Numerical
9 4
17 1
25 2
33 1
41 2
Total 10 × 2 = 20 (Score)

Auditory-Language
3 3
11 1
19 4
36 4
44 3
Total 15 × 2 = 30 (Score)

Auditory-Numerical
7 4
15 1
23 1
31 4
39 4
Total 14 × 2 = 28 (Score)

Auditory-Visual-Kinesthetic
1 4
18 3
26 4
34 4
42 4
Total 19 × 2 = 38 (Score)

Social-Individual
4 3
12 2
20 4
28 4
45 4
Total 17 × 2 = 34 (Score)

Social-Group
8 1
16 4
24 2
32 2
40 2
Total 11 × 2 = 22 (Score)

Expressiveness-Oral
6 4
14 4
22 4
30 4
38 4
Total 20 × 2 = 40 (Score)

Expressiveness-Written
2 1
10 1
27 1
35 1
43 1
Total 5 × 2 = 10 (Score)

Score: 34–40 = Major learning style
20–32 = Minor learning style
10–18 = Negligible use

Transition Planning Inventory (TPI) Results for Juan Rodrigiez

Juan Rodrigiez is a 10th grade boy with specific learning disabilities who attends an urban school. Juan's parents and special education teacher have just completed his special education re-evaluation which included a transition evaluation. The Transition Planning Inventory (TPI), a comprehensive transition assessment, was used as part of the battery of assessment instruments. Results gleaned from two of the nine planning areas are listed below. These areas are Community Participation and Daily Living. The scale rating is NA (not applicable); 0, 1, 2 (strongly disagree); 3, 4, or 5 (strongly agree); DK (don't know).

Community Participation

Knows basic legal rights	Parent = 1;	Student = 3;	School = 1
Participates as an active citizen	Parent = 1;	Student = 2;	School = 1
Makes legal decisions	Parent = 0;	Student = 0;	School = 0
Locates community services and resources	Parent = 3;	Student = 3;	School = 2
Uses services and resources successfully	Parent = 1;	Student = 2;	School = 1
Knows how to obtain financial assistance	Parent = 0;	Student = 0;	School = 1

Daily Living

Maintains personal grooming/hygiene	Parent = 3;	Student = 3;	School = 3
Knows how to locate place to live	Parent = 2;	Student = 3;	School = 1
Knows how to set up living arrangement	Parent = 1;	Student = 2;	School = 1
Performs everyday household tasks	Parent = 2;	Student = 4;	School = 2
Uses local transportation system	Parent = 1;	Student = 2;	School = 1

TPI Evaluation Summary for Juan Rodrigiez

The items listed below are subcompetencies from the Transition Planning Inventory (TPI). They are divided into strengths and needs which further clarify the exact skills that Juan either possesses or does not possess in the areas of daily living and community participation. These subcompetencies are formatted in the TPI in an objective manner that lends itself to IEP development.

Strengths

Community Participation

Demonstrates ability regarding how to volunteer at an organization, club, social group, or other community service organization.
Demonstrates ability to locate post office, emergency assistance, recreational services, religious groups.
Demonstrates skills in locating public pay telephones, vending machines, and restrooms.

Comments At the IEP conference, Juan said he marked the area "knows basic legal rights" as "strongly agrees" because he knew about laws. His parents and teacher then told him why they had it marked as "strongly disagrees" (see needs below). He then understood that he still had transition needs in the area of "knows basic legal rights."

Daily Living

Ability to perform personal hygiene functions.
Ability to dress appropriately, purchase and maintain clothing, and organize and store clothing.
Demonstrates ability to use basic household appliances safely.
Ability to perform floor maintenance (include sweeping, mopping and vacuuming).
Demonstrates ability to wash and store dishes and other cooking and eating equipment.

Demonstrates ability to pick up items around residence and return to proper setting.

Manipulates money (includes selecting coins and/or bills to total a specific amount, making change, using an automatic teller machine and/or debit card, and identifying coins and bills and their values).

Comments At the IEP conference, Juan said he marked the area "knows how to locate place to live" as "strongly agrees" because he knew someone that had an apartment and they could show him how to get one when he was ready. Also, he had moved with his parents before and knew how to pack boxes. His parents and teacher then told him why they had it marked as "strongly disagrees" (see needs below). He then understood that he still had transition needs in the area of locating and setting up a place to live in the community. Juan's rating of himself reflected his current financial needs and not his needs in the future. When that was discussed at his IEP meeting he understood why his teacher and parents had rated "strongly disagree" and had areas of need listed on the evaluation summary.

Needs

Community Participation

Assistance setting up living arrangements (evaluate and select from various options using resources in the community).

Assistance making legal decisions, understanding legal terms (legal documents, civil versus criminal, felory versus misdemeanor), and accessing legal assistance.

Daily Living

Help obtaining financial assistance (paying bills on time, applying for loans, building a credit history, opening a checking/savings account, budgeting, using credit cards, purchasing large items).

Using local transportation systems when needed (local transportation options, knowledge of process for using public transportation, getting a driver's license, traveling independently, purchasing insurance, planning routes to various destinations and timeframe, budgeting for transportation costs.

Transition Exit Form: Interagency Responsibilities

Student Name: Heidi Camper Date of IEP: May 5, 20--

School: Lakewood High School Soc. Sec. No.: 388-64-0000

Projected Date of Graduation or Program Completion: June 10, 2010 Date of Birth: June 13, 1990

IEP Committee Members: Mr. Edwards (*Teacher*) Earl & June Camper (*Parent*) Heidi Camper (*Student*) Dr. Bagley (*Admin. Rep.*)

Mr. Keys: DVR (*Name* / *Agency*) Ms. Amacher: Tech College (*Name* / *Agency*) Mr. Akay: Center for Ind. Living (*Name* / *Agency*)

		Responsibilities					
		Parent/Guardian/Student		**School**		**List Community Agency**	
Transition Needs	Recommendations for Placements, Services, or Other Options	Action	Time Line	Action	Time Line	Action	Time Line
1. Financial/ Income Security	Tech College tuition and living expenses	Apply for college grants	03/10				
2. Voc. Train./ Job Placement/ Postsec. Ed.	Application to tech college	Student completes application with school counselor	01/10	High school counselor secures application	01/10		
3. Secure Living Arrangements	Heidi will need independent living arrangements while attending tech college	Student has meeting with Center for Ind. Living representative	05/10	School counselor sets up meetings	05/10	Center for Ind. Living rep. meets with student	05/10

		Responsibilities					
		Parent/Guardian/Student		School		List Community Agency	
4. Adequate Personal Management	Needs to have independent living Skills assessed	02/10		Special ed. staff assesses personal care skills	01/10		
5. Access to and Enjoyment of Leisure/Recreation Activities	Heidi needs to learn about leisure/ rec. options in new community		09/10			Div. of Rehabilitation Services will help Heidi learn about community options	08/10
6. Efficient Transportation System	Needs transportation from apartment to tech college	Parents will assist with transportation and drivers license	07/10				
7. Provision of Medical Services	Student will need periodical medical check-ups	Student tours medical facility at college	05/10			Medical services available at tech college	As needed
8. Link age to and Use of Advocacy/ Legal Services	Student will need advocacy and support at tech college			Tech college counselor will provide support	on-going		

		Responsibilities					
		Parent/Guardian/Student		School		List Community Agency	
Transition Needs	Recommendations for Placements, Services, or Other Options	Action	Time Line	Action	Time Line	Action	Time Line
9. Appropriate Personal/Family Relationships	No additional needs at this time						
10. Other Instructional Support While Attending College						Tech college transition specialist will provide instructional support at college	on-going

Vocational Assessment Profile

Results for Spencer McGillacutty

Date(s) of profile completion: 2/24/10

Compiled by: Hannah Morris and Talia Gallagher and Andy Jenson

I. Identification information

A. Name: Spencer McGillacutty

B. Date of birth: 3/17/90

C. Social Security #: 354-267-0000

D. Address: 31½ Maple St.

E. Phone: (414) 542-0000

F. School district: Milwaukee

G. Primary school contact: Grace Simpson

H. Year of expected graduation/exit: 2010

I. Disability (check all that apply):

( ) Mental/Cognitive disability
( ) Mild
( ) Moderate
( ) Brain injury
( ) Autism
( ) Deafness or hearing impaired
(✓) Other ADHD
( ) Behavioral disability
(✓) Speech and language impairment
( ) Physical impairment
( ) Other health disabilities
(✓) Learning disability
(✓) Visual impairment

J. Vision/hearing screening (check all that apply):

Does individual use assisted devices such as:

( ) Hearing aid
(✓) Glasses
( ) Braille reader
( ) Other ____________

K. Physical/health restrictions:

List additional information regarding medications, allergies, recurring health problems, physical restrictions, or limitations.

Ritalin, seasonal allergies, peanuts

L. SSDI Application (check all that apply):

( ) Receives: amount per month ____________
( ) Completed, awaiting determination
( ) Not applied

Other sources of income and amounts:

Stocker at Sendiks amount $416 (Tax excl) /mo.
________________ amount ________ /mo.
________________ amount ________ /mo.

M. Additional Information (check all that apply):

(✓) Physical exam date: 08/09
( ) Psychological exam date: 09/08

(✓) Most recent IEP/transition plan date: 09/08

( ) Most recent resume date: ____________________

II. Residential/Domestic Information

A. Family (parent or guardian) address (if different from student's)

same

B. Phone Number: ____________________

C. Names, ages, and relationships of family members:

1. Oliver McGillacutty, III Age: 42 Relation: father
2. Anne McGillacutty Age: 40 Relation: mother
3. Simon McGillacutty Age: 14 Relation: Brother
4. Jeremiah McGillacutty Age: 8 Relation: Brother
5. Age: Relation:

D. Residential status (check all that apply):

(✓) Lives at home with natural parent(s) ____________

( ) Lives with guardian ____________

( ) Lives in residential facility ____________

( ) Lives with spouse ____________

( ) Other (specify) ____________

E. Family supports

Estimate the extent to which this student's family can assist him/her with respect to the following areas:
Rate the following areas (1) none or minimal support, (2) some support, (3) full support

(3) Finances (3) Housing (3) Transportation

(3) Education (3) Work/Education

F. Description of neighborhood and location in community:

Shorewood, family oriented community

G. General types of employment near home:

Grocery store, Restaurants (Sp!)

H. Transportation available:

Mother provides transportation

I. Potential employers among family or friends:

Lexus car dealership (owned by father)

III. Summary of student skills (attach resume)

A. Describe work related abilities:

not limited physically, very tactile

B. Describe occupational interests:

Computers, Technology, Graphic design

C. Describe work related experiences:

Grocery store stocker

D. Describe leisure/recreational interests/hobbies:

Soccer team, computers

E. Quality considerations: Rate the following items as to the importance for the student/family on a scale of:
(1) not important, (2) somewhat important, (3) very important

(3) Opportunity for interaction with nondisabled coworkers

(2) Opportunity for high wages
(2) Opportunity to receive health benefits
(2) Opportunity to receive vacation and sick pay
(3) Potential for long-term employment
(3) Opportunity for supported employment
(3) Proximity to transportation
Comments: ______________________________

For sections F through R, please check all that apply and identify supports the students may need after school exit.

F. Job-Seeking Skills (check all that apply):

(✔) Describes own job interests and skills	( ) Needs assistance
(✔) Uses resume during interview	( ) Needs assistance
(✔) Initiates job-seeking tasks	( ) Needs assistance
( ) Demonstrates job interview skills and can interview independently	(✔) Needs assistance
(✔) Describes past work experience	( ) Needs assistance
(✔) Completes application forms	(✔) Needs assistance
( ) Prepares a resume	(✔) Needs assistance
(✔) Other: be specific Job tryout/career exploration	( ) Needs assistance

Describe the Supports Needed in each area of Job-Seeking Skills in which the student needs assistance.
____
____

G. Work-Performance skills (check all that apply):

( ) Arrives, takes breaks, leaves at right times	( ) Needs assistance
( ) Obtains more work when needed	( ) Needs assistance
( ) Completes assignments and tasks within timeline	( ) Needs assistance
( ) Adjust to job demands	( ) Needs assistance
( ) Travels independently to job	( ) Needs assistance
( ) Makes transitions smoothly from old to new tasks	( ) Needs assistance
(✔) Checks and corrects own work	( ) Needs assistance
(✔) Follows company rules/procedures	( ) Needs assistance
(✔) Calls in when sick	( ) Needs assistance
(✔) Follows written work schedule	(✔) Needs assistance
( ) Other: be specific ______________	( ) Needs assistance

Describe the Supports Needed in each area of Work Performance Skills in which the student needs assistance.
____
____

H. Working with others (check all that apply):

(✔) Follows directions	( ) Needs assistance
(✔) Asks for help	( ) Needs assistance
(✔) Works well with others	( ) Needs assistance
(✔) Interacts well with customers	( ) Needs assistance

( ) Self-care skills at independent level ( ) Needs assistance
( ) Other: be specific ______________________________
______________________________ ( ) Needs assistance

Describe the Supports Needed in each area of Working with Others in which the student needs assistance.

____
____
____

I. Travel skills (check all that apply):

(✔) Can use mass transit ( ) Needs assistance
(✔) Uses taxi ( ) Needs assistance
( ) Drives automobile (✔) Needs assistance
( ) Uses maps or bus schedules ( ) Needs assistance
( ) Reaches destinations on time ( ) Needs assistance
(✔) Other: be specific driver's license
______________________________ (✔) Needs assistance

Describe the Supports Needed in each area of Travel Skills in which the student needs assistance.

Needs to enroll in driver's education class.
____
____

J. Health and safety skills (check all that apply):

(✔) Recognizes safety and warning symbols ( ) Needs assistance
( ) Monitors own medications/takes medication appropriately (✔) Needs assistance
(✔) Follows safety practices ( ) Needs assistance
(✔) Responds to emergencies ( ) Needs assistance
( ) Schedules and attends medical/dental care (✔) Needs assistance
( ) Other: be specific ______________________________
______________________________ ( ) Needs assistance

Describe the Supports Needed in each area of Health and Safety skills in which the student needs assistance.

Medications should be available in nurse's office.
____
____

K. Meal planning (check all that apply):

(✔) Displays manners ( ) Needs assistance
(✔) Obtains prepared foods ( ) Needs assistance
(✔) Prepares nutritious meals ( ) Needs assistance
(✔) Purchase groceries ( ) Needs assistance
(✔) Other: be specific can benefit from
visual or written aids (✔) Needs assistance

Describe the Supports Needed in each area of Meal Planning in which the student needs assistance.

____
____
____

L. Money management (check all that apply):

( ) Can identify "best buy" consistently — (✔) Needs assistance
(✔) Can accurately exchange money for goods — ( ) Needs assistance
( ) Uses checking and savings services — (✔) Needs assistance
( ) Writes checks correctly — (✔) Needs assistance
( ) Balances checkbook — (✔) Needs assistance
( ) Can independently use an ATM machine — (✔) Needs assistance
( ) Other: be specific ______________________
______________________ — ( ) Needs assistance

Describe the Supports Needed in each area of Money Management in which the student needs assistance.
Needs assistance in budgetting strategies

M. Recreation/Leisure Activities

List recreation and leisure activities in which the student routinely participates.
Soccer team
Chat online

List recreation and leisure activities in which the student would like to participate.
Computer programming

N. Academic skills (reading, writing, mathematics) (check all that apply)

(✔) Uses simple mathematics independently — ( ) Needs assistance
( ) Uses mathematics for problem solving — ( ) Needs assistance
(✔) Uses computers/software — ( ) Needs assistance
( ) Can keyboard effectively — ( ) Needs assistance
(✔) Writes in complete sentences — ( ) Needs assistance
( ) Uses phone book independently — ( ) Needs assistance
( ) Uses study skills independently — ( ) Needs assistance
( ) Reads newspapers, books — ( ) Needs assistance
( ) Reads with understanding — ( ) Needs assistance
( ) Other: be specific ______________________
______________________ — ( ) Needs assistance

Describe the Supports Needed in each area of Academic Skills in which the student needs assistance.

O. Telling time (check all that apply):

(✔) Tells time accurately — ( ) Needs assistance
( ) Can follow his/her own schedule — ( ) Needs assistance
( ) Needs to follow prompts — ( ) Needs assistance
( ) Other: be specific ______________________
______________________ — ( ) Needs assistance

Describe the Supports Needed in each area of Money Management in which the student needs assistance.

____

____

P. Communication skills (check all that apply):

(✔) Speaks English clearly (✔) Needs assistance
( ) Speaks language other than English clearly ( ) Needs assistance
( ) Other:be specific ______________________
______________________ ( ) Needs assistance

Describe the Supports Needed in each area of Communication Skills in which the student needs assistance.

Speech therapy to continue
Needs tp improve written and oral expression

Q. Social interaction skills (check all that apply):

(✔) Communicates basic needs ( ) Needs assistance
(✔) Listens and follows directions ( ) Needs assistance
( ) Resists negative peer pressure (✔) Needs assistance
( ) Initiates, maintains, and ends conversation (✔) Needs assistance target goal
( ) Effectively deals with teasing or negative comments (✔) Needs assistance
(✔) Uses telephone effectively ( ) Needs assistance
( ) Expresses feelings in appropriate manner (✔) Needs assistance target goal
( ) Writes letters to friends and family (✔) Needs assistance
( ) Cooperates and shares in group activities (✔) Needs assistance
(✔) Respects others' property and privacy ( ) Needs assistance
( ) Recognizes and deals with interpersonal issues (✔) Needs assistance
( ) Makes appropriate decisions (✔) Needs assistance
(✔) Assists others when needed ( ) Needs assistance
( ) Follows through on plans and decisions ( ) Needs assistance
( ) Manages own anger and frustration ( ) Needs assistance
( ) Adapts to changing situations ( ) Needs assistance
( ) Functions appropriately under pressure ( ) Needs assistance
(✔) Responds appropriately to affection ( ) Needs assistance
( ) Takes part in recreation/leisure activities ( ) Needs assistance
(✔) Interacts appropriately with authority figures ( ) Needs assistance
( ) Writes letters to friends and family ( ) Needs assistance
( ) Other: be specific______________________
______________________ ( ) Needs assistance

Describe the Supports Needed in each area of Social Interaction Skills in which the student needs assistance.

____

____

IV. Predictions/Recommendations

Make a tentative prediction regarding this student's future course(s) of study or future employment.

____

____

Program Inventory

Results for Spencer McGillacutty

Person(s) Requesting Inventory Completion: Special Ed. staff Date: 2/27/10

Program Title: Computer Programming Instructor: Mr. Jenson

Text Title: Intro to programming Reading Level: 12th grade

Teaching Preferences of Instructor

Indicate the frequency of teaching methods used below:
1 = Used daily; 2 = Used occasionally; 3 = Never used

Information Input (Instructional Methods)

(Information Sources)

- 2 textbooks
- 2 worksheets
- 1 lecture
- 2 discussion
- 2 Internet
- 3 video
- 2 computer
- 2 compact disc
- 1 audio tapes
- 3 slides
- 1 simulations
- ____ other ____________

(Structure of Instruction)

- 1 teacher-directed
- 2 independent
- 2 small group
- 2 peer tutoring
- 3 one-to-one adult
- 1 large group
- ____ other ____________

Information Output

(Assignments)

- 2 worksheets
- 2 short papers
- 3 term papers
- 1 oral reports
- 2 group discussions
- 1 demonstration
- 1 written reports
- 1 portfolio
- 2 panel presentation
- 2 word problems/math
- 3 artistic expression
- ____ other ____________

(Test Formats)

- 2 short answer
- 2 essay
- 3 multiple choice
- 1 oral exam
- 2 true/false
- 1 demonstration
- 2 matching
- 2 online
- 3 word problems/math
- ____ other ____________

Grading Options Traditional A–F with honors option

Extra Credit Options Two projects per semester

Homework Requirements Twice weekly

Make-up Policy Only if a medical or family ____________________

____

____

Attendance Policy Must attend 95% of classes ____________________

____

Behavior Policy ____________________

____

Curricular Requirements for Program

Put a check next to the most important skills a student should possess upon entry to this program.

Entry-Level Skills

________	following directions
________	safety skills
________	paying attention
________	staying on task
________	working independently
✔	oral expression
✔	written expression
________	social skills
✔	working in groups
________	spelling
________	math/calculation skills
________	note taking
✔	keyboarding
________	artistic/drawing
________	measuring
________	independent research
________	problem solving
________	other ____________

Instructional Support Options

(within classroom)

limited	special education teacher
limited	classroom aide

(in resource room)

✔	taped textbooks
________	assistive technology
________	alternative testing
________	note taker
________	outlining
✔	test preparation
✔	assignment assistance
✔	computer assisted instruction
________	research assistance
________	study guides
________	other ____________

Learning/Working Styles Inventory

For Spencer McGillacutty

NAME: Spencer McGillacutty **DATE:** March 2010

Study each statement carefully and choose one of the four answers that best describes how you feel about what is said. Put an "x" in the space containing the number of your choice.

4 = MOST LIKE ME **3 = SOMEWHAT LIKE ME** **2 = NOT MUCH LIKE ME** **1 = LEAST LIKE ME**

	Statement	4	3	2	1
1.	When I am trying hard to learn or study something, I pace the floor		X		
2.	I remember what I learn by closing my eyes to recall it				X
3.	Taking notes in a notebook helps me learn best		X		
4.	When learning information for the first time I read it aloud	X			
5.	I like studying with one or more friends		X		
6.	Studying alone is enjoyable to me	X			
7.	I study better when sitting at a desk or table				X
8.	When I study, I like to sit in a soft chair, on pillows, or on a couch		X		
9.	A well-lit room helps me study better	X			
10.	I learn best in a room that is dimly lit				X
11.	Studying in a warm, cozy room makes it easier for me to learn		X		
12.	I feel more comfortable in cool weather	X			
13.	Studying is best for me when it is quiet	X			
14.	Noise helps me to study or concentrate				X
15.	Speaking helps me express my ideas better than writing does				X
16.	It is easier for me to write what is on my mind than to speak it		X		
17.	Working in jobs out-of-doors is enjoyable to me	X			
18.	I prefer jobs requiring me to work indoors				X
19.	I like working on a job that requires me to work at a desk or table				X
20.	Moving from one area to another to work is something I enjoy	X			
21.	I enjoy lifting and moving items on my job	X			
22.	Lifting or moving things on my job is not what I like to do				X
23.	Looking up information in a library is enjoyable to me		X		
24.	I enjoy working with people more than I like working with data			X	
25.	I prefer working with things rather than with people	X			
26.	Tapping my foot or fingers helps me to study or learn	X			
27.	When I read materials, important facts are easy to remember		X		
28.	Using an outline helps me study		X		
29.	I learn best through class discussions and lectures			X	
30.	The things I do best I do with my friends		X		
31.	The things I do best I do alone, without my friends				X
32.	When I study, I like to sit in a straight chair				X
33.	I learn best when I am sitting on the floor in a relaxed area		X		

B-7, Form 3

Item				
34. A well-lit area helps me think more clearly	☒	3	2	1
35. I like to study in a dimly-lit area	4	3	2	☒
36. I can think or concentrate better when I am warm	4	3	☒	1
37. When I am cool, I think more clearly	☒	3	2	1
38. Noise keeps me from thinking or concentrating on my work	☒	3	2	1
39. Before studying new information, I turn on the radio or television	4	3	☒	1
40. I enjoy being called upon to explain answers or situations	4	3	2	☒
41. I express myself better in writing than in speaking	4	☒	2	1
42. Working out-of-doors relaxes me	☒	3	2	1
43. Working indoors relaxes me	4	3	☒	1
44. I enjoy working in one area	4	3	2	☒
45. Working in one area for a long period of time bothers me	4	☒	2	1
46. Lifting and moving things helps me show others how strong I am	☒	3	2	1
47. I seek jobs that do not require me to lift or move objects	4	3	☒	1
48. Working with facts or figures is enjoyable to me	4	☒	2	1
49. I would rather work with people than with things, facts or figures	4	3	☒	1
50. I would rather work with things than with people, facts or figures	☒	3	2	1
51. When I can relate to something I have done, I understand it better	☒	3	2	1
52. I enjoy reading	4	3	☒	1
53. When I read, I remember best when I underline the important facts	4	☒	2	1
54. To remember important facts, I need only to listen carefully	4	3	2	☒
55. I like my friends to assist me in completing my assignments	4	3	☒	1
56. Studying is something I like to do by myself	4	☒	2	1
57. I like to have all my materials handy when I study	4	☒	2	1
58. When sitting on my bed, I study or learn new information better	4	☒	2	1
59. Bright lights help me think better	☒	3	2	1
60. Dim lights help me think better	4	3	2	☒
61. Being in a warm area helps keep me alert	4	3	2	☒
62. Cool surroundings help me stay alert	☒	3	2	1
63. Loud or soft noises bother me when I am trying to study	☒	3	2	1
64. I study best in a noisy area	4	3	☒	1
65. I would rather call a friend on a telephone than write a letter	4	☒	2	1
66. When I want to express my ideas, I jot them down first	4	☒	2	1
67. If I could choose my job setting it would be out-of-doors	☒	3	2	1
68. If I could choose my job setting it would be indoors	4	3	☒	1
69. I would rather work in one area than moving to different areas	4	3	2	☒
70. I would rather have different work areas than just one work area	☒	3	2	1
71. Moving or arranging things is something I seek in a job	4	☒	2	1
72. Letting others know how strong I am on a job is not important	4	3	☒	1
73. I seek jobs that require me to work with facts or figures	☒	3	2	1
74. Working with people is something I seek in a job	4	3	☒	1
75. Something I seek in a job is working with things	4	☒	2	1

Hand Scoring

1. The numbers listed under each of the nine construct areas designate the statements on the instrument which measure that particular style. For example, statements 1, 26, and 51 all measure the kinesthetic style of learning.
2. To determine the score for each style look at the worksheet below and do the following:
   a. Look up the response given for each statement and write it in the right hand column.
   b. Total the numbers.
   c. Multiply the sum of the numbers by 2.
   This determines the score. Example: (suppose these are the responses given on the inventory)

   KINESTHETIC
   1. 3
   26. 4
   51. 3
   10 x 2 = 20 20 is the score for KINESTHETIC.
3. Figure the score for each of the 25 areas. If the score is 19 through 24, the style is considered to be a major learning style for the participant. From 12 through 18 is a minor learning style for the individual. A score below 12 indicates the participant uses this style to a negligible extent.
4. After computing each score, the scores may be graphed on the profile sheet.

NAME S. McGillacutty	LEARNING STYLES WORKSHEET	March 2005	DATE	
Kinesthetic: 1- 3 26- 4 51- 4 Total 11 x 2 = 22	Individual: 6- 1 31- 1 56- 3 Total 5 x 2 = 10	Warm Environment: 11- 3 36- 2 61- 1 Total 6 x 2 = 12	Written Expressive: 16- 3 41- 3 66- 3 Total 9 x 2 = 18	Lifting: 21- 4 46- 4 71- 3 Total 11 x 2 = 22
Visual: 2- 1 27- 3 52- 2 Total 6 x 2 = 12	Formal Design: 7- 1 32- 1 57- 3 Total 5 x 2 = 10	Cool Environment: 12- 4 37- 4 62- 4 Total 12 x 2 = 24	Outdoors: 17- 4 42- 4 67- 4 Total 12 x 2 = 24	Non-Lifting: 22- 1 47- 2 72- 2 Total 5 x 2 = 10
Tactile: 3- 3 28- 3 53- 3 Total 9 x 2 = 18	InFormal Design: 8- 3 33- 3 58- 3 Total 9 x 2 = 18	Without Sound: 13- 4 38- 4 63- 4 Total 12 x 2 = 24	Indoors: 18- 1 43- 2 68- 2 Total 5 x 2 = 10	Data: 23- 3 48- 3 73- 4 Total 10 x 2 = 20
Auditory: 4- 4 29- 2 54- 1 Total 7 x 2 = 14	Bright Light: 9- 4 34- 4 59- 4 Total 12 x 2 = 24	With Sound: 14- 1 39- 2 64- 2 Total 5 x 2 = 10	Sedentary: 19- 1 44- 1 69- 1 Total 3 x 2 = 6	People: 24- 2 49- 2 74- 2 Total 6 x 2 = 12
Group: 5- 3 30- 3 55- 2 Total 8 x 2 = 16	Dim Light: 10- 1 35- 1 60- 1 Total 3 x 2 = 6	Oral Expressive: 15- 1 40- 1 65- 3 Total 5 x 2 = 10	NonSedentary: 20- 4 45- 3 70- 4 Total 11 x 2 = 22	Things: 25- 4 50- 4 75- 3 Total 11 x 2 = 22

B-7, Form 3

Profile Sheet

NAME: Spencer McGillacutty

DATE: March, 2010

				MINOR							**MAJOR**					
	6	**8**	**10**	**12**	**13**	**14**	**15**	**16**	**17**	**18**	**19**	**20**	**21**	**22**	**23**	**24**
KINESTHETIC														X		
VISUAL				X												
TACTILE										X						
AUDITORY						X										
GROUP								X								
INDIVIDUAL			X													
FORMAL DESIGN			X													
INFORMAL DESIGN										X						
BRIGHT LIGHT																X
DIM LIGHT	X															
WARM ENVIRON				X												
COOL ENVIRON																X
WITHOUT SOUND																X
WITH SOUND			X													
ORAL EXPRESSIVE			X													
WRITTEN EXPRESS.									X							
OUTDOORS																X
INDOORS			X													
SEDENTARY	X															
NON-SEDENTARY														X		
LIFTING														X		
NON-LIFTING			X													
DATA												X				
PEOPLE				X												
THINGS														X		

APPENDIX

C Sample Transition Assessment Materials and Tools

Burnsville–Eagan–Savage School District Transition Assessment Tools

Assessment	Grade 8	Grade 9	Grade 10	Grade 11	Grade 12
Academic Skills Assessment Learning Styles					
Inventory (LSI)	X	X	X		
Curriculum-based Assessments			X		
Achievement Tests			X		
C.I.T.E. Learning Styles Inventory					
Assessment of Future Planning Student Needs and Goals					
Transition Planning Inventory (TPI)	X			X	
Transition Behavior Scales (TBS)	X		X	X	
Future Planning Inventory (FPI)	X	X			
Life Skills Assessment Brigance (Adaptive Behaviors)	X			X	
Test for Everyday Living (TEL)		X			
Life-Centered Career Education (LCCE)				X	
Transition Planning Inventory (TPI)				X	
Street Survival Skills Questionnaire (SSSQ)				X	X
Evaluation of Future Outcomes/Goals (required)					
Transition Planning Inventory (TPI)	X	X	X	X	X
Enderle-Severson Transition Rating Scales	X	X	X	X	X
Vocational Inventories (required)					
Interest Determination Exploration and Assessment System (IDEAS)	X	X	X		
Career Winds (computer)	X				

Published with permission of the Burnsville-Eagan-Savage Independent School District #191, Burnsville, MN.

Assessment	Grade 8	Grade 9	Grade 10	Grade 11	Grade 12
Occupational Aptitude Survey and Interest Schedule (OASIS)	X	X	X	X	X
Career Planning Survey (CPS)			X		
Career Exploration and Evaluation Program (C.E.E.P. results)			X	X	X
Minnesota Career Information System (MCIS)			X	X	X
Bridges (computer)			X	X	X
Career Decision Maker (CDM)			X	X	X
Learning Styles Inventories					
Informal Learning Styles Inventories (i.e. C.I.T.E.)	X	X	X	X	X
Life Skills Assessment					
Brigance Life Skills Inventory—Revised (Adaptive Behaviors)	X	X	X	X	X
Test for Everyday Living (TEL)				X	X
Life-Centered Career Education Knowledge/Performance Battery (LCCE) - ***ongoing***	X	X	X	X	X
Transition Behavioral Scales			X	X	X
Vineland Adaptive Behavioral Scales				X	X
Street Survival Skills Questionnaire (SSSQ)			X	X	X
Scales of Independent Behavior-R (SIB-R)				X	X
Evaluation of Level of Self-Determination and Self-Advocacy Skills					
I PLAN—Kansas Learning Strategies					
ARC Self-Determination Scale				X	X
Self-Determination/Self-Advocacy (STEPS)				X	X
Other Informal Self-Advocacy Checklists	X	X	X	X	X
Other Career Assessments					
ASVAB (Armed Services Vocational Aptitude Battery)				X	X
ACT (American College Test)				X	X
SAT (Scholastic Achievement Test)				X	X
College Placement Tests					
Community College				X	X
Technical College				X	X

Assessment	Grade 8	Grade 9	Grade 10	Grade 11	Grade 12
Assessment of Future Planning Student Needs and Goals					
Transition Planning Inventory (TPI)	X			X	
Transition Behavior Scales (TBS)	X	X	X		
Future Planning Inventory (FPI)	X			X	

Transition Planning Checklist

Individual Student Planning Activities

Student's Name: ____________________

Items in bold are mandatory actions

Age	Action	Person(s) Responsible	Yes	Comments
By age 14	**1. Begin Student <u>Transition Program Planning Folder</u>/complete personal data and Individual Student Transition Portfolio (in <u>Transition Program Planning Folder</u>)** ■ **One month prior to annual IEP meeting, send out letter confirming Initial Transition/IEP conference and transition information materials**	IEP Manager		
	2. Conduct 3 year evaluation including initial vocational evaluation or conduct transition evaluation if not up for 3 year re-evaluation ■ **Follow due process** ■ **Transition Planning Inventory (TPI)** ■ **Vocational Interest Inventory** ■ **Supplemental Inventories as appropriate for** - **disability area** - **Career Winds** - **Life Centered Career Education** - **Tests for Everyday Living** - **Other**	IEP Manager		
	3. Conduct IEP conference—address all five areas of transition	IEP Team		
	4. Bring <u>Transition Program Planning Folder</u> to IEP meeting to share and update with IEP team.	IEP Manager		
	5. Review progress towards transition goals to consider additional needs and services	IEP Manager		
	6. After IEP planning and meeting, keep <u>Transition Program Planning Folder</u> in Due Process File	IEP Manager		
	7. Obtain Minnesota Identification Card ■ Student with Disability discount - Dakota County License Center located in the Burnsville Transit Station - Cost is $12.50 if first page of IEP is supplied - Bring 2 of the following forms of identification: * Original birth certificate * Social Security card * Student picture ID card	Parent/Guardian		
	8. Explore volunteer work option	IEP Team		
	9. Develop awareness of student disability area and learning style	IEP Team		
	10. Participate in career awareness activities (i.e. job shadowing, career exploration, career day/career fair, summer youth employment, Tree Trust)	IEP Team		

Published with permission of the Burnsville-Eagan-Savage Independent School District #191, Burnsville, MN.

Age 14 continued	Action	Person(s) Responsible	Yes	Comments
	11. Plan coursework to match career interests and needs	IEP Team		
	12. Develop leisure/recreation skills and access options in community (i.e. Community Ed. Catalog, public library, YMCA)	IEP Team		
	13. Become involved/aware of extra-curricular activities in school ■ Sports ■ Drama ■ Clubs	IEP Team		
	14. Secure Social Security card	Parent/Guardian, Student		
	15. Apply for medical assistance, if appropriate	Parent/Guardian		
	16. Apply for Social Services, if appropriate	Parent/Guardian		
	17. Apply for Supplemental Security Income (SSI), if appropriate	Parent/Guardian		
	18. Invite community agency personnel	IEP Manager		

Age	Action	Person(s) Responsible	Yes	Comments
By age 15	**1. Update Transition Program Planning Folder and Individual Student Transition Portfolio (found in Due Process file)**	IEP Manager/ Student		
	2. Conduct IEP Conference—address all five areas of transition	IEP Manager		
	3. Bring Transition Program Planning Folder to IEP meeting to share and update with IEP team	IEP Manager		
	4. Review progress towards transition goals to consider additional needs and services	IEP Manager		
	5. After IEP planning and meeting, keep Transition Program Planning Folder in Due Process File	IEP Manager		
	6. Develop awareness of student disability area and learning style	IEP Team		
	7. Participate in career awareness activities (i.e. job shadowing, career exploration, career day/career fair, summer youth employment, Tree Trust)	IEP Team		
	8. Plan coursework to match career interests and needs	IEP Team		
	9. Develop leisure/recreation skills and access options in community (i.e. Community Ed. Catalog, public library, YMCA)	IEP Team		
	10. Become involved/aware of extra-curricular activities in school ■ Sports ■ Drama ■ Clubs	IEP Team		
	11. Secure Social Security card	Parent/Guardian, Student		
	12. Apply for medical assistance, if appropriate	Parent/Guardian		
	13. Apply for Social Services, if appropriate	Parent/Guardian		
	14. Apply for Supplemental Security Income (SSI), if appropriate	Parent/Guardian		
	15. Invite community agency personnel	IEP Manager		
	16. Explore transportation options/driver's license	IEP Team		
	17. Consider participation in job seeking/keeping curriculum	IEP Team		
	18. Obtain Minnesota State ID card (see Age 14)	Parent/Guardian, Student		

 Published with permission of the Burnsville-Eagan-Savage Independent School District #191, Burnsville, MN.

Age	Action	Person(s) Responsible	Yes	Comments
By age 16	**1. Update <u>Transition Program Planning Folder</u> and <u>Individual Student Transition Portfolio</u> (found in Due Process file)**	IEP Manager/ Student		
	2. Conduct IEP Conference—address all five areas of Transition	IEP Manager		
	3. Bring <u>Transition Program Planning Folder</u> to IEP meeting to share and update with IEP team	IEP Manager		
	4. Review progress towards transition goals to consider additional needs and services	IEP Manager		
	5. After IEP planning and meeting, keep <u>Transition Program Planning Folder</u> in Due Process File	IEP Manager		
	6. Develop awareness of student disability area and learning style	IEP Team		
	7. Participate in career awareness activities (i.e. job shadowing, career exploration, career day/career fair, summer youth employment, Tree Trust)	IEP Team		
	8. Plan coursework to match career interests and needs	IEP Team		
	9. Develop leisure/recreation skills and access options in community (i.e. Community Ed. Catalog, public library, YMCA)	IEP Team		
	10. Become involved/aware of extra-curricular activities in school ▪ Sports ▪ Drama ▪ Clubs	IEP Team		
	11. Secure Social Security card	Parent/Guardian, Student		
	12. Apply for medical assistance, if appropriate	Parent/Guardian		
	13. Apply for Social Services, if appropriate	Parent/Guardian		
	14. Apply for Supplemental Security Income (SSI), if appropriate	Parent/Guardian		
	15. Invite community agency personnel	IEP Manager		
	16. Explore housing options	Parent/Guardian, Student		
	17. Obtain driver's license or Minnesota State ID card (see Age 14)	Parent/Guardian, Student		
	18. Consideration of employment (i.e. competitive employment, Work Experience Program, job training, supported employment) to develop positive work history	IEP Team		
	19. Explore legal representation (guardianship/conservatorship)	Parent/Guardian		
	20. Visit Career Center	Parent/Guardian, Student		
	21. Consideration of postsecondary opportunities (i.e. TESA, Transition Plus, supported employment, tech colleges. 4-year colleges, military)	IEP Team		

Age	Action	Person(s) Responsible	Yes	Comments
By age 17	**1. Update <u>Transition Program Planning Folder</u> and Individual Student Transition Portfolio (found in Due Process file)**	IEP Manager/ Student		
	2. Conduct IEP Conference—address all five areas of transition	IEP Manager		
	3. Bring <u>Transition Program Planning Folder</u> to IEP meeting to share and update with IEP team	IEP Manager		
	4. Review progress towards transition goals to consider additional needs and services	IEP Manager		
	5. After IEP planning and meeting, keep <u>Transition Program Planning Folder</u> in Due Process File	IEP Manager		
	6. If special education services are to continue, include adult service providers and district coordinators when considering future outside agencies	IEP Manager		
	7. Develop awareness of student disability area and learning style	IEP Team		
	8. Participate in career awareness activities (i.e. job shadowing, career exploration, career day/career fair, summer youth employment, Tree Trust)	IEP Team		
	9. Plan coursework to match career interests and needs	IEP Team		
	10. Develop leisure/recreation skills and access options in community (i.e. Community Ed. Catalog, public library, YMCA)	IEP Team		
	11. Become involved/aware of extracurricular activities in school ■ Sports ■ Drama ■ Clubs	IEP Team		
	12. Secure Social Security card	Parent/Guardian, Student		
	13. Apply for medical assistance, if appropriate	Parent/Guardian		
	14. Apply for Social Services, if appropriate	Parent/Guardian		
	15. Apply for Supplemental Security Income (SSI), if appropriate	Parent/Guardian		
	16. Invite community agency personnel	IEP Manager		
	17. Explore housing options	Parent/Guardian, Student		
	18. Obtain driver's license or Minnesota State ID card (see Age 14)	Parent/Guardian, Student		
	19. Consideration of employment (i.e. competitive employment, work experience program, job training, supported employment) to develop positive work history	IEP Team		
	20. Explore legal representation (guardianship/conservatorship)	Parent/Guardian		

Age 17 continued	Action	Person(s) Responsible	Yes	Comments
	21. Visit Career Center	Parent/Guardian, Student		
	22. Consideration of postsecondary opportunities (i.e. TESA, Transition Plus, supported employment, tech colleges, 4-year colleges, military)	IEP Team		
	23. Develop career focus	IEP Team		
	24. Consideration of alternative living arrangements	Parent/Guardian		
	25. Apply for Rehabilitation Services	Student/Parent/ Guardian		
	26. Formal vocational evaluation, if appropriate	Rehab. Services		
	27. Awareness of accommodations provided at postsecondary schools	IEP Team		
	28. Take college ACT tests (recommend Spring of Junior year)	Student, Guidance Counselor, IEP Team		
	29. Explore transportation needs and options	Student/Parent/ Guardian		

Age	Action	Person(s) Responsible	Yes	Comments
By age 18	**1. Update <u>Transition Program Planning Folder</u> and <u>Individual Student Transition Portfolio</u> (found in Due Process file)**	IEP Manager/ Student		
	2. Conduct IEP Conference—address all five areas of transition	IEP Manager		
	3. Bring <u>Transition Program Planning Folder</u> to IEP meeting to share and update with IEP team	IEP Manager		
	4. Review progress towards transition goals to consider additional needs and services	IEP Manager		
	5. After IEP planning and meeting, keep <u>Transition Program Planning Folder</u> in Due Process File	IEP Manager		
	6. If special education services are to continue, include adult service providers and district coordinators when considering future outside agencies	IEP Manager		
	7. Develop awareness of student disability area and learning style	IEP Team		
	8. Participate in career awareness activities (i.e. job shadowing, career exploration, career day/career fair, summer youth employment, Tree Trust)	IEP Team		
	9. Plan coursework to match career interests and needs	IEP Team		
	10. Develop leisure/recreation skills and access options in community (i.e. Community Ed. Catalog, public library, YMCA)	IEP Team		
	11. Become involved/aware of extra-curricular activities in school ▪ Sports ▪ Drama ▪ Clubs	IEP Team		
	12. Secure Social Security card	Parent/Guardian, Student		
	13. Apply for medical assistance, if appropriate	Parent/Guardian		
	14. Apply for Social Services, if appropriate	Parent/Guardian		
	15. Apply for Supplemental Security Income (SSI), if appropriate	Parent/Guardian		
	16. Invite community agency personnel	IEP Manager		
	17. Explore housing options	Parent/Guardian, Student		
	18. Obtain driver's license or Minnesota State ID card (see Age 14)	Parent/Guardian, Student		
	19. Consideration of employment (i.e. competitive employment, work experience program, job training, supported employment) to develop positive work history	IEP Team		
	20. Explore legal representation (guardianship/conservatorship)	Parent/Guardian		

Age 18 continued	Action	Person(s) Responsible	Yes	Comments
	21. Visit Career Center	Parent/Guardian, Student		
	22. Consideration of postsecondary opportunities (i.e. TESA, Transition Plus, supported employment, Tech colleges, four-year colleges, military)	IEP Team		
	23. Develop career plan	IEP Team		
	24. Consideration of alternative living arrangements	Parent/Guardian		
	25. Apply for Rehabilitation Services	Student/Parent/ Guardian		
	26. Formal vocational evaluation, if appropriate	Rehab. Services		
	27. Awareness of accommodations provided at postsecondary schools	IEP Team		
	28. Take college ACT tests	Student, Guidance Counselor		
	29. Explore transportation needs and options	IEP Team		
	30. Register for Selective Service (mandated if male)	Student		
	31. Complete site visits of postsecondary schools of interest (Fall of year)	Student		
	32. Apply for admission to postsecondary schools (Fall/Winter of year)	Student		
	33. Complete postsecondary school entrance requirements - Physical - Immunizations - TABE testing (technical college) - ASVAB testing (military) - ACT testing (college)	Student		
	34. Complete financial aid packet (January or February of year, obtain packet from Guidance Counselor)	Student		
	35. Explore transportation options/resources after high school	Student		
	36. Student-led IEP meeting	Student		
	37. Register to vote (County Auditor's office)	Student		

ISD 191 INDIVIDUAL STUDENT TRANSITION PORTFOLIO

Date(s) Updated: __________, __________, __________, __________, __________

Name: ____________________ Birthdate: ____________________

Address: ____

City: ____________________ State: __________ Zip Code: __________

Phone: ____________________ Social Security Number: ____________________

School: ____________________ Country: ____________________

Graduation Date: ____________________ IEP Manager: ____________________

School Counselor: ____

Description of my disability(s):

____

____

Personal counseling/therapy: ______________________________

Location of important documents (SS card, birth certificate): ____________________

____

Registration number for selective service: ____________________

Benefits Received (check all that apply):

- ❑ Medical Assistance
- ❑ Minnesota Care
- ❑ SSI (Supplemental Security Income)
- ❑ MFIP (formerly AFDC)
- ❑ Private grants for training
- ❑ VA benefits

Log of dates and times that I attended Transition/IEP Meetings:

Date: _______________ Time: _______________ Location: _______________

____

____

____

Transition Assessments I have taken:

8th Grade

Date	Name of Test	Transition Area	What I learned about myself

9th Grade

Date	Name of Test	Transition Area	What I learned about myself

10th Grade

Date	Name of Test	Transition Area	What I learned about myself

11th Grade

Date	Name of Test	Transition Area	What I learned about myself

12th Grade

Date	Name of Test	Transition Area	What I learned about myself

Employment

Circle the number that corresponds with your employment interest and with the amount of support you believe you will need to get the kind of job you want.
1 = none, 2 = minimum, 3 = moderate, 4 = maximum

Type	8th & 9th Grade		10th Grade		11th Grade		12th Grade	
	Interest	Support	Interest	Support	Interest	Support	Interest	Support
Competitive—independent (part-time or full-time)	1 2 3 4	1 2 3 4	1 2 3 4	1 2 3 4	1 2 3 4	1 2 3 4	1 2 3 4	1 2 3 4
Competitive—supported (short-term)	1 2 3 4	1 2 3 4	1 2 3 4	1 2 3 4	1 2 3 4	1 2 3 4	1 2 3 4	1 2 3 4
Apprenticeship	1 2 3 4	1 2 3 4	1 2 3 4	1 2 3 4	1 2 3 4	1 2 3 4	1 2 3 4	1 2 3 4
Supported employment (long-term)	1 2 3 4	1 2 3 4	1 2 3 4	1 2 3 4	1 2 3 4	1 2 3 4	1 2 3 4	1 2 3 4

I am interested in job shadowing experience or mentorship (check grade)

_______ 8th _______ 9th _______ 10th _______ 11th _______12th

My Goals/Activities for Employment:

____

____

Work/Volunteer Experience I Have Had:

	Type of Job	Employer	Paid/Volunteer	Dates	Supervisor
1.					
2.					
3.					
4.					
5.					

Vocational Tests and Inventories:

Date	Name of test	What I learned about myself

References:

	Name	Address	Position	Phone
1.				
2.				
3.				
4.				
5.				

Possible Agencies to Contact:

Agency Name	Phone
Rehabilitation Services (RS)	(651)552-5000
Dakota County Social Services (DCSS)	(952)891-7480
Metropolitan Center for Independent Living	(651)646-8342
Community Action Council	(952)985-5300
Governor's Council on Disabilities	____________
Legal Advocacy for Persons with Disabilities	____________
Minnesota State Council on Disabilities	(651)296-6785

Other:

1. ____________
2. ____________
3. ____________

Adult Service Providers Contacted about Jobs and Job Training:

	Agency Name	Contact Person	Phone	Status/Outcome
1.				
2.				
3.				
4.				
5.				

Home Living

Circle the number that corresponds with your home living interest and the amount of support you believe you will need to get the kind of home living you want.
1 = none, 2 = minimum, 3 = moderate, 4 = maximum

	8th & 9th Grade		10th Grade		11th Grade		12th Grade	
	Interest	Support	Interest	Support	Interest	Support	Interest	Support
Live alone or independently	1 2 3 4	1 2 3 4	1 2 3 4	1 2 3 4	1 2 3 4	1 2 3 4	1 2 3 4	1 2 3 4
Live with friends or roommates	1 2 3 4	1 2 3 4	1 2 3 4	1 2 3 4	1 2 3 4	1 2 3 4	1 2 3 4	1 2 3 4
Live with parents or foster parents	1 2 3 4	1 2 3 4	1 2 3 4	1 2 3 4	1 2 3 4	1 2 3 4	1 2 3 4	1 2 3 4
Live with other relatives	1 2 3 4	1 2 3 4	1 2 3 4	1 2 3 4	1 2 3 4	1 2 3 4	1 2 3 4	1 2 3 4
Live with husband or wife	1 2 3 4	1 2 3 4	1 2 3 4	1 2 3 4	1 2 3 4	1 2 3 4	1 2 3 4	1 2 3 4
Live in supervised setting	1 2 3 4	1 2 3 4	1 2 3 4	1 2 3 4	1 2 3 4	1 2 3 4	1 2 3 4	1 2 3 4

Circle the number that corresponds with your interest in learning more about the curriculum area listed and the amount of support you believe you will need to reach your home living goal.
1 = none, 2 = minimum, 3 = moderate, 4 = maximum

	8th & 9th Grade		10th Grade		11th Grade		12th Grade	
	Interest	Support	Interest	Support	Interest	Support	Interest	Support
Managing personal finances	1 2 3 4	1 2 3 4	1 2 3 4	1 2 3 4	1 2 3 4	1 2 3 4	1 2 3 4	1 2 3 4
Getting around the community	1 2 3 4	1 2 3 4	1 2 3 4	1 2 3 4	1 2 3 4	1 2 3 4	1 2 3 4	1 2 3 4
Caring for personal needs	1 2 3 4	1 2 3 4	1 2 3 4	1 2 3 4	1 2 3 4	1 2 3 4	1 2 3 4	1 2 3 4
Selecting/managing a household	1 2 3 4	1 2 3 4	1 2 3 4	1 2 3 4	1 2 3 4	1 2 3 4	1 2 3 4	1 2 3 4
Buying/preparing food	1 2 3 4	1 2 3 4	1 2 3 4	1 2 3 4	1 2 3 4	1 2 3 4	1 2 3 4	1 2 3 4
Making adequate decisions	1 2 3 4	1 2 3 4	1 2 3 4	1 2 3 4	1 2 3 4	1 2 3 4	1 2 3 4	1 2 3 4

Goals/Activities that I would like to do for Home Living:

____

____

____

Tests/Assessments and Inventories in Home Living:

Date	Name of test	What I learned about myself

Possible Agencies to Contact:

Agency Name	Phone
Rehabilitation Services (RS)	(651)552-5000
Dakota County Social Services (DCSS)	(952)891-7480
Metropolitan Center for Independent Living	(651)646-8342
Community Action Council	(952)895-5300
DARTS (Dakota County Regional Transportation Services)	(651)455-1560
Governor's Council on Disabilities	____________
Legal Advocacy for Persons with Disabilities	____________

Other:

1. ____
2. ____
3. ____
4. ____
5. ____

Adult Service Providers Contacted about Home Living:

	Agency Name	Contact Person	Phone	Status/Outcome
1.				
2.				
3.				
4.				
5.				

Community Participation

Circle the number that corresponds with your community participation interest and the amount of support you believe you will need to get the kind of community participation you want.
1 = none, 2 = minimum, 3 = moderate, 4 = maximum

	9th Grade		11th Grade	
	Interest	Support	Interest	Support
Transportation	1 2 3 4	1 2 3 4	1 2 3 4	1 2 3 4
Health care	1 2 3 4	1 2 3 4	1 2 3 4	1 2 3 4
Volunteer activities	1 2 3 4	1 2 3 4	1 2 3 4	1 2 3 4
Agency support	1 2 3 4	1 2 3 4	1 2 3 4	1 2 3 4
Clubs and organizations	1 2 3 4	1 2 3 4	1 2 3 4	1 2 3 4
Community service	1 2 3 4	1 2 3 4	1 2 3 4	1 2 3 4
Other ________	1 2 3 4	1 2 3 4	1 2 3 4	1 2 3 4

Transportation—How I Get Around

____

____

Health Concerns I Have:

____

____

Medications I Use:

Date	Medications	Why I take it

Goals/Activities that I would like to do for Community Participation:

____

____

Activities/Assessments and Inventories in Community Participation:

Date	Name of test/activity	What I learned about myself

Possible Agencies to Contact:

Agency Name	Phone
Rehabilitation Services (RS)	(651)552-5000
Dakota County Social Services (DCSS)	(952)891-7480
Metropolitan Center for Independent Living	(651)646-8342
Community Action Council	(952)985-5300
DARTS—Dakota County Regional Transportation Services	(651)455-1560
Governor's Council on Disabilities	____________
Legal Advocacy for Persons with Disabilities	____________
Local Service/Youth Organizations	
Minnesota Valley Transit Authority (MVTA)	(952)882-7500

Other:

1. ______________________________
2. ______________________________
3. ______________________________
4. ______________________________
5. ______________________________

Adult Service Providers Contacted about Community Participation:

Agency Name   Contact Person   Phone   Status/Outcome

1. ______________________________
2. ______________________________
3. ______________________________
4. ______________________________
5. ______________________________

Recreation and Leisure

Circle the number that corresponds with your recreation and leisure interest and the amount of support you believe you will need to participate in the recreation and leisure activities you want.
1 = none, 2 = minimum, 3 = moderate, 4 = maximum

		9th Grade		11th Grade	
	List	Interest	Support	Interest	Support
Hobbies	____________	1 2 3 4	1 2 3 4	1 2 3 4	1 2 3 4
Sports participation	____________	1 2 3 4	1 2 3 4	1 2 3 4	1 2 3 4
Spectator sports	____________	1 2 3 4	1 2 3 4	1 2 3 4	1 2 3 4
Cultural activities	____________	1 2 3 4	1 2 3 4	1 2 3 4	1 2 3 4
Rest and relaxation	____________	1 2 3 4	1 2 3 4	1 2 3 4	1 2 3 4
Vacation and travel	____________	1 2 3 4	1 2 3 4	1 2 3 4	1 2 3 4
Physical fitness	____________	1 2 3 4	1 2 3 4	1 2 3 4	1 2 3 4

	List	9th Grade Interest	9th Grade Support	11th Grade Interest	11th Grade Support
Community center programs	________	1 2 3 4	1 2 3 4	1 2 3 4	1 2 3 4
Parks and rec. programs	________	1 2 3 4	1 2 3 4	1 2 3 4	1 2 3 4
Church groups	________	1 2 3 4	1 2 3 4	1 2 3 4	1 2 3 4
Other	________	1 2 3 4	1 2 3 4	1 2 3 4	1 2 3 4

Goals/Activities that I would like to do for Recreation and Leisure:

____

____

Activities/Assessments and Inventories in Recreation and Leisure:

Date   Name of test/activity   What I learned about myself

1. ____
2. ____
3. ____
4. ____

Possible Agencies to Contact:

Agency Name	Phone
Rehabilitation Services (RS)	(651)552-5000
Dakota County Social Services (DCSS)	(952)891-7480
Metropolitan Center for Independent Living	(651)646-8342
DARTS—Dakota County Regional Transporation Services	(651)455-1560
Governor's Council on Disabilities	________
Legal Advocacy for Persons with Disabilities	________
Local Service/Youth Organizations	________
Park and Recreation Departments	________
Community/Adult Education	________
Other:	

1. ____
2. ____
3. ____
4. ____
5. ____

Adult Service Providers Contacted about Recreation and Leisure:

Agency Name   Contact Person   Phone   Status/Outcome

1. ____
2. ____
3. ____
4. ____

Postsecondary Education and Training

Circle the number that corresponds with your postsecondary education and training interest and the amount of support you believe you will need to participate in the postsecondary education and training you want.
1 = none, 2 = minimum, 3 = moderate, 4 = maximum

	9th Grade		11th Grade	
	Interest	Support	Interest	Support
Community college (2 year)	1 2 3 4	1 2 3 4	1 2 3 4	1 2 3 4
Military	1 2 3 4	1 2 3 4	1 2 3 4	1 2 3 4
Technical college (1 semester to 2 years)	1 2 3 4	1 2 3 4	1 2 3 4	1 2 3 4
Four-year college/university	1 2 3 4	1 2 3 4	1 2 3 4	1 2 3 4
Trade or business school	1 2 3 4	1 2 3 4	1 2 3 4	1 2 3 4
Apprenticeship program	1 2 3 4	1 2 3 4	1 2 3 4	1 2 3 4

Goals/Activities for Postsecondary Education and Training:

____

____

____

____

Program of Study I Am Interested in:

____

____

Schools/Vocational Programs I Have Visited:

Date — Name of school/training — What I learned

1. ______________________________
2. ______________________________
3. ______________________________
4. ______________________________

Schools I Have Applied to Attend:

Date — Name of school/training — Status of application

1. ______________________________
2. ______________________________
3. ______________________________
4. ______________________________

List of Contact People at Schools/Training Programs:

Name of School — Name of Contact Person — Phone

1. ______________________________
2. ______________________________
3. ______________________________
4. ______________________________

Entrance Exams I Have Taken:

Date Taken Accommodations Requested/Used Score/Rank

ACT

____

____

PSAT

____

____

ASVAB

____

____

Technical college entrance exam

____

____

Financial Aid I Have Applied for:

Date Name of aid Status of application

____

____

Accommodations and Assistive Technology That I Use:

____

____

Possible Agencies to Contact:

Agency Name	Phone
Rehabilitation Services (DRS)	(651) 552-5000
Dakota County Social Services (DCSS)	(952) 891-7480
Postsecondary Admissions Advisor	________
Office of Disability Services	________
Military Recruiter (specific service branch)	________
Metropolitan Center for Independent Living	(651) 646-8342
Community Action Council	(952) 985-5300
Governor's Council on Disabilities	________
Legal Advocacy for Persons with Disabilities	________
Minnesota State Council on Disabilities	(651) 296-6785

Other:

1. ____

2. ____

Interagency Guide for Transition Planning

Student's Name ____

This guide was made possible through the Dakota County Community Transition Interagency Committee (CTIC)

Transitioning to Adult Life

The Dakota County Community Transition Interagency Committee (CTIC) has taken a leadership role in the effort to make provisions for effective transition planning and services to young adults of Dakota County with disabilities. The goal is to ensure that young people with disabilities who are attending school experience a smooth transition to adult life. Transition planning was designed to prepare students to make a smooth transition and to assist them with overcoming obstacles.

Transition services are a coordinated set of activities based on the individual student's needs and takes into account the student's preferences and interests. Areas to address include postsecondary education or vocational training, employment, independent living, community participation, and recreation/leisure.

In Minnesota, every school district must ensure that all youth with disabilities are provided the special instruction and related services that are appropriate to their needs. The youth's needs and the special education instruction and services to be provided shall be agreed upon through the development of the individual educational program (IEP) or the individual interagency intervention plan (IIIP). The plan must address the youth's need to develop skills to live and work as independently as possible within the community. The youth's plan must include a statement of the needed transition services, including a statement of the interagency responsibilities or linkages or both before secondary services are concluded. The statement of transition service needs should relate directly to the youth's goals after high school and show how planned activities are linked to these goals. A youth's "Future's Plan" identifies his/her goals, interests, and needs as they relate to future employment, home living, community participation, recreation/leisure, and postsecondary education.

Addressing a youth's transitional needs requires collaboration and creativity. The process must involve planning with youths, parents, special educators, vocational educators, and adult service system representatives such as social services, Independent Living Services counselors, Rehabilitation Services counselors, and possibly employers.

Team Member Page

Team Member Names	Title	Phone Number
______________________	____________	______________
______________________	____________	______________
______________________	____________	______________
______________________	____________	______________
______________________	____________	______________
______________________	____________	______________
______________________	____________	______________
______________________	____________	______________
______________________	____________	______________
______________________	____________	______________

Brief Resource List

Dakota County Social Services—Developmental Disabilities Intake—Birth to 18: (952) 891-7459; Age 18+: (651) 554-6000
Dakota County Social Services—Mental Health Intake—Birth to 18: (952) 891-7400; Age 18+: (651) 554-6000
Dakota County Economic Assistance Intake—(651) 554-2611
Dakota County Public Health Intake—(651) 554-6115
Rehabilitation Services—(952) 997-4850
DARTS Transportation—(651) 455-1560
Metro Mobility Transportation—West Metro: (612) 332-7161 East Metro (651) 636-5000

For a detailed list of transition resources please contact the Community Transition Interagency Committee of Dakota County (CTIC) at (651) 423-8503 or on the web at www.isd917.k12.mn.us/ctic.htm

Interagency Guide for Transition Planning

The intent of this document is to serve only as a guide—all youth must be considered uniquely

Youth's Name: ____________________	**Date Guide Initiated:** ____________________
Agencies Involved: ________________	**Dates Reviewed:** ________________________

Principles / Philosophy

- A Future's Plan identifies a youth's goals, interests, and needs *related* to future employment, home living, community participation, recreation/leisure, and postsecondary education.
- The youth and his/her team will develop incremental steps toward the youth reaching his/her future goals *starting at grade 9 or by age 14*.
- Transition is a combined effort, no one individual or agency is solely responsible to develop, implement, and coordinate a youth's transition.

Summary of Youth's primary preferences, interests, needs, and future goals:
Date______________________________

Time Frame	Transition Planning Domain	Options to Consider	Action / Services to Be Completed	Transition Team Member(s) Responsible	Completion Date
Age 14	**General**	Ensure assessments of transition needs have been completed. Provide information on County Social Services (i.e. eligibility for case management services). Identify Youth's disability and learning style. Review the initial transition planning/IEP meeting notes & corresponding IEP meeting that was held at age 13. Begin identification of long range goals, taking into account the student's preferences and interests. Consideration of future transition service needs including the five planning areas. Identify graduation date via credit-based standards or by IEP/IIIP. Develop a graduation plan.			
	Home Living	Review current support services at home (if applicable). Consider future living setting, (e.g., on own or group home). Initiate increased independent living skills (e.g., self care and life skills at home).			

Time Frame	Transition Planning Domain	Options to Consider	Action / Services to be Completed	Transition Team Member(s) Responsible	Completion Date
Age 14	**Postsecondary Education and Training**	Begin researching / identifying postsecondary training possibilities; (e.g., technical college, university, trade school, military).			
		Determine coursework to match career goals based on interests, needs and abilities.			
	Recreation & Leisure	Pursue leisure options for group or individual activities. Explore referral to mentor/peer program. Explore school district extra curricular activities. Explore structured recreation/leisure via YMCA, community education, park & recreation, etc.			
	Community Participation	Find opportunities to volunteer. Consider "Service Learning Options" through school district. Gain awareness and skills through community experiences (i.e. restaurants, movies, library). Acquire and use self-advocacy skills.			
	Employment	Research job/occupations for skills and training requirements. Identify pre-employment skills. Establish volunteer/job shadow opportunity / business tours.			

Age 15	**General**	Consider completing a "Future's Plan". Review long range goals. Review graduation date and plan.			
	Home Living	Consider future living environments (e.g. on own, group home). Increase responsibilities at home to enhance independent living skills. Review current support services at home (if applicable). Determine school coursework to meet home living needs.			
	Postsecondary Education and Training	Continue to research and identify postsecondary training possibilities (e.g. technical college, university, trade school, military). Determine coursework to meet requirements for postsecondary training that matches future goal attainment.			
	Recreation & Leisure	Pursue leisure/recreation opportunities in the community and school. Explore referral to mentor/peer program. Explore school district extracurricular activities. Explore structured recreation/leisure via YMCA, community education, park & recreation, etc.			

Time Frame	Transition Planning Domain	Options to Consider	Action / Services to be Completed	Transition Team Member(s) Responsible	Completion Date
Age 15	**Community Participation**	Pursue volunteer opportunities Consider "Service Learning Options" through school district. Incorporate money management skills into community experiences. Gain awareness and skills through community experiences (e.g., restaurants, movies, library, shopping). Consider completing application for Supplemental Social Security Income (SSI). Continue volunteer opportunities / service learning. Explore available public transportation options. Determine appropriateness for driver's education and/or formalized driving assessment. Obtain a Minnesota Identification Card. Acquire and use self-advocacy skills.			
	Employment	Provide opportunities for career exploration, (i.e., career fairs, career center visits, job shadowing). Provide opportunities for vocational skill development (i.e. work experience program, vocational classes). Provide opportunities for community based employment (e.g., competitive, summer youth employment program work experience program). Select coursework to coordinate with employment/volunteer interests.			

Age 16	**General**	Offer completion of a "Future's Plan." Review long-range goals or the Future's Plan. Review graduation date and plan. Provide Transfer of Rights information to parents and youth.			
	Home Living	Consider future living environments (e.g. on own, group home). Review current support services at home (if applicable). Increase independent living skills (e.g. self-care and life skills at home.) Determine school coursework to meet home living needs. Consider future needs for supported or independent living skills training.			
	Postsecondary Education and Training	Continue to research and identify postsecondary training possibilities (e.g., technical college, university, trade school, military). Determine if transition services will be extended beyond age 18 (via enrollment in a transition program). Consider taking ACT or SAT by spring of junior year.			

Time Frame	Transition Planning Domain	Options to Consider	Action / Services to be Completed	Transition Team Member(s) Responsible	Completion Date
	Recreation & Leisure	Pursue leisure/recreation activities in the community and school. Explore referral to mentor/peer program. Explore school district extracurricular activities. Explore structured recreation/leisure via YMCA, community education, park and recreation, etc. Consider joining a league (e.g. softball, bowling). Explore new avenues to build social outlets.			
Age 16	**Community Participation**	Pursue volunteer opportunities. Consider "Service Learning Options" through school district. Continue volunteer opportunities/ service learning. Incorporate money management skills into community experiences. Gain awareness and skills through community experiences (e.g., restaurants, movies, library, shopping). Consider completing application for Supplemental Security Income Experience using public transportation. Identify best transportation resources.			

		Determine appropriateness for driver's education and/or formalized driver's assessment. Identify assistive technology or adaptive equipment needed to access community. Obtain a Minnesota Identification Card. Acquire and use self-advocacy skills.			
Age 16	**Employment**	Participate in job seeking/keeping curriculum/experiences. Invite Rehabilitation Services counselor to IEP meeting. Consider applying for Rehabilitation Services (RS) services. Initiate/continue job-shadowing experience(s). Visit Minnesota WorkForce Center and find out what's available there for employment and career resources. Consider completion of a vocational assessment (if transition assessments and school data do not provide needed information for planning) to identify employment skills, abilities, and interests, and to identify how the disability affects employment. Provide opportunities for community-based employment, (i.e., competitive, summer youth employment program (Tree Trust), and work experience program).			

Time Frame	Transition Planning Domain	Options to Consider	Action / Services to be Completed	Transition Team Member(s) Responsible	Completion Date
Age 17	**General**	Review long range goals or "Future's Plan." Review graduation date and plan. Provide Transfer of Rights information to parents and youth.			
	Home Living	Consider future living environments (e.g. on own, group home). Review current support services at home (if applicable). Increase independent living skills (e.g. self care and life skills at home). Determine school coursework to meet home living needs. Consider future needs for supported or independent living skills training. Explore development of "natural supports."			
	Postsecondary Education & Training	Determine if an updated psychological evaluation and adaptive functional/behavioral scale needs to be completed. Consider postsecondary direction: transition program, tech college 2–4 yr., college, military, supported employment. Apply for postsecondary education and training programs. Become familiar with accommodations needed in a postsecondary education and training program.			

		Apply for disability accommodation services at the selected postsecondary education or training site. Learn how to increase self-advocacy.			
Age 17	**Recreation & Leisure**	Pursue leisure/recreation activities in the community and school. Explore referral to mentor/peer program. Explore school district extracurricular activities. Explore structured recreation/leisure via YMCA, community education, park and recreation, Special Olympics, etc. Consider joining a league (e.g. softball, or bowling). Explore new avenues to building social outlets.			
Age 17	**Community Participation**	Determine appropriateness for guardianship. Continue volunteer opportunities/ service learning. Gain awareness and skills through community experiences (e.g., restaurants, movies, library, shopping). Select and use multiple modes of travel. Determine appropriateness for driver's education and formalized driver's assessment. Identify assistive technology or adaptive equipment needed to access community. Obtain a Minnesota Identification Card. Acquire and use self-advocacy skills.			

Time Frame	Transition Planning Domain	Options to Consider	Action / Services to be Completed	Transition Team Member(s) Responsible	Completion Date
		Transfer from Child Medical Assistance (TEFRA, Waiver, MFIP) to adult Medical Assistance or MA-EPD. Apply for SSI, MA, MSA. Begin with SSI as basis for MA.			
Age 17	**Employment**	Participate in job seeking/keeping curriculum/experiences. Invite Rehabilitation Services counselor to IEP meeting. Consider applying for Rehabilitation Services (RS). Initiate/continue job shadowing experience(s). Visit Minnesota WorkForce Center and find out what's available there for employment and career resources. Consider completion of a vocational assessment (if transition assessments and school data do not provide needed information for planning) to identify employment skills, abilities, and interests, and to identify how the disability affects employment. Provide opportunities for community based employment (i.e., competitive, summer youth employment program (Tree Trust), work experience program).			

Age 18–21	General	Review long range goals or "Future's Plan." Review graduation date and plan.			
	Home Living	Review current support needs at home (if applicable). Increase independent living skills (e.g., self-care and life skills at home). Determine school coursework to meet home living needs. Determine needs for supported or independent living skills training. Identify informal supports. Explore development of "natural supports." Complete application for Minnesota Supplemental Assistance (MSA) through Dakota County Economic Assistance Department if Youth will pursue residential housing. Make final decision regarding living setting following graduation.			
	Postsecondary Education & Training	Determine if an updated psychological evaluation and adaptive functional/ behavioral scale needs to be completed. Consider postsecondary direction: transition program, tech college 2–4 yr., college, military, supported employment. Apply for postsecondary education and training programs. Become familiar with accommodations needed in a postsecondary education and training program.			

Time Frame	Transition Planning Domain	Options to Consider	Action / Services to be Completed	Transition Team Member(s) Responsible	Completion Date
		Apply for disability accommodation services at the selected postsecondary education or training site. Implement plan for postsecondary training/skill development. Practice self-advocacy.			
Age 18–21	**Recreation & Leisure**	Explore structured recreation/leisure via YMCA, community education, park & recreation, Special Olympics, etc. Explore new avenues to build social outlets Consider joining a league (e.g. softball, or bowling). Consideration of adult formalized social/recreational activities (e.g., Project Explore). Participate in preferred activities of interest for both alone and with others. Have a plan for staying physically active.			
Age 18–21	**Community Participation**	Finalize court process for guardianship (if applicable). Complete application for Medical Assistance. Transfer Youth to an ongoing adult transition County Social Worker. Register for selective service (males). Register to vote. Match transportation to employment and living settings.			

 Published with permission of Dakota County Community Transition Integrancy Committee (CTIC), Rosemount, MN.

		Identify assistive technology or adaptive equipment need to access community. Obtain a Minnesota Identification Card. Acquire and use self-advocacy skills. Explore participation in adult community education.			
Age 18–21	**Employment**	Participate in job seeking/keeping curriculum/experiences. Invite Rehabilitation Services counselor to IEP meeting. Consider applying for Rehabilitation Services (RS). Initiate/continue job shadowing experience(s) if appropriate. Visit Minnesota WorkForce Center and find out what's available there for employment and career resources. Consider completion of a vocational assessment to identify employment skills, abilities and interests, and to identify how the disability affects employment (if transition assessment and school data do not provide needed information for planning). Provide opportunities for community-based employment (i.e. competitive, summer youth employment program (Tree Trust), work experience program).			

Time Frame	Transition Planning Domain	Options to Consider	Action / Services to be Completed	Transition Team Member(s) Responsible	Completion Date
		Explore appropriate options for supported employment if appropriate. Tour supported employment programs if appropriate. Make final decision of supported employment program if appropriate. Obtain & maintain suitable employment to be kept after completion of formal education. Develop a plan for continued employment supports. Monitor employment.			

Burnsville-Eagan-Savage Independent School District #191

Post High School Follow-Up Survey: Class of 2003

Student No.: ____________ **Primary Disability:** ____________________ **Fed. Setting:** ____________________

Gender: ____________ **Ethnic Code:** ____________________

1. First, we are interested in knowing how you might spend your free time. . .
   During the last month, have you exercised, for example, taken a walk in the park or worked out at a gym?
   - ❑ yes
   - ❑ no

2. During the last month, have you spent any free time away from home, for example, at sporting events, restaurants, the mall, or movies?
   (*mark all that apply*)
   - ❑ yes, by myself
   - ❑ yes, with my friends
   - ❑ yes, with a family member
   - ❑ no

3. When you want to go somewhere, how do you usually get there?
   (*mark up to three boxes*):
   - ❑ drive a car or motorcycle
   - ❑ walk or ride a bicycle
   - ❑ ride the city bus
   - ❑ take a taxi
   - ❑ get a ride from family or friends
   - ❑ ride a special bus or van
   - ❑ none of the above

   Comments regarding leisure activities or transportation:

4. If the following services were available, which would be of most interest to you?
   (*mark up to three boxes*):
   - ❑ accessing healthcare
   - ❑ arranging recreation and leisure activities
   - ❑ choosing a place to live
   - ❑ finding a ride
   - ❑ gaining legal help or advice
   - ❑ learning home-living skills
   - ❑ managing money
   - ❑ training for a job
   - ❑ finding a job

5. Next, we would like to know if you are registered to vote for people in public office, for example, the President of the United States?
   - ❑ yes
   - ❑ no

6. If you answered "no" to question 5, do you know how to register to vote?
   - ❑ yes
   - ❑ no

7. The next few questions are about your living arrangements. . . whom are you currently living with?
   (*mark one box*):
   - ❑ by myself
   - ❑ with friends
   - ❑ with my spouse or children
   - ❑ with my parents or other family members
   - ❑ with my foster parents
   - ❑ with house mates in a group home
   - ❑ other

8. What part of your living expenses do you pay?
   (*mark one box*):
   - ❑ all (rent, doctor bills, insurance, car, food, etc.)
   - ❑ some
   - ❑ none
   - ❑ don't know

9. Do you receive monthly government checks, for example Social Security, Welfare, Medical Assistance, or unemployment benefits?
   (*mark one box*):
   - ❑ yes
   - ❑ no
   - ❑ don't know

10. Are you working with someone at a community/county agency to find a different place to live?
    (*mark one box*):
    ❑ yes
    ❑ yes, but on a waiting list
    ❑ no
    ❑ don't know

    Comments regarding living arrangements:

11. The next few questions are about your work experience. . . How many different paid jobs have you had since leaving high school?
    (*mark one box*):
    ❑ none
    ❑ 1 job
    ❑ 2 jobs
    ❑ 3 or more jobs

12. Are you currently working (or in the military)?
    ❑ yes, **please go to question 15**
    ❑ no, **please go to question 13**

13. If you are not working now, are you. . . ?
    (*mark one box*):
    ❑ going to school
    ❑ staying home, actively looking for paid employment
    ❑ staying home, not actively looking for paid employment
    ❑ training for a job
    ❑ participating in a day program
    ❑ volunteering
    ❑ none of the above

14. Are you working with someone at a community/county agency to help with job training or job placement?
    (*mark one box*):
    ❑ yes
    ❑ no
    ❑ don't know

Please skip to question #22

15. Who was most helpful to you in finding your current job?
    (*mark one box*):
    ❑ myself
    ❑ a friend
    ❑ a family member
    ❑ someone from my high school (for example, a teacher or work coordinator)
    ❑ someone at a community/county agency (for example, a job placement person or rehabilitation counselor)

16. What is your current job title, for example, cashier?
    (*write it in the space below*):

    ____

17. Which one of the following best describes your job?
    (*mark one box*):
    ❑ working at a regular job (part time or full time)
    ❑ serving in the military
    ❑ working and going to school
    ❑ working with a job coach
    ❑ working at a center with persons who have disabilities
    ❑ working at some other job setting:

    ____
    (specify)

18. How many hours do you work per week?
    (*mark one box*):
    ❑ less than 10 hours
    ❑ 10 to 20 hours
    ❑ 21 to 30 hours
    ❑ 31 to 40 hours
    ❑ more than 40 hours

19. Have you received any promotions in the following areas?
    (*mark all boxes that apply*):
    ❑ increase in wages
    ❑ special bonuses
    ❑ increased responsibility
    ❑ improved health benefits
    ❑ paid vacation
    ❑ none of the above

20. How much money do you earn per hour?
    (*mark one box*):
    ❑ less than $2.00 an hour
    ❑ $2.00 to minimum wage
    ❑ minimum wage to $8.00
    ❑ $8.00 to $10.00
    ❑ $10.00 to $15.00
    ❑ more than $15.00 an hour

21. How long have you been working at your current job?
    (*mark one box*):
    ❑ less than one month
    ❑ 1 to 6 months
    ❑ 6 months to 1 year
    ❑ 1 to 2 years
    ❑ over 2 years

Comments regarding employment situation

Please refer to the following programs for questions 22 through 25:

- GED program—*Graduate Equivalent Diploma, a program to earn your high school diploma*
- Apprenticeship program—*on-the-job training in a trade or industry*
- Private Trade/Vocational School—*skills training (for example, cosmetology or business)*
- Technical College/Institute—*1 to 2 year skills training (for example, Dakota County Technical College or Brown Institute)*
- Community College—*a 2 year program (for example, Normandale or Inver Hills Community College)*
- University—*a 4 year program*

22. Have you **considered** enrolling in any of these 6 programs?
    (*mark all boxes that apply*):
    ❑ GED program
    ❑ apprenticeship program
    ❑ private trade/vocational school
    ❑ technical college/institute
    ❑ community college
    ❑ university (4 year program)
    ❑ none of the above (please skip to question 31)

23. Have you **applied** to any of these 6 programs?
    (*mark all boxes that apply*):
    ❑ GED program
    ❑ apprenticeship program
    ❑ private trade/vocational school
    ❑ technical college/institute
    ❑ community college
    ❑ university (4 year program)
    ❑ none of the above (please skip to question 31)

24. Have you at any time **started** taking classes for any of these 6 programs?
    (*mark all boxes that apply*):
    ❑ GED program
    ❑ apprenticeship program
    ❑ private trade/vocational school
    ❑ technical college/institute
    ❑ community college
    ❑ university (4 year program)
    ❑ none of the above (please skip to question 31)

25. Have you **completed** or are you **planning to complete** any of these 6 programs?
    (*mark all boxes that apply*):
    ❑ GED program
    ❑ apprenticeship program
    ❑ private trade/vocational school
    ❑ technical college/institute
    ❑ community college
    ❑ university (4 year program)
    ❑ none of the above

26. In the most recent program you started did you receive any special help, for example, test/note taking, tutoring, getting around the campus?
    ❑ yes
    ❑ no

27. In the most recent program you started, what was your area of study, for example, accounting, automechanics, or nursing?

    ____
    (write area of study on this line)

28. In the most recent program you started, which of the following best describes your student status?
    (*mark one box*):
    ❑ part time student
    ❑ full time student

29. In the most recent program you started, who helped you the most to choose and enroll in the program?
    (*mark one box*):
    ❑ myself
    ❑ a friend
    ❑ a family member
    ❑ my employer
    ❑ someone from my high school who? ______________________
    ❑ someone at a community agency, for example, a rehabilitation counselor
    ❑ none of the above

30. While attending one of the 6 programs, in which of the following areas, if any, were your required to take developmental classes to improve your skills?
    (*mark all boxes that apply*):
    ❑ math
    ❑ reading
    ❑ writing
    ❑ none required

Comments regarding postsecondary training or education:

31. Who answered the questions on this survey?
    (*mark one box*):
    - ❑ student
    - ❑ a family member
    - ❑ student and a family member
    - ❑ some other involved person

32. Which best describes your student status at the end of school year 2001–2002?
    (*mark one box*):
    - ❑ graduated with diploma
    - ❑ dropped out
    - ❑ completed high school requirements and remained in the Transition Program
    - ❑ working on diploma at an alternative site

33. Do you feel your high school experience helped prepare you for what you wanted to pursue after high school?

34. Is there anything you can think of that could have been provided or addressed in high school that would have helped you after graduation?

35. Based on what you know now, what would you have done differently in high school?

36. Were you ever *unable* to access resources to meet your needs in the past 2 years?

37. Is there anything you would like to share with the district about your first 2 years out of high school, that we did not ask?

38. Would you be willing to share your post-high school experiences with current #191 high school students?

Interviewed by: ______________________________ **Date:** ______________________

APPENDIX

Reevaluation Report for Joe Site (9th Grade)

Reevaluation Summary Report for Joe Site (9th grade)

Student Name: Joe Site
Birthdate: October 10,19—
Age: 15
School: Wilson High School
Grade: 9th
Initial Evaluation ________
Reevaluation ___X___

Reason for Referral

Student is currently in 9th grade at Wilson High School. This evaluation was conducted based on agreement of parents and school to begin the transition planning process for Joe Site as well as to examine concerns regarding academic achievement and functional performance of the student. This evaluation will look at the student's skills and abilities to determine educational programming needs.

Background Information (9th grade)

Student was originally referred to special education in third grade because of parent and teacher concerns regarding low grades, lashing out, and disrespectful behavior toward school staff as well as impulsive behavior. He had high levels of off-task behavior and talking-out behavior. In third grade his physician diagnosed him with Attention Deficit Hyperactivity Disorder (ADHD). Low grades, talking out, and disrespectful behavior continued at similar rate of frequency. Student diagnosed with Oppositional Defiance Disorder (ODD) by hospital in spring of third grade. Student identified as student with disability under IDEA in spring of third grade year. Student's disability label was identified by a multidisciplinary team as Other Health Disability (OHD) in spring of third grade year.

Attendance Record

Student has missed fifty-six days of school in the last three years. During 7th grade student missed a total of twelve days (two in-school suspension, five illness/excused, three out-of-town with parents, and two other). During 8th grade student missed a total of eighteen days (five in-school suspension, six illness/excused, three out-of-town with parents and four other).

During 9th grade year, (as of April 30), student has missed twenty-six days of school (seven in-school suspension, six illness/excused three out of town with parents, and ten other).

Medical History of Student

According to parents, student was within normal ranges for development tasks in activities such as walking, sitting, talking, etc. Parents do not see personal self-care needs for student. No medical concerns reported by parents beyond ADHD as diagnosed by physician.

Test Results

Intellectual/Cognitive Functioning

Wechsler Intelligence Scale for Children – Third Edition (WISC – III) has been administered to measure the student's intellectual ability during the spring of his 9th grade school year.

Student has a verbal IQ of 90 (standard score, SS)
a performance IQ of SS 103, and
a full scale IQ of SS 96.

His testing is very consistent since his initial evaluation as a student receiving special education services. Intellectually, student functions in the average ability range.

Academic Performance

Student had a GPA of 1.45 out of possible 4.0 in 8th grade. Student participates in general education classes and has failed classes in 8th grade in Reading, Science, and Social Studies. Student's teachers in 8th grade reported his abilities in Math, Art, and Physical Education as "average ability." His teachers rate his ability as a moderate problem in Reading and Written Language and a severe problem in Social Studies and Science. During the first three quarters of 9th grade, student's GPA is 1.55 out of possible 4.0.

Woodcock Johnson Tests of Achievement Third Edition (WJ–III ACH)

Test was administered by school psychologist in early spring of 9th grade year. Test results are as follows:

Standard Battery Age Norms

	Standard Score	Percentile
Broad Reading	96	40
Broad Math	98	44
Broad Written Language	90	26
Math Calculation Skills	100	50
Written Expression	90	26

Summary

Student's academic skills are in the average range with his lowest scores in written language area. Written language scores are in average to low-average range compared to same-age peers.

Information Processing

No concerns in areas of *storage* (adding information to existing information), *organization* (structuring, categorizing, or sequencing information), *acquisition*, *retrieval* (recalling or locating stored information), *expression* (communicating information), or *manipulation* (applying, using, or altering information).

Communication Skills

According to teacher report, student appears to have age appropriate expressive and receptive communication skills.

Sensory Status

Student's sensory status appears to be within normal limits. However, parent reports student is fabric defensive and does not like to wear socks in any season including winter. Teacher notes student is usually without socks on most school days. Student passed hearing and vision screen. Vision R 20/20, L 20/20. Student does not wear glasses.

Motor Skills

Student participates in general physical education classes and appears to have age-appropriate gross and fine motor skills. Joe appears to enjoy physical education.

Present Health

Student is 5 feet 7 inches tall and weighs 146 pounds. All required immunizations are updated. Student was admitted to hospital in January of eighth grade year presenting problems of defiance, aggression, irritable mood, and multiple school suspensions. Discharge summary confirms diagnosis of ADHD and ODD. Student presently takes medication with possible side effects, including: nervousness, fast heart rate, insomnia, reduced appetite, growth suppression, chest pain, or involuntary movement.

Health Needs

There are no apparent health needs at school at this time.

Emotional/Social/Behavior

Parent report student's current school problems center around the student's "defiant and disrespectful behavior." Student reports being "bored" with school. Parent reports that student does not have much trouble making or keeping friends. Student likes physical activities. He prefers "hands-on activities."

Student's teachers report student "is disrespectful, lashes out, becomes angry, and shuts down" when presented with academic activities he does not like. Teachers note severe problems with verbal aggression, violent behavior, mood swings, and threatening behaviors toward others. Student has had fourteen days of in-school suspensions in the past three years of school. His absenteeism from school for all reasons is trending upwards. In 7th grade he missed twelve days of school for all reasons, in 8th grade eighteen days and in 9th grade (through April 30) student has missed twenty-six days. Behavior incidents appear to have occurred most often in academic classes, with less disruption in classes with hands-on activities and movement (Art, Physical Education).

To identify any emotional or behavior problems that might be interfering with the student's ability to perform well in school, a behavior rating scale was completed by a parent and two teachers.

Behavior Assessment System for Children (BASC)

Validity indexes were within acceptable ranges.

BOLD = Clinically Significant

Asterisk = At Risk

Clinical Scale	Parent	Teacher 1	Teacher 2
Hyperactivity	66*	56	51
Aggression	**71**	63*	50
Conduct problems	**84**	51	56
EXTERNAL COMPOSITE	**78**	57	53
Anxiety	54	48	52
Depression	**77**	50	49
Somatization	64*	55	43
INTERNALIZING COMPOSITE	68*	51	48

Attention Problems	62*	59	64*
Learning Problems		53	55
SCHOOL PROBLEM COMPOSITE		56	60*
Atypicality	44	43	47
Withdrawal	52	51	47
BEHAVIOR SYMPTOMS INDEX	67*	54	53
Adaptive Skills Scale			
Social Skills	35*	32*	39*
Leadership	40*	42	33*
Study Skills		39*	40*
ADAPTIVE SKILLS COMPOSITE	36*	37*	35*

Clinical Scale Teacher ratings of student behavior produced no scores in Clinically Significant range. Parent rating resulted in multiple areas of Clinically Significant (Aggression, Conduct Problems, External Composite score) and At Risk ratings.

Adaptive Skills Scale All raters (both teachers and parent) rated student At Risk in Social Skills. Both teachers rated Study Skills and Adaptive Skills Composite as At Risk. Scores in Social Skills, Study Skills, and Adaptive Skills Composite suggest deficits in the skills to interact successfully with adults and peers. This scale is a measure of the skills associated with accomplishing academic, social, and community goals, including the capacity to work well with others.

BASC Self-Report of Personality

The BASC Self-Report of Personality was also completed by student to examine his own skills and behaviors as perceived by student. Validity indexes are within acceptable limits.
BOLD = Clinically Significant
Asterisk = At Risk

Clinical Scales (student self-report)	T-Scores
Attitude toward School	**75**
Attitude toward Teachers	**73**
Sensation Seeking	66*
SCHOOL MALADJUSTMENT COMPOSITE	**77**
Atypicality	44
Locus of Control	63*
Somatization	49
Social Stress	48
Anxiety	40
CLINICAL MALADJUSTMENT COMPOSITE	47
Depression	62*
Sense of Inadequacy	51
EMOTIONAL SYMPTOMS INDEX	48
Adaptive Scales	
Relations with Parents	55
Interpersonal Relations	41
Self Esteem	50
Self-Reliance	42
PERSONAL ADJUSTMENT COMPOSITE	49

Student's ratings of Attitude toward Teachers, Attitude toward School, and School Maladjustment Composite were in the Clinically Significant range. This is consistent with academic classroom behavior which is often disruptive and aggressive. Student often uses verbal threats as "jokes." Example: "I'll sit on you and shave your head." This or a similar response is sometimes heard by teachers when the student is given independent seatwork and asked to work independently during class time. Teachers believe this behavior is meant as "attention getting" and represents the student's need for personal power in the academic setting.

Student believes his biggest problem in school is "talking back to teachers and getting in trouble."

Classroom Observations

Math Class

In math class, special education paraprofessional did an observation during class time. Out of fifty systematic observations done in thirty-second intervals, student was found to be "on task" 55% of the time compared to 85% by peers. Student blurted out responses in class and was defiant when asked to work. Is out of seat 25% of time.

Art Class

Out of fifty systematic observations done at thirty-second intervals, student was "on task" 100% of time as compared to 85% by peers. Student worked independently with no out-of-seat behavior or inappropriate blurting responses.

Reading Class

Out of fifty systematic observations done in thirty-second intervals, student was "on task" 75% of time compared to 85% by peers. Student blurted out questions or comments when he struggled with words in reading assignment or did not understand reading. Is out of seat 20% of time.

Functional Behavioral Assessment (FBA)

An FBA was completed with input from parent, student, and teacher interview and classroom observation—**Target Behavior** was student's refusal to work in class.

Based on assessment data, team hypothesizes that student engages in work refusal behavior as a way to escape/avoid tasks he does not like to do. At the same time, he gains attention from adults and staff for emotional needs.

Behavior Reduction Strategies

1. Provide student with opportunity to move in classroom. Provide two desks for student. One in preferential seating in front of room to minimize distractions and one in back of room to provide a destination for movement in class.
2. Allow student to choose between acceptable alternative tasks.
3. Provide assignments that are "hands-on." If possible, include motor activity and use of tools.
4. Involve student in development of a plan to meet his educational goals in the class. Specifically identify what he needs to do to be successful.
5. Clearly identify the consequences of behavioral choices.

Possible Reinforces

Building models
Riding bike
Working on bike
Playing basketball/shooting baskets
Praise
Positive comments/Good grades

Transition Assessment

Federal laws mandates that students, families, and schools begin planning for transition from school to adult life beginning at age sixteen. As a part of the 9th grade educational re-evaluation, the following assessment tools were used to gather transition assessment information: (1) Future Planning Inventory, (2) Interest Determination Exploration and Assessment System (IDEAS) (3) Pretest from STEPS—Self-Determination and Self-Advocacy Skills curriculum and (4) Brigance Life Skills Inventory.

Future Planning Inventory

In spring of 9th grade year, student, parents and special education teacher completed the **Future Planning Inventory**. Student completed his assessment with assistance from school counselor.

Vocational Interest/Goals

Results indicate student is unsure of career interest after high school. Parties agree that student needs to explore career options.

Postsecondary Education Interest/Goals

Student is currently uninterested in exploring postsecondary education.

Home Living

At this time, student and parents anticipate student will live at home in the year after high school.

Recreation and Leisure Options

Results indicate student is involved in numerous leisure activities including swimming, fishing, canoeing, softball, and riding bike. Student attends movies and sporting events. Student listens to music, watches TV, participates in shopping and lawn care, plays video games. Student would like to participate in football or soccer (fall season sports) and baseball (spring season sport) as extracurricular activities during high school.

Transportation Options

Student currently gets around the community by walking, riding bike, and depending on others. Student, parent, and educator agree that student needs to learn to drive vehicle and needs to get learner's permit when possible.

Financial/Agency Support

Student and parents do not see need for financial support or the assistance of adult support services in postsecondary education, help getting a job, or home living assistance at this time.

Health Related Needs

Last physical examination was in February of this school year. Student takes medication as noted earlier in this Evaluation Summary Report.

Greatest Concern

Student's greatest concern for 9th grade is "Getting along with my teachers in my classes in high school."

Interest Determination Exploration and Assessment System (IDEAS)

The IDEAS interest inventory was given to the student during English class in spring of 9th grade year. Student areas of high interest included the following three career areas: (a) mechanical/fixing careers, (b) nature and outdoor careers, and (c) protective services.

Steps to Self-Determination (STEPS)

Student completed **Self-Determination Knowledge Scale—Form A** in spring of 9th grade year. Based on the results of this criterion-referenced test:

- Student appears unclear regarding how to set goals and work toward attaining those goals.
- Tests results indicate weakness in career planning skills.
- Student is unclear regarding process of "active listening." He is also unclear regarding effective communication strategies including passive, assertive, and aggressive communication styles.
- Student identified three of five components of self-determination model. Student perceived compliance (follow the leader and avoid conflict) as components of the model. He did not include important components (know yourself or value yourself). Suggests external locus of control and a desire to be compliant.

Brigance Life Skills Inventory

Results of this criterion-referenced assessment instrument indicate that student currently lacks skills in (a) basic banking (including checking), (b) use of credit and credit cards, (c) budgeting for expenses, and (d) independent living after high school (e.g. apartment living, roommates).

APPENDIX

Selected Assessment Tools For Transition Planning for Students with Mild Disabilities

Future Planning and Self-Determination and Self-Advocacy Assessment Instruments

The ARC's Self-Determination Scale Available online through the Beach Center on Disability. The University of Kansas at: www.beachcenter.org

Choice Maker Instructional Series (Choice Maker Self-Determination Assessment) Sopris West Publishing, 4093 Specialty Place, Longmont, CO 80504. (303) 651-2829 or (800)547-6747. Online at http://sporiswest.com

This assessment instrument is sold as a Component of the Choice Maker Curriculum.

Future Planning Inventory Assessment System This assessment Instrument is included in Appendix A for your use.

The Self-Determination and Self-Advocacy Skills Questionnaires These assessment instruments are included in Appendix A for your use.

Steps to Self-Determination: A Curriculum to Help Adolescents Learn to Achieve Their Goals, Second Edition. (Self-Determination Knowledge Scale (Forms A and B)) PRO-ED, Inc., 8700 Shoal Creek Boulevard, Austin, TX 78757. (800)897-3202. Online at www.proedinc.com

This assessment instrument is sold as a component of the Steps to Self-Determination curriculum by both PRO-ED and the Council for Exceptional Children (CEC).

Additional Resources and Curriculum for Future Planning, Self-Determination, and Self-Advocacy

My Future My Plan: A Transition Planning Resource for Life After High School (Sheets & Gold, 2003)

The Self-Advocacy Strategy (Van Reusen, Bos, Schumaker, & Deshler, 1994)

Dare to Dream: A Guide to Planning Your Future (Webb, Repetto, Beutel, Perkins, Bailey, & Schwartz, 1999)

FUTURE Planning Strategy (Begun, 1995)

The McGill Action Planning System (MAPS) (Vandercook, York, & Forest, 1989)

Personal Futures Planning (Mount & Zwernik, 1988)

NEXT S.T.E.P.: Student Transition and Educational Planning, Second Edition (Halpern, Herr, Doren, & Wolf, 2000)

Self-Determination for Youth with Disabilities: A Family Education Curriculum (Abery, Arndt, Greger, Tetu, Eggebeen, Barosko, Hinga, McBride, Peterson, & Rudrud, 1994)

Student-Led IEP's: A Guide for Student Involvement (McGahee, Mason, Wallace, & Jones, 2001)

Whose Future Is It Anyway? A Student-Directed Transition Planning Process, Second Edition (Wehmeyer, Lawrence, Kelchner, Palmer, Garner, & Soukup, 2004)

Learning Styles Assessment Instruments

Barsch Learning Styles Inventory Academic Therapy Publications, 20 Commercial Boulevard, Novato, CA 94949-6191. Online at www.academictherapy. com

C.I.T.E Learning Styles Inventory (computer version) Piney Mountain Press, Inc., P.O. Box 86, Cleveland, GA 30528. (800)255-3127. Online at www.pineymountain.com and http//:wvabe.org/cite.htm

Kaleidoscope Profile Performance Learning Systems, 224 Church Street, Nevada City, CA 95959. (800)506-9996. Online at www.plsweb.com

Learning and Working Learning Styles Inventory Piney Mountain Press, P.O. Box 333, Cleveland, GA 30528. (800)255-3127. Online at www.pineymountain.com

Learning Styles Inventory Price systems, Inc., Box 3067, Lawrence, KS 66044. (785) 843-7892. Online at www.learningstyle.com

Career and Occupational Assessment Instruments

Armed Services Vocational Aptitude Battery U.S. Department of Defense. Online at www. asvabprogrm.com

Barriers to Employment Success Inventory JIST Publishing, 8902 Otis Avenue, Indianapolis, IN 46216. (800)648-JIST. Online at www.jist.com

Career Exploration Inventory (CEI) JIST Publishing, 8902 Otis Avenue, Indianapolis, IN 46216. (800)648-JIST. Online at www.jist.com

The Career Game JIST Publishing, 8902 Otis Avenue, Indianapolis, IN 46216. (800)648-JIST. Online at www.jist.com. Also available at: Rick Trow Productions, Inc., P.O. Box 291, New Hope, PA 18938. (800)247-9404. Online at www.careergame.com

California Occupational Preference Survey (COPS) EDITS, P.O. Box 7234, San Diego, CA 92167. (800)416-1666

Explorer Rick Trow Productions, Inc., P.O. Box 291, New Hope, PA 18938. (800)247-9404. Online at www.careergame.com

IDEAS: Interest Determination, Exploration and Assessment System NCS Assessments, 5605 Green Circle Drive, Minnetonka, MN 55343. (800)627-7271. Online at www.personassessment.com

Minnesota Importance Questionnaire (MIQ) Vocational Psychology Research, N657 Elliot Hall, University of Minnesota, Minneapolis, MN 55455-0344. (612)625-1367. Online at www.psych.umn.edu/psylabs/vpr

Prevocational Assessment Screen Piney Mountain Press, Inc., P.O. Box 86, Cleveland, GA 30528. (800)255-3127. Online at www.pineymountain.com

OASIS–3: Complete Aptitude Kit PRO-ED Publishing, 8700 Shoal Creek Boulevard, Austin, TX 78757-6897. (800)897-3202. Online at www.proedinc.com

OASIS–3: Complete Interest Kit PRO-ED Publishing, 8700 Shoal Creek Boulevard, Austin, TX 78757-6897. (800)897-3202. Online at www.proedinc.com

The Harrington-O'Shea Career Decision Making System (CDM) American Guidance Service, Inc., 4201 Woodland Road, P.O. Box 99, Circle Pines, MN 55014. (800)328-2560. Online at www.agsnet.com

The Self-Directed Search (SDS) JIST Publishing, 8902 Otis Avenue, Indianapolis, IN 46216. (800)648-JIST. Online at www.jist.com

Pictorial Inventory of Careers Talent Assessment, Inc., P.O. Box 5087, Jacksonville, FL 32247. (800)634-1472. Online at www.talentassessment.com

Reading Free Vocational Interest Inventory: 2 Elbern Publications, P.O. Box 09497, Columbus, OH 43209. (614)235-2643.

Red Hot Jobs Rick Trow Productions, Inc., P.O. Box 291, New Hope, PA 18938. (800)247-9404. Online at www.careergame.com. Also available at: JIST Publishing, 8902 Otis Avenue, Indianapolis, IN 46216. (800)648-JIST. Online at www.jist.com

Wide Range Interest and Occupation Test (WRIOT 2), Second Edition PRO-ED Publishing, 8700 Shoal Creek Boulevard, Austin, TX 78757-6897. (800)897-3202. Online at www.proedinc.com

Work Adjustment Inventory (WAI) PRO-ED Publishing, 8700 Shoa Creek Boulevard, Austin, TX 78757-6897. (800) 897-3202. Online at www.proedinc.com

Work Values Inventory JIST Publishing, 8902 Otis Avenue, Indianapolis, IN 46216. (800)648-JIST. Online at www.jist.com

Career and Occupational Resource

Occupational Outlook Handbook, 2004–2005 Edition JIST Publishing, 8902 Otis Avenue, Indianapolis, IN 46216. (800)648-JIST. Online at www.jist.com

Project C3: Connecting Youth to Community and Careers Online at www.c3online.org

Transition and Functional Living Skills Assessment Instruments

Brigance Inventory of Essential Skills Curriculum Associates, Inc., 153 Rangeway Road, North Billerica, MA 01862-2021. (800)225-0248. Online at www.curriculumassociates.com

Brigance Employability Skills Inventory Curriculum Associates, Inc., 153 Rangeway Road, North Billerica, MA 01862-2021. (800)225-0248. Online at www.curriculumassociates.com

Brigance Life Skills Inventory Curriculum Associates, Inc., 153 Rangeway Road, North Billerica, MA 01862-2021. (800)225-0248. Online at www.curriculumassociates.com

Checklist of Adaptive Living Skills Riverside Publishing Company, 425 Spring Lake Drive, Itasca, IL 60143-2079. (800)323-9540. Online at www.riverpub.com

Enderle-Severson Transition Scales ESTR Publications, 1907 18th Street, South, Moorhead, MN 56560. (218)287-8477. Online at www.estr.net

Life-Centered Career Education Knowledge and Performance Batteries Council for Exceptional Children, 1920 Association Drive, Reston, VA 22070. (888)CEC-SPED. Online at www.cec. sped.org

Life-Centered Career Education Council for Exceptional Children, 1920 Association Drive, Reston, VA 22070. (888)CEC-SPED. Online at www.cec.sped.org

Responsibility and Independence Scale for Adolescents Riverside Publishing Company, (800)323-9540. 425 Spring Lake Drive, Itasca, IL 60143-2079. Online at www.riverpub.com

Scales of Independent Behavior Revised Riverside Publishing Company, 425 Spring Lake Drive, Itasca, IL 60143-2079. (800)323-9540. Online at www.riverpub.com

Self-Esteem Index PRO-ED Publishing, 8700 Shoal Creek Boulevard, Austin, TX 78757. (800)897-3202. Online at www.proedinc.com

Social Skills Rating System American Guidance Service, P.O. Box 99, Circle Pines, MN 55014. (800)328-2560. Online at www.agsnet.com

Street Survival Skills Questionnaire (SSSQ) McCarron-Dial Systems, P.O. Box 45628, Dallas, TX 75245. (214)634-2863. Online at www.mccarrondial.com

Student Self Concept Scale American Guidance Service, P.O. Box 99, Circle Pines, MN 55014. (800) 328-2560. Online at www.agsnet.com

Transition Behavior Scale Hawthorne Educational Services, 800 Gray Oak Drive, Columbia, MO 65201. (800)542-1673. Online at www.hesinc.com

Transition Planning Inventory PRO-ED Publishing, 8700 Shoal Creek Boulevard, Austin, TX 78757. (800)897-3202. Online at www.proedinc.com

Transition-to-Work Inventory JIST Publishing, 8902 Otis Avenue, Indianapolis, IN 46216. (800)648-JIST. Online at www.jist.com

Vineland Adaptive Behavior Scales The scales are available in three editions: Survey Edition, Expanded Edition, and Classroom Edition. Available from American Guidance Services, P.O. Box 99, Circle Pines, MN 55014-1796. (800) 328-2560. Online at www.agsnet.com

Index

Note: Page numbers in **bold** indicate blank instruments